William Adolph Baillie-Grohman

Camps in the Rockies

Being a narrative of life on the frontier, and sport in the Rocky Mountains, with an account of the cattle ranches of the West, with illustrations, and an original map based on the most recent U.S. Government Survey. Third Edition

William Adolph Baillie-Grohman

Camps in the Rockies

Being a narrative of life on the frontier, and sport in the Rocky Mountains, with an account of the cattle ranches of the West, with illustrations, and an original map based on the most recent U.S. Government Survey. Third Edition

ISBN/EAN: 9783337197131

Printed in Europe, USA, Canada, Australia, Japan

Cover: Foto ©Andreas Hilbeck / pixelio.de

More available books at **www.hansebooks.com**

CAMPS IN THE ROCKIES.

BEING A NARRATIVE OF LIFE ON THE FRONTIER, AND
SPORT IN THE ROCKY MOUNTAINS, WITH AN ACCOUNT
OF THE CATTLE RANCHES OF THE WEST.

BY

WM. A. BAILLIE-GROHMAN,
K.C.E.H.,
AUTHOR OF "TYROL AND THE TYROLESE," "GADDINGS WITH A PRIMITIVE
PEOPLE," ETC.;
Member of the Alpine Club.

WITH ILLUSTRATIONS, AND AN ORIGINAL MAP BASED ON THE MOST RECENT
U.S. GOVERNMENT SURVEY.

THIRD EDITION.

London:
SAMPSON LOW, MARSTON, SEARLE, & RIVINGTON,
CROWN BUILDINGS, 188, FLEET STREET.
1882.
[*All rights reserved.*]

PREFACE.

When the outspoken frontiersman happens to be bored by a stranger, and desires to rid himself of his unwelcome company, he will address him with his usual drawl: "Say, Mister, are you aware that nobody is holding you?"

In laying before the reader an humble record of several little expeditions to some of the least known portions of the Rocky Mountains, I shall have to ask him to camp, to use another Western expression, on the trails of all sorts of beasts and uncouth characters; the least interesting and decidedly the most monotonous of these tracks will, I am afraid, be those of the irrepressible "Ego." For this personage, and for all his faults, I have to claim the good-natured reader's indulgence, and I hope that, remembering the good old adage of *noblesse oblige*, he will not suit the action to the above bit of very savage frontier humour, by summarily ridding himself of his company.

Having spent, for the last two-and-twenty years, all my leisure in the uplands of Europe, after an early training in the sport of the chamois and deer stalker—killing my first deer in the Alps before I was ten years old—I had long wished to make the acquaintance of the great Mountain System of the New World, the home of such lordly game as the grizzly, the bighorn, and the wapiti—the latter our own stag, produced on a wholly magnified, one might say *American*, scale. Three years ago this wish was consummated, and the fact of my having returned for a fourth visit to the Western hunting-grounds needs no further comment.

Portions of "Camps in the Rockies" have been previously published in the "*Field*," where they mostly appeared with the signature "STALKER," and in the "*Fortnightly Review*," and "*Time*," and I have to thank the respective Editors and Proprietors for their courteous permission to republish them in their present shape.

For many details on my map, I am indebted to Mr. S. F. Emmons and Mr. W. H. Holmes, two chief officials of the United States Government Geological Survey, through whose kindness I have had access to the Hayden Survey Publications for purposes of compilation.

THE AUTHOR.

CONTENTS.

	PAGE
PREFACE	v

CHAPTER I.
AN INTRODUCTORY CAMP 1

CHAPTER II.
CAMPS ON THE WAY 33

CHAPTER III.
LIFE IN CAMP 52

CHAPTER IV.
OUR DUMB FRIENDS IN CAMP 87

CHAPTER V.
CAMPS AMONG WAPITI 112

CHAPTER VI.
CAMPS ON THE TRAIL OF THE BIGHORN . 154

CHAPTER VII.
CAMPS ON TIMBERLINE . . . 182

viii *Contents.*

CHAPTER VIII.
Camps in the Teton Basin 205

CHAPTER IX.
Beaver Camps 233

CHAPTER X.
Indian Camps and Winter Camps 261

CHAPTER XI.
Camps in the Canyons of the Colorado . . . 296

CHAPTER XII.
Camps in Cowboy Land 320

CHAPTER XIII.
Western Reminiscences 365

Appendix 397

LIST OF ILLUSTRATIONS.

The Walls of the Grand Canyon of the Colorado . *Frontispiece*
A Mauvaises Terres Peak 156
A Rapid in the Colorado Canyons 304
Mauvaises Terres Country in the Lower Course of the Colorado . 316

CAMPS IN THE ROCKIES.

CHAPTER I.

AN INTRODUCTORY CAMP.

Our Outfit—Western air and Western cities—A bad start—Different ways of visiting the West—My companions—The people and their ethics—Three chief qualities, and what they have accomplished.

On a bright, breezy June morning a couple of years ago, a motley "outfit," consisting of three men, a boy, a huge four-horsed, canvas-covered waggon laden with provisions for six months, and some thirty or forty head of horses, was on the eve of starting for the Rocky Mountains from a certain Western "city" situated on the elevated table-land of Wyoming.

"Outfit," it may at once be mentioned, is an expressive Western term, covering every imaginable human, animate, and inanimate being or article. The Missourian speaks of his wife and little ones as the outfit he left behind him when he came West. The Plainsman calls a funeral or a wedding, his domestic kitchen utensils or his rifle, "that yer outfit." The Western hunter will tell you he never knew one of "them thar English lord chaps' 'outfits,' them top-shelfers who come over a' hunting, to be without 'bear-coated wipes' (rough towels), rubber baths, string-shoes (laced boots), and a corkscrew in their pocket-knives." The single occasion I ever heard of that production of civilization, a lady's maid, penetrating into the more approachable Western wilds, an old trapper—who, happening to observe that the woman, in the absence of side-saddles, was riding her horse in man's fashion—asked me whether "them outfits as I heerd called lady maids *always* straddle their horses?"

Ours, for the author is one of the three men, is an outfit that has nothing of the top-shelf about it. Two of the pack-horses carry bundles of rusty iron beaver-traps; the saddles and harness on the work-horses are wonders of patching and raw-hide home manufacture. The men's wardrobe—at least what little they have on their bodies this sunny June morning—displays a similar acquaintance with trapper tailoring as does the leather work with trapper harness-making. There is, however, a very workmanlike, "ready-for-all-emergencies" air, about the little caravan. The rifles carried across the saddle-bows are bright and shining with constant handling; the faces, at least of three of the party, are as brown as chestnuts; and their conversation smacks of the wilds they have but left to re-provision and to meet their old boss.

They and I are old friends, for it is not my first expedition of this kind. Five or six months before, in the dead of a Rocky Mountain winter, I had returned from a like trip—my second one—as ragged, unkempt, and disreputable-looking a being as ever "ran his face" among a civilized community, and got "policed" as a cut-throat. In the Cunarder's ferry-boats I had sped to Europe and

An Introductory Camp.

back; and now once more, with my old companions, we are about to foist ourselves on bountiful Nature, to "grub and board" where food and houseroom are free, and where the alien is as welcome as the copper-coloured native.

The sun has been up two hours, when, after a great deal of business-like bustle, the final "All set!" from the mouth of genial Port, the leading spirit of the expedition, rings out. "All set!" echoes from each of the horsemen in front and in the rear of the waggon, and with this Western "All right; go ahead!" the little party bids goodbye to civilization, and begins to move north-westward. It is a broad high-road, scarcely less than 800 miles in width, with the bright sun as our guide, for on the vast ocean of land we are about to cross we shall be days—or rather, weeks—before catching sight of more definite landmarks.

The next town north-westward of us is "'way up" in Montana, 600 miles or more off; but we are not steering for it. We are glad to turn our backs on that one yonder, and we hope not to set foot into a street for at least six months; indeed "if," as Port expresses himself, "we go light on the flour, we needn't for the next nine months."

Whatever may be the demerits of the West in the eyes of some, no one has ever dared to question the amazingly inspiriting qualities of the atmosphere of these trans-Missourian highlands. Dry and sparkling as perhaps none other on the globe, it seems to be composed not of one-fifth, but of five-fifths of oxygen. As your city-worn lungs inhale it, fresh life is infused into your whole being, and you feel that it is air which has never before been breathed.

The following fact speaks for its recuperative qualities.

An American friend, the victim of a pulmonary disease of long standing, two years ago took my advice and went West. His guide, whom I happened to meet some time afterwards, informed me that when the invalid engaged his services "he was kinder coffiny-looking; that he appeared to walk about only to save funeral expenses." Three weeks later, according to the same authority, it was a pleasure to see him, with a crippled bear after him, barking up a tree "as if every darned thing on him, boots and all, wanted to climb"—a statement partially confirmed by the hero, who has perfectly recovered. Its wonderful effect upon men's animal spirits have been compared to that of champagne, without its headaches and blues; with the further difference, that this rejuvenating fillip is enduring and health-endowing. You seem to be growing younger, not older; and you begin to understand the plainsman's opinion of it, when he told you that out West men take twice as much killing, and horse-thieves have to hang five minutes longer than anywhere else.

I had travelled five or six thousand miles on end as fast as steam would take me: an exceedingly bad sailor, the racket of five nights and five days in the train had not removed the cobwebs from my inner man. What nought else in so short a time could have accomplished, four-and-twenty hours in this bright atmosphere, and a glorious night's rest under buffalo skins—or robes as they are called in America—with the sky for a roof, had brought about. Mounted on my old favourite "Boreas," the slow but sure prince among mountain shooting-ponies, my "Express" slung over my back,[1] I cantered along; the keen,

[1] The frontiersman when on horseback usually carries his rifle in front of him across the Mexican saddle, attached by a simple leather arrange-

crisp breeze sweeping over the plains from the yet invisible Rocky Mountains, puffing out my loose flannel blouse-shirt, life on that fresh June morning seemed again quite worth living for.

There is nothing about the landscape, except its treeless barrenness, to indicate that we are 7000 feet and more above the Atlantic and Pacific Oceans. There are no mountains to be seen, and neither trees nor shrubs are visible. Behind us lies the mushroom matchboard "city," as direly forsaken by nature's beautifying hand as is the scenery surrounding it. In the middle of arid highland barrens—which, measured from their northern to their southern, from their eastern to their western, extremities, are just thirty times the size of England—there is an indescribable crudeness about this bubble attempt of man to leave his mark on Nature's vastness. The glare of the intensely bright light beats down with searching brilliancy upon the city's grotesque unpicturesqueness. Around us, in front of us, at our side, is the immeasurable nothing of the sagebrush desert. The streets of the settlement begin in it, and end in it with the same startling abruptness. Built yesterday—inhabited to-day—deserted to-morrow, is written on everything. Some of the dwellings indeed have already reached that last stage; roof-and-windowless cabins, they have about them a pathetic look of woebegone desolation; for while among other surroundings the ruin of a log-cabin can at least claim a certain picturesqueness of decay, the same sight on the Plains of the West carries with it all the

---

ment to the "horn"—a position which in my eyes is more riskful than slung over one's back, for the first tumble with your horse is liable to snap the slender English stock; and then—where are you?

suggestive signs of human misfortune, and instinctively one passes in mental array the hundred-and-one catastrophes by which possibly the dwelling was rendered tenantless. But such thoughts cannot live in the sparkling life-giving air of the West. A bright future—as bright, I hoped, as the past I spent in those wilds I was now bent for—is looming up. But steady; not quite so fast, my dear sir. Before you can taste all the promised delights in the yet distant sportsman's idyl, you have to get there. Four hundred and fifty miles—five long dreary weeks' travel, replete with the minor ills of the Plains, will try the patience of man and beast. Did not, when I was purchasing our stores the previous day, the keen-eyed, tobacco-chewing vendor, with pitying compassion in his voice, solemnly conjure me to sink capital in various luxuries in the tinned meat and canned fruit and vegetable line? "For," as he added, "you'll find it all-fired mean travelling this season. We ain't had such a dry spring since this yer town was started." Did not the spirit merchant, while furiously masticating his quid, and playfully invoking the most familiar dwelling-places of evil spirits, exclaim in accents of profound amazement, "Say, mister, you surely don't mean to start out on a six months' trip at this darned dry season with only a five-gallon keg of whis-key, and four of you to drink it?" But my men and I knew too much of Western "tangle-leg" and its vile poisonous qualities. That good old "cowboy" saying, which tells you that one drink of it tempts you to steal your own clothes, two drinks makes you bite off your own ears, while three will actually make you save your drowning mother-in-law, was not invented for us; "for," as Henry the boy cook quizzically put it, "our clothes arn't worth stealing, our ears are too big and too tough, and our outfit ain't got no mother-in-laws about it."

So, forewarned, but not forearmed, we start for our distant goal. But, as is the case in most similar undertakings, first days are apt to be lost days. We had not got out of sight of the "city" when we were reminded of this.

"Dog-garn them horses!" a loud voice exclaims; a lightning-like streak of the long "black-snake" whip accompanying the words; and plunging madly forward as they hear the dreaded "whiz," the two restive leaders in the team have broken the coupling chains; and with the link-bars jingling and clattering at their heels, they are off, tearing over the sagebrush desert, as genuinely stampeded two bronchos as you can wish to see.

The next instant the whole train is in dire confusion. The little band of as yet perfectly unbroken horses, round whom one of the men and the boy have been incessantly circling, herding them in with whip and voice, have taken the alarm; and, kicking up their heels, have done likewise. The pack-horses in front of them, "bossed along" by me, have, notwithstanding my frantic efforts, followed the example, for most of them are as fresh as frisky three-year-olds, and a long spring, spent in perfect liberty on their range, has made them unused to tight girths and to the rattle of sundry pans and pots about their packs. They are now streaking it over the plains; tails flying, and bucking off their loads in fine style. Except our three saddle-horses and the two staid old wheelers, not a horse remains. Dispersed in forty odd different directions, we have only the cold comfort of knowing that they are probably still somewhere in the

100,000 square miles of Wyoming. No time, however, is wasted; for those horses must soon be caught, or, fresh as they are, they will roam—goodness knows where to. The wheelers are taken out; one is turned out loose, the other is mounted, bare-back, by the driver, and we are off. Two take this side; the other, that side, of the 59,588,480-acre paddock.

Five minutes later, the old waggon is standing there forlorn and forgotten—a sad picture of the vicissitudes of Western life.

Late in the afternoon, two of the party return. The boy and I managed to gather in the pack-horses and the two leaders, who, not quite so wild as the unbroken horses who have never had a saddle on their backs, have not run so far. Tired, dust-begrimed, hungry and thirsty, we get back to the stranded "prairie-schooner," i.e. the waggon. The rest of the afternoon and long evening is passed in collecting the packs bucked off by the brutes, and which are strewing the Plains—here a bundle of traps, there the fifty-pound iron powder-keg, yonder the whiskey-cask; and a few hundred yards further, the two strong, raw-hide sacks containing the cooking utensils and table-ware. As everything is of sound, solid, enamelled cast-iron, the typical "This side up, with care," anxiety of anxious housewives, is not one of the ills to which we are heir.

Leaving the waggon where it is, we return to the spring from whence we started that morning.

It is quite dark by the time the pungent smoke from the sagebrush camp-fire has subsided, and our primitive supper of bacon and corn is finished. The absentees have not yet returned. "As bad a break as ever I sees, Boss," remarks Henry, "and no two ways about *that*." " Guess them doggarned horses have funeralized us all-fired meanly; shouldn't wonder if the whole outfit has gone back to their old range, hundred and fifty miles south." And, to cut a long story short, the "darned mean cusses" did return to their home range, one of the men going in pursuit, while Port returned the next morning; and we made another start of it, leaving the other man, with his flying column of unbroken stock, to catch up with us as best he could.

While we are waiting for the men at our smouldering camp-fire, let me introduce the most prominent personages of these pages, and say a few words on the *raison d'être* of my presence in a trapper outfit.

There are three ways of visiting the Far West, either for pleasure or for sport. The orthodox mode, to which only rich men can aspire, is at present also the most usual manner, for as a rule none but men of more than independent means visit trans-Missourian countries for pleasure. The frontiersman calls them, as we have heard, "top-shelfers;" they are accompanied by their servants from England, they hire some Western "hunters" as guides, and their expedition is provided with an amazingly complete camping outfit. They are asked very high wages —and they pay them.

The second way is cheaper, but far less independent. It is to get letters to, or, if you chance to be of commanding personal attractions, endeavour to make friends with, the officers in charge of such of the frontier military forts that are near good game ground. There are many of this kind in the northern Territories; and there, if properly introduced, you will meet with rare hospitality, and readiness to further your object; you will be supplied with stores, waggons, horses, troopers—everything you want. The American officers, notwithstanding the weary loneliness of their desolate posts, hundreds of miles from the nearest companionable being, are as a rule no sportsmen, but they will nevertheless enter with zest into your plans; and if they see that their presence is not unwelcome, one or the other of them will accompany you on your little shooting expeditions, and will make a very welcome addition in the number of mouths to be fed with venison, and hence also to the number of wapiti or bighorn you can legitimately kill. There will be plenty of whiskey—indeed, very often its supply is far too abundant; and on returning to camp from a long day's stalk, you now and again find the cook or the other underling troopers in a state not conducive to good cooking or handy service.

The third is the cheapest, the freest, the most pleasant manner provided its rough sides have no terrors for you. It is to eschew the usual run of Western guides, who take their parties year after year over to the same well-beaten ground, and to choose for your companions regular trappers or fur-hunters.

I have tried all three ways. My first trip, on which I was accompanied by a friend, partook of the top-shelfer's outfit. We were laden down with unnecessary camp luxuries, stored away on two waggons. I shot very little game, I saw the people as they are not; and owing to that very bad habit of asking questions, I was told more tall stories than the proverbial Colonel from Texas could invent in a year, for, as the frontiersman will himself tell you, the West is a country where "talk is cheap and lies worth nothing." Had it not been that on this trip I made the casual acquaintance of my future companion, genial Port, there would not have been a single redeeming feature about my first experience. The second manner had never very great attractions for me; though at a considerably later period I had occasion to be one of a party of three Englishmen, who have every cause to remember the remarkable hospitality of the commanding officers in a certain Wyoming fort, who fitted us out in right royal style, with men, horses, waggons, and escort, enabling us to visit the Ute Indian country in the depth of a very severe winter. Far more preferable is the third way, i.e. to join a trapper outfit, and at a cost which, under the circumstances, and in comparison to the ten or fifteen pounds per diem cost of many "top-shelfer" expeditions, must be called exceedingly moderate, turn, for all intents and purposes, trapper yourself. Only the most remote districts are visited by the genuine fur-hunters—by no means a numerous class; for the much-persecuted beavers and other valuable fur-bearing animals have long retired to the few uninvaded districts, and there only can they be found in paying numbers. You enjoy the good-fellowship of thoroughly trustworthy men; and while they do their trapping or wolf-poisoning, you, who are tacitly considered the " boss," or master, and are also addressed as such, can roam about at your own free will, gradually extending your expeditions as you become versed in the necessary art of woodcraft. Of course, for the newly arrived "tenderfoot" this roaming about, and not losing himself or getting into other more awkward dilemmas, necessitates some preliminary experience in woodcraft. But this, under the tuition of the very capable trapper-masters, is, if he has had previous training in other parts of the world, soon acquired; and when once mastered, the pleasure of knowing himself perfectly independent will vastly enhance the charm of life in the woods and in the mountains.

But it is not every sportsman fresh from the East or from Europe, who has either the time, opportunity, or desire to hunt for men of this stamp. The Union Pacific lands him at Cheyenne or Denver; and while in his innermost soul he hides a feeling of defrauded curiosity at not finding dead men lying about the streets and festooning the odd trees about the town, he expects to fall into the arms of a revised edition of a Bridger, Kit Carson, or old Joe Clark. At the first glance, perhaps his disappointment on this score is not so great; for the modern representatives of those old scouts of classic renown who forthwith interview him in front of the hotel bar, are got up in embroidered buckskin suits, broad sombreros, cartridge belts, and a six-shooter at the waist. Their hair is long, and their name some startling imitation of " Buffalo Bill " or "Wild Will." They tell him they are old Indian fighters, who know the whole West as they know their pockets.

I can, alas! speak from experience of the wiles and of the traps that waylay the newly-arrived sportsman; for I was green, very green, when I first crossed the Missouri, and hence I fell a singularly easy prey to certain "Bearclaw Joes" and " Scalp Jacks."

As a warning to others, I may relate how I was taken in, for my tale will also give an idea of the manner and ways of getting up such names. Out West, everything, from a mining stampede to the achievement of making a particular whiskey saloon a favourite with the public, requires " getting up;" and names fare no better.

An Introductory Camp.

I was fresh from England, for the four or five months I had spent in New York, Newport, and other Atlantic resorts, could hardly be called a proper schooling for the West. Let the Western town where the following incident occurred, be nameless. During my fortnight's stay I had interviewed more than a dozen of so-called hunters, who came up to offer me their services—and get a free drink. One of them was especially taking, and the most startling adventures had "camped on his trail" from the time he left his mother's lap. Indian fighting, bear shooting, and elk and buffalo slaughtering, from the Saskatchewan to the Panhandle, had been his life's vocation. Naming certain regions I desired to visit, he claimed to be intimately acquainted with every Indian trail that crossed the densely timbered district. I am not sure that I should not finally have been tempted to engage the great hunter, had not a sudden *dénouement* taught me a very salutary lesson.

The buckskin suit, the broad Texan hat, no less than the long hair that fell down to his shoulders, were all as greasy as became a great Indian fighter; but I remarked that his sporting accoutrement was decidedly new, and had evidently seen but little wear and tear. The ponderous cartridge-belt round his waist was as brand-new from the saddler's shop as his big six-shooter and Winchester rifle from the gunmaker's. Nailed to the stock of his rifle were the front claws of a grizzly, and on my making some cautious inquiries respecting it, and the name by which he had introduced himself to me—"Bear-claw Joe"—he proudly informed me, that though he had had that rifle but a short time, it had already annihilated the biggest bear in the Territory, a fierce hand-to-claw fight having preceded the monster's demise. During the terrible combat the bear had got the stock between his jaws, and the dents the man proceeded to show me on his weapon—but which, I innocently thought, looked more like harmless hammer marks—were the result, which led his comrades to give him that name. Knowing something of bears in other parts of the world, serious doubts began to rise in my mind that the oft-repeated stories of the terrible ferocity of the grizzly were sad exaggerations, and my adventurous ardour to add this prize to my list of slain became grievously dampened. However, fortunately for the reputation of old Ephraim, the dead " give away " that was in store for the bad man who ventured to impugn the ferocity of his kind, removed the shadowy blemish from his character. " Bearclaw Joe " and I were walking through the streets of the town, when we happened to pass one of the five or six meat and game shops the town boasts of. On a strong iron hook attached to the outside hung the carcass of a big grizzly. Naturally I was interested in the sight, and stopped to examine the slandered one's corpse. My companion seemed in a hurry, and when finally I pointed out that the bear's forepaw had been cut off, his haste to get away increased. Everything, however, would have passed off unsuspected had not, just as we were turning away, the owner of the shop come to the door, and addressed my companion in words which, somewhat toned down, ran as follows: " You cussed bull-whacking son of a dog! what in Texas did you mean cutting off that er' forepaw last night? Neighbour S. saw you do it, you Texas-begotten steer-smasher! " What would have followed had my friend " stayed with him " I know not; but fortunately the next corner was put between the two in the shortest of time, while the greasy locks of the thief streaming behind him were the last I saw of noble "Bear-claw Joe." On making inquiries, I learnt that the great hunter was nothing but a bull-whacker (teamster), and had been led to lay aside for a season his bull-persuading "black snake" whip, tempted by the big wages he could make "trundling tenderfeet outfits through the country!"

The genuine trapper is a very different being to the usual run of these self-constituted guides. You can generally know him by his unobtrusive and taciturn manners in the presence of strangers.

Of the old guard of famous Rocky Mountain "Fur company" voyageurs there are but very few left; the two or three I know are grizzly septuagenarians. The present race are younger men, who have passed a long apprenticeship under old veterans. The genuine trapper one very rarely meets in towns or other haunts of frontier civilization. They are out all the year round, visiting outlying settlements only every six months, to get their stores (provisions). Many of them have not slept in a bed for fifteen or twenty years, and they love not the luxuries of civilization, living a life as independent of social fetters as it is well possible to imagine. Very few of them ever marry; and death, which has stared them in the face times out of number, finally surprises them, in the shape of scalp-hunting redskins or a fierce eight-day snowstorm in a shelterless region, or an infuriated she-grizzly, or in any one of the many other guises in which the grim master is wont to call in the lonely hunter's checks. Few miss them; and when one fails to put in his appearance at the frontier store where in spring and autumn he was in the habit of purchasing his modest "grub outfit," a casual "Guess the old stag has gone up!" and a regretful sigh on the part of the enterprising owner of the general emporium, where the unworldly old buck used to trade his valuable peltry for third-class flour and adulterated coffee, will be about all that mankind can spare for the wanderer.

Among the rough and uncouth champions of the wilds, beneath a very shaggy exterior there are hidden many of the large-hearted qualities of ideal man in his primitive state. You find among them men—true men—on whose word you can build, and on whose quiet, cool-headed though subdued courage you can implicitly depend. Happily not a few of our best sportsmen who well know the West have on different occasions stood up for the sterling stuff of the genuine frontiersman.

Port, the leading spirit in our party, is such a man—about thirty-four years of age, tall, squarely built, with very sound bodily strength, and as sound constitution, which, as he will tell you, not even the two nights he slept in a proper bed in eleven years have succeeded in undermining. His face is tanned to a Sioux brownish-red; and a fine beard, kept very cleanly, hides the lower portion of his pleasant features. A glance at the outer shell, a look into the grey-blue eyes, betray the character of the man before you. Very silent in the presence of strangers—always a good sign in this Western country—his appearance pleased me from the first. He was "riz" in West Kansas in its earliest days, when the eastern portion of that State was the "bleeding Kansas" of which twenty years ago we heard so much. Settlements were far apart; and the dreaded invasions of the bloodthirsty red man, chiefly the Cheyennes, followed by the unheard-of ravages of the fiendish white man's Border-Roughian War, that turned such men as Quantrell and the James boys into beasts more savage than hyænas, made Port from his earliest youth acquainted with rapine.

Before he left his mother's lap he saw blood shed; before he could walk he saw men strung up and shot; and before he could read he had killed his Indian. He left his home at the early age of nine; "going West" was his fancy, and the yet untrodden wilds of the Rocky Mountains his dream. He passed a long trapper apprenticeship under one of the old guard of fur-hunters, and his subsequent career, as Indian scout in some of the most sanguinary Indian wars on the Plains, developed in him all those qualities which make him such an invaluable companion in a country where certain risks are not absent if the party is so numerically weak as ours is. It takes moments of danger to discover a man's true grit—the "bottom sand," as a plainsman would say. On the one or two occasions of such a nature, when I happened to be at his side, his self-reliant coolness convinced me that in times of risk, no less than at the quiet camp fireside, I could have no trustier companion.

The manliness about Port and other men of his calling is not that of the bravado, or that of the "bad man" of literature; but the quiet, unobtrusive manliness of a character that, while it knows not what pusillanimous fear is, yet knows what death is—of a nature that, while born and bred to carry life on the open palm, is yet for ever ready to do grim battle in its defence.

Port is full of quiet, dry, hammer-and-tongs humour. His sallies, in their pointed but good-natured criticism, spare neither present nor absent ones. This sparkling bantering wit, the happy creation of the moment which, when once you have bidden good-bye to white woman's face, and have exchanged your town garb for that far more comfortable flannel jumper, has, in its racy *abandon*, charms that go hand in hand with the life you lead and with the wild scenery about you.

The two remaining men will take up less space. What I have said of Port holds good for Edd and Henry. The first of the two is Port's junior by several years. Born in the East, he came West twelve or thirteen years ago, and has ever since been hunting and trapping; though the tour under consideration is the only one on which he has been in our outfit.

Henry, the boy cook and general factotum, is a lad of seventeen, who has been with me for the two last expeditions. "Skipping" three years ago his Iowa home, where his father, so I am told, holds the position of judge, he came West, and luck guided him into Port's camp. He is more of a character than Edd, and bids to become a genuine old mountaineer in an astonishingly short time. Intelligent, full of Western humour, life in the wilds has already removed from him the polish of a more civilized existence.

From Master Henry, who, I have strong proofs, is much attached to me, it would go hard to get out a "thank you," except perhaps for some unusual or specially gratifying gift; but I cannot say I like him much the less for it. At first I was often exasperated by this habit, but the boy soon showed me he meant not what his manner implied.

A ludicrous interview, to which a half-starved "cattle boss," who happened to stray into the vicinity of our camp and partook of our hospitality, subjected me, shows that "thank you" is, according to the laconic and not over polite manners of the West, a superfluous form. The meal over, I happened to be left alone with the now good-humouredly satiated "cow-puncher." "Say, mister," he began, "aint you the boss as runs this outfit?" To my affirmative answer he replied, "Well, say, that's kinder strange. Why I'll be darned if you wasn't the only cuss who said thank ye when the grub pile was trundled over to yer side." I told him that I hadn't got over that habit yet; to which he naively replied, "Them's bad habits of civi-ly-sashon. Out here them tony chin music don't pan worth a cent."

Henry is full of Western repartee. An acquaintance once remonstrated with him in quite undeservedly severe words for some defective cooking. Being no particular favourite among the men, the boy answered him "right smartly." "Wa'al," he said, "I was born for a cook, but the devil stole the pattern and ran off with it. I kinder reckon he must have loaned it to you." There was no more fault-finding.

An absent one I must not forget, for notwithstanding his red skin he proved himself a trustworthy fellow, and, for an Indian, a fair hunter. This is "old Christmas"[2] a Soshone, who was with us on and off for some time. At first he could not praise our camp too highly; it was "boss," "heap good," and "heap eat, and heap buckskin," alluding to the victims of my Express, which, whether elk, deer, or bighorn, are all called "buckskin" by Indians, and were disposed of by him among his voracious brotherhood with an amusing assumption of condescending hauteur. All went well, as I say, until we ran out of

[2] For obvious reasons, I have had to lengthen his name by a syllable.

grub, and for more than a fortnight had to "go it" on meat "straight," without bread, coffee, sugar, or salt. This was bad, and none of us felt it more than "old Christmas." One evening we were sitting round the fire, consulting over the dismal outlook—200 miles to the next post, and all the horses "plum played out"—when Port, in his most serious tone of voice, remarked in a sort of stage whisper across the fire to me, "Well, I guess we'll have soon to go on old Christmas 'straight.'" Overheard by the red man, as was of course intended, we saw a peculiar look spread over his stolid face; and the next morning old Christmas, with his horses, had "vamoosed." When, months afterwards, we returned to the Agency, we found our reputation among the Indians sorely blackened by the name they had given us, "The outfit who scare poor Indians."

So now, reader, you know my companions. They are thoroughly good fellows, genial, and devoted to me; and a pleasant and never broken accord—the paramount conditions for an undertaking of this kind—has long been established between us.

Before concluding this introductionary chapter, let me say a few words on the West generally, the people and their ethics.

Mentally and physically, ethnographically and topographically the West is a land of experiment. Everything is tried and tested—the soil, the climate, and Nature generally, no less than man; his spirit, his endurance, his honesty, and his depravity, one and all, are experimented on with a ruthless vigour of which it is difficult to form an adequate idea. No contrivance can be too new, no idea too original. Reverence for old landmarks and time-hallowed institutions the frontiersman knows not, for there are none of these venerable finger-posts to mature civilization. Nothing on the face of the broad Earth is sacred to him. Nature presents herself as his slave. He digs and delves wherever he fancies; forests are there but to be felled, or, if that process be too slow and laborious, to be set ablaze; mountains are made to be honeycombed by his drills and sluices; rocks and hills exist but to be blasted or to be spirited away by the powerful jet from the nozzle of his hydraulic tube. Landscape itself is not secure, for eminences may be levelled, lakes laid dry, and the watercourse of rivers may be turned off, as best suits his immediate desires.

The same hands that tackle nature in such a robust though shockingly irreverent manner, show little respect for the mandates and dignity of a more orderly social condition. They build a church that in weekdays can be used as a grain elevator; and with the same unceremonious haste that a "graveyard" is started, it will, should the soil happen to prove rich in precious ores, be turned into a silver mine.[3] The Western man makes his own laws—not

[3] The well-known Deadman's Claim in Leadville is not the only instance of a cemetery being turned into a silver-mine. From a late work on Leadville I take the following details:—"It was winter; Scotty had died, and the boys, wanting to give him a right smart burial, hired a man for twenty dollars to dig a grave through ten feet of snow and six feet of hard ground. Meanwhile Scotty was stuffed into a snow bank. Nothing was heard of the gravedigger for three days, and the boys going out to see what had happened to him, found him in a hole, which, begun as a grave, proved to be a sixty-ounce silver-ore mine. The quasi sexton refused to yield, and was not hard pushed. Scotty was forgotten, and stayed in the snowbank till the April sun searched him out, the boys meanwhile making prospect holes in his intended cemetery."

a day before they are required; and he enforces them himself. He is his own judge, father confessor, and executioner; but one and all are mere experiments. The laws, the judge, and the sheriff are just as much on their trial as the culprit.

If we look at the result of all this twenty years' experimentalizing, we see the unfinished rough sketch of a country, vast and great, as few ever were, and as none other now is—peopled, as would seem to me, not by the strange medley of race and temperament as is so often remarked, but rather by a community about which there is a singular unanimity of purpose and a startling uniformity of character. The Western man is essentially a cosmopolitan in regard to the largeness of his ideas and the unprejudiced sympathy with the thoughts, manners, and eccentricities of others. Just as the tattered garb of the miner hides often some sterling qualities of a strong manhood, the whole community, rough and unpolished as it appears to the superficial observer, comprises the essential characteristics of a great people. Good manners are called the final flowers of civilization, some say they are the sign of its decay; and as a clever American writer has pointed out, the polishing of a people is a slow process. In the case of the Western nation, the conditions are of an exceptional kind; for not only are those under which manners are to be formed glaringly new in the absence of the traditions of caste and of history, but they are doubly new in the addition of the dogma of equality.

There are three very admirable qualities to be found in the Western character. The first is the sturdy capacity of self-help, and genial readiness for mutual succour—the latter a concomitant result of the former;

secondly, his alert common sense, leading him to shun and to deride the hypocrite and the pretentious : and thirdly, the manliness that under all circumstances does honour to itself by the uniform respect paid to woman.

If I add still—what I do with great pleasure—that the frontiersman is the most hospitable being imaginable, I say not only what is true, but what makes itself pleasantly manifest to the stranger. The poorest cowboy or miner will exhibit an unselfish and genuinely hearty hospitality, such as only can be found in a frontier country, where civilization has not yet managed to cast over the individuality of man her gloomy and repellent shroud, of so called " good manners."

But enough of this tedious generalizing. In the eyes of most Englishmen, and, in fact, of Europeans who have not visited those regions themselves, the West—the "far" West, I mean—is a very lusty, not to say rowdy country, where blasphemy, murder, and swindling are more than rife. They judge by what they have read; and their opinion would be perfectly justified, were it not that with few exceptions authors have seemed to centre their attention on the careful collection of as many instances of barbarism and crime as their pens could lay hold of, thus presenting the country in a most unfavourable, and, I am prepared to say, incorrect light. This is perhaps bold fault-finding, and hardly compatible with the diffidence I feel in obtruding my own personal experience when it is so strongly at variance with the dictum of far abler writers; but as I am very convinced of its reasonableness, I may perhaps be excused on the ground of my more extensive travels and more prolonged sojourn among frontier populations. If we look at the list of books on the West, it is startling to see on what very short acquaintance many of their authors have put pen to paper. There decidedly must be some quite irresistible attraction in the solution of the Indian question, and in the fact of filling pages and chapters with homicidal tales; for there is a singular unanimity in all Western books on that score. A ride across the Continent in a stage-coach, or a fortnight's "fly" about the country in a palace car, where they of course never saw a wild Indian, seems in many cases to be considered sufficient to warrant the expression of very decided opinions on what the Indians should do and the white man should not—for of course those philanthropic traits that are component parts of all great characters *must* be aired; and with touching magnanimity they show mercy—on paper—at the cost of other people's scalps. All this has contributed to make the word "author" rather a byeword among Western men, and the being who sports it a person to whom it is hardly worth while telling a good lie; anything will do for them "inkslinging tenderfeet."

Seriously speaking, there is, I suppose, no country in the world on which so much has been written, based on less personal experience.

If there is anything that the educated American of the Atlantic States resents, it is the spirit of patronizing protection, often exhibited in an unwarrantable manner, by English writers when criticizing the ethics of the United States. The self-assured Western man, less thin-skinned than his Eastern brother, rather enjoys this; for to his keen humour it presents always welcome opportunity to get off some good story at the cost of the author. There *are* some good ones abroad, for he is an adept at reading characters; and to the average frontiersman, nothing affords more enjoyable fun than playing on the gullibility of strangers.

It is amazing what questions travellers will ask; but it is very much more amazing what answers they will believe, or at least apparently do so, to judge by " facts " in their books culled from the mouths of romancing " bad men."

The late tragic occurrence at Washington, the work of a maniac, infused fresh life into revolver literature, and raised another great wave of shooting tales. Quite recent authors have given the world a good many pages of frightful homicidal stories—not of their own experience, but what "oldest inhabitants" and railway-train friends told them.

So far as I can remember, there is not a single one among the host of past and present authors on the West who ever saw a man either shot or lynched out West; and yet what startling pictures of lawlessness do they not give us! We laugh at the American tourist who at Holyrood mistakes the butler for the Lord Chamberlain, and in Westminster Abbey addresses a chorister as the Dean; but surely the mistakes our tourists make are equally startling, for they believe very harmless blusterers to be desperadoes of the worst type, and that to visit the West without a revolver in each coat-tail pocket is risking their lives in a very reckless manner.

Everybody, or nearly everybody, has heard of those two old Western revolver stories of the divine and the English tourist. The one of the eminent divine from New England, who travelling in Colorado for his health, one day went in search of a barber's shop in a Western city, and on entering the establishment observed, it is said, a big double-barrelled gun leaning against the wall. Having a constitutional awe of fire-arms, he hastily asked the barber if the gun was loaded. A half-shaved native, who occupied the chair, turned around his lather-beaten face and exclaimed,—

"Stranger, ef you're in an all-fired hurry, you'll find a six-shooter what is loaded in my coat-tail pocket!"

The other, the story of an English tourist who proposed to visit Arkansas, and asked a citizen if he ought to provide himself with a revolver. "Well," replied the citizen, "you mout not want one for a month, and you mout not want one for three months; but ef ever you did want one, you kin bet you'd want it almighty sudden!"

These are both characteristic emanations of Western humour and gross exaggeration, tales which are nowhere more zestfully enjoyed than right in the very country they belie. The latter is suggestive, and its point may well be taken to heart by intending visitors. For three very good reasons the tourist should abstain from carrying about with him these arms, with which he is far more likely to hurt himself than anybody else. The first is, that as long as he is sober, and does not visit places where he has no more business to be than a visitor to London has to frequent Ratcliffe or the slums off the New Cut after dark, he will assuredly never want them. Secondly, if by mingling with bad company, or in consequence of visiting places where he should not venture, he should require an arm of defence, he will be sadly "left;" for long before he could extricate his weapon, the aggressor, if he is a Westerner on the shoot, would have emptied his six chambers into him. And thirdly, if this disagreeable contingency did occur, on the ground that he has no revolver the man who killed him will in all probability have something unpleasant occur to him; while if he has one, let it be even in the remotest corner of his pocket, the case is likely to resolve itself into justifiable manslaughter committed in self-defence, and the murderer will get off scot free.⁴ Though the latter is but "cold-mutton" comfort, it is at least some satisfaction to know that if one does get "rubbed out" the person who accomplished it will have the same happen to him.

Were Americans given to write books on travel they could, I am very inclined to think, by visiting any European country—England by no means excluded—in this superlatively superficial manner, singling out not the best nor the average, but the worst classes of the population, furnish, by simply collecting all police court and assize reports, a very harrowing calendar of crime. Comparisons are odious, so I will not pursue this theme. Let the newspaper-reading critic sketch out for himself such a list, while, for example, undertaking a fanciful journey of say 7000 miles on end through England. It would contain several species of crimes which are entirely unknown in the West. On one of my Atlantic crossings a fellow-passenger afforded me much amusement. He was a Western man, who had visited the old world to see

⁴ The act of bringing your hand to your hip, where the pistol is generally carried, is a gesture warranting a man, in the eyes of a Western jury, to defend himself, and if he kills his adversary it is justifiable manslaughter. The act of drawing the pistol first is called getting the "drop on you," which is done with marvellous rapidity, leaving untrained hands not the remotest chance of self-defence. I have often seen men throw up their hats, *then* draw their pistol, cock, and fire twice, putting two bullets through the hat before it reaches the ground.

"Your old You-rope," and to exhibit, as he proudly informed me, the first horned frog ever seen in "your country." He was full of quizzical 'cuteness, and some of his opinions of Europeans things evinced the peculiar sharp wit of the frontier. He had no very high opinion of European manhood, as shown in certain phases of crime evincing a total disregard of the fundamental principle of manly regard for woman. "If all that thar kicking and mauling of women whar tu happen out West, you bet you'd see an all-fired lot of lynchin' in that 'ar section of the country"—words that tallied very conspicuously with my own experience of trans-Missourian regions; for I am strongly convinced that without exception there is no country where women are treated so respectfully as in the West, a criterion that stands, as they say, on its own legs.

Let us look at the Western man in the common walks of life. He is, as he will tell you himself, a "'cute man of business; and don't you forget it." His customers make him that. And business with him means the business of getting rich as fast as he can—often with policy as his honesty. Outside his vocation, in the common relations of life he is an uncommonly honest fellow, much more so than many men who can claim a far higher degree of polish, but to whom mean pettifogging is not a matter of abhorrence.

In the West, a man, as I said, is apt to act as his own judge in all personal offences, and also as the executioner of his own sentences. There are many varieties of the former; but as, in his self-confident hurry to get rich, he has forgotten to build a gaol and provide a police force, there is naturally only one species of the latter—he must either ignore or kill. Hence, as men deem life too valuable to jeopardize it for some pettifogging meanness, or verbal affront, or slander, they are, as a rule, careful of their words and actions.

If these doctrines of morality, which make men honest and civil-mouthed at the point of the revolver, are ethics that do not come up to a very ideal standard of man, they are, however, usefully practical, and answer their purpose remarkably well. In no country in the world is there so little bullying, either physically or morally, as in the West, for there the turning worm is apt to handle his fire-irons just as dexterously as he who would override and crush him.

If a man is "dragging on his anchor," either in consequence of natural affinity to crime, or bad company, or drink, with the result that he takes to a criminal life, you can be sure he will start into his new career with much the same cool daring enterprise as were he building a town or a railway. The first horse or mule he stole has forfeited his life; what matters whether far worse crimes dye his hands? He has as much or as little chance to escape into some distant district, and hide his identity under a different name, a broad sombrero, with an ever-ready six-shooter to arrest the first unpleasant inquiry, whether he has "found a set of horseshoes" (horse-thieving) or whether he has called "hands up" to the armed guard of a bullion convoy, and, to prove satisfactorily that *he* meant business, has shot two or three who stupidly resisted. These are the desperadoes, the pet children of literature on the West—personages one reads about so much, but somehow never, or at any rate very rarely, meets.

Quite apart from this class of criminals, but in close connexion with Western ethics, stand the "manslaughterers," who have killed in "self-defence." Both these terms are stretched a good deal beyond their European meaning. We would call the one a murderer, the other murder; but in doing so we would show our ignorance of the very *raison d'être* of frontier life—a condition of things upon which the standard of old and well-regulated communities is not applicable.

The West rejoices in the absence of "nobs" and "snobs" —worshipped lords and those that worship them; and the spirit, as an American author with some truth remarks, which disowns the one and discountenances the other, "is not the noisy gascon of uncurbed democracy; it is the self-asserting, prideful scorn that comes of independent power and strength."

The Western man minds his own business, a circumstance grimly paraphrased by Brigham Young's injunction to his "Latter Day Saints."[5]

The qualities of a man stand on their own merits; he falls or rises by them, unabetted in either of these processes by extraneous wealth, family, or condition. We can understand, therefore, that the air of the West is a frightfully uncongenial atmosphere for vanity and self-importance. Airs and "frills," cant and braggadocia, find, as the same writer with truth remarks, no customers. The true gentleman is heartily liked, but the swell is as heartily hated. They have no objection to good clothes

---

[5] To the men he said: "Keep still and mind your own business." The women he told: "If you see a dog run by the door with your husband's head in his mouth, say nothing till you have consulted with the Church."

on the back of men who know how to wear them without ostentation. The dandy—and it is easy to be a dandy in the West—strolling through the streets of a mining town, is apt to be unpleasantly reminded of this. As likely as not he will hear himself hailed, " Hold on tha'r, stranger ! When ye go through this yer town, go slow, so folks kin take you in." Or in dry quizzical tones he will be asked, " Mister, how much do you ask for it ? " " For what, sir ? " " Why, for the town ; you look as if you owned it."

We recently heard how a Scotch Duke visiting the West rode on the cow-catcher of a locomotive. Though it was not just a thing a Western man would do—at least, if he did not get paid for such a purposeless job —it yet evinced such a pleasing aberration from the usual stiffly-starched, brilliantly white cloak of British superiority, that the Western people as a man rose, and hailed him with acclamation. No act of the traveller could have possibly gained him so immediate popularity as this experimental ride.

If ever men have the right to be proud of what they collectively have achieved, they are the frontiersmen —be they miners, railway or town builders, or cattle-men. Nothing in the World's history can be compared to the creation of the last five-and-twenty years beyond the Missouri. Indeed, the Western man has outdone himself. In 1865 the astute and much-travelled General Sheridan said, when speaking of the unfeasible nature of the first great trans-continental line of railway, that " he would not buy a ticket for San Francisco for his youngest grandchild." Four years later he himself travelled in a Pullman car from the Atlantic to the Pacific coast; while to-day there is complete a second line across the

Continent, and three more in a more or less advanced state —20,000 miles of railway being at the present moment travelled over in the West, where, twenty years ago, there was not a single foot of track.

It is only about thirty-five years since parties of men began to cross the Continent, and only about twenty since the first emigration to the Rocky Mountains. It took two and a quarter centuries for the descendants of the Pilgrims to make their way in force to the Missouri. A tenth of those centuries sufficed for the exploration and peopling of by far the greater half of the North American Continent.

CHAPTER II.

CAMPS ON THE WAY.

Ills of Plains travel—Exceptional seasons—A Plains fire—A funeral—The " Bad Medicine "—Fasting on coffee and bread—A veteran meat hunger—Mosquitoes—Final release on Timberline.

I THINK it is Ruskin who says there are three material things essential to life, and no one knows how to live till he has got them ; *i.e.* pure air, water, and earth. Every one of these three necessaries is remarkably well represented in the West.

The air, as we have heard, is decidedly the purest and most invigorating of the globe. There is plenty of water —at least in the northern districts; and as day after day we let our eyes roam over the boundless Plains, the superabundance of earth becomes monotonous. Unfortunately, however, the two latter are rarely present together. There is constantly too much of the one and too little of the other, and *vice versá*.

I have mentioned that five dreary weeks' travel ensued after our successful second start before we reached our goal; let me touch upon some of the most striking events, which, though not one of them was in the least uncommon, will give in their *tout-ensemble* a good idea of the ills of

Plains' travel. In justice, however, to these much reviled Plains, I must premise, that the season of 1880 was in several ways an exceptional one. On none of our previous or subsequent expeditions has Nature placed so many obstacles in our path.[1]

The winter of 1879-80 was, out West, a severe and long one—though nothing like the next one. Very much snow fell in the Rocky Mountains. Spring, the rainy time, was, on the Plains that season conspicuous by its absence. Winter and snow one day (it snowed near Cheyenne, in the first week of June), and great summer heat the next. The West is at best a country of extremes, such as we know not in Europe. A variation of 80° or 90° Fahr. in twelve hours is by no means unusual; and in most parts of Central and Western Wyoming, not a square foot of which is lower than 6000 feet over the sea, very few summer nights passed that the water in our camp-bucket was not coated with a film of ice; while at noon the thermometer in the shade would be up to 85° or 90°. In winter the extremes will occasionally be even greater; and in the last winter I was out (1880-81), the cold was twice below −50° Fahr. or some 80° or 85° degrees of frost.

As a natural consequence of the absence of the usual daily rains during several weeks, the grass, the sole verdure on these elevated highlands, failed to spring forth, and great suffering among the semi-wild cattle that roam

---

[1] I must also mention, that I could have lessened the distance of 450 miles by nearly half, had I started from a point further West, and nearer to the foot-hills of the Rocky Mountains. As it was early in the season, I desired to look up some of the cattle ranches of Wyoming, and hence chose a much longer route than was necessary for strictly sporting purposes.

at will over very nearly all those regions, ensued. Tens of thousands died for want of water and food. The whole country presented a forbiddingly barren and burnt-up aspect; and very soon the great dearth of water, and the meagre growth of parched grass began to tell on our horses, obliging us to travel slower every day.[2] All the streams and creeks rising on the Plains proper "gave out," *i.e.* went dry; while, in perplexing contrast to them, the few great rivers traversing the Plains that head or have their source in the Rocky Mountains, where vast masses of snow were succumbing to the warm June sunshine, were more than bank full. Thus it happened that for a week at a time we would suffer from want of water; whereas the next week we would be camped for several days on the banks of a great river, such as the Platte or Big Wind River, while waiting for the waters to subside so as to allow us to ford or swim the foaming torrents twenty feet deep and a quarter of a mile broad, which at other seasons of the year would be scarce four feet deep, and fifty or sixty yards across.

For days we were a prey to the pangs of thirst, such as only is known on the alkaline deserts of the Plains; and were compelled to ride for water from dawn till midnight—to be several times disappointed even then. Dry camps, *i.e.* waterless ones, were frequent; while at other times we had only cattle or buffalo-wallow water to quench our thirst. Coffee-making, in these instances, became a farce, the natural condition of the liquid resembling that beverage in all but smell and taste.

Port, who had lived in Arizona and New Mexico, where

---

[2] We had taken no grain for the horses with us, as in ordinary seasons nobody would think of doing so.

the scarcity of water develops a keen scent for the remotest sign of its presence, proved a wonderful water-finder, Holes, often three and four feet deep, had to be dug; and even then the precious liquid would accumulate so slowly that it took three or four hours to collect a cupful of water for each human and animal being. I need not say what weary times those were, when, after thirteen or fourteen thirsty hours in the saddle, the two spades or picks would have to be taken in turns, and by the light of sagebrush torches a water-hole dug. The tired animals, suffering from the pangs of fierce thirst, would crowd round us and watch the proceedings with intelligent understanding; and when the hole was dug, and a camp cup placed in the bottom to catch the valuable drops, one of us had to guard it to prevent the eager brutes from tumbling into the hole. While traversing one of these dreary waterless stretches of "droughty" Plains, we got a severe but salutary lesson illustrating how easily devastating Plain fires "get out." We had nooned at a wallow, and when we started again the small fire we had made to cook some beans had apparently long gone out. We had proceeded about two miles, and just were losing sight of the little "bottom" where we had camped, when, happening to look round, I perceived a huge volume of flames envelope the spot where we had camped. Fires in the dry season are generally serious things, lasting frequently four or five months; and though timber, if there is any, is perfectly valueless, they are often very disastrous to straggling settlements, but especially to the cattle roaming over the country. Hence, the Territorial legislature has recently put a heavy fine (100*l.*) and imprisonment on the offence of "letting out" plain or forest fires.

Though we had already got beyond the last white settlement, we were still in cattle land; and a timbered range of mountains eight or ten miles off would assuredly have been sacrificed, had we not resolved, after a brief moment's consultation, to try our best to put it out. Leaving Henry with the horses, the two men and I rode back as fast as our excited horses could carry us. A very gentle but steady breeze was blowing, and long before we got to the scene we heard the crackle and roar of the flames, spreading at a great rate among the sagebrush. Dry as tinder, and of good size, this shrub of the desert makes about the hottest and quickest fire possible. Our saddle blankets were the only available article with which to fight the flames. But alas! by the time all three were well soaked in the copper-coloured wallow water, there was not a drop left, and the next water was, as we knew, eighteen miles off. Taking the blankets, we rode bareback to the further extremity of the conflagration. Running before the wind, the flames were leaping onwards very nearly as fast as a man can walk. So, to have any chance with what is here called counter-burning, we had to begin several hundred yards or so ahead. One of us, taking a lighted sagebrush in hand, walked along, setting fire to the dense growth, while the other two did their best to keep the new fire under control by confining it to a strip some twenty or thirty feet wide. This was hot work, and had to be done very quickly. Three times did we fail to complete the belt before the main fire was upon us, coming on with a rush and a subdued roar very grand to behold from a safe distance, but uncomfortably awkward at close quarters. Each time we had to retreat and begin again a considerable distance ahead. The fourth attempt at last succeeded, favoured as we were by the lull in the breeze usual just before sundown. It was the last effort, for we were thoroughly exhausted, and blinded and scorched, staggered about like inebriates. It was a close shave, too, for the flames of the main fire were within a few yards of us when we completed the belt, and the last few seconds we were working right in the flames. Half blinded, our hands and faces, hair and beards singed, our boots burnt, nothing whatever left of our saddle-blankets, two of us minus our shirts, which we had torn off to beat out the flames of the counter belt, black as negroes, we threw ourselves on the ground, too exhausted even to speak. It was nearly dark by the time we extinguished the last sagebrush, and long after it when we regained our horses. It had taken us several hours to master the fire, and as the men expressed themselves, "nothing but a strip of sagebrush country, a mile long and a quarter of a mile in width, blackened and burnt, to show for it."

That night's camp—a dry one, it is needless to say—was one of the most uncomfortable ones I remember. Not a drop of water to cook, wash, or quench our burning thirst. Thereafter we took care that the camp fire was out before leaving it. This, on referring to my diary, I find, occurred on July 14th. The next day, one of the very hottest I can remember to have experienced on the Plains, brought new disaster, in the shape of a stampede of the unbroken horses, who in an unguarded moment made a break for their home range, now over 300 miles to the south. Port, by riding down one of his favourite saddle-horses, managed to head them off, and overtook us with them the following day, coming up to us in a grand rush—the only way a single man can hope to drive a band of untrained horses so as to keep them from straying. The 17th, 18th, and 19th July were in their way also replete with unpleasant experiences. Before I proceed to tell them, let me explain how it happened that we were then travelling with a heavy waggon and a band of more than perfectly useless wild horses. Both were to be left at Port's isolated ranche, 250 miles from our starting-point, and about half way to our final goal, the Big Wind River Mountains, the highest and longest chain of the northern Rocky Mountains. The horses Port had bought quite recently, and owing to my unexpectedly early return, and the fact that no men to drive them for us could be hired in the place we started from, we had to do so ourselves. We were gradually approaching the place where they and the waggon were to be left, and everything was to be "packed," *i.e.* carried on sumpter or pack horses—a far quicker mode of travelling than with a waggon, however amazing be the roughing capacities of these conveyances,[3] and however wonderful be the skill, the daring, and the swearing powers of a Western driver.

Give him a handy six-team, his powerful blacksnake whip, and the universe to fill with his Titanic language, he will take you, and a light load of twenty or thirty hundredweight, across almost any chain of mountains there is in the United States or in Europe.

I have myself crossed very steep mountain ranges

---

[3] The regular Plains-waggon, of which there are several patterns, all of well-known name and repute, are wonders of practical usefulness and strength, combined with comparative lightness. Everything about them—from the very powerful lever-brake to the axle-nuts and bolts—can be taken asunder with perfect ease. The body is an oblong box-like contrivance, that can be adapted for every kind of load, even of such an heterogeneous nature as timber, sacks of flour, or hay.

10,000 feet high with one, traversing places where a stranger would suppose a horseman could not possibly get through. On reaching a ravine or gulch with sides too steep to venture to cross it in the ordinary manner, the waggon is forthwith unloaded, and the whole machine—wheels, pole, box, and axles taken apart, and carried piecemeal over by the men, and then set up again, and the journey resumed. Mining prospectors, who travel in a party, usually take one of these waggons, with a good team of four or six horses; and there are very few places indeed where they cannot get through one way or the other. In crossing rivers too deep to ford, the box is used as a boat, fastened by a long rope in the fashion of a ferry, to a tree or rock higher up the stream. Thus flour and other damageable stores can be got across perfectly dry.

Hitherto the waggon had not given us much trouble, the country was of the usual Plains type—hill land of an undulating character, hardly ever calling into use the dreaded blacksnake whip, Port's simple "Git!" with a mild addition or two, being sufficient to keep the team to their collars. Every day or two we would pass an isolated cattle ranche, deserted by the owner and his men, who were away on the summer "round-up," *i.e.* collecting their bovine property. On one such occasion, soon after starting out, a little incident happened illustrating in a grim fashion the saying that frontier life is hard on cattle and women.

While crossing a range of hills we happened to pass a little settlement, consisting of four families, living in miserable, tumble-down, windowless adobe hovels. The males were all away "tie chopping," and during their absence diphtheria had swept off, in less than four-and-twenty hours, the entire infant population, consisting of five children, who were now lying dead in the huts. In my absence, and at the prayers of the distracted mothers, the two men who were with the waggon emptied some dry-goods (grocery) packing-cases, and turned them into coffins for the little ones, and, moreover, after unloading the rest of the contents, drove the wretched mothers with their dead little ones to the nearest settlement, fifteen miles off, where diphtheria had caused a children's graveyard to be started. I mention this little incident for two reasons—firstly, because it speaks well for the kindly heart and ready help the genuine frontiersman invariably evinces ; and also as a proof—at least apparently so—of the spontaneous origin of this fell disease, which in the West is the one sore danger for children. I was assured by the afflicted women that they had neither been visited nor had seen living being for seven days previous to the appearance of the disease, while the next habitation was quite eight miles off, on the other side of the range of hills.

But to return to our own little troubles. The third day after the fire, the character of the landscape we were passing through underwent a signal change. We were travelling across country, and had struck what is known as the Upper Shirley Basin—ten years ago a very famous resort for Indians and game. A stream, named very appropriately the " Bad Medicine," passes through it, and we had to cross it three times in four days. Western rivers are all very arbitrary and self-willed powers in the land. Many have a bad name for most dangerous quicksands, others for their extraordinarily rapid rise. Some of the larger creeks in the northern "bad-lands" are known to rise twenty and thirty feet in half an hour, in consequence of rainstorms. Again, others take it into their heads to sink out of sight just when their precious liquid is most wanted, and keep out of man's way for ten or twenty, in places even for sixty, miles. I know not of one single river or stream west of the Missouri that has not some more or less memorable awkward quality or characteristic about it ; but for a coalescence of all possible vileness on the part of a creek give me the "Bad Medicine," where we struck it on our last trip.

The Shirley Basin is entirely of the *mauvaises terres* or bad-land character, the chief characteristic of which is a verdureless, spongy, or claylike soil, riven by great gaps with treacherous banks. Through this rotten and water-worn country the creek had carved itself a tortuous bed, with overhanging banks fifteen or twenty feet high, so that its bed at the water-level was broader than the opening at the top, giving it in places the character of a semi-subterraneous stream. The "Bad Medicine" is strictly a Plains river, so when we reached it we found it suffering from the general drought, and no water save occasional stagnant pools in it. This, however, did not facilitate matters, for it was the bed of the stream not its water that puzzled our ingenuity. The banks were so rotten that, when on our first striking it I approached the brink, fortunately on foot, it broke under me, and I fell some twelve feet, landing on a mud bank, in which, had not a rope been thrown to me, I would have very quickly disappeared. When, therefore, I say that we crossed this Styx with waggon and horses three times in three days, the reader can fairly picture to himself the nature of the job. The first crossing was managed by cutting down the banks (we had then two picks and two shovels with us), and making a very steep roadway to the water-level. Next, no timber being near, we had to collect great quantities of sagebrush to make a foundation for a banked dam across the creek, sufficiently solid to let the heavy waggon pass over it: this took us nearly the whole day. The two miles we pulled on that evening brought us to a worse place, where, without twice the labour, we could not build a similar dammed bridge. So the waggon had to be unloaded, taken asunder, and everything carried across piecemeal. The third crossing, near which there were some trees, was performed by means of a timber bridge we threw across the yawning gulf, taking us rather more than a day's hard work. Thus in nearly four days we travelled rather less than four miles. Forty-eight hours later we struck the Platte river at one of the few fords, where, a month later, a man could wade across. It was now a huge mountain torrent, the yellow masses of water rushing over some rapids with a roar we heard a mile off. It was far too high and swift to risk swimming it; so we had to pitch camp, and wait till the waters subsided, which they did very rapidly, for the season was already unusually far advanced for these freshets. When we finally ventured it, the water was about six feet deep, obliging everything to swim. None of the horses, with the exception of the saddle animals and one or two of the pack-ponies, had ever undergone a similar experience, and we had some very ludicrous "breaks" on the part of the terrified beasts when they found themselves swept off their legs. There were two colts, born not quite a week before; these we did not dare to trust to the rushing torrent, so their four legs were strapped together, and with one tucked under the arm we swam our own horses across, the anxious mothers following at our heels. It took us six hours to get the whole outfit to the other side; but it was most useful practice, for our subsequent journey along the course of the Big Wind River was replete with similar crossings.[4]

The following evening we reached Port's ranche, where we halted for a day to rig out the pack-train in proper ship-shape. Hitherto we had been travelling very slowly, on an average not more than ten or twelve miles a day; but now, rid of the troublesome band of horses and the lumbering waggon, we proceeded very much quicker, doing often four or five miles at a stretch on a trot—a deal of jingle and rattle of pots, pans, and steel-traps accompanying the performance. Effecting an early start, we used to ride till eleven; then if we happened to strike water, noon for a couple of hours, and proceed till dusk, the distances between water, which if possible we ascertained ahead, governing the speed of travel. To pack and unpack eleven sumpter or pack animals four times a day, not to mention your own saddle animals, is a job not as easy as it looks in writing, for you have to combat with

---

[4] I may here mention a danger which "tenderfeet" expeditions are liable not to notice till it is too late. Most horses out West are ridden with Mexican curbs, furnished with tongue-bits with rowels, of cruel device and of great power. In swimming rivers, attention should be paid to give horses a perfectly free head, if they have these curbs. I saw a half-breed's horse drowned, he himself very nearly sharing its fate, by his tugging at the reins and thus forcing open the horse's mouth. The stream was rapid and rough, so the water surged into the poor brute's mouth, and presently it sank under its rider.

the profoundest stratagems on the part of the wily old stagers to frustrate your frantic tug at the lash rope; and you can be sure that even if, by perseverance worthy of a better cause, you have at last managed the famous "diamond" or "Kit Carson" hitch to the lash rope, it is only life-long practice that develops the skill of a good packer. To see Port pack nine or ten horses inside of five-and-twenty minutes—the loads being of course laid handy by the rest of us—was better than a course of lectures on equine metaphysics. Kindly and easy of hand to those of the horses that had recognized the uselessness of resistance, he "meant business, and no two ways about it," with those that had a "buck" or a kick left in them. A "real mean broncho" is an object worth close attention. He snorts with rage, bites, rears, bucks, kicks, ducks his head and throws it up again, arches his back, and dashes himself to the ground; foam flies from his mouth, fire is in his eyes, while his ears are pressed flat against the head; but the powerful purchase gained by an outstretched leg pressed against his flank enables the brawny-armed Port to subdue that unnecessary expenditure of vileness in a very short time, and for the next five minutes that horse will go "teepering" about on his toes for the "cinche" or girth that holds the pack-saddle to its place, and the lash-rope that is thrown over the load and round the animal are as taut as a strong man's arms can make them.

One of the most unpleasant results of the great drought which seared the Plains in 1880, was the quite unprecedented scarcity of all game. Except antelopes, for the tasteless venison of which we all have a strong aversion, game is always rare on the Plains proper; but it was much more so the season I am speaking of, for even the prongbuck (or antelope) had deserted his usual runs, and had betaken himself to regions where water and grass were less scarce. Our outfit sported in the way of provisions only the very simplest articles. Besides 500 pounds of flour, an adequate quantity of coffee, tea, sugar, and salt, and some dried apples and beans, we could not boast of a single tin of preserved meat, vegetables, or such luxuries of camp life, with which toothsome but bulky commodities most pleasure expeditions are loaded down. Hence, when game failed us in such a very unexpected manner we were reduced to a very heart-breaking diet of bread, beans, and coffee. Then the beans gave out, and for sixteen days—endlessly long days they seemed—we lived exclusively, or, as the phrase is, "grubbed straight," on bread and coffee. Not even when we reached the spurs of the Rocky Mountains did we strike game, till we had penetrated far up, close to Timberline on the main chain. Where at other times of the year wapiti and bighorn roamed in great numbers, there was not a single animal left. We longed for venison, and we had meat on our brain. The worst of our starvation diet was, that it played such havoc with our fine, healthy animal spirits nothing ever before had managed to subdue. I believe there are few more temper-trying, though in reality harmless extremities, than a ravenous appetite whetted to outrageous dimensions by twelve or fourteen hours in the saddle in the keen Western air, and only such unsubstantial fare as bread and coffee—let the former be ever so doughy, and the latter consisting of muddy dregs —wherewith to appease it.

Day after day four disgusted white men and one grimly

glum red man would assemble round a cheerfully blazing camp fire to play, as Port expressed himself, Old Harry with the flour-sacks and coffee-bags—to rise with an uncomfortable sense of vacuity no tightening of the waistband or gathering in of the six-shooter belt could remove. Meat we must have: it was the cry in the early morn, when after a good night's rest a glorious "break-fast" hunger (*sic*) would sit down with us to the first meal of the day; meat was the cry at noon, and meat was the last word at night; indeed, in the case of at least one of the party, even in dreamland would the appetite receive unnecessarily stimulating fillips by fata morgana visions of boiling ribs of elk, and juicy tender loin-steaks of a prime three-year-old bighorn. One morning, I remember, a grim laugh was raised by Henry. The evening before I had been telling the men—for conversation *would* keep to suggestive topics—how a very celebrated surgeon (Professor Billroth, of Vienna) had succeeded in removing portions of the stomach from cancer patients, who finally recovered. Henry, it seems, had been sleeping that night with Port, who had reason to complain of his restlessness, and when twitted with it, as with rueful faces we were sitting round the morning coffee and bread, he laconically remarked "that 'most anybody would be restless if they dreamt that thar boss bone-carpenter was 'dressing' (*Ang.* gralloching, used when opening a deer) their insides, and kinder couldn't find no stomach *to take out.*" A good sound hunger is a very nice thing— nothing nicer in fact when just about to be appeased; but to have that selfsame hunger grow older, outstrip baby proportions, assume a more aggressive manly form, and finally turn into a regular grizzly old veteran hunger, getting up with you from your meals and lying down with you at night, bathing with you in the cool beaver pool or mountain stream, sitting on your horse through long dreary rides, gnawing at your vitals, wrecking your even temper, turning your pleasure-trip into a wretched parody —this, I say, was hard to bear. And as I look back to those days, I cannot hide from myself that the very fact of our not having cut each other's throats, or snapped each other's heads off, speaks volumes for the innate good qualities of those four white men. The red man, juicy old Christmas, who knew our savage pleasantry from previous occasions, had suddenly discovered urgent business on the other side of the range, and had ridden off with the carcass of an unlucky prairie dog dangling at his saddle-bow.

Thirst and hunger are bad enough, but what are they in comparison to a scourge that swept down upon us when we struck the timbered foothills of the Rockies, *i.e.* the dreaded mountain flies—a species of mosquito, the most terrible of the genus *Culex?*

The contrasting extremes of the camel and the gnat are very applicable, when pointing out how very ridiculous it seems that a big, burly, bearded son of his mother should cut such mad capers, occupy such ludicrous positions, use such Titanic language, evince such an abnormal shortness of temper, and altogether present the appearance of a maniac, just because an animal, the body of which is smaller than a pin's head, chooses to make of his person a playground for its microscopic antics.

For the common weal of mankind I hope there is no such mosquito-ridden place on the green Earth as certain marshy lakes about the base of the foothills of the snow-capped Big Wind River Mountains. It was in the last days of July, the worst time; and the whole district was overwhelmed by enormous clouds of these torments, the creation of the abnormal drought which had laid dry lakes and creeks. Never before having been troubled to any extent by mosquitoes, we were totally unprovided with veils, or any material that could be substituted, the nearest thing to gauze, being empty canvas flour sacks, which *faute de mieux* came in very handy. One or two of our horses were white; and to give an idea of the myriads of the enemy, I may mention that when seen from a little distance they appeared of uniform dark colour. Life became an intolerable misery, men and beasts suffering alike. For while we, ludicrous scarecrows, were dragging ourselves along, with swollen faces and half-closed eyes, in the despairing listlessness of men who for a week knew not what a night's rest was, and who for a fortnight had not sat down to the semblance of a square meal, the poor brutes of horses were staggering along under their light loads, reduced to walking skeletons by the bloodthirsty pests.

But everything has an end, so also our unpleasant experiences. In the latter part of July we reached Fort Washakie, the most isolated of the military posts in the West. On leaving it, after a stay of a couple of days, we bid good-bye to fellow-beings, for till the end of November I saw only on two occasions strange white faces. On August 10th we reached Timberline on the Sierra Soshoné, and on the following day struck a delightful oasis in the uppermost belt of forest. Here we made the first permanent camp of nearly a week. Four-and-twenty hours later a snowstorm cleared the air of mosquitoes; and on the same day I killed four big wapiti

stags. With the first dinner where meat graced our table
the spell was broken. For more than four months we
roamed over incomparable mountain territory, for weeks
camped at altitudes varying between 10,000 and 12,000
feet over the sea-level—to-day perhaps on the borders of one of the hundreds of small exquisitely-beautiful mountain tarns that dot the great backbone of the
Big Wind River Mountains; to-morrow at the brink of a
deep gloomy canyon,[5] of mysterious depth and supreme
grandeur; while on the following day, night would surprise us close to Timberline, in the dense green wilderness
of the pathless forests of the Western slopes, where we
would spread our robes under the broad branches of a
stately silver pine; the following evening's camp-fire
lighting up great fantastically-shaped and grotesquely-
coloured walls of rock, closing in on every side a
small emerald-tinted meadow lining the bank of a
turbulent mountain stream, to which snug cliff-bowered
retreat access could only be gained by following the
beaver's example, and wading our horses through the
gloomy canyons the waters had worn through the surrounding mountains. A couple of weeks hence we would
probably be a couple of hundred miles away, threading our
way through the grotesque *mauvaises terres* scenery, grandly
coloured, and of the superbly *bizarre* formation, by which
the Sierra Soshoné, that unexplored sea of nameless peaks
cut up by deep gorges of tortuous course, is distinguished.
Every day, every hour, new scenery, new vistas of
Alpine landscape, burst upon our eyes. Game abounded, and
from the grizzly to the muledeer exceptionally large speci-

---

[5] In writing the word cañon, I prefer to follow its phonetic rendering.

mens rewarded the stalks of many hours along bad-land ledges, or the day's ride through forests.

The desire to avoid wearisome geographical details has led me to refrain filling these pages with matter of little interest to the general reader. I must, however, give those who may entertain a lurking desire to visit the Rockies some little clue to my wanderings. In the Appendix I have embodied a brief outline of the country and of its history in the way of previous explorations; here I will only say that the district in question, taken as a whole, has been tracked by three Government exploring expeditions on the Western, Northern, and South-Eastern extremities. Many portions visited by us were, so far as the information of leading authorities goes, never before visited by a party of white men. Until quite recently (1879) the country was most unsafe for small expeditions; and I am not aware that any shooting-party had ever, up to 1880, penetrated into the recesses of the Sierra Soshoné, or visited the Western slopes of the Wind River chain between Togwotee Pass and the head-waters of the Dinwiddy. The occasional trappers who had been there before us did so by turning squawmen, *i.e.* marrying Indian wives, and by turning Indians themselves had thus been able to intrude into those pleasant hunting-grounds.

CHAPTER III.

LIFE IN CAMP.

Camp incidents—Appearance of camp—Baking—Good appetites—Charms of free travel—Lake scenery—Naming camp—Nature of camps—Return to camp at night—Camp homes.

I HAVE purposely delayed speaking of our every-day life till we had reached the hunting and trapping grounds; to get at which, as the reader has heard, we had to pass through a series of little trials and petty hardships, sorely trying our mental and physical tempers.

Now everything is again bright and pleasant; and, if not exactly *couleur de rose*, the vast stretches of blue-green pines and silvery-trunked spruce through which we are constantly travelling, and the beautiful emerald-green "beaver-meadows" we frequently traverse, present more gratefully nature-like tints to eyes scorched by the glare of the verdureless Plains; while the magic air of timber-line regions exercises its rejuvenating powers on lungs that for weeks have breathed the alkaline dust of the same desert-like expanses. The camp fireside is again the meeting-place of cheerful faces and unbounded spirits; while the best of sport, amid grand Alpine scenery, gives keen zest to our every-day lives, and provides a never-failing fund for anecdote and chaff.

There is a peculiar charm in the independent mode of trapper voyaging. Entirely emancipated from the rest of mankind, unrestrained by the fetters and by the exigent demands of civilization, you roam about as free as the deer you constantly startle from their covert. You pitch camp, or scoop out a primitive "dug out," with the enfranchised liberty of the beaver. The great unknown lies before you; and, none but a character blunted to all natural feeling could fail to experience the pleasant, though sadly travestied, flush of the embryo "Weltentdecker," adding a subtle charm to pursuits dear to the sportsman's and to the naturalist's heart.

The next best every-day scene of our travels will convey the pleasant freedom that marks the life of our party.

"Boreas, the doggarned old hoss, has, after all, a better nose than any of us for finding a camping-place," remarks Port, one September evening, as, riding at the head of our little pack-train, through a glade traversing a grand old forest, he comes up to where I am sitting on a fallen pine, awaiting the party. And it is not an idle compliment either; for truly the old horse seems always to sniff a good camping-place from afar. As usual, I have taken an evening stalk on foot through the twilight forest, not so much for sporting purposes as to stretch my legs after a long day's ride, and also to examine the ground for tracks of wapiti and moose.

Boreas has, as on all such occasions, the reins thrown over his neck, fastened to a spring buckle cunningly concealed behind the horn of the Mexican saddle, and after receiving a slap or a mild kick, as a signal that he is not wanted and need not wait for me, ambles off alone after the pack-train, strolling ahead of it, till he finds an espe-

cially inviting bit of grass, upon which he will feast till
his companions get half a mile or so ahead, when he will
repeat his tactics. The sun is down, and both horses
and men are on the look-out for camp. A loud neigh—
"nicker" the trapper calls it—from Boreas, and an
answering one from his favourite mare, causes the above
remark. Looking round, we discover the equine camp-
finder standing 200 yards off, with head outstretched in
the middle of a most inviting little clearing, evincing
in his pose, as plainly as had he spoken: "This is
the boss camping-place for us." As yet we can see
no water—that most essential element in choosing the
camp site; but so convinced are we of my favourite's
sagacity, that the train is immediately swung to the side,
and very soon we catch sight of a clear little brook, half
hidden under tall rye-grass and the drooping branches of
stately spruce-pines. Ten minutes later the grass is littered
with the packs: here a heavy load of three sacks of flour,
there the elk-hide side-panniers, containing the "dry"
stores, *i.e.* those most to be protected against water when
fording and swimming the larger creeks and rivers;
yonder the powder-keg and sundry big bales of furs,
interspersed by "bunches" of steel traps. On a pile of
pack-saddles lie our four rifles, while sundry saddle-bags,
buffalo-coats, and carelessly flung-down Colts are strewing
the ground all round. The horses, just sufficiently tired
by their day's work to thoroughly enjoy a good roll, and
not stand about, as often, poor beasts, they do, with
drooping heads and pinched flanks, too tired to feed, are
relishing that pleasure to the fullest, while the example
of the two colts—general pets of the camp—racing each
other round and round, cutting the most amusing capers,

and nickering with wild delight, is followed by our two canine camp-followers, playing their doggish game of hide-and-seek with all the vivacity of youth and vigour.

It is the *beau-idéal* of a trapper's or hunter's camp, guarded by the great peak that overshadows the picturesque glade. The grass in rich plenty, reaching up to the knees of the horses, is green; not the tint of our pastures at home, but a green that matches the silvery trunks of the stately pines and the blue-green of their boughs, sweeping in languid curve the tall rye-grass at their feet. The smoke of the camp-fire, pleasantly perfumed by the cedarwood which produces it, rises in blue circles, higher and higher as the blaze increases, till at last it blends with the Alpine blue of the sky. The clear brook, traversing the glade sounds an irresistible invitation to enjoy a dip.

Let us look round. How content, how pleasant and pleased, everything looks! For a moment we wish we could roll in the green fragrant mountain-grass as do the horses and the dogs. Happy carelessness of what the past has brought and what the future ma bring—of the long weary rides through desolate parched deserts; of dreary " dry camps;" of swollen rivers swum by shrinking animals; of the deep snow, that presently will cover the mountain-side; of cold and hunger—blissful ignorance and forgetfulness are stamped on human, equine, and canine physiognomy, as each member, in his manner and way, is enjoying to the full the present.

Here, dotting the quiet peaceful glade before us, is animal life, the impulsive joyous spirit of healthful vigour, fanned to keen freshness by the cool bracing breeze straight down from the snow-fields. There, right round us, wrapped in solemn stillness and majesty, life of another kind—that of Nature as she was created, as yet undefiled by the desecrating hand of man.

But duty cuts short these musings; for in an "outfit" composed of the elements, and based on the simple principles of trapper fashion, as ours is, there is always plenty to do. A long day's ride has made us all hungry as Indians; so if we are to begin at the beginning, that very beginning is the supper.

The fire brought to proper cooking proportions—*i.e.* the coals raked to the front for baking, and the logs so arranged that pots and pans preserve their equilibrium—we all go to work. One man bakes; but that man is not I, for I was found wanting, since on one of my first attempts to do so, one cold drizzly night on a previous expedition I had to bake in the dark, and my pipe—an otherwise inseparable companion—was subsequently found in the loaf. Baking is altogether a very hateful occupation. Your face gets scorched, your knees get sooty, your fingers blistered, and it taxes not only your patience, but also your vocabulary of "Government talk." On cold days in winter you have got to wash your hands in a mush of water and ice; for hunger is a mighty impatient master, and there is no time to heat water in the camp kettle. The flour-sack is sure to be at the very bottom of the pack-sack, and the baking-powder, or "saleratus" (the grandest word in the trapper's very abridged dictionary), cannot be found, or when it is found everything around it in the pack bears the marks of your mealy fingers; for naturally, in the manner of man, you have first mixed the flour, and then only look about you for "that yar white powder as makes bread git up and hump itself," as an old trapper called it. But it is only in "real mean" weather, when the snow or frozen sleet beats down upon your devoted head, unprotected by tent or other shelter—for our outfit was singularly bare of your luxurious camp paraphernalia of Nimrods who travel in the Adirondacks with tent, camp-stools, and camp-bed—and the wind, a genuine No. 12 gale, whirling your flour from the pan, that you realize what baking really is. Then, probably, the giggling wretches who do not bake will hear some choice and not unfamiliar quotations, while their "Hurry up!" will set at defiance that good old trapper's proverb, "To make haste slowly, pans the best." It is always a comical sight to see big strapping fellows, their six-shooters at their waist, metamorphosed into cooks: their horny hands, but ill fit to handle pots and pans, their awkward touch, their heavy tramp, and withal their clumsy way of setting about things,—one and all combine to make a cowboy or trapper-cook a ludicrous sight. But more than comical it is to watch, on a fierce winter's night, a big hulking giant, wrapped in a buffalo-coat, make his preparation for baking, while a snow-hurricane is blowing, and damp wood is on the fire. With his back to the wind, the pan in which the flour is mixed—in nine cases out of ten the gold pan, in which at odd times he washes for that precious metal—carefully held inside his coat, as a loving mother would fondle her babe; between his teeth the tin cup full of water, from which, by a dexterous jerk of the head, he spills into the pan the requisite amount of the liquid; between his knees the flour-sack, and tucked under his arm the saleratus tin: thus the shaggy monster bakes!

Practice alone can make you an adept at it, as I found

out on a certain terrible December night, when Indians, as we thought, had stampeded our horses, the men having set out in pursuit, while I, being temporarily disabled by a thrust of a dying elk, was to guard camp and—bake. The gale howled, and turn wherever I would the snow beat with fierce violence against my face. Hundreds of times had I watched the men mix the flour under precisely similar circumstances; and were not my teeth as able as theirs to hold the tin cup of water, and was not my buffalo-coat as windproof as that of the trapper's? All very true; but yet my first attempt to clinch the ice-coated metal between my teeth resulted in a cold bath for my knees, while the second trial succeeded in so far as the holding was concerned. I could grasp the cup as long you liked, but, to save my life, I could not give that dexterous jerk necessary to spill some of the water into the pan, where the flour was in the meanwhile, notwithstanding the windproof quality of my coat, whirling about in utter disregard of my clothes. My bulldog grip continued, and at last I summoned up courage to give that fatal jerk. It is needless to say that the whole contents was landed in my face, where it very soon turned into a thin layer of ice, not increasing my good humour. Water was plentiful, so the cup was refilled; and, as I was determined to succeed, a second attempt at jerking was made. This time it was somewhat nearer the mark; for the liquid went down my neck only. That suicidal "reback action" of the water, as the men called it, was difficult to overcome. It would go back, instead of forward, be the jerk ever so gently and nicely adjusted. By the time my perseverance did succeed there was no flour left in the pan to mix, and the saleratus tin had rolled off, "running down the slope before a stiff breeze." When the men finally returned, I was no little proud of my two loaves, but less so of my flour-bedraggled appearance, leading the men to more than suspect "what a job it was to bake!"

No wonder, the reader will say, when I tell him that grumbling on the score of bread was not infrequent. It was either too salt, or too doughy, or too crisp, or too much saleratus in it, or burnt to a cinder, which latter, as we had only a frying-pan to bake in, and the fire generally of huge dimensions, would occur, notwithstanding the best intentions. It was, therefore, agreed among the men, that the first who should grumble was to relieve the then baker. Two or three days afterwards, when we had only a very miserable camp-fire, the bread was a mass of dough inside. The boy was the first to forget the penalty for grumbling. Taking a hearty bite at the bread, he exclaimed, "Doggarn this bread! I'll be darned if it ain't a mass of—" Then the paste gummed up his mouth; but recollecting at the same instant in what danger he was, he blurted out, half choked by the dough, "but I like it."

This time his quick wits had saved him; but he fell victim a day or two later, when, taking up a loaf just from the frying-pan, he dropped it as quickly, saying, "Cuss that hot bread!" The *vox populi* of the camp declared that "hot" was sufficient to convict, so he had to take the baker's place.

While the boy fetched the water, ground the coffee in a tin cup with the muzzle of his six-shooter—our coffee-mill having come to an early grave at the heels of the "kitchen mule," the others occupied themselves with the meat and bread. There were three frying-pans in the outfit: one, a very big one, was for the bighorn haunch or black-tail tender loin-steak; the other for the bread; while the third and smallest one fell to my lot. In it I fried, broiled, stewed, or boiled such odds and ends as struck my fancy. Beaver tail and bear liver were general favourites, not so elk brain or kidney. Cooking these little tidbits of camp-fare reminds me always of that most delightful occupation of the juvenile mind, making mud-pasties on the sands by the sea. Let the liver be a blotched mass of half-cooked gore, or the brain a jelly-like mass, or the kidney cinder on the outside and raw inside, yet you find it nice, and are happy. These latter delicacies the men never touched; for trappers are very fastidious in the choice of their meat, and I believe they thought me next to a barbarian for gourmandising on kidneys, which they consider "unclean, and not fit for a dog."

Once I inveigled a stranger to taste my favourite stew; but I am sorry to say it was not favourably received. "By the jumping Moses, you've been and gone done it!" he cried out. And when I asked him what I had gone and done, he replied, "Why, pisoned me, man, like a cayote." The fellow was a Hoosier (native of Indiana), and his language was the strangest mixture of Pennsylvania Dutch and Kentucky negroisms, and a liberal infusion of "we uns" and "you uns," and "gone done it" and "gwine to gone done it," I ever heard.

Cooking did not take long, and the "All set!" was a welcome signal to repair to our festive board. The water-proof sheet spread on the ground near the fire where the smoke was least troublesome; four tin plates, and as many cups and knives and forks, do not take long to lay, especially if they are tumbled out of their usual receptacle in a heap, every man "grabbing a root," *i.e.* helping himself to his own.

What a glorious thing a good, healthy appetite is!

Indeed ours was so glorious, that before leaving frontierland and entering the wilds we were well known for it, I am ashamed to say, at all the camps, ranches, and hunters' camps where we had partaken of hospitality. At one place the "boss," after watching in silence our attacks on the grub pile, remarked very good-humouredly, "Wa'al, boys, I'll be doggarned if I won't back you at grub-lifting against any other outfit in this yar country. By G—— I will, if it takes my bottom dollar and cleans me out to bed-rock." At one "road ranche"—a roadside inn, where you have to pay for your meals at a fixed rate—which I passed on my return to civilization, and where I struck the first potatoes after having gone five months without vegetables of any shape, the fellow who "ran" the house, after seeing me "through" my meal, asked me if I was thinking of returning to "these yer diggings." On my answering him, and innocently asking why he wanted to know, he said, "Wall, you see, stranger, times ain't been way up hereabouts, and our p'tater-patch yonder ain't as big as a county; but if you take back-tracks, I'd have to make it about that squar', sure."

The very next day (I was travelling in the mail-sleigh from a remote fort to the next little town, 160 miles off), luck would have it that, at a similar log-hovel hostelry, I struck butter, the first I had tasted for nearly half a year. I was hungry, and the butter looked fresh, and little besides bread on the table. A woman "ran" the house, a sour-looking Rocky Mountain "lady," whose life, to judge by her grim humour, must have consisted of one series of reverses, her birth being one of them. During my meal she sat opposite to me. She had not spoken a word, for on my entrance she only pointed to the table in the taciturn Western way; and moreover there was not time for gossip, as the mail-driver was in a hurry to finish his day's drive, with the thermometer down to −35° Fahr. My meal over, I threw the customary fifty-cent piece on the table, and was about to hurry out, when she spoke up :—"Stranger, you ain't got no mother-in-law, that's sartin. Hadn't my cow just calved, I would donate you them ar' four bits" (fifty cents) "to buy yourself one. You kinder want one to teach you what four bits' worth of butter hefts" (weighs).

But I am rambling away from our trapper-camp. Supper over, the work of the evening began. First of all the stock wanted looking after. If it were an Indian country—the case most of the time—three or four of the horses had to be picketed or hobbled; but before doing that, it was necessary to let them feed. Probably they had wandered off a mile or so while we were at supper, and hence it took the man whose turn it was to attend to them the best part of the evening to get them back into the next neighbourhood of the camp, pick a good patch of grass, water them, and secure those whose turn it was. The others looked to the washing up and "straightening out" of things generally. I fancy many a good and true man's lips will curl with disdain as he reads that rifles have to be cleaned, cartridges require loading, clothes need patching with sailor's needle and buckstring thread, horses have to be shod, coffee browned, gaping holes in boots and moccasins want the awl and last, straps and pack-harness require splicing, the pack-sacks cry out for patches, and pack-saddles for odd screws, and no end of other suchlike pleasant and unpleasant pastimes, not to mention our groom's duties of saddling our horses and taking them to water when they are thirsty. But, then, reader, you and I, I hope, always comfort ourselves with the knowledge that the guns, the boots, and the horses are our own, while the lips that scoff at these menial occupations are not. Everything that fell to my share accomplished, my pocket-book with my daily notes had its turn. Often an hour or two was spent in jotting down, in a scrawling hand —the powder-keg between my knees serving as table— some very inspired thoughts that could not wait. When, at very rare intervals, a chance was looming up of sending by Indians letters to the next frontier fort, often 150 or 200 miles off, the evening was devoted to epistolary duties; the result of such hours, in the shape of letters, being pinned to the inside of some morose old buck's blanket, or nailed to the board on which the papoose was strapped, the latter being of the two the surest way. Later on in the season, when winter storms and intense frosts were in regular attendance, writing became a more embarrassing undertaking, till finally it had to be abandoned altogether.

"Going to bed" is a very simple affair. Boots or moccasins are taken off, and carefully covered by the robe you lie on, for they must not be exposed to the frosty air, or they will freeze hard, in which case you will in the morning hear some unchristianlike conversation. This is about all you take off; what extra clothing in the shape of a knit jersey, or even buffalo-coat, you put on, depends upon the temperature. Your pockets are emptied, and their contents placed in your hat, alongside the six-shooter, underneath your pillow, which probably will be the saddle; while the rifle is equally carefully laid alongside the boots, so as to be handy, and perfectly protected against rain or snow. Trapper-beds are snug and warm, and as simple as the toilette of the occupants. A bearskin or two, with a blanket, if you have one, under you, and two robes as cover, with a large sheet of waterproof tarpaulin, to turn rain and snow, spread over the whole, is all that is wanted.[1] If you pitch camp while it is yet light, a "soft" spot for your roost can be looked up, though generally the discovered softness will be more illusionary than real, and such being the case, old mountaineers usually do not trouble themselves about it. After dark the less you bother about stones or projecting rocks under your bed the wiser you are. Remove those that are loose, and as you "twist to fit the bumps" regard those that are not loose with the supreme contempt the sound sleep of the Rocky Mountains will enable you to manifest.

Two things are of importance anent making beds. The first is to lie with your feet towards the direction from whence the wind blows, for if you do not observe this precaution you will risk having your cover and blankets lifted bodily off you by a sudden gust. Secondly, choose as level a spot as you can, for if the plane of your bed slopes ever so slightly to one side you will surely roll out of your warm nest in the night, and if you lie with your legs downwards you will in the morning find yourself "'way down," where when you went to sleep you left your feet.

Avoid, if you possibly can, to sleep with another man; sacrifice rather a blanket or a robe than risk passing an uncomfortable night at the side of a restless sleeper. Of course there are cases where, if you find yourself in a strange camp without your own bedding, you will have to share beds. On one of my previous trips I once was witness of a ludicrous scene in the way of bedfellow trou-

[1] See Appendix.

bles. It was in a stockman's camp, which I reached late in the evening, my horse being too worn out to take me the remaining twelve or fifteen miles to my own fireside. The boys, in the hospitable way peculiar to them, let me have a "bed" to myself, while two of them *shared*. I had not got fairly to sleep when I was roused by some angry and not very select biblical quotations. The trouble was in the double bed next to mine; and presently the cause was developed. It seems that one of the men, knowing the other to be a restless sleeper, addicted to violent kicking, had buckled his big Spanish spurs with two-inch rowels to his stockinged feet. Against these his restless bedmate had come to grief; and the other man's dry, "Wa'al, I reckon'd you *would* hurt yourself," raised a titter all round.

Another little anecdote of a Western Judge and an Irish navvy sharing beds is worth telling. The former addressing himself, self-importantly, to his humbler companion asked whether he had ever slept in the old country with a judge? To which Pat responded: "No, sure that I havn't; but sure, ye mightn't have been a judge in the ould countree."

The camp, if a stay of a day or two is intended, rapidly acquires a homelike look. Long six-inch nails, carefully removed on leaving, are driven an inch or two into the trunks of the trees that surround our quarters. On them are hung up the various articles that otherwise would be lying about in primitive disorder. One trunk is the larder tree, on the next are hung all the traps, the third is a sort of general wardrobe, while the fourth has my stout leather "hold-all" slung up. What a wealth of recollections does not that "hold-all" conjure up!

Called by the men the "boss's Saratoga trunk," it has undergone on its three expeditions a wonderful amount of roughing. The receptacle of the most heterogeneous knick-knacks, it can, if ever a trunklike receptacle could, tell fabulous tales of travel. When only half filled—nearly cut in twain by the strangling pack-ropes, pulled across the saddle as taught as Port's or Edd's strength would let them. When full—squashed a dozen times a day out of all pristine shape and contour between handy trees standing close together, and past which the horse or mule carrying it, with the peculiar obstinacy of all pack animals, *would* force a passage. Soused by frequent immersions into rivers and creeks; now rolling down steep slopes, with the brute to whose back it is roped using it as buffer, and finally, after cannoning against rocks and trees, when he is brought up at the bottom with a dull thud that jars your tenderest chords. Disappearing in the distance, dragging and bumping along the ground, for it is still attached by the rope to the stampeded horse, who, after "lighting into bucking," has partially rid himself of his burden, and is now showing the country to my invaluables. To see a horse go head over heels down a precipitous bank, and land at the bottom either "ended up," as the trapper calls a position of wholly disturbed equilibrium, or see the waters of a rapid-flowing mountain torrent closing over his head, is very funny, for you have long come to the conviction that nothing short of absolute instantaneous annihilation can hurt or harm a pack-horse. But your smile is apt to change into a look of agonized fear if the loud laughing shouts of the men inform you that, not sacks of flour or packs of skins, which you at first imagined to be on that very horse, are its burden, but the devoted "hold-all," for ever being sat on, ducked, kicked, dragged, scraped, hoisted, flung about, and otherwise maltreated. Like a flash of lightning the contents of the hapless bag are passed in review. The stockings and flannel garments cannot be damaged; the reloading tools of the rifle are all of iron, and have been ducked many a time without harm. Boots, the three or four small books, the store of tobacco, a tin case with fuzees and matches, a similar receptacle for the entire store of the men's strychnine, which, to prevent accidents, I have taken charge of—for hitherto it was usually "packed along" in uncomfortable proximity to our flour and sugar, —the stout waterproof writing-portfolio, with sheet-tin sides, some extra pipes, knives, &c. One and all are by their nature, or by that of their covering, not liable to be damaged, were the "hold-all" to be thrown from a church steeple, or to be engulfed in the Niagara. But what of that little bottle of cayenne powder—the only bottle-like breakable in the outfit—which I received as a present at the Fort? Broken to tiny splinters in a bumping race, the contents have been nicely distributed through the whole sack; and when opened it made us all cry a yard off, and what is more, continued to make us cry and sneeze by fits and starts for the next month. But everything has its bad and also good sides; even that cayenne powder had redeeming points, for it accomplished what nothing else seemed capable of performing, namely, it cured a mischievous young Newfoundland dog of a perplexing trick of carrying off personal property, to play with in private. All kinds of things had thus been lost —socks, handkerchiefs, winter gloves, and other articles of our simple toilette. With playful bound, the young thief espied that evening an innocent-looking glove lying on the ground near camp, and with the usual canine gambols it was tossed up—only once, mind you, for the next instant that dog was weeping over his sins. On the whole, it would be hard to say who cried more, we from laughter or the pup from cayenne. He never touched gloves again.

Or, to give another instance of suchlike mishaps, what of that single paper of " paint," [2] which, after my last attempt at trading with a morose old Arrappahoe Indian, I had forgotten to restore to its proper water-tight receptacle of sheet-tin, and left knocking about the " hold-all," perfectly unprotected against the unforeseen sousing the mal-intentioned Old John had in store for it ! We all laughed at his frantic efforts to get out of the whirlpool into which his own obstinacy had driven him. But I for one no longer laughed when, by a final vigorous leap, the horse gained dry ground, and the water that had inundated the " hold-all " trickled forth a bright vermilion-hued liquid. I never knew a thimbleful of colour dye so much; and no doubt the family of beavers, in whose pool a day or two afterwards I did my washing, must have thought the same.

We were in the habit of giving every camp where we stayed more than one night, and even many so-called twelve-hour camps, a distinctive name. For not only is

[2] One of the best mediums of trading with Indians is " paint " *i.e.* Chinese vermilion, put up in small packets, similar to Seidlitz powders. They use it for painting their persons ; and, next to whiskey, which it is a criminal offence to trade or give to Indians, it is a very favourite article amongst most wild tribes of the North-west. I had taken several pounds with me, to trade horses and peltry for the men. The papers containing the powdered paint are known as " a paint."

this a great aid when referring in after-time to one in particular, not to be obliged to have recourse to the very roundabout trapper geography—which at best was only possible in that portion of the frontier country where the creeks and mountains had names, and also not to be obliged to use strange-sounding descriptive terms, as, for instance, " the camp six miles up the second creek, on the west side of the south fork of the west fork of the Cottonwood creek." Not only may this " Cottonwood creek " be *primâ facie* wrong, but there are such an innumerable number of Cottonwood, Beaver, Great and Little Sandy, Muddy, Sweet-water, and Stinking-water creeks in the West, that, at best, this sort of designation is worse than useless. So with us every camp received its name, and was henceforth known by it. Usually called after some incident—and few camps were without that—which occurred at it, one could instantly identify the place indicated by the speaker when he referred to some locality visited by us two or three months previously. Looking through my diary I come upon rather odd names. " Hunger camps," paraphrased in all sorts of ways, more explanatory than euphonious, of course abounded on the first part of the trip. Some others were more practical than funny, as, for instance, the " Live skunk," the " Dead skunk," the " Sick rattler," the " Knife in the thigh," the " Pipe in the loaf," the " Boss baker," the " Peppery glove," the " Trampled coffee-mill," the " Split flour-sack," the " Big bear," and the " Lost-stocking camp." Others were pathetic : " No horse," " Gone up," " Big Lie," " Boss Lie "—the two last referring to romancing guests, for I am speaking also of previous expeditions, where we more frequently came into contact with story-tellers of Western grit and bottom; while a dozen of more than usually famous "Stampedes," each designated by the leading equine criminal's name, rendered some of our camp sites memorable. A few were of grim import, thus "Deadman's camp," where we found a man's body in the brush close to our roosts, after wondering all night what on earth smelt so badly; "White-woman's-hand camp" when one of the dogs (we were camped near the old emigrant trail) discovered a mummified human hand, which, to judge by its size, was that of a woman. Several combined the ludicrous with the grim. Thus, for instance, on two occasions the Plains water, more than usually impregnated with alkaline salts, made us, accustomed as we were to its disturbing effects, remember the first as "Ache camp" (there was a prefix to the first word). The second instance, a more flagrant case than the first, Henry, with his usual quick originality, helped us out of the difficulty of inventing a distinctive name, by remarking that as we all had the ache of "the wurst sort," that name was the best one for this uncanny spot. At the time we were travelling through cattle-ranche country, where every two or three days we would meet cavalcades of wild young Texan "ranchers" or cowboys. At the camp fireside, where topographical notes upon the country would, as usual, be exchanged, a laugh was frequently raised by the catch answer inquirers would receive, who on hearing us talk of the "sudden death" qualities of that 'er water at "worst sort camp," they asked: "Worst sort of what camp?"

Among the 1879 camps I find another strangely named one, *i.e.* "Wisdom-tooth camp," where an acquaintance, to whom I have before referred, was laid up, cutting, at a somewhat late day in life, his masticating ivory.

Life in Camp.

Not a few were descriptive names. One instance will suffice: it was "Fish-in-bed camp," on the borders of "Fish-in-bed lake," where, one fine September morning I caught a two-pound trout, and shot a fine wapiti stag, right from my "bed," spread within a foot or two of its placid surface. The stag had come down to water in the early dawn, and, happening to see his outline through the mist, my Express ended his career. Half jokingly, I flung—half an hour or so later, at Port's suggestion, just as the sun was tipping the crags overhead—my line into the shallow water at my side. A minute later a big lazy trout had committed suicide, obliging me to get up and land him.

In judging these simple and decidedly unromantic camp appellations, the reader must not forget that we were breathing the Western air, which is an effective vermin-killer in point of æsthetic sentiment. Most deadly of the men's caustic humour was that of young Henry. Let one instance explain what I mean. We had made camp in a more than usually beautiful spot near a lake, and I was sitting on one of the side panniers near the fire smoking my pipe and doing the lazy. Suddenly my meditations were interrupted by Port's voice informing me that the pack I was sitting on seemed to be on fire. Raising the lid, I found that one of the tin boxes containing matches had got on fire, probably when the sack was thrown from the pack animal. I had been sitting on a volcano, for, cheek by jowl, with the match tin was the fifty pound powder-keg and the whiskey. Henry, who saw that I was about to scold him, for I had told him several times to keep the matches and the powder apart in the packs, to which he usually would answer, "I guess if they do blow up, we'll find it out," saved himself by his quick wit. His quizzical, "By golly, that *would* have been rough on the whiskey," turned the escape I had had at once into ridicule. It was my idea to call the camp, in view of the sufficiently narrow shave, "Pilgrim's Progress Camp," but that was too "tony" for the men, so I let them have their way, and the spot was henceforth known as the "Boss's go *down* to heaven camp."

In the old world beautiful localities are usually distinguished by euphonious appellations that somehow give one an idea of the place which is not as a rule disappointed when we come to visit it. In the Atlantic States of America this is often carried to unpleasant extremes. Names that carry the weight of beauty or at least that of mellow old age are given to outrageously unpicturesque localities and glaringly new edifices. In the West, away from big-named cities, the other extreme is the rule. The old *Coureurs de bois* were the essence of practicalness unrelieved by a particle of imagination. We find such names as *six cailloux* (the six pebbles) spoken of as *Siskyou*, the Indian tribe *Bois Brulés* are known as *Bob Rulys*, the *Bois Blancs* as Bob Longs. The river known to the Spanish of Mexico as *Les Animas* (the souls), and to the French as the *Purgatoire*, is called by the western man, *Picket-wire*, reminding one rather of the frontier rendering of Wilkes Booth's words after shooting Lincoln, *Sic semper tyrannis*, *i.e.* into *six serpents and a tarantula.*

A word or two is due to explain to those of my readers who may not have travelled with a trapper pack-train, the nature of camps. There are three kinds; the "travelling," the "light-pack," and the "permanent" camp. The first is the one made every evening while *en route,* pitched at the termination of the day's travel, at the first suitable place that presents itself, where water, wood, and good grazing for the horses can be found. When the first-mentioned essential is absent, and a camp must be made to rest man and beast, it is called, as we have already heard, a *dry camp*—one of the most unsatisfactory experiences of Western travel. Where wood, not even the rank sagebrush or greasewood, or buffalo chips are procurable—a catastrophe, however, of rare occurrence—a *cold camp* is the result. The *permanent* one is where a stay from a day or two to several weeks is made. *Light-pack camps* are made when short branch trips become desirable. You take but quite the most necessary things—grub for two or three days, the blankets or skins of one bed to accommodate two men, and everything is packed on one pack-horse. These are by far the most enjoyable ones; for you can travel faster, are but slightly bothered with the pack-animals—for the single one you have with you, the steadiest of the lot, can be led—and you can get over and through places where the whole train could not possibly succeed, except with considerable loss of time and great risk to the less sure-footed animals. We were constantly making these light-pack camps. Often I would start off alone, or Port would accompany me, while the rest either travelled on, and met me at a specified landmark, or made a permanent camp, with a view to trapping. On one or two occasions we "strung out" our camps even longer; that is, we made several light-pack camps, each getting lighter as we did away with unnecessaries, and left behind us horses we did not want. Thus several times we had our stores câched at one place, 100 or 120 miles off; then we left six or seven horses, and a lot of unnecessaries, in charge of Henry. Twenty miles further, the second man remained back with three horses, "trapping a creek out;" while Port and I went twenty or thirty miles further, to some of the little lakes, where he and two pack-horses remained, with the same object; my own goal being higher up, close to the snow-fields, where only Boreas, my favourite hunting pony, could get to. After an absence of one, two, or three days, I returned to Port; and, taking what are technically called " back tracks," we picked up, *seriatim*, the other three camps. This telescoping of camps is a very pleasant mode of giving some of your horses the rest they are in want of, besides enabling the men and me to cover more ground than otherwise would be possible—they with their traps, and I with the rifle.

Awkward, or unexpected, interruptions now and again disturb the connecting part of these light-pack camps. Thus, for instance, a snow storm would come on, and while it would be very bad in my neighbourhood, it would just " blow a little " twenty or thirty miles off, where the " outfit " was camped; and hence, while they would act upon the pre-arranged plan, and move on a day or two's travel to where we were to meet, the storm would imprison me in my camp, which, generally, of the very lightest order, consisted of a couple of robes, a cup, plate, and a frying-pan. If my little store of grub, flour, coffee, and sugar held out, and a quarter of a Bighorn or a Blacktail was festooning the nearest tree, all well and good; but if flour ran short, and I had killed no game before the storm surprised me, the consequences were short commons, and a bad time generally. I remember on both of my last trips, such "disvobulations," as the men called them, breaking grub and all other connexions in a most tyrannical and sudden manner—days that were not as pleasant to live through as they are now in the retrospect.

With us, travel partook of the usual features of exploration. None of us had ever been through or near the districts we were about visiting. We had nothing to guide us, for the only faulty chart that at the time existed of the Upper Wind River and Sierra Soshoné country—a copy of which I had procured through the kind offices of the General then commanding the North-Western Division, had, along with another essential commodity, *i.e.* my miniature medicine-case, being engulfed during one of the crossings of the Big Wind River, and, no doubt, had long found their way into the Mississippi and the Atlantic Ocean. And even had we retained the chart's services it would not have helped us, for not only, as I subsequently discovered, was it faulty, but its scale was much too small to be serviceable for mapping out the daily course.[3] Every two or three days we would sight a great peak, such as Fremont's, or the Teton; and as we knew where they were, the lay of the country could be marked by those means. The Big Wind River mountains afforded us all the sport we wanted. The men found rare trapping ground, and I was kept busy with the big heads of Wapiti and Bighorn—events of which I shall presently have to speak in a more detailed manner.

---

[3] Even to-day there exists no serviceable map of the whole Wind River and Sierra Soshoné country.

To most men the life I led would appear undoubtedly the essence of old-fashioned crabbedness. And yet if many of them could for once experience the glorious sense of freedom that fills the whole being in those far-off wilds which crown the great dome of a vast Continent, I think they would presently look back upon idle, colourless, city existence in a murky and vitiated atmosphere, no longer as the brightest and most joyous of existences, but rather as one which to endure is a necessary evil, but from which to escape fills you with the light-hearted transport of your schoolboy days.

What, for instance, can be more delightful to the lover of sport and of Nature than a long day's ramble about Timberline, in the clear, sparkling atmosphere of those altitudes.

If you are an admirer of forest scenery, there are vast stretches of literally trackless forests. Some composed of veteran spruce pine, where the trees grow close together, and you can wander for miles without catching sight of the sky; others, on the uppermost reaches of timber vegetation, spread over the upland slopes in more detached masses, patches of snow still lingering in gulches on the northern declivities of the range. Here the scenery resembles Alpine landscape: the Wengeren Alp reproduced on the summit of the Rockies. If you are a lover of the curious in Nature, visit yonder stretches of burnt forest, set afire probably by a July or August thunderstorm. If not endowed with rare endurance and provided with an axe, you will fail to penetrate very far into the maze of fallen trees; and should there be a strong breeze blowing, the crashing of lifeless trees who, though their roots are charred to cinders, have somehow retained an upright position, will warn you not to venture into the devastated wood.

Alpine lake scenery is replete with charming details, and here among the hundreds of lakelets you have the opportunity of studying their character in a diversity represented in very few places I know of. Numerous as they are, no two are alike in expression. Let the surroundings be as analogous as two drops of their water, yet a subtle something gives identity to each. In not a few instances it will be so unappreciable that words cannot depict the difference. Or again, there will be a curve of the shore, a peculiar tint of the water, the presence or absence of a wooded promontory, the great trunk of an uprooted pine, half floating on the placid surface, half stranded on the pebbly beach; while on the next this wreck of Nature will be replaced by a colony of quaintly-tufted duck, one and all specific features, endowing the picture with a distinct personality. One lake you will see with a great Wapiti stag or quaintly uncouth Moose[4] standing knee-deep in the water, or the presence of beaver will give it the peculiar charm of inhabitedness; while the next one, just as picturesquely situated, will have about it a lifeless, desolate air, that detracts from its idyllic loveliness. Some are shut in by beetling walls of great height, which impress you with a sense of prison-like melancholy. In the middle of one, I remember, a rocky tooth rose from the water in weird form. On the top an eagle had built its nest; reminding me of the historical Old Rocky Mountain eagle, the sole inhabitant of an island below

---

[4] In the Northern extremity of the Big Wind River chain Moose can now and again be seen; it is about the most southernmost point to which they extend.

one of the first falls of the Missouri, in Montana. The
bird and its nest was minutely described by the first
explorers of the West, Lewis and Clarke, who penetrated
to the headwaters of the great river in 1805.[5] Other
lakes, higher up above timber-line, surrounded by Titanic
boulders and rocks, thrown together in amazing confusion,
look as inhospitable as their surroundings are savage.
Some are deep, and their water of an exquisite beryl blue
and of such crystal clearness, that from overhanging cliffs
your gaze penetrates to a depth of astonishing profundity;
others are shallow and black-looking, with no visible
afflux or influx; some swarm with fish, others lack every
sign of living thing in or around their gloomy depths;
and not a beaver-sign, not a track of Wapiti, Bighorn,
or Deer is visible on the shore. In several instances I
found them to lie in tiers over each other; thus on the
southern slopes of what I believe is Union peak there are
no less than eleven small lakelets lying in six tiers over
each other. The lowest is at an altitude of about ten, the
highest close to 12,000 feet, huge perpendicular steps in
the mountain formation separating each set. Such is the
diversified character of these mountain tarns, on many of
which the eye of white man had presumably never rested.

Let the reader stretch himself at my side, on the soft
sward on the banks of such a tranquil mountain lake,
10,000 feet above the Atlantic and Pacific, to one, or per-

[5] Most of the subsequent explorers describe this bird, or at least
what they supposed to be the same bird. Thus Reynolds, who saw
him in 1860, and Roberts in 1872, speak of him as crippled by age,
and the latter reports his pinions as badly dilapidated. A later
traveller says: The jolly old sentinel, passing away the golden days
of a ripe age in one eternal 4th of July, looked old enough to have
participated in the affair at Bunker Hill!

haps to both of which it sends its waters. It is a lovely autumn afternoon; the forenoon's stalk has been a successful one, for yonder, his noble antlers half immersed in the limpid waters of the lake, lies stretched out the majestic form of a master of the forest, a giant among Wapiti. Arduous has been the stalk after the wary monarch of the woods, and many a smaller brother escaped with his life as, bent upon bagging the big one, I stepped with the noiseless tread of moccasined feet through the dense timber or along the creeks—for my guide, the fresh tracks of my quarry; for my sole companion, the old Express rifle which has rolled over many a one before.

An eight-hours' stalk in the keen, bracing atmosphere of these altitudes makes one hungry, and the slices of Bighorn meat and the chunks of camp-baked bread, washed down by the contents of a battered old hunting-flask, disappear with rapidity—adding, when the appetite is once appeased and the pipe is set ablaze, fresh beauties to the lovely scene rolled out before me. The tranquil lake, with not a ripple on it, stretches away to the distant abruptly-rising cliffs, that lead up to snow-fields and to the grandly built-up peak. The lake is encircled on three sides by an unbroken chain of sombre pine forest, and the little bays, and wooded forelands jutting out into the water, are fringed with groves of the hardy willow peculiar to these altitudes.

With hands crossed under my head I lie there, and let the gentlest of breezes, soughing through the tapering tops of the stately pines, play with the open collar of my flannel shirt. Utter seclusion has always great charms, and nowhere more so than here. The nearest human habitation is ten days' ride off, and for many weeks not a strange human being has crossed my path. And yet this loneliness is not oppressive, for dumb friends break the monotony and enchain attention. As the sun sinks, gilding the cyclopean masonry of the buttresses overhead, my chum and special crony, the "old man" beaver, with his spouse and kittens, will presently issue forth from their underground habitation, and furrow the glassy surface of the lake with silvery streaks as they swim from bank to bank, cutting or collecting feedsticks—the winter's provender—or tall saplings to repair, on the most approved principles of beaver hydrostatics, some damage to the family dam. My friends of the deer tribe are sure to come down to the water; and if the day has been warm, or the flies and mosquitoes troublesome in the dense timber to which most game retires during noon, I shall witness such a bathing scene as would make the heart of a Landseer throb. The wary otter, out on his foraging expedition, is creeping along the banks of the lake, and woe to the trout that comes within the reach of his extraordinarily agile grab.

A flight of wild geese, wanderers from northern latitudes bent for the south, alight on the lake, the loud splash of their descent frightening away the beaver and a quaint little family of blue-winged teal, who have been circling and diving about for the last hour or two in the little bay, not ten yards from where I am lying, skimming over the water, uttering their low plaintive "teat, teat," the blue of their wings glistening like polished steel. They disappear at last at the end of a long silvery pathway made by their wings on the glass-like surface. [6]

[6] It is remarkable that these beautiful birds seem equally at home in the extreme north as in the centre of America. During

The gentle breeze has died away, as it often does after the sun has set. The glorious colours, tinting the heavens with ever-changing brilliancy, have at last given way to that peculiar clearness of the atmosphere which lights up the distant snow-clad peak with an ashen hue, and makes the forest seem nearer to us than ever. Night is closing in apace, a gauzy mist rises from the lake, while stray stars are already visible, reminding me that I have a long walk to camp, across strange country. The pipe is re-filled, and shouldering my rifle I stroll homewards. Crossing long stretches of open upland, dark forms of deer or elk flit hither and thither, and as likely as not old Ephraim, the grizzly of the Rockies is setting out on his nocturnal raid. The bold outline of yonder peak is a landmark, and the north star my guide, leading me through the forest, across gulches, and along the gloomy depth of canyons as safely as had I a beaten trail before me. The sombre woods, looking so silent and gloomy from the distance, are, as I enter them, alive with strange noises. My moccasined feet do not allow me to walk very fast, for there is a wealth of sharp pointed branches strewing the ground, and in the darkness, with only fitful moonbeams finding their way through the network of pines, the foot instinctively seeks its way in a cautious manner. Stealthily

---

the breeding season they are as plentiful on the Saskatchewan as they are at the mouth of the Mississippi. Audubon says that they are to be found as far north as the 57th parallel, and as far south as the island of Cuba. Unlike the green-winged teal, which brave the coldest weather, they depart at the first sign of ice. It is interesting to note that Audubon and Bachman believed that the habits of the blue-winged teal proved a *double* migration. On the highland lakes to which I refer I have often seen them. They swim very buoyantly, and generally close together.

I thread my way through the timber, while around me is to be heard that quaintest of sounds emitted by the Wapiti stag at this season of the year. At night, in the silent forest, this tone, not unlike the notes of an Æolian harp, has a weird charm about it, that matches well the grand melancholy vastness of Western mountain landscape. My faithful guide-star leads me past a small forest tarn, a mere pool in comparison to the one just left. Here again there is a family of beaver at their nocturnal work of dam-building; and as I proceed along the shore studded with willows, the paterfamilias crosses the mirror-like surface lit up by the bright moonlight, infinitely brighter than in the Old World, a silvery ripple marking the course of the dark bullet-shaped head—all that is visible of the indefatigable little labourer. He is making for a willow-bush a yard or so from me, where, ready for transportation, lie a number of slender stems, from two to seven feet long, which he has cut under water during daytime. Watching him as I stand motionless, hidden by a friendly shadow, he raises himself out of the water, his silken coat, reflecting the bright moonbeams, appearing as of burnished silver. Firmly grasping between his powerful teeth a stem at the big end, where it is some inch and a half in diameter, he dives backwards and proceeds to return to his dam, with the leafy stem trailing beside him. A twig breaks under my weight, and the noise frightens the beaver, who, with a loud slap of his broad tail on the water, dives under, leaving the stem to float in the centre of gradually widening circles, to mark the spot where the cautious animal sought safety in his element. The noise has not only disturbed the beaver, but also a fine Wapiti stag, who has been lurking unobserved in the thick undergrowth near me, where he failed to scent or hear my approach. With one grand bound he has cleared the brush, and is standing up to his knees in the lake, his whole attitude that of keen watching. He is a noble fellow—an old warrior, too, for his shaggy neck is nearly twice the usual size, and one of the main prongs of his massive antlers is broken off short. Full five minutes he stands there, gazing intently towards the tree under whose sweeping boughs I am standing. The breeze is favourable, and the deep shadow hides my form so effectually, that, notwithstanding my proximity, he cannot see his human foe.

Stepping out from behind the tree, I snap my fingers. A toss of the head, and the stag is off, crashing madly through the timber in his headlong flight, while the peculiar noise of his antlers striking against the reverberating trunks of lofty pines, can be heard for some time.

Other strange sounds fall on the ear as I proceed with quickened step towards camp, sounds that you never hear in daytime, when, usually, oppressive stillness reigns in the great upland forests. The hoot of the owl is one of the most quaintly weird; but it is not like the unearthly wail of the puma, or mountain lion, demoniacal and ghoullike as no other sound in the wide realm of nature. As it re-echoes through the forests you involuntarily shudder, for it is more like a woman's long-drawn and piteous cry of terrible anguish than any other sound you could liken it to. Once heard, it will never be forgotten; and it can no more be compared to the jabber of the cayote or the howl of the hyena, than a baby's cry of displeasure resembles its mother's piercing shriek of terror as she sees the little one in a position of danger. Out only at night, they are of all beasts of prey the most watchful, and most difficult to shoot; and though their fearful call, in very close vicinity, has frequently stampeded our horses, and startled some of us from sleep, I have only been near enough to shoot, and kill, one single specimen in all my wanderings. Half an hour more, and I reach the last stretch of meadow, bathed in a flood of moonlight. Grazing on it in peaceful quiet are our trusty friends the horses. From afar they have seen me, and their snorts show their watchfulness; for here the grizzly is at home, and pony meat is better than ants and berries. My well-known voice pacifies them, however, at once, and brings the old horse, my favourite, trotting up to me to get his wonted piece of bread, while the two colts, favourite playfellows of his, dash past me in a spirited race, their heels high up in the air. Both these lively young animals, general pets of the camp, were foaled on the trip, and, wonderful to say, managed to outlive great hardships. The commotion among the faithful workers has been noticed in camp by the two watch-dogs, well trained to their work. They dash out into the darkness; but their angry bay changes into a bark of pleasure and welcome as they recognize me, and, whining with doggish delight, bound towards the belated wanderer.

Half a dozen big trunks of dry Alpine cedar-wood have been thrown on the fire by the men—a sure sign that supper is ready, for no cooking can be done at a blaze as big as a small loghouse afire—and the broad flames leap high up, licking the far-reaching branches of the next pine.

The camp scene, as I see it from the dark recess of the forest, bathed in the brightest of lights, and surrounded by shadows of quaint shape and varying effect, is a picturesque sight. There is little about it that reminds one of civilization—no tent, camp-stools, and other luxuries of modern " campers," strew the ground. The two men and the boy, all aglow with Rembrandt colours, are wild rough-looking customers, their six-shooters in their belts, and their rifles leaning against a handy tree. They have finished their supper—for, having a very erratic " boss," they never wait for him—and are grouped round the fire, smoking the pipe of good-fellowship ere they begin the work of the evening. A dozen steel traps and a pile of fur gleaming with silvery sheen, as the silken coats of several beaver and one wolverine catch the light, are scattered about at their feet. Two hours' work for two men means that heap, for the animals have to be skinned most carefully, and the peltry stretched and pegged out. After my own supper, of a panful of trout fried in bear's fat, and a tender loin steak of a bighorn, has been done justice to, my briar—tied with a piece of buck-string round my neck, for pipes have a most uncanny knack of getting lost, and this one is the last but one out of the half-dozen I started with—is pulled forth, filled, and its comforting contents are lighted at an ember from the bright log-fire. Leaning back in the hollow of my saddle, which has furnished me with a convenient prop during the meal, the sporting news of the past twelve hours is exchanged. The men are no great arithmeticians; so, after counting the heap of peltry, and making a rapid summary, I help them to form a correct estimate of their take, and of the precise number of dollars their day's labour has put them ahead. My own brief tale is soon told: "Jumped a grizzly, missed a good head, but got a better one;" and, while the plans for the morrow, the fetching in of the aforesaid good head, and the strategical distribution of the entire stock of traps, are being duly matured in council, time has passed, and I must fain turn to my several little camp duties.

The evening wears on, and as the lazy ones watch the glittering skinning knife busily at work—chaff the only plaister, if the keen edge of the oddly-shaped tool peels the wrong hide—I presently set out to take a last look at our horses, and at our only watch, the "dipper," as the constellation of the Great Bear is called out West, and which by its varying positions indicates time as correctly as the sun at daytime. Everything is quiet; the horses are grazing peacefully, and the only audible sound we can hear is the distant whistling of Wapiti. Dragging behind me as I return to camp a dead pine, I pile it on the fire, and by the bright flames which leap up, the bear and buffalo-skin bed, is smoothed and occupied. Soon, wonderfully soon, the sound sleep of the Rocky Mountains hushes the camp

CHAPTER IV.

OUR DUMB FRIENDS IN CAMP.

Our horses on the glade—Boreas, my favourite horse—His origin and development—His good and bad qualities—Baldfaced Hattie—Vixenish temper—Getting bucked off—Some of our other horses—The rattlesnake and its peculiarities—The skunk and his individuality.

HITHERTO I have spoken of our faithful dumb helpmates in a very casual manner, hardly worthy of the important place they necessarily occupy in the record of our trip; so ere winter snows, long weary rides, and the scantiest of "feed" have reduced their plump outline to anatomy woeful to behold, let us make their acquaintance.

We have not far to go, for there, with grass reaching half-way up their knees, they are rambling over the forest glade opening on a little Alpine lake. They are apparently enjoying to the full the "shining hours" of the long afternoon.

It is an off-day, or rather an off-afternoon, for an early ride of twelve miles has brought us hither long before noon. Charmed by the beauty of the spot and the richness of the feed, we have for once metamorphosed, in the delightfully independent manner of our travel, what was intended only as a noon camp into a night camp, thus giving us and our horses a long, unbroken afternoon of welcome rest. An ample repast has laid a pleasantly substantial *fond* for an idle spell with our pipe and our thoughts.

Not often did I indulge voluntarily in such hours of complete, downright laziness; for once, however, I succumbed to the temptation. A stately pine-tree, standing alone, and erect as a sentinel, in the centre of the forest-girt glade which rises in swelling lines from the perfectly smooth surface of the lake, offers an invitingly shady bower; for though we are in close proximity to snow-fields, and only a week has passed since the last snowstorm buried us for two days, yet, during the noon hours of the gloriously bright September day, shade is acceptable. So, armed with my recently replenished tobacco-pouch, I retire under the drooping boughs of the pine, and not, as the men apparently expected, to the crags overhead or to the quiet sombre forests, where a Bighorn, or a Wapiti, or even a Grizzly, would perhaps reward a leisurely afternoon's stalk. "Guess the boss has eaten too much dinner," is a remark overheard by me as I stride towards my tree; it shows, I sadly fear, of what unpoetic elements your true frontiersman's character is composed.

I am soon lying on my back, hands folded under my head, and knees crossed on high, my moccasined feet forming a buff and very domestic foreground to as pretty a vista of Alpine scenery and genuine mountain life as pen can sketch. Between the tree and the pebble-strewn shore of the tarn, its forested shores curving in and out around beryl-green bays and pine-crowned promontories, there is the sloping meadow on which the horses are feeding.

With whom shall I commence? Who but Boreas, my old favourite, is worthy to take the first place? He is a "buckskin," or claybank-coloured,[1] cob-built pony. His sturdy exterior, the mould of his shoulders and strong limbs, betray endurance, but not fleetness; and ten minutes on his back would convince you that you are astride of a remarkably lazy horse.

But there is a good side to every unpleasant event, and primitive trapper-life teaches you to hunt up both aspects of the little trials that may overwhelm you. The good point of this laziness is, that it keeps him in a far better condition than were he a more willing or spirited animal.

Boreas, as I have said, cannot exactly be called a fast horse. When I was "trading" for him the vendor asked me, "Kin ye ride, stranger?" Rather a useless sort of question, I thought, for I had just dismounted from trying his paces in my habitually cautious manner; and having found him an essentially quiet horse, I owned, with a returning wave of bravery, that I thought I could "a little," adding the query whether, in his opinion, I should be able to run antelope with him? For I was then still filled with the tenderfoot's passion of breaking down horses and *not* getting antelopes; and his answer, given in the dry Western intonation, while a sort of far-away yearning look stole over his features, ran thus: "In course you kin, stranger, and a better cayuse for that y'er 'ntlope running you jist niver forked. No darned 'ntlope could live near him; and if ye engineer him right up and down, when you

---

[1] This neutral tint is by far the best colour for a shooting pony, a matter of considerable importance. To one who has no experience, the colour would seem far too light; but this is not the case, as the most ordinary trial will show.

glimpse a band, ye'll have all the sport ye want, and needn't hold him either, for fast running niver did hurt him." [2] I hadn't been in the West very long when those words were addressed to me, so I thought there was just a little bit of exaggeration about that "living" business of the antelopes, who, as I had found out, required remarkably fleet horses to keep them as much as in sight. Two days afterwards I had opportunity to try the powers of my new acquisition after the fleet game of the Plains. It was my turn to have that far-away yearning look steal over my features. His former owner's words came true. The antelope did not continue to live near him. I had all the sport I wanted, and the speed of the chace no more hurt my steed than did the excitement attendant upon it. Some Texas cowboys, who watched me from a distance, subsequently made some considerate inquiries, showing what a lively interest they had taken in my sport. They wanted to know whether I had driven stakes into the ground to see that I was moving; and whether I felt *very* tired, for " that six-year-old club had no slouch of a lazy time, and them legs did seem kinder willin' to shove the old hoss along." Such, and more, were their unkind remarks. They pained me; and while I now perfectly understood why my horse's name was "Bibleback," [3] I forthwith decided to change it to a more suitable one, the name

[2] This "never did hurt him," was used, as I afterwards learnt, in the usual Western sense, indicating quite something else than I inferred. The frontiersman says of an irreligious fellow: "Religion never hurt him;" or of a bumptious official,—" That man's office is hurting him."

[3] When I asked the vendor why he was called "Bibleback," he replied in his twangy voice :—" Wa'll, stranger, I reckon because the hefty (weighty) preachin' that's been done on his yar back."

which the reader already knows. Boreas was not an expensive horse as Western horses go ; he stood, or rather, as I am still his owner, he stands me in just forty-five dollars (£9). The way I got him was rather singular. On starting on my first trip I had invested in a more expensive animal named Dickie. From causes then inexplicable Dickie somehow went dead lame before we were three days out, and I had either to ride a spare but uncomfortably frisky cayuse, with a lot of unbrokenness clinging about its vicious nature, or sit on the waggon, while my late purchase was tied to the rear of the "schooner." Fate decreed that we should meet a few days later a "bull-whacking outfit"—a convoy of heavy ox-waggons, on their way to one of the outlying frontier forts with Government stores. Among the half-dozen horses that were running loose behind the long string of huge waggons was the "claybank" Bibleback. He was not much to look at ; lean, shaggy-coated, he looked every inch a "bull-whacker's cayuse," but he was the best of the lot. The leader, or "waggon-boss," a lanky Arkansian, came strolling down to our camp, and after an apparently very careless survey of the lame one, and a long string of hard words to show that he did not belie his occupation or origin, presently opened on the trade.

"Trading," I must here mention, is the favourite amusement of your genuine Western man. In other words, it is barter in kind, now and again with a dollar or two thrown in to kick the beam if it so be wanted, and always with a drink to finish up. Everything, or very nearly everything, the frontiersman owns is " traded." His " ranche," or log-house home, is probably swapped for an old-pattern Winchester repeater, " as wouldn't shoot straight even round the corner," as he will privately inform you with a wink; and when you ask why the other party had not tried its shooting qualities, he tells you— " Fact is, stranger, thar wasn't anything but his hat to shoot at (on the level and stoneless Plains), and that was so full of holes as would have taken all the yar hats in cryation set up behind it to show a bullet hole; so the old man took the shooter along mor'n (more for) its looks." To us, who are supposed to possess the much-desired articles of barter—whiskey, powder, or cartridges, and the every-day " grub " items, such as flour, coffee, and sugar—some typical " trades " were offered. For our camp-stove and six pounds of coffee we could once have got a pack-mule; for a horse and a gallon of our precious whiskey, a silver-mine, consisting of six " recorded " claims, were offered; and when we showed some hesitation, a pair of boots was added to the allures of the mine.

We could have become " house-owners " ten times over, at trades varying between a horse, a pint of whiskey, or a hundred Winchester cartridges. To trade coats, saddles, blankets, harness, spurs, for hats, cartridges, six-shooters, coffee-mills, or frying-pans, with a horn-handled spoon or a pewter plate thrown in to make a level trade of it, seems to be the legitimate source of most of the possessions of the poorer ranks of the frontier population. But the most flourishing of all trades is the one in horse-flesh, *i.e.* an exchange of horses, the minor good quali-ties of the one, should there be any great difference in their merits, being made up if possible by 'cuteness on the part of its owner. I have often watched these " horse trades," and every time came away a "better" man, at least in the Western sense of the word. Naturally each of the traders thinks himself the 'cuter of the two; both laugh in their sleeves at the stupidity of the other, both grumble to each other's face, and finally, both are generally equally unscrupulous in taking advantage of previous knowledge of little vices which their property happens to possess. In my own case—for I have yet to narrate on what basis Boreas was traded for Dickie—the blemishes were, alas! too apparent, as, tied to the hind end of the waggon, the latter limped along in a most woebegone fashion. The "steer smashing trainboss" looked me squarely in the eye when I told him, in reply to his question, that when I started, the horse was perfectly sound, and had gone lame the third day out—a statement which he seemed to believe. More I could not tell about the cause of the lameness, which was on his near front leg, for we had no opportunity to consult a Vet. to decide the nice question whether the mischief was a mere passing or a serious shoulder lameness. His fine sleek exterior and capital points, being an expensive horse, however, had made a deep impression upon the bull-guiding genius, hence his hints that perhaps we might make a level trade between the sound Bibleback and the lame Dickie—who not only was perfectly useless to me in his present condition, but also a source of bother— overjoyed me. Had he known what a green one he had to deal with, he could have got five-and-twenty dollars and Dickie for the sound Bibleback, and indeed I had expressed myself to this effect to my companions. Suppressing my pleasurable emotions, though I dared not look at the rest of the party lest I should laugh, I had the unconscionable impudence to demand five dollars and the sound horse for the lame one. This settled the matter, for had I closed at once on the level trade, the bullwhacker would have perceived my eagerness, and probably would have backed out, or the five or more dollars would have been on his side instead of mine. As it was we had ten minutes' higgling over the "fiver," which I finally waived, and Bibleback changed owners on a level trade—my first, and remembering certain subsequent transactions, by no means my worst trade in horseflesh out West. A month later nobody would have recognized in the sleek, sturdy, "bob-tailed" cob Boreas, the ill-conditioned gaunt Bibleback. Not the same could be said of Dickie, for his injury turned out to be an incurable shoulder lameness, from which he had previously suffered and been temporarily cured previous to my getting him. When months afterwards I visited the Fort for which my bullwhacking friend was bound, who should be offered to me, as a quite unusually inviting bargain, but Dickie "just gone a bit lame," who, according to the account I received, had made the fortune of the whiskey-store keeper by the innumerable "trade" drinks called forth by his so frequently changing hands. In the three months that had intervened, everybody in the Fort and the country about seemed to have owned him; and when I told the then possessor that I was the person who had introduced Dickie to that section of Wyoming, he looked at me, as much as to say, "Now that *won't* wash, Sireebob; you ain't clever enough for that—no, not by half, you bet."

Boreas's origin is, as I have said, the lowest of the low, for out West a bullwhacker's horse is on a par with the slowest "growler's" nag in murky London streets; and a bullwhacker's *spare* horse sinks him to a level lower than the costermonger's much abused specimen of beasts born to a cruel and degenerate fate. Notwithstanding these plebeian connexions, he is, however, above price to me, for he has turned out a jewel among shooting-ponies. His endurance, wind, surefootedness, and a singularly developed bump of locality, are beyond praise; and while now and again certain vices—for what strong character, either human or equine, has not some failings?—come to the fore in an unpleasant manner, they yet contribute in an indirect way to make him what he is. He has taken to hunting, as were he "riz" to it from his earliest colt-days. Game in sight, it is wonderful to see how the old fellow warms up to his work, for his speed has amazingly increased since those "stake-driving days." But it is not on the level or broken, but on the steep mountain slopes, or in the dense timber, that his qualities shine forth. I think very few horses have executed such mountaineering feats as my old four-footed friend, for he has been in places where a good many two-footed beings I know would not care to venture. If I see game, and the final approach has to be performed on foot, I slide from his back, drop the reins over his head, and am off. Let me be absent one hour or ten hours, he will be there when I return, and welcome me with that peculiar, remarkably unmusical, sawbuck "nicker" of his, by which I could tell him out of a thousand horses. When I say he will be there, I must except one contingency, the result of his innate dislike to grizzly. If one of that race is about, then he will *not* be there; but be making good, steady time back to camp. He does not mind black or brown bear, and for wolves he has rather a liking; but between him and Uncle Ephraim there is no love lost. He scents him at a distance; and the wriggle of his body, toss of his head, and snort by which he testifies his discovery, has served on more than one occasion as a welcome signal.

Some trappers manage to train their hunting-horses to follow them about like dogs. In this I have succeeded only partially, a patch of good grazing-ground upsetting all my teachings. Another peculiarity is his deeply-rooted aversion to be packed with more than a certain quantity of game. With unvarying regularity he draws the line at about sixty pounds ; so if he already has the hind-quarters of a bighorn or of a mule-deer slung to his saddle, and he perceives me approaching with a fresh load, he just gives one toss of his head and a swish of his tail, and, let the distance be half a mile or ten miles, he proceeds to lead the way home, his head kept high so as not to step on the reins. Now and again if he is in particularly good humour, and he has perceived that I have thrown away the second load, he will, after a mile or two, let me regain the saddle, but I cannot bet on that as a certainty; on the whole, I think I would rather stake "a pile" on the contrary. In camp, when he reaches it, they well know what has occurred. If the reins are fastened to the spring buckle of which I have already spoken, they know the boss has sent him home ; but if they are dragging, and no game festoons his saddle, they are informed that he "struck bar ;" while if he is laden with the usual hind-quarters, they know the boss has shot a second beast, and will presently appear very heated, and brimful of uncharitableness.

His bump of locality is perhaps the most extraordinary of his gifts ; unfortunately he only chooses to develop it on the home stretch. Let the distance be one or thirty miles—let the ground be ever so puzzling, the rocks ever so steep, the forest dense and full of windfalls or treacherous mire-holes, the snow-storm fierce, or the mountain fog of pea-soup consistency, Boreas carries me, at day or at night, safe and sound, if he knows his head is turned homeward. T'other way it takes, as my men jokingly assert, three-inch rowelled spurs and a three-foot oak-club; but that is a sad exaggeration. The only two times I have really been lost—once in a very dense mountain-fog, the other time in a bad snow-storm—was owing to my doubting the proficiency of Boreas's path-finding abilities. On the first occasion I thought I knew the way better than he did, for I had been twice over the ground on foot, and he had only been once; while the other time I let my course be governed by my compass, rather than by the unmistakable pulls to one side by which Boreas intimated his non-acquiescence with the direction. As it turned out, he was right and the compass wrong, the latter being unsettled by the presence of large masses of iron in the rocks. On both occasions I spent the night out at considerable altitude, and I can tell you that now I know better than to pull rein when once I am on the home turn.

Grizzlies, as I have said, he detested, and one of the most uncomfortable incidents of my protracted acquaintance with him was caused by this apparently unprovoked dislike. I was out after bighorn, and had left Boreas at the base of some steep cliffs. On my return six or seven hours afterwards, his presence, as the Irishman said, was conspicuous by his absence. The soft soil betrayed the cause—the tracks of an adult grizzly. The distance to camp was not very great, some eight or nine miles. Before I reached camp I heard signal-shots,[4] which I promptly answered;

[4] An advisable precaution for travelling through the wilds is, to

and inferring that something serious had happened at camp, I hastened down. I found the men standing round Boreas, who had reached camp in a state considerably the worse for a very hasty flight through dense timber and rolls down precipitous slopes, "looking," as they declared, "as if he had fallen down and trampled on his nose." He was bruised all over, and bleeding from various cuts, and of his accoutrements next to nothing was left. His bridle was wrenched off short, his saddle blanket was gone, and of the saddle absolutely nothing left but the cinche, or girth, and splinters of wood, and those were astride of his belly. Arriving in this sorry state, the men fancied something had happened to me—that, in fact, I had "gone up" in consequence of some misadventure, and hence were greatly relieved when, after several ineffectual signals, they heard my answering shots just as they were starting out to look for what remained of me. We had only one spare saddle in the outfit, and that was only the "tree" or frame of an old Government pack-saddle one of the boys had traded from an Indian for some "paints." This little mishap occurred in August, and until the end of November I forked that pack-saddle, which in the course of an afternoon the dexterous Port had supplied with the necessary rawhide loops, cinche, and bearings, and two odd-looking stirrups of wood. I need not add that it was about the hardest, most uncomfortable, and most impiety-engendering saddle man ever was astride of.

preconcert some way of signalling. With us, two shots, fired consecutively as fast as possible (quicker than you would be able to shoot when aiming), was a signal that was always to be answered by all who heard it. It was only used twice on the whole trip—once by Port, and once by myself; but, nevertheless, it is a precaution that, in emergencies, can be of very great help.

But now I must close Boreas's record, for were I to give all his adventures they would fill a couple of chapters. Near him, on the glade in front of me, feeds a small, wiry mare. On her forehead she has a large white spot, her profile leans towards the Roman, and her eyes even in repose betray that she's "a real mean cayuse." Let me speak of the baldfaced Hattie, for that is her name, as tenderly as lies in human nature, for, alas! she is no more, being one of last winter's victims. Port got her as a perfectly unbroken three-year-old, trading her from a Texas cattle-boss, who had just brought her from her wild home. She was not even "rope-broken," *i.e.* accustomed to the rope-halter. To manage this "breaking in" without a "corral," or fenced-in enclosure, where this is usually performed, would have exercised the ingenuity of one less accustomed to handle unbroken stock than Port was. She was as wild as a fawn, as fierce as a young tiger, and her four legs, when one of her kicking tantrums was upon her, exhibited the agility of forty ordinary limbs. But all this was subdued by that pliant young ash to which one fine morning we managed to lead her, tying one end of the rawhide "lariat," or lasso-rope, to the trunk of the tree about eight feet from the ground, while the other was fastened round her neck. Then casting loose the hawser by which we had hauled her up to the tree, we sat down to await the end. It presently came: laying her ears well back, and giving a few introductory kicks, she dashed off at full speed. The lariat was about fifty feet in length, so that there was ample space to get up speed by the time she got to the end of the tether. The tree bent like a bow, but it held, and so did the rawhide rope—with the result that the mare "swapped ends," *i.e.* turned a clean summersault, and was laid flat on her back with a good deal of force, teaching her a well-known cowboy lesson no horse is likely to forget—if its neck stands it. When she regained her legs she seemed the most astonished mare you ever saw, and one, too, who never again " ran agin a rope."

She is the only genuine " bucker "[5] in the outfit, and she is the only *bonâ fide* bucking horse that ever threw me, and that for the very good reason that she was the only one I ever bestrode. The occurrence of my parting company with her happened in the presence of a number of Texas cowboys, and the event was hailed with such yells of mischievous delight on the part of the bystanders as I never shall forget, for your genuine cowboy—a masterly rider, born in the saddle—is an unmerciful critic of horsemanship. Indeed they are the only human beings, I believe, who can sit a horse that has learnt bucking in Texas, and has not been broken of it in his youth. I do not exactly know what possessed me to mount the bald-faced one that afternoon; anyhow, I did get on her, while two of the fellows held her. As a London omnibus cad would say, I was nearly " near side up and off side down." However, I managed to stick to her during the first preliminary flourishes with those forty legs of hers, after the boys had cast her loose. " She is just a' feeling of you ! " they shouted; and presently she settled down to business, to as fair and square a spell at bucking as ever shook the life out of a white man. Not being a Texan, or feeling in me the talent of gripping with my knees an animal bow, I was shot off at the fourth or fifth buck, delivered,

---

[5] Bucking is, I believe, an endemic vice of Texas—a circumstance easily explicable by the peculiarities of management, no less than of surroundings.

as is the wont of a genuinely "mean one," with lightning-like rapidity. The movement of the animal consists of lowering the head between the front legs, and suddenly arching the back, all the muscles of which act as so many bowstrings, the whole thing being accompanied by a leap into the air, and coming down on all four legs stiffened out as were they pokers.

A few stray bucks, with intervals between each, are easy enough to weather; it is the continuance and the amazing rapidity that accomplish the rout of riders not trained to such horses from youth. The first buck, lifting you perhaps only a couple of inches from the pigskin, shakes you; the second, following so quickly as hardly to leave you time to ascertain that the first is over, puzzles you; the third makes you lose your balance; the fourth pitches and tosses you; and the fifth accomplishes the brute's design, namely, dumping you off. My performance—to revert to a sore subject—was greeted with endless laughter and loud shouts, "Stay with her, boss; stay with her." And when finally I left her, "I landed," as the boys said, "kinder squar'ly;" "I hurt the ground," "I was rough on the bunch grass," "I tried to make a hole in the earth," and other suchlike humorous expressions greeting my ears when I could again hear, for the violence of my fall had very nearly shaken out of me the few little senses I had left. The next minute there was recorded in my neighbourhood a solemn vow, that has not been broken since, and I doubt if that same person will ever share the fate set forth on a wooden cross at the head of a lonely Western grave, of

> " William Jake Hall,
> Got a buck and a fall;

> Killed dead as a Slug,
> By a Texas Plug.
> Born in Georgy,
> '48 Anne Domini."

Breaking a horse of bucking is, as a profession, about one of the most riskful ones that exist, and few professionals attain mature age. The wages are very high, and only quite young men are able to withstand the terrible shaking, few of them being able to continue longer than a few months at a time. The first organs to suffer are the lungs, spitting of blood being, as I am told, the invariable result of this vocation. There are two ways, I understand, of sitting a bucking horse; tersely rendered, the one is to "follow the buck," the other to "receive the buck." Both have warm adherents, though I certainly met more "followers" than "receivers," a circumstance I can perfectly understand, for the strain upon the rider's body of the latter process must be terrific.

My first acquaintance with the wayward temper of the baldfaced one was made three years ago in a steep canyon, the very precipitous slopes of which left hardly room for a two or three feet trail to pass up its long course. Right in the middle of it, on about the worst spot, something suddenly went wrong with her, the precise nature of which we never had a chance of discovering. It was enough, however, to make her "light into bucking." The first thing I saw was a two-pound tobacco canister, followed by my tooth-brush and sponge-bag, describing a graceful parabola down the dizzy depth of the gorge—for unfortunately my "hold-all," carelessly fastened, was part of the bald-faced one's load—where they of course were lost to me. Buck followed buck, the vixen very highly enjoying the fun, vastly increased by the security of her position. Neither of the men at the head or at the end of the long file of horses could approach her on account of the narrowness of the trail; till finally Port, by wriggling past the legs of the horses ahead, did manage at considerable risk to approach her. It was high time; a few more bucks, and the rest of my "duds" would have followed the canister. Fortunately I had a spare tooth-brush, otherwise this disaster might have been of overwhelming consequences.

To our other friends I cannot devote as much space. There, near the vixenish Hattie, stands Kate, a good-natured, old-maidenish mare, exhibiting, when "bar" are about, not unreasonable nervousness, for she has a "game" leg. She demonstrated to me once how great things can come of little beginnings. With her lame leg she started a stone, which rolled down a slope, the stone started a grizzly, the grizzly started a very formidable growl, the growl started Boreas, and Boreas not only started himself, but the whole band of horses, causing a disastrous stampede. Kate is full of character; she does not like to be petted, and resents kindly pats with lightning-like kicks, delivered with unerring aim.

Close to her, under the far-reaching sweep of a pine, stand the two clowns of the party, "Bigbelly" and "All-eat," both horses of mature age and mature humour, but most lively temperaments. No trail is too wide that they do not manage to find a handy tree against which to "snag" their packs, no stream too shallow for them to tumble down and duck their loads, no meadow bottom so dry that they cannot find mire-holes in which to get "stalled," no descending slope too gentle to offer them welcome opportunity to reach the bottom "ended over," as

Western vernacular typifies a state of general head-over-heelishness; no ascent so gradual that their pack-saddles cannot be wriggled back, giving them the necessary excuse for a headlong stampede into the densest brush or timber they can find; and finally, no chance is ever lost by either to indulge in a five minutes' spell at "bucking." There they stand, in looks meek and submissive, the head of one close to the tail of the other—an arrangement more ingenious than you would think at the first glance, for it enables them to whisk the troublesome flies off each other's heads.

There, not far from "Old John," another victim of last winter, stand the Sorrel Mare and the Bay Mare, as a rule patient, good-natured brutes, though neither can bear matters going wrong with their packs. Further off are "Whitie," an Indian pony who *can* buck, and the "Bessie Mare" who can *not*, but who is a remarkably fast half-bred —American cross-bred with Texan—animal, who, hence, comes in for all the quick work. Poor thing! she too fell victim to the severity of that unprecedented winter. The remaining three or four horses, being possessed of no special characteristics, I shall leave to oblivion.

I cannot close this chapter on dumb friends without some short notice of dumb foes in camp. Conspicuous among them are two much-abused pests of the upland plains of Wyoming, Idaho, and Montana, *i.e.* rattle-snakes and skunks. The former have given their name to a considerable range of high hills in Central Wyoming; but these Rattlesnake Mountains, across which I passed on this as well as on a previous occasion, hardly deserve their notoriety, for there are other portions of the West far more deserving the name. Once I was camped for many weeks among these hills, and saw not more than about a dozen rattlers, all told. They are in reality, notwithstanding their fatal fangs, as it is needless to tell those who know them from personal experience, very harmless beasts, when once you know their manner of attack and the sound of the rattle that *always* precedes their "striking," as the act of precipitating is called. It is a noise not at all like what you expect it to be. I had never heard it in my life before visiting these hills, and it was only owing to this circumstance that I had a sufficiently narrow escape. For the warning of others I may relate it, though there is nothing in the least sensational about it, but on the contrary a good deal of the ludicrous. I was out after some Bighorn, and by hand-over-hand climbing had ascended an excessively steep "knife-back" cliff of moderate height. The top, of amazing sharpness, whence I hoped to get a good look at the slope on the other side of the ridge, was as jagged as a saw, offering a good chance to peep over without yourself being seen. I had gained one of these craggy indentures by wriggling up to it in serpent fashion. Very intent upon sport, I had raised my head to peep over, when close to my right ear I heard a peculiar sound. For the first second I paid no attention to it, but eagerly scanned the precipitous slope on the other side. Something, I don't know exactly what, made me turn my head; and there, on a level with my face, not fifteen inches off lay coiled on a protruding slab of rock a moderate-sized snake, her head raised, and "forked lightning" playing.[6] I did not know it was a

---

[6] The rattlesnake (*Crotaline Ana*) prefers arid wastes. It has recently been found that this animal can do almost entirely without water. Mr. Stradling writes of it:—"During eleven months that I

rattlesnake; nor was I aware that the position, with the head raised high and curved back, is the one to be dreaded most, inasmuch as it immediately precedes the "striking."

The beast, however, looked so venomous that instinctively I instantly ducked my head, and threw myself to one side; and the snake, who at that moment struck, of course overshot the mark. My movement was, however, so violent and unpremeditated that I lost my foothold, and not being able to regain it I rolled down the entire cliff. It is decidedly nicer to write about than to undergo such a roll, for the height, some forty or fifty yards, was sufficient to land me at the bottom a sorely bruised being, "feeling funnybones all over." The rifle, which was cocked, had fared much better, for somehow on such occasions the thought instantly flashes across one's mind that much more depends upon keeping whole your rifle than your skin. Mischief to the latter can be remedied, and in the wondrously invigorating Western air, sores and wounds of every kind heal remarkably quickly; but damage to your trusty friend, if at all of a serious nature, means ruin.

I well remember how among the "boys" I once raised a great laugh, a laugh whose mocking intensity is still ringing in my ears, by this very instinctive carefulness. We were going through some very broken country, and were ascending a precipitous slope, by a game trail that went zigzag up its face. Port, with four or five of the horses, was ahead, I being in the centre, leading "Boreas," or rather, I walking ahead and he following me, while

have had a rattlesnake under close observation, it has shed its cuticle four times; has eaten fifty or sixty large rats . . . . is now four feet eight inches long; but during the whole time it has never drunk water nor bathed."

close up behind us came the rest of the horses and men. Those in front were just getting out of my sight, when suddenly I heard a shout ahead, and looking up saw " Baldfaced Hattie " charging down the narrow trail as fast as she could come ; both her side packs, containing pots and pans, were off, and dragging behind her. Down she came, snorting with terror at the jingle and rattle of the pans. If ever I saw a "stampeded mare with a teakettle tied to her tail" it was the terror-stricken baldfaced one. A collision was inevitable, for the trail was not broader than a couple of feet or so, having on the one side a declivity which was almost a precipice, on the other an overhanging bank some four or five feet in height, merging into a very steep upward slope, on which stood, four or five yards higher up, a weatherbeaten cedar, which notwithstanding the steep angle had managed to strike root. One thing or the other had to be done, and that quickly, for when I saw the mare she was not more than ten yards off. I decided for the upward slope; and as I happened to have my rifle in my hand, where it hampered me least, my, as I suppose very frantic-looking leap up the bank, was successful ; another hop and a stride and I had reached the tree. But just as I was about to turn round in order to witness the collision between Boreas and Hattie, I felt the soft clay-like ground give way under my feet, and I had the sensation of slipping back. A frantic clutch I made for the tree was too late ; I broke my nails, but could not stay my backsliding. Next I dug the stock of my rifle deep into the soft soil; it stopped me for a tenth of a second, but no more, for the whole bank seemed to be sliding under my feet. At that moment the safety of my faithful arm flashed across my mind, and feeling it securely imbedded in the soil, I relinquished my grip on it, and leaving it standing there upright as a sentinel, I went back and back, and finally over the bank, landing on my back right between the forefeet of the two collided horses. How I got out between the plunging and rearing beasts with whole bones I know not; I did, however, and was greeted by a never-ending roar of facetious Western laughter. My leap up the bank was declared to be the biggest thing they had ever laid eyes on, "doggarned well worth while crossing the staked plains to see." While other questions purporting kind inquiries "why I had not stayed with the rifle?" whether I "was scared at the tree?" or whether I "thought the mare would eat me?" were put to me by the two most uproarious of my audience, a couple of starved cowboys we had accidentally met, and who for several days previously had drunk of my coffee and eaten my bread—the latter, however, not of my baking, for then I should have excused them as madmen. The "boss's thundering big jump" remained a favourite joke for several days.

Of skunks—an animal in shape like a big polecat, with a very bushy tail—a multitude of amusing stories could be told, for the Plainsman is generally brimful of tales of the "Essence pedlar;" and all the ingenuity of Western humour is expended upon the building up of "good stories," that often bid fair to outrival the notorious bear stories, not only in the way of facts but also in humorousness. Leaving them to the frontiersman to tell—for nobody narrates them better—I desire to advert to a more serious matter, namely, the wide-spread belief in the West that the bite of the skunk produces hydrophobia, and hence is usually attended by fatal results, an exaggeration of certain facts which is apt to inflict very needlessly deadly terror upon persons who have had the mischance of being bitten by one of these pestiferous little brutes.[7]

Nobody who has ever watched a skunk is likely to forget the peculiar mincing step and leisurely zigzag course by which he retreats, till finally, when attacked, suddenly asserting himself, and raising the hinder parts, with the tail elevated over the back so that the long silken hair heretofore trailing in one direction falls in a tuft on all sides, the sense of smell immediately indicates the flagrant fragrance. According to Audubon, the skunk can squirt his terrible scent a distance of fourteen feet; and though the animal is very particular not to soil his own pelt, he generally is the very first to retreat, if retreat is possible.

Lacking the chief qualities of other Mustelidæ—the sagacity and prowess of the wolverine, the scansorial ability of the marten, the agility of the weasel, the aqueous accomplishments of the otter, and the fossorial capacity of the badger, its nearest relation—it is evident that the tardy skunk, of little strength and spirit, had to be distinguished by additional means of self-defence.

---

[7] Of this I am able to speak from experience, having on my first trip to the Rocky Mountains been bitten by a skunk, and having had for more than a year the ever-present dread of possible inoculation of that most horrible of diseases, hydrophobia, hanging over me. It is entirely owing to this circumstance that I have since taken pains to collect authentic information, and also to examine all available scientific records on rabies generally—the results of which I have endeavoured to embody in a few pages in the Appendix, as being a subject, I fancy, which can interest but those about to visit the West.

That his wonderful audacity and confidence in the terrible weapon, of which he makes use with startling assurance and accuracy, is not misplaced, is proved by the large number of skunks in certain districts.

Skunks are, as is well known, by no means shy animals. They are generally about at night, and will enter human habitations with surprising temerity. An old prospector, "French Louy," whom I met in the Rattlesnake Hills, a great place for skunks, had a pet one who used to sleep in the bunk at his feet very nearly every night. The cabin was so strongly scented that we smelt it a little distance off; indeed, as it was night, and none of us had ever been to the place, we were guided to it by the perfume, for we had already heard of this strangest of pets. The old fellow, a great character in his way, was rather hurt at our objections to the scent. "He no stink; he smell just *sufficement* to know he is dar;" and when I informed him that I quite believed it, he rejoined with his favourite oath, "Soup de Bouillon Almightee! why-for do you come here if you are so par-tic-u-laire?"

As a warning to those unacquainted with the West, I may mention, that skunks evince a special predilection for bacon. Indeed, I am convinced I have to ascribe the bite to which I have already alluded to this circumstance. My hands having been blistered by the dry heat and by a very hard-mouthed brute of a horse, I had, failing all other species of grease, applied some bacon fat to the sore places, drawing on a pair of gloves before turning in under my robe. One of the skunks had evidently winded the enticing scent of the bacon; and finding one of my hands, covered by a glove, outside the robe, had given it a hearty nip.

Long before I was fully aroused, and had whipped out my six-shooter from under my saddle-pillow, the enemy had scuttled off, his vanishing form dimly visible in the moonlight semi-darkness. The previous night three skunks had walked off with a good-sized piece of bacon, which had been left lying in a dish on the ground.

Many people have a great terror of skunks, a fear instilled into them by tall stories. I once travelled with such a personage, a countryman, who had been stuffed up with Western tales; and our camp, as long as we were in the skunk regions, was nightly the scene of reckless revolver practice and bad language. His shots at the vanishing enemy, fired a few feet from my ear, now and again woke me (I am a very sound sleeper), but of course always too late to prevent the invariable result—an answering discharge, far more terrible and fatal than my friend's nervous aim. If the skunk is not alarmed or frightened off, he will presently wander away, a comparatively very faint perfume being all that he leaves behind him—for *he* only fires as a means of self-defence.

CHAPTER V.

CAMPS AMONG WAPITI.

Our great hunger—Appeasing it by four bulls—Their stalk—Early snow-storm—My great head—His home and his death—Stag-lore—My first Wapiti—My young guide and his family—Male and female market hunters—A natural game park—Unsophisticated game—Moonlight stalking.

IN a previous chapter reference was made to a hungry sixteen days, eventually brought to a pleasant termination by a successful Wapiti hunt.[1] Let me introduce this chapter on sport with an account of that memorable stalk—for memorable I must call it, to do justice to certain antecedent features. Camped on a delightful glade in the last belt of timber, where we had ineffectually sought refuge from mosquitoes, and where our worn-out horses could recruit on the best of mountain grasses, the morning of the 13th of August was just dawning, when our camp-fire burst into brilliant flames, shedding round it a circle of grateful warmth, of which four shivering, hungry human beings, with strangely disfigured faces (one of my eyes, fortunately my left one, was entirely closed by a bite or

---

[1] Wapiti are called elk out West; and the stag is spoken of as a "bull"—both anti-phraseological instances.

sting more than commonly poisonous) are not slow to
take advantage. I am probably the warmest of the lot, for
I have just returned from an invigorating, though very
brief, dip in a beaver pool close by, over which the frost
during the night has cast a film of ice. A rub down
with a rough towel has brought out a glorious glow, but
alas! has also roused to outrageous keenness that old
man hunger of which I have already so bitterly com-
plained. Hands are rubbed very vigorously; and in
Government terms the men stigmatize the depravity of
that "doggarned water in the camp bucket, friz up like
a Mormon's tongue when you ask him how many wives
he's got." At last the coffee is steaming in our cups, and
a huge pile of bread, the result of three bakings, is heaped
on the waterproof-sheet—our ordinary table-cloth—spread
on the sward as near as possible to the fire. We have
"put ourselves outside" of that pile, and four cups of coffee
each, long before the sun has topped the "sawback"
ridge overhead. Having settled each man's rayon for the
day's sport, we are off in good time. We all mean business,
you bet; and there won't be any careless shooting, you
can stake your hair on *that*. Henry, with his huge smooth-
bore double-barrelled gun—stock, locks, and barrels held
together by cunning rawhide fastenings, is to take the
lowest level, where there is thick covert and a chance
of Muledeer. Port with his Winchester, and Edd with
his Sharp rifle, take the right; while to my choice falls the
left slope of the great chain on which, close to Timberline,
we are camped.

I am in light climbing order—a flannel blouse-shirt,
my cartridge-belt and field-glasses round my waist
and shoulders, a chunk of bread of yesterday's baking,

a favourite author in cheap waistcoat-pocket edition, and a pair of moccasins in my "rücksack,"[2] complete my usual outfit when hunting on foot. The rocks overhead are of wonderfully bizarre formation. Partly of volcanic origin, they are piled over each other in the most grotesque and Titanic disorder imaginable. There are great pillars 500 feet high, at their base considerably smaller than further up. Some of the cliffs look like the battlemented walls of a Norman keep, sorely battered by time. Over all rise the tops of two peaks, the highest in this district, quite 3000 feet above my standpoint.

The air is marvellously light, but as it is my first day this season in high altitudes, the exceedingly rarefied atmosphere tells, after a couple of hours' climb, upon my strides; I stop oftener—to admire the view, and my pipe requires more care than does commonly that inseparable companion. The field-glasses are constantly in use, but not a sign of living being can I descry. In another hour's ramble I have reached the first patches of last winter's snow, firm *névé*-like masses that fill the steep ravines. Yonder is a great projecting rock, from which I hope to get a good view of the whole slope. And half an hour later, by dint of some hand-over-hand and knee-over-knee climbing, I have reached my place of outlook. Of the view that burst on my eyes, splendid in its vastness, I will not speak. The crag, quite detached from the main mass of mountains, flanks on one side a pass like depression in the great chain, while on the other three sides it falls off in stupendous precipices. A large snow-

---

[2] A canvas game-bag, carried by two straps, not unlike a knapsack; its weight bearing more on the small of the back. It is a most useful article; when empty it can be stuffed into your pocket, while it will hold a buck chamois or roedeer. See Appendix.

field, painfully glittering in the brilliant sun, covers the pass, but as I fancy it is an unlikely place for game, I confine my scrutiny to the rocky slopes that stretch away on both sides of me for many miles. The heat and stillness is oppressive, for even the breeze has died away—an unusual circumstance in the morning—while the sky has assumed a peculiar purple tinge. Hours pass, as, stretched out in a comfortable sprawling attitude on the top, just sufficiently large to permit me occupying this spread-eagle pose, I keep scanning the cliffs for Bighorn, the only game I expect to find at this great altitude. When my eyes get tired of peering through the powerful glasses, my book comes in very handily. For more than an hour I have not turned my head in the direction of the snow-field at my back. What is therefore my astonishment when, on happening to wriggle round so as to see down to the snow, I perceive quite a band of animals on it. "Bighorn, by Jove!" I exclaim. "But no; by all that's green they are Wapiti," for I can plainly see the antlers. The pipe is consigned to the pocket, the little volume returns to the rücksack, and my heavy stalking-boots are replaced by the noiseless moccasins.

The distance is about half or three quarters of a mile, air-line; but I have to take a great round; and the slope up which I have to run is steep, and the air rarefied to a trying extent. Fortunately no extra clothing handicaps my movements; and, as a Westerner once remarked after watching me—from a safe place—making the best of time towards a handy tree with a crippled bear after me, I am "all legs, with elbows for handles." On reaching the lower extremity of the snowfield, where a rivulet, formed by the melting of the snow, has worn a great cavern in the *névé*, I come to a halt. "If they have stopped for an hour, they will wait another ten minutes," I think—and there is too much at stake to risk mischance. So I pause for a moment, to regain my wind, and bathe my temple and wrists with the refreshingly cool ice-water. A singular change has come over the sky, where great banks of most threatening-looking clouds—the first I have seen for many weeks—have appeared. The wind, too, which out West is so singularly steady, has sprung up, but from the wrong quarter, and presently it begins to blow big guns. No time is to be lost. So, with a final look at my rifle, I begin a tedious stalk up the snow. Fortunately, a recent landslip from the crag I occupied has sent numerous fragments of rock down the slope, where they lie deeply imbedded in the drift, thus affording me some little cover. That most momentous question, whether the stags are still there, is filling me with anxiety, for since leaving the rock I have had no opportunity to see the upper extremity of the *névé* where they were, but have worked my way solely by certain landmarks. Now I must be close to them; and a boulder larger than the rest, protruding two feet over the snow, is as good a place as any for a cautious survey of the ground. Slowly, very slowly, I raise my head over the stone, and presently catch sight of the tips of a pair of antlers, moving to-and-fro, apparently not more than five-and-thirty yards off. Glorious view! But how unsteady my hands have suddenly got; and what uncommon vigour is manifested by my heart, as if I had not previously seen thousands of the noble game? But it is that venomous old hunger which has wrecked my nerves, making them a prey to my unsportsman-like thoughts of steaming pots that float with fairylike *vraisemblance* before my eyes; proving, to use the words of an American, to whom I afterwards related the episode, "how quickly the optical waves were propelled inward to the seat of hungry war, to return to the protoplasm of intellect freighted with rejuvenating culinary dreams!" Turning on my back, I take from my belt a dozen or so of cartridges, which, after blowing the snow off, are placed in my stalking cap, on the stone in front of me. With the rifle to my shoulder, I raise myself slowly to a standing position—the only one enabling me to see the animals. With eager eyes I scan the ground. There they are, fifteen or twenty lordly Wapiti, mostly bulls, standing and lying about, some feeding on the sparse blades on the border of the snowfield, others couched in a state of repose on the cooling snow.

Though so close, none but a hind has seen the strange apparition; so while she is staring stupidly at me, I have an instant's respite to pick out good heads. One big old bull, about forty yards off, gets the first greeting. Need I say that, all the aiming I have in me, is put into that shot? The second barrel is turned on another a few yards further off. While the former has fallen in his tracks, the latter receives the fire without making a single sign that he is hit; but I am pretty confident of my shot; so after reloading, which I do without taking my eyes off the herd, who now, after the first moment's spell-bound terror, are in the act of making off, fire is opened on a third and fourth victim. Both are hit, but very indifferently, and they continue their flight: four or five shots more have to be expended before they are my meat. All this time the second stag is standing there, erect, and apparently unhurt. He has a very fine head; so, after slipping fresh cartridges in, I keep him covered. Presently a slight swaying motion can be noticed; and through the huge body of the noble beast there passes a convulsive shudder. His front legs refuse to carry him, and he slowly sinks on his knees; the next instant his head droops, and he rolls over—a dead Wapiti.[3] The altitude of the spot, not a foot under 11,000 feet—and probably nearer 12,000 feet—is an uncommon one for Wapiti; but more extraordinary is the fact, that, while two of the stags I killed have their antlers perfectly cleaned, the other two are in as perfect a state of velvet, without the slightest sign of rubs on their fur-like covering. Well, there they lie, the four slain ones, and you will not be surprised to hear that my inner man goes forth, and greets them right gladly, for I fancy my sensations resemble those,—of course altogether on a lower level—which moved the spirit of the "cowboy," who, after a long parting, saw his girl—for I feel "like I'd reach out and gather her in."

The circumstance of their different heads was, however, so curious that, before entering upon my gralloching duties I spent half an hour in a successful search for a clue.[4] I was prompted to do this before anything else, by the very threatening look of the sky; and I had not got through brittling the first stag, when the snowstorm was upon me. Considering the very early season of the year, the intensity of the storm was somewhat surprising to me; and I bitterly rued the valuable half-hour I had, as I then thought, wasted in my search.

The storm commenced with a slushy hail, drenching me to the skin in the first three or four minutes, which presently,

[3] See Appendix: Wapiti.   [4] Ibid.

influenced by the intensely cold wind, turned into regular snow. I persevered, however, and accomplished the most essential portion of my butcher's work, so that at least the meat should not spoil; and a portion of the fat, which to us was invaluable, was secured. More I failed to accomplish, for my fingers refused to hold the knife, which danced about as had I been stricken by the worst form of palsy, while my teeth kept up a lively chattering. Not often have I felt the intensity of cold as on that August day. Fortunately I had begun on the first stag by cutting out the tender loin; and with two tongues, all safely stowed away in my rücksack, I was soon making good time down the slope. My sole flannel upper garment, frozen stiff, had turned into icy armour, crinkling at every movement. On reaching camp I found things in a decidedly uncomfortable condition, for not expecting such an early snowstorm, we had left everything strewn about on the ground; and what we had not left open, the hurricane-like wind which preceded the snow had scattered. The only dry thing was the tent, and that, as usual, was securely rolled up and stowed away in its proper waterproof canvas sack, for hitherto we had never once used it. At first nothing could be found under the snow, and the whisky keg, last of all; for I need not say, that under the circumstances the cask was the first thing I looked for. At last I discovered it under a heap of drifted snow, and nearly knocked my front teeth down my throat in my attempt to bring the cup to my lips. Very shortly after my arrival, Port and Edd, the former's beard a mass of icicles, turned up. They were quite as miserable-looking as I was; but their faces became wreathed with sunny smiles when they heard that meat—glorious meat! was in camp. My discovery of the whisky-keg benefitted also them, and with lighter hearts we began to set things straight. When, after some search, we found some dry wood, all our hands refused to hold the match, to light it. Teeth had to do duty; and, aided by the wonderfully developed trapper's knack of making a fire under the most unfavourable circumstances, we had a roaring blaze shortly afterwards. The snowstorm had vanished as rapidly as it had appeared; so that when after an hour's work, we finally sat down to dinner, the sun was shining brightly. I need not say that the meal was a remarkably square one, with two very eager and hungry-looking dogs, quite forgetful of their usual good manners, sitting by us and staring us hard in the face. One very delightful result of the storm was that it cleared off all mosquitoes; for that year we had seen the last of them. Henry, who had lost his way in a dense forest at the foot of the mountain we were on, turned up only the next morning. Strange to say, he had seen nothing of the snowstorm; and while we had been suffering intense cold, he had to complain of heat, the difference of altitude being hardly over 4000 feet. As he reached camp early, we had plenty of time left to bring the meat and heads into camp before night. We managed to get two of our steadiest pack-horses a good way up the steep slopes, to a point not more than half a mile from the snowfield, and left them there securely picketted. In two loads to each man, we took down to the horses as much meat as they could carry, two sets of antlers, and about fifty pounds of fat, or so-called "elk-tallow," besides a goodly load for each human back. The stags were in splendid condition ; but we had some trouble in cutting up the carcasses, for they were frozen hard, and we had either to cut the meat out in shapeless chunks with the timber-axe and knife, or saw it in strips with my powerful antler-saw.

Never was venison more welcome, and never did savages "eat with a more *coming* appetite," for, as Port said, it kept on "coming" till the relays of frying-pans were empty. The "Four-bull camp hunger" soon became a standard measure in our little trapper republic, and it was one of the camps that we loved to talk about in times of "famine and pestilence."

Game of the larger species, to be seen to full advantage ought to be watched in their proper home; and though some of the deer species, such as the barren-ground cariboo, and the reindeer, afford exceptions to the rule that the stag is the child of forests, the Wapiti decidedly does not. Nowhere but in forest landscape can the glorious proportions of this great deer be fully appreciated. To run Wapiti on horseback, as now and again at one season of the year the sportsman has a chance to do on the upland Plains, puts him on a par with a quarry that occupies a far lower rank in the scale of game worthy of real sportsmanlike ardour, viz. the bison, or buffalo. And though I have done so on one or two occasions myself, and have keenly enjoyed the run, I am by no means proud of my performance.

I know of few more inspiring sights than a fine stag in his true home, the beautiful Alpine retreats high up on certain of the great ranges of the Rocky Mountains. Scenery, grand as it may be, receives fresh charm when framed in by a noble pair of branching antlers ; and I know no trophy of days spent in the far-off wilds that will recall stirring memories in more lifelike and warmer colours, or fill your soul with such longing desire to return speedily to the well-known glade in the forest, where in a fair struggle the bearer of yonder head found in you his master.

As I write these lines, which I happen to do in a quiet old Tyrolese "schloss," the arched corridors of which are lined with trophies of the chase in the Old and New World, the shadow of such a great head is thrown across my table, for the low winter's sun is casting its last rays through the quaint old diamond-paned and marble-arched window at my back. It is my largest head. The skill of the taxidermist has not been uselessly expended upon this cherished souvenir of the Rockies, and the grand old fellow looks down with a very lifelike calmness of mien from the broad expanse of the tapestried wall reserved to him, where in stately exclusiveness he has found his last home.

Twelve months ago the great stag was roaming seven or eight thousand miles away, through the dense forests and across the timber-girt barriers of the main backbone of the North American "divide." At the break of day he bathed in the clear waters of one or the other of its hundreds of nameless, never-visited lakelets: in the morning he drank of water that flowed into the Atlantic, while his evening draught deprived the Pacific Ocean of some drops rightfully belonging to it; for his home was on the great watershed of the Continent.

Here one beautiful, breezy, October morning he and I met; but hunter and hunted were both equally unprepared for each other's presence. With my rifle at my side I was lying on a prominent knoll, examining with my glasses a band of his species grazing on a broad glade somewhat lower than my position, and about three or four hundred yards off. There was nothing worth killing among the lot, though there was many a portly old stag stalking over the barren, for it was "whistling time," as the rutting season is called,[5] when the old males join the smaller fry—a sight which, though it no longer stirs my pulse, is yet one I always love to watch. I had done so scores of times in different parts of the West; this year on the grassy highlands shut in by *mauvaises terres* peaks, of weird shape and weirder colouring, in some of the more central portions of Wyoming; the next season on the frontier of Montana, where the forestless Sierra Soshoné rises from the undulating Bighorn basin. The proud stag, filled with the dominant instincts of the season—love and war—exhibits at this time the full virile vigour of his prime. His neck swells, and he steps with a consciousness of power which at other seasons is replaced by a less noble, timid cautiousness.

Well, I had scanned every one of the two or three hundred animals disporting themselves with a pleasant consciousness of security in the utter seclusion of their retreat, for probably none of them had ever before set eyes on a human being, when I heard a slight, rustling noise behind me. I was above actual Timberline, and only dwarfed cedars and some tall bushes were about me. I turned my

---

[5] The term is derived from the peculiar sound emitted by the stag at rutting time. It is very hard to imitate, or to describe. It is neither a whistle nor a bellow. Not unlike some tones produced by an Æolian harp, it might also be compared to the higher notes produced by the flageolet, and of course is entirely different from the red deer's call.

head—and there, not ten yards off, just issuing from the cover, stood the biggest Wapiti I had ever seen. His neck was nearly black, the rest of the body a grizzly grey-brown, and the antlers of truly gigantic size. We looked at each other for a second; then, still keeping my eyes riveted on his, my hand was slowly, very slowly, extended, to where, a foot or two off, my rifle was lying, for a quick movement is in like cases a fatal policy. But what had succeeded numbers of times with other quarry, more wary even than the Wapiti, failed in this instance. Something or other, perhaps a nervous twitching of my face or other involuntary motion, alarmed the stag, and long before I had the rifle up to my shoulder, he had turned and put the dense undergrowth between him and me.

To say that there was gnashing of teeth and scalding heart-burning would faintly describe the intensity of my disgust. The whole thing was the work of a second; but on my eyes, trained to speedy impression, was photographed the number of tines and the extraordinarily heavy beam of the antlers, outmatching everything I had killed or seen up to then. What was most singular about him was, that he came up without once whistling—a very unusual thing for a Wapiti to do at the height of the rutting season. The reader, if he be a sportsman—and no other is likely to follow me through this chapter—can fancy that the apparition had awakened in me all the bad passions of the craft, and I determined to bag him, if it were at all possible. As the sequel will show, it was destined to be a stern chase.

The first thing to do under the circumstances was to ascertain whether the stag was seriously alarmed, in which case pursuit would have been next to hopeless, or whether he was only momentarily scared, and also to discover the direction he had taken. I had been camped a day or two in the vicinity, and knew the general character of the ground for several miles round. I was also aware that the eminence on which I stood was encircled at the base, on every side, by a belt of perfectly barren ground. Waiting a minute or two as patiently as I could, to let the stag get far enough off not to hear me, I proceeded at a trot to the bare top of the knoll, about 200 feet above me. A minute or two after getting there, I perceived the stag debouch from the forest below me, and cross the said open ground. He did so very leisurely, so I judged he was not really alarmed. The distance was great—some six or seven hundred yards at the very least; but so eager was I to get him, that had he halted I am afraid I would have succumbed to the temptation of chancing a shot—under the circumstances, about the most foolish thing to do. Fortunately, however, he kept on his even, though slow, trot, and in half a minute or so had gained the forest on the other side of the belt of bare ground. When I started from camp that morning I intended to return by night; and as I conjectured that this chase might be a long one, and possibly entail sleeping out, I deemed it wiser to take a little grub, and procure some warmer clothing than the flannel shirt which was my only upper garment. My camp was not far off, and not very much out of the direction the stag had taken, so putting the best of my long pair of legs foremost, or as my men called it, "untangling forked lightning," I soon reached the little tarn, close to the pebbly beach of which two piles of buffalo robes and bearskins, and the remains of a big camp-fire indicated our vagrants' domicile. After scribbling with a burnt stick from the fire on the skin surface of the nearest buffalo robe, "Gone after big elk," so as to let the men know the reason of my absence if I did not turn up at dark, I snatched up half a loaf of bread, my coat, and my faithful rücksack, and was off. Always ready packed for such emergencies, I knew the latter contained, small as was its volume and weight, the most essential things with which to pass a night or two in the woods without uncommonly great hardships. A quarter of an hour later I was on the track of the Wapiti. The ground was very broken, and the forest soon "pettered out" into detached patches, while groups of strangely-gnarled cedars and spruce, which finally gave way to an undulating "barren," strewn, wonderful to say— for I was on the very top ridge of the great chain, and no high peaks about—with huge detached boulders, whose origin only science could demonstrate. Here it was very difficult to track, for the ground was frozen hard. Fortunately, there were frequently recurring patches of snow from the last storm, and there my work was easier. On the other side of the barren there were strange-looking mounds, tipped with little groves of trees. These mounds had precipitous banks, and in places spurs of the same soft soil, a sort of loam, connected them. On this ground I could easily track him; and there, too, I saw from the tracks that he was no longer trotting, but walking. With varying fortune I followed on, doing my best not to lose the slot. As there were scores of old and new spoors about, I was obliged to distinguish mine more by the size than by anything else. It was no easy task, particularly as I had to keep a sharp look-out ahead, for the stag might be grazing on any one of the numerous forest-girt glades I was constantly crossing. I suppose I must have been about two or three hours peering my eyes out of my head, when in the distance

I heard a regular "whistling" concert. There seemed to be hundreds of Wapiti, and I was left in no doubt that I was about to run on a large band. Probably the big stag was among them, for his track led straight into the middle of them. I climbed a rocky hillock, thirty or forty feet in height, and there awaited the herd, for on account of the wind, which was athwart my course, I was afraid, not knowing the extent of the area covered by the band, to risk proceeding any further on their lee side. On they came, slowly grazing their way; at first a few detached bodies, each consisting of a few females with their more than half-grown calves at their side, herded along in each instance by a large stag, kept very busy by his amorous attentions, and by the persistent impudence of young bucks, at whom many a vicious dig was levelled. Then gradually more and still more hove in sight, till at last the undulating barren was a moving mass of Wapiti—fighting, feeding, love-making, and "whistling," while I on my rocky perch was in the very midst of them. Some of the fighting was of a very determined character; and remembering their great size —for only good stags engage in these desperate struggles —it is a grand sight to see two such lordly combatants rush at each other, their huge antlers crashing together with amazing force. Unlike the European stags—who, if their horns do not get interlocked, fly asunder as soon as the charge is delivered, to repeat the furious rush again and again—the Wapiti try rather to push; and, not being as quick as our European stag, who generally rips his antagonist's side, the wounds are mostly about the neck and shoulders.

As I was very intent looking out for my big stag, I hardly paid sufficient attention to the general aspect of the scene, and did not even take time to approximately count the band, as is my wont on such occasions. At a rough estimate, there were six or seven hundred animals in it. Among them were two exceptionally large old bulls, each surrounded by a group of hinds far more numerous than those of the ordinary seraglios. A second's scrutiny with my powerful glasses proved, however, that neither was the one I was looking for. The main body was passing me on the safe side, but some had taken the leeward one—a matter of some anxiety to me, for I feared they could not help getting my wind. Nothing happened, however, the breeze, I presume, carrying the betraying taint over their heads. There I sat, and had to sit for two long hours. The open barren was apparently a well-known pleasaunce to the band, for they were in no hurry to leave it.

My impatience can be imagined. Things looked very dark, for if the stag did not show up with the band it would of course be impossible to trail him any farther over ground tracked all to bits by such a number of animals. At last the coast was sufficiently clear to permit my stealing down and gaining the forest from whence the herd had issued, and through which my quarry must have passed. What to do next I knew not; but I determined to continue my search as long as it was light, and if it proved futile, to get back to camp by night. The forest, I discovered, was not very extensive. On the other side of it again was very broken ground, full of ravines and bad-land gullies. In one of these, larger and deeper than the rest, there grew a bunch of cottonwood-trees, with thick brush-cover round the base. I was running down the excessively steep slope of soft loam, when I heard twigs snapping, and other unmistakable signs of a stag breaking cover. I could not stay the impetus of my course, but managed to swerve off to one side, so as to get a better view of the opposite slope. Hardly had I done so when there, not more than seventy yards off, the big stag burst from the cover, his peculiarly grizzly colour convincing me of his identity the very first second I saw him. He was making down the gully at a double-quick trot, and a sharp corner would hide him the next moment; so, without knowing very clearly what I did, I threw up my rifle and fired. Had I hit him? I knew not, for my shot was a very quick one, and I was standing in a most awkward position on a steep bank, the soil of which was continually giving way under my feet. I imagined I heard the bullet strike, but the distance was too short to make out distinctly that reassuring sound, so well known to the rifleshot. The stag had vanished, without a sign or drop of blood to show I had hit him. As can be imagined, I was vastly excited, and had a grizzly at that moment started up in my path I think I would have shouted to him to get out of my way. The first thing to do was to see whether I had wounded my game. By marking the ground I soon found in the clay bank which formed the background to the Wapiti at the moment I fired, the hole made by my bullet; and with my jack-knife I dug out the missile. The short distance it had penetrated into the clay, and the circumstance that its top was flattened, and that under the recurving bits of lead blood-stains could be seen, proved incontestably that the ball had passed through some part of the animal, unluckily without striking any large bones. Notwithstanding that I knew from experience what an astonishing amount of lead Wapiti will often carry off, I was greatly elated at what I had discovered, and also far too impatient to do what would have been the wisest thing under the circumstances, namely, to return to camp, and on the following morning track the Wapiti with the dog. Giving him not more than half an hour's grace, I was on his slot very much too soon. At first I found drops of blood only on the near side of the track, then they appeared on both sides; that on the near side, being of dark, that on the off, of lighter colour, and flecked with bubbly froth—the latter, a sure sign the lungs were injured. Hence as I had shot him quartering, I had hit him low, and rather too far back, and the bullet, ranging forward, had penetrated the right lung.

It must have been about five when I shot, so little more than an hour remained for tracking. Urged on by the hope of every minute coming up with the dying stag, I foolishly proceeded. I had not gone more than a mile when I struck a "couch" of the sick animal, which evidently he had just left. The blood was still warm, and by the quantities I judged the animal would have died very shortly had he not been roused to a last frantic effort by hearing, or rather winding, my approach. It is wonderful how far even the much smaller and feebler European stag will wander if he is thus alarmed. Life seems to receive a fresh lease; and only too often will a stag, fatally wounded and not left to die in peace, elude the hunter and outrun his hounds.

I was disgusted, and gave up further pursuit for that night; for dusk was approaching, and I had to look for a camping-place. After a little search I discovered an inviting spot beneath a grove of spreading old trees, occupying a very sheltered nook under some high cliffs where fuel was abundant. The "iron store" of my rücksack furnished an ample, though simple, supper; and one of my usual little waistcoat-pocket companions helped me to wile away the long hours of the evening. Stretched out before the fire, with a log under my head, my stalking-cap and handkerchief as pillow, my face turned from the bright warm flames throwing a sufficiency of light upon the closely printed pages, several logs piled upon each other on my *cold* side as a wind-brake, while my other one was undergoing pleasant toasting— I have passed many a more dreary evening in drawing-rooms, many a more sleepless night in civilized beds. There is, however, a most uncanny chilly spell just preceding dawn, which usually wakes one. It is about the only time one really feels—at least, in fine weather—the hardship of camping out without coverings, and with the thermometer, for hours, a good many degrees below freezing-point. Then it is, while the camp-fire is piled highest, that the few precious drops of whiskey—saved especially for this moment—taste uncommonly like more, and that the human form divine is voted solid and lumpish. The portion of your body that you can warm at the grateful fire seems ludicrously small; while the periphery of the rest of your shivering anatomy exposed to the icy blast appears vastly extended. How willingly you would sacrifice some of your impermeable depth for increased surface, to be able to unfold, as it were, your shivering humanity, and thaw it at the bonny blaze, as you or your butler dries the sheets of the *Times* in front of the cosy breakfast-room fire.

Fortunately, dawn in the West is not like the gradual awakening of Nature we know it to be in the old world,

The change from night to day is far more rapid; and, what I have remarked in another place, namely, the newness of Nature, seems to be betrayed also in this instance. She rouses herself with the vigorous impetuosity of robust youth which revels in contrasting extremes.

The crumbs of last night's supper gave a scanty breakfast; and I was on the track of my quarry at the first show of light. I will not weary the reader with an account of that long day's pursuit. The last gasp for life of the dying stag had carried him many a mile; fortunately, not very much out of my way back to camp, otherwise I should have been in the most unpleasant fix of passing another night under a handy tree—this time, a wretchedly food-less and spirit-less being.

It was late in the afternoon when I came up to the monarch of the Great Divide. There he lay, where death had at last ended his gallant flight. He had been dead many hours, for his body was quite rigid, and his eye lustreless and broken. He was released with merciful suddenness; for yonder, not five yards off from where he lay, I could plainly see by his slot that he had been trotting with measured stride, when all at once his vital forces collapsed, and he pitched forward on his head, the lowest prongs of his antlers digging themselves for more than a foot into the soil—so deep, that unaided I could not release them.

Of the many thousands of Wapiti I have seen, he was by far the largest, and must have weighed quite 10 cwt., for his antlers alone, on their arrival in Europe, turned the scales at forty-four pounds. His skin was a very peculiar grizzly, and I was most anxious to save it; but it was much too late to do anything that day, even had I been able to turn the stag on his back, which, without much loss of time, I found impossible. Cutting out, as I always do, his two canine teeth, I found them to be of quite enormous size, nearly double that of any others I ever got. So uncommonly large were they, that when I subsequently happened to show them to one of the sub-chiefs of the Mountain Crow Indians, he offered me the pick of his ponies[6] for them.

With them in my pocket and his tongue in my rücksack—the former as a very tangible proof of the great size of my quarry—I left for camp, to return on the morrow for head and skin.

It was after dark when a tired, and hungry, but withal good-humouredly satisfied person struck our camp. A single signal-shot had rung through the sombre forest and across the tranquil tarn, so when the belated one emerged from the inky gloom into the bright circle of ruddy light round the huge camp-fire, he found awaiting him a cheery welcome and a glorious supper.

Next morning, Port and I, with a pack-horse, rode over to the dead stag. I have mentioned that I was anxious to save the skin, as its colour was unlike anything I had seen:[7] but Uncle Ephraim had this time acted the proverbial host, and when we got to the spot the carcass had disappeared. Two large bears had made a very satisfactory supper off it, and, as is usual with them, had câched (concealed) the remainder in a hole they had dug, leaving but the upper portions of the antlers protruding.

---

[6] See Appendix.

[7] I have since observed a like instance of grizzly Wapiti; but, notwithstanding ardent efforts, I failed, owing to a disgraceful miss, to secure the owner of it.

Considering that the surface of the ground was frozen, and that the hole must been quite three or four feet deep, it was a surprisingly quick piece of câching. With pointed sticks we dug out the upper portion of the carcass, which was uninjured, and thus rescued not only the best head of my collection, but also the one to which are attached the pleasantest memories.

Many an idle half-hour have I passed on yonder corner lounge, from whence the grand outline of the majestic head can best be seen. No doubt some future Ruskin of the chase will build up and propound the hitherto unenunciated bearing of Nature's works upon Art. For one of his examples let him take the spreading antlers of the stag, creations not only of graceful beauty, but also of architectonic boldness, with their pearled burr, their cannelured beam, their tapering tines, their spreading sweep, while the angles formed by the tines and the main beam may well be supposed to have served as primitive models for the first Gothic arches. All have engrossed from the earliest prehistoric times the pictorial attempts of the human race. Things which administer to the domestic daily wants of man, as did the staghorn for thousands of years, are wont to lose in his eyes the impressiveness of their beauty; and yet we see on the potsherd discovered in long-hidden "Pfahlbauten," or on the Aquitanian relics of prehistoric men, the rude attempt to outline the hart's form. From the Rigvedas to records of later days which narrate how silver images, such as *Cervi argentei*, were placed in ancient fanes and Christian churches, in commemoration of legends not dissimilar to that of Rome's foundation, we learn how the stag busied chisel, pencil, and pen. And, if we pass to later periods, to mediæval times, we find that in the vast forests of the main Continent of Europe, a cultus of worship of the stag's chase had sprung up; and when monarchism succeeded the rude reign of patriarchism, the stag became the royal game. The right to kill him was the exclusive privilege of the highest of the land. Ecclesiastic as well as secular sovereigns devoted their lives to his chase; while *Notabilia Venatoris* was, in the Sixteenth, Seventeenth, and Eighteenth Centuries, the sole science of polite society.[8] In those days the courtier received from his earliest youth strict training in the arts of venery, and he had to know more about the seventy-two signs by which the slot of a "royal" could be recognized than of any other polite art. Those were the good old days, when nothing less than the *Cerf de douze-cors* was killed. and such very singular customs prevailed as *f.i.* the presentation on a silver salver of the droppings of the "royal," the object of the day's chase, to the royal mistress, by the master of the hunt kneeling at her feet—a ceremony which, by-the-bye, was *de rigueur* also at the court of our good Queen Bess.[9] Most of the Continental potentates were great hunters. So late as the commencement of the present century, we hear of one of these grizzly Nimrods, devoting his whole life to the chase of the stag, doffing his hat every time he passed the head of the largest hart he had killed, which hung with many hundreds of others in the galleries of his favourite "schloss," and insisting that the gentlemen of his court should do the same. His ancestors from time immemorial were great staghunters; and the chronicles of that ancient house teem with the most

---

[8] See Appendix : Wapiti.

[9] In Turberville's "Noble Arte of Venerie" (1575), this is quaintly illustrated.

extravagant eccentricities, some even more singular than the following instance, the fancy of Duke William the Red, who would order a great triumphal arch to be raised in the centre of the forest, and by dint of the extraordinarily complete *equipage de chasse* force the stags to run through the arch, where rosaries made of the orthodox number of wooden beads, only much larger than usual, would be dexterously thrown over the antlers. "Thus prepared for death," as the chronicler, from whom I take this, says, "they would rush on to meet it at the hands of the royal hunter."

The beauty of outline displayed by a pair of good-sized and normal-shaped stag's antlers—I am referring here only to those of the red deer and Wapiti—is perhaps not of a kind to strike the eye of the casual observer.

There is probably no formation in nature so difficult to portray correctly as a stag's head. It took even Landseer six years to grasp its wealth of ever-changing form; and nothing will give one a better idea of the difficulties in this respect than to turn over the earlier sketches of great animal painters. Not to speak of several German masters in this department, who ultimately were worthy rivals of Landseer's skill, at least as far as red deer are concerned, and whose original sketches I have had occasion to examine, a study of the latter's very numerous early attempts to depict this configuration of undulating lines will show what I mean.[1]

---

[1] Some idea of this circumstance can be gained by examining Landseer's sketches, giving many of his more youthful works, in the *Art Journal* for 1876; and, if I remember rightly, also for the preceding year. Of course, the original sketches bring this even more strikingly before one's eyes.

But I am wandering far from Wapiti shooting; and though I could fill many a page with matter anent stag-lore and "antlermania," it is a subject which is anything but of general interest in the two great countries in the language of which these jottings are written.

The shooting of my very first Wapiti, under the guidance of an urchin some fourteen years old, was a somewhat ludicrous affair; and as its recital will give the reader an idea of a Western family of market-hunters, I am tempted to relate it. The locality was Laramie Peak, once a well-known sporting-ground a hundred miles north of Cheyenne, in Wyoming, but now too near to frontier settlements to afford good sport. I had been following some mythical Bighorn on the peak—it was on my first trip, and I was yet of pleasant greenness—and was returning in the evening to our distant camp, when a shot in close proximity attracted me to a small glade-like opening in the forest. When I reached the spot I saw, lying in the centre of the treeless space, a large animal; and, going closer, I found it was a Wapiti, apparently in the throes of death, for his legs were moving, and his body was not yet quite motionless. Going still closer, till I was about ten yards off, I perceived that the game had been brittled, and that the paunch and intestines were lying close to it, alongside of an outlandish rifle, with a barrel some four or five feet long. No sportsman was visible; a grey pony, *rigged* in Indian fashion, was grazing peacefully in close vicinity, its slashed ear betokening it to be of Indian origin. Strange to say, the Wapiti, though brittled was still moving, and, to my no little astonishment, I heard guttural sounds issuing from his inside. He was lying on his back, his antlers dug into the earth; and on my stepping closer, the sounds took the shape of words, and these again the form of some of the hardest and most blasphemous oaths of the American tongue ever heard by me. Certainly, if that Wapiti had not died of a legitimate bullet, he must have succumbed to the language now issuing in sepulchral tones from his belly.

I was naturally much surprised, for, great as were my expectations of the wonders which the "Great West" was to unfold to me, a speaking and swearing Wapiti was not among the sights I had hoped to meet. No doubt "bad medicine" hovered about this wild and lonely spot. I was not a little relieved, therefore, when the evil spirit presently took the shape of a pair of heels clad in moccasins, which made their appearance at the incision cut to brittle the game. A pair of legs clad in leathers reeking with blood, next made their appearance; and soon body and head of a very diminutive creature, covered from head to foot with gore still warm and steaming, had wriggled itself out of the carcass, dragging out behind him the lungs, heart, and a part of the windpipe. A stream of tobacco juice, squirted from the mouth, which at once broadened into a grin, and a terse greeting, made up largely of blanks, "stranger," and two or three "guesses," dispelled my last doubts respecting the humanity of the creature. The boy—for such the being turned out to be—an urchin fourteen years old, but very dwarfed for his age, had soon informed me that he had "gone and done the bull" with his needle rifle, whose merits for range and precision he wearied not to extol, and which presently he handed to me for inspection. Not unlike our Enfield rifle of prehistoric day, it was of immense bore, and decidedly a foot and a half longer than its owner was tall. The metal fastenings of the barrel to the stock were gone—raw hide or "buck-string" had taken their places—and the stock was of home-made origin, studded with brass nails, and notched in the most fantastic manner. The owner, however, informed me with much pride, that he had shot already over two hundred elks and blacktails with it, not forgetting two cinnamon (grizzly) bears, which he had potted, I presumed, from a safe place. The boy had come upon a gang of moving Wapiti, and, picking out the biggest bull, had rolled him over by a very true shot some two hundred yards off. Questioning him why he hid himself in the Wapiti, his grinning answer informed me that it was his usual manner of getting at the lungs, for his arms were far too short to reach them in the usual way, and he was not strong enough to cleave the breast-bone and brisket with his knife.

While talking he had whipped out an Indian scalping-knife (sharpened only on one side of the edge), and in less than half an hour had skinned the huge stag in the most workmanlike manner—a fire of guesses respecting the weight of meat and tallow, interlarded with frequent discharges of tobacco-juice, accompanying the greasy work. The green hide, weighing about a hundredweight, was of course too heavy for the boy to lift on his pony; and, as he explained to me that he was going to take it home, leaving the carcass "empty and clean," covered with boughs, to be fetched on the morrow, I was expecting he would ask me to help him put the hide on his horse. But so used does the merest child get to the great Western axiom of self-help, that he preferred accomplishing this in his own way, which he did with the quick readiness of long practice. Taking his raw-hide lariat from his saddle, he gave it a turn or two round the horn, and bringing up the pony to the Wapiti which was still lying on the skin, he twisted the lariat round the neck of the hide, gave the horse a kick, and the next instant the skin had been pulled from under the stag, and was dragging behind the pony, who, however, soon stopped, evidently well up to his work. Going up to him, the boy tied the loose end of the lariat to the two hind legs of the hide, and taking the rope across the smooth saddle, and placing one leg against the horse's flanks as a purchase, had in a twinkling hoisted one half of the fleshy mass saddle-high. Doing the same with the fore part, it was then easy to arrange the skin in the most convenient manner. The rapid and practical manner of the urchin's arrangements proved that, though youthful in years and diminutive in stature, he was an old hand at packing elk hides. Not a knot was slung superfluously; with rapid but silent steps he moved hither and thither, now covering the huge carcass with fresh boughs, or with one circular sweep of his sharp knife extracting the Wapiti's tongue and fastening it to his saddle; then tightening the primitive rope and cord girth of the old pony, he had soon brought his preparations to a finish.

Before mounting he spread a square of the tattered saddle blanket, which he had taken from under the old ruin of a saddle on the pony's back, over the carcass of the stag, while a rag of a handkerchief he wore round his head instead of a hat was fastened to a stick, and stuck flag fashion into the ground close to the dead game, with the object of frightening away the wolves and bears—a precaution which for the first night is often effectual.

Then the great gun and the small boy got on the top of the pony, which the latter did by using the former as a sort of leaping pole. It was quite dark by this time, and being in a perfectly strange country, I gladly availed myself of the boy's invitation to partake of a "squar'" meal," and share a buffalo robe with his big brother, rather than chance losing my way in the forest, especially as the boy had informed me that next day some grand sport could be enjoyed. A big gang of elk, numbering, he said, quite 2000, had been seen by him in the afternoon, a small detached portion of which he had struck later on, and out of which he had killed his stag.

His home was several miles off, so trudging at the rider's side, he was soon telling me of his shooting, or, as he called it, "gunning." His father had moved to the neighbourhood three or four years previously, when Indians were still roaming through the Laramie Peak country. He was now making a living as market-hunter, supplying the next settlement, forty-five miles distant, with game, selling it all to one man, who kept a "road-ranche" (inn), and at the same time was the grocer, dry-goods store keeper, sheriff, and postmaster of the settlement. All game—only the hind-quarters are used for food—fetched three cents per pound ($1\tfrac{1}{2}d.$), which, however, was not paid in cash, but in kind—coffee, sugar, flour, ammunition, and all those numerous articles in which a Western merchant deals. Money they hardly ever saw; horses and cattle were traded—a certain number of sacks of flour or pounds of plug tobacco forming the usual base of their barter. In due time we reached the log shanty, standing in a wide clearing, fenced in by stout rails. Here the stock was kept during night, while in daytime the horses and cows grazed over the mountains. Loud barking, and a peculiar shrill call, answered by the boy with a loud halloo, gave us a welcome. A flood of light issued from the open doorway, and a crowd of men, half-grown youths, and two or three women, were soon grouped round the tired old horse. A minute later I had found my way into the hut, where a kindly "Come right in, stranger," welcomed me.

The hut, about fifteen feet by eighteen feet, was divided into two compartments, one the kitchen and living room, the other the sleeping-quarters for the females and two married couples, while the sons were housed in a barn close by. Everything looked clean and comfortable, though exceedingly primitive. Wapiti skins lined the walls, and buffalo robes formed the carpet, while a large table in the centre was laid out for supper, with plates and cups of tin, and buckhorn knives and forks. Everything but the cooking and eating utensils was home made, from the buckskin garments of the men to the coarse homespun dresses of the women. A large rack, occupying one wall, held some twelve or fifteen different arms, from the Winchester repeater—bartered, as the father presently informed me, for a bale of otter and wolf skins, the real value of which was perhaps ten times the price of the cheap gun—to the antiquated Kentucky pea rifle. Every arm had its name. Here was an "Uncle Ephraim" or a "Track-maker," there an "Aunt Sally" and a "Sister Julia;" and every one had some special degree of merit and long gunning yarns attached to it. Besides the father and mother, three sons, and two daughters, there were just then on a visit an aunt, with two half-grown sons and a little girl, so that the supper-table, of ample proportions, was somewhat crowded. The ring of faces, from the old man's grizzled head to the seven-year-old damsel's fresh little physiognomy, afforded an interesting study. Happy content was impressed upon every feature, and soon loud laughter rang through the tumble-down shanty. Except a certain primitiveness of manner, there was little to remind one of the isolated position of this little community. The next settlement of whites was forty-five miles away, and except the grown-up son, who in summer and autumn took the game in a heavy waggon once or twice every fortnight to market, none of the members ever came into contact with civilization. In winter they were entirely blocked up, the narrow glen through which communication was alone possible becoming impassable. The newest paper was four months old, and for winter literature a bale of old illustrated weeklies were annually traded for wolfskins, and these were the only "reading matter" the family possessed. In the presence of their elders the young fellows' conversation exhibited a marked absence of foul-mouthed language, in which they otherwise indulged with remarkable force of expression.

Many an amusing yarn of their gunning adventures and primitive life enlivened the evening hours, and it was late when I and the sons and cousins retired to our barn, if such a building could be called, having only three walls, and breezy spaces quite six inches wide between the beams of which it was built. Hides were nailed on the outside to dry, and a row of Wapiti hind-quarters were hung on the top beam. In the middle of the night I was awakened by deep formidable growls, and constant scratching on the beams close to where I lay. Not knowing what to make of it, I awoke my neighbour, who, on listening for a second, quieted me by telling me they were only "bar" trying to reach the wapiti quarters. Two minutes later he was snoring again, evidently less put out by a bear's visit than I was. We were up before sunrise, and when, after a dip in the icy-cold waters of a neighbouring stream, I reached the hut, I found the family already assembled at breakfast.

Everybody, except the youngest daughter and the little niece, was going after the "gang" of elk. The ponies (some nine or ten) were already hitched to posts in front of the shanty, and all the antiquated rifles—the "Sister Julia," "Track-maker," and "Greased Lightning," the latter being the name of my dwarf friend's shooting-iron —were cleaned and laid ready for use. The little hunting party presented a quaint and yet not unpicturesque sight—men and youths, women and girls, all, male and female alike, armed with long rifles and revolvers, and mounted on shaggy ponies—and certainly it had about it the spice of novelty. After hearty good-byes to the young girl and the child standing in the open doorway, we started off at a round pace. Old Newland—for that is the name of this isolated family—lent me a horse for the day, as I was eager to catch a glimpse of this big gang. The previous evening young Newland had seen them some nine or ten miles off, going in a westerly direction; it was therefore decided to make sure of them by cutting them off on their usual route, well known to the family, for it was the usual autumn move of elk. The party kept together, except my boy friend and I, and by going in a more westerly direction, sought to strike the band before the main body came up. We had not gone far when I saw two big bulls moving over a very steep slope on the peak, at the base of which we were riding. We at once came to a dead halt, and decided to follow them on foot, the ground being too broken and steep for horses to venture on. The elk evidently did not belong to the main gang, for they were coming from an entirely different direction. Probably they were in sight or had the wind of the herd, and were now about to join them. Dismounting, we climbed the precipitous mountain side, rising, at an angle of quite fifty degrees, as rapidly as we could, and in the course of about twenty minutes had reached the spot where I had seen them. Turning, suddenly round, I saw spread out at our feet, some four or five hundred feet below us, and perhaps half a mile off, a plateau, on which were grazing a vast number of Wapiti. It needed not the boy's "That be them," to assure me that it was the big gang. Sitting down on a convenient rock, I had a long look with my glass, endeavouring to get some correct estimate of the number. That there were not two thousand, I saw very soon. There were three large groups, each of about four or five hundred, and each again divided into smaller bands. They were moving slowly westward, grazing as they proceeded. It was a grand sight, especially to one who had never before witnessed the like.

Knowing that the main party would strike them presently, we decided to follow the two big bulls we had first sighted. The ground was excessively broken, and covered with loose stones, making it nigh impossible to move noiselessly with boots or shoes. The urchin, with his soft moccasins—to which, at that period of my trip, I had not yet taken—had naturally great advantage over me, and he took a special delight in leading me over the roughest ground, where stones were constantly set rolling by my awkwardly heavy shooting-boots. Jumping from rock to rock, his huge rifle, carried in his right hand, used as "alpenstock" to steady himself, the little fellow moved along at a very rapid pace. We soon sighted the bulls, who were trudging along a small dry watercourse half a mile off. Here my youngster got excited, and, forging ahead at a "level" run, I was left behind, with no chance of approaching the game with the necessary noiselessness.

Scrambling up the next high rock, I scanned the ground, and saw that the ravine selected by the bulls turned sharply some few hundred yards ahead, enabling me, by crossing a slope of huge boulders thrown pell-mell together, to cut off the game should they remain in the gulch. There was no need to keep quiet; so, putting my best foot forward, I ran, or rather leaped, the distance in good time. On reaching the desired spot I saw the two Wapiti right under me, still in the watercourse, and the moccasined boy-stalker just settling down to open fire at eighty or ninety yards. I had run nearly as far as he had, but was considerably "pumped," and, besides, my shot would be quite double or treble as far as his. Before he had time to shoot, the game had got my wind, and swerving sharply, ascended the very precipitous sides of the gulch. Whipping out my glass, I watched the boy's fire. Taking the leader first, which was the smaller of the two, he hit him out of his seven shots every time, but so indifferently that the stag's movements were not impeded.

They were now close to the top, and twenty yards more would take them out of our sight. I had to fire over the boy's head, as the last movement of the game had brought him right between them and me. The boy evidently had never heard an Express bullet ping over his head, for immediately after my first shot he jumped up, evidently not a little startled. A second, third, and fourth followed in quick succession, passing some fifteen or twenty feet over his head; and when my fire came to an end, both bulls and the boy were lying stretched on the ground —the two former dead, the latter sorely put out by "that thar singing cannon," as he persisted in naming my ·500 bore Express, which, before he had seen its effect and heard its report, had appeared to him somewhat popgun-like in comparison to his punt rifle. We found both bulls to be good-sized animals, but with small heads, which seemed, however, very fine ones just then. The bigger one had his back broken by my Express, and no other injury; the other one was riddled by bullets—the boy's seven and one of mine, which latter had knocked him over. It was my first Wapiti—indeed, the first one I had ever shot at—and of course I was highly elated with my success. Moreover, the boy paid me the compliment that, for a "tenderfoot," I had done "mighty well." Higher still did I rise in his esteem when I presented him with my bull, hide and all, reserving only the head.

Being anxious to return to my camp, where I knew my people would be uneasy on my behalf, I left the boy skinning the animals, and again to dive into his gory hiding-place, and struck off across the range to where my camp was situated. On reaching the height I saw with my glass, four or five miles away, the big gang, now moving at a rapid pace, followed by black spots dodging about the herd. Three hours later I was back in my camp. Months afterwards I heard the result of their big "fall" hunt. They killed that day, if I remember rightly, some twenty odd head.

To strike Wapiti where there are plenty is not so much a matter of luck—as is the case, for instance, with bear—but rather the result of an accurate knowledge of the ground your expedition intends to cover. Where there will be hundreds in September, there may not be a single head six weeks later.

So, for instance, in the Laramie Peak country I doubt if there was a Wapiti there a week before "moving time." I had been there for two or three weeks, and had not come across a single track. This was several years ago (1879), and now, I suppose, not even while "moving" do these animals visit that otherwise very handy range of mountains. A week after this not unsuccessful *debût*, we struck a favourite whistling-place of elk. It was in the eastern extremities of the Rattlesnake Range, where the peculiar formation of the barren "bad-lands" is here and there rendered less repulsive by the occasional presence of forests growing on level plateaux, formed by deep eroded ravines cutting up the whole country into a number of flat-topped hills, of much the same height but varying extent. The one we were about to visit was a solid square; the sides, about 400 feet high, were, if not absolutely precipices, yet of amazing steepness, and none but Western horses could have scrambled to the top. It was no easy matter to find a practicable approach, and I remember we went very nearly round the entire mountain square before we found a Wapiti trail broad enough to allow our pack-horses to pass up. The top was about four miles in circumference, and, as I have said, comparatively level; in the centre a grass-covered barren, while a fringe of very dense forest formed the outer circle. On this land-girt island, as one might call it, there were a couple of good springs of water, and the barren was covered with peculiarly fine bunch-grass. After rather an eventful ascent up the narrow trail, with the precipice on one side, for our horses were as yet unaccustomed to this kind of work, we reached the top, and found not only the forest but also the open literally swarming with Wapiti. We were not yet quite beyond the fringe of frontier settlements, a Fort was fifty miles off, and a ranche not more than five-and-thirty; but the remarkably unsophisticated fearlessness of the game, which to me then was most surprising, and the absence of the slightest trace to indicate that human beings had ever been there, led us to suppose that except Indians, who were still roaming about the neighbourhood, the forbidding nature of the surrounding country, which was a desert-like wild, had kept off human approach. We pitched camp where forest and barren met, right in the middle, as it were, of whistling Wapiti. We could see them from the camp-fire, as half a mile off they were grazing on the barren. Our noon meal over, which I hastened as much as I could, to the disgust, I am afraid of the men, Port and I left for a stalk, if so the ludicrously easy approach to the unwary game deserved to be called. The only thing to which attention had to be paid was the wind. With that in our favour, Port actually brought me up to within sixty or eighty yards of a band grazing on the level open, quite 500 yards from the nearest trees or bushes. Of course we had to wriggle along, seeking cover behind straggling and stunted sagebrush, not higher than ten or twelve inches.

This was my first lesson in Western stalking, and strangely easy it seemed to me, though, I cannot deny the glorious sight of many hundreds of splendid stags, with heads which then seemed of the very largest dimensions, but which now would appear very moderate ones,[2] carried me away, and awoke that reprehensible love of slaughter inherent in most men's natures. Picking out only the very best heads I made an easy right and left, my first one at this grand game, the next two shots being misses, or next to it, for one of them grazed my third bull's back, while with my fifth I grassed him. I had killed the three biggest stags out of the herd, and though I could have continued pinging away with my long-range Express, I had sufficient control over myself to eschew putting fresh cartridges into the rifle. Not so, however, when after gralloching and sawing off the horns of the victims, we struck a mile or so further on another band. Among them again some fine antlers, of which I secured three pairs, thus acquitting myself (as I had stalked the latter by myself) to the entire satisfaction of Port, who was usually not given to pay compliments. By the end of the second day in this natural game-park, I had enough of Wapiti shooting—or rather, the wanton waste that I would have perpetrated had I continued to let my rifle have free scope, would have been unjustifiably great, for beyond our own immediate wants and a couple of pony-loads of meat I had promised the people at the nearest ranche, there were, in the absence of Indians, no other customers for the venison. I killed nine bulls—all good heads—in that locality,

[2] The size of Wapiti antlers varies considerably. The largest are never found on the Plains, but always in high altitudes, in timber; at least this is the general opinion of all trustworthy hunters, and is fully borne out by my own experience.

and, without exaggeration, could easily have trebled the number. My men, I need not say, were somewhat amused at this, for they very well saw how my hands itched to grab for the Express every time a Wapiti broke cover near us. The Western hunter seems to fancy the game resources of his home perfectly limitless, and exhibits a supreme indifference to the reverse side of the " first come first served," hence is often astonished at what he calls English squeamishness. To a friend a Western guide once said, "You have come a good many thousand miles to shoot, and now that we have at last struck game where it is plenty, you shrink from depriving the rascally Redskins or a parcel of skin-hunters of what is just as much yours as theirs. Certainly you Britishers are strange chaps." We remained a day or two longer, but I devoted my attentions exclusively to Bighorn, the tracks of whom we had seen on some very broken bad-land cliffs on the Western extremity of our "park." Except in the perfectly wild regions, such as the Wind River and Soshoné Ranges, I have never seen game so fearless as in this spot. One morning we found a grouse perched on the sailcloth that covered our buffalo-robe beds. Only when the inmate threw his rugs back did the bird take flight. Antelope bucks, always curious at this season of the year, used to approach quite close, eyeing the blaze of the camp-fire with astonishment.

Stalking on bright moonlight nights during the stags' rutting season has ever been one of my favourite sports; and of the many good harts I have killed in the Old World, to none are attached such pleasant recollections as to those few rolled over after a long and exciting stalk through the tranquil hours of a fine moonlight October night in the Alps. At first disappointed on missing the blood-stirring "call" of the European "royal" as he challenges his foe across valley and tarn, the whistle of the American stag has, as I have already said, a weird charm not easily to describe. Every kind of stalking is much easier in the New than in the Old World, not only on account of the greater quantities and greater fearlessness of the game, but also owing to the nature of the ground, and to the fact that during autumn the wind blows constantly from the same point, changing only at the approach of bad weather. All these circumstances combine in making Wapiti hunting a toilless pleasure—in fact, in the long-run rather too much so. There are few of those exciting moments when, with breath indrawn the little finger is wetted to discover the direction of the breeze, which with us is of such changeful temper; none of those memorable half-hours stretched motionless at full length in the grass, pendent with heavy dew, as with beating heart you watch the stag issue from the sombre forest heavy with the fragrant perfume of the pine, stalking forth in all the strength and pride of a monarch on to the little dell where the bright moonlight throws quaint shadows of his noble proportions, his breath issuing from his dilated nostrils upon the frosty air in vapoury clouds blending with the gauze layer of luminous steam which envelopes Mother Earth. No proud call re-echoes through the silent night from crag to crag those welcome seconds during which, with bared feet and crouching form, the blood rushing wildly through your tingling veins, you stride over fallen trees, cross the dark brook, wending your noiseless step through the maze of lichened pines, as, with your rifle to your shoulder, you approach the heedless quarry, thereby betrayed. And no such experiences as, when you have approached to within a dozen yards and already perceive through the network of brush and pine branches the faint outline of the stag lit up by a fitful moonbeam, you behold him suddenly dash away, and with inflated neck, bristling hair, and head thrown well back, crash through the dense timber: for upon his fine ear there has re-echoed an answering call to his challenge, and long before you have time to feel your discomfiture your quarry is far away, rushing onward to meet his rival in combat.

In European wild preserves, let them be ever so well stocked, such a chance does not present itself twice in the course of one night. If you have either alarmed or missed your stag, further pursuit is useless for that occasion, while here ten minutes will put you on the track of another calling Wapiti. It is no wonder, therefore, that the Western chase is after some experience found to be wanting in some of the more refined charms of the same pursuit in Europe. While in the Old World you are not as a rule overfastidious regarding the size of the head you bag, in the New World great slaughter would be the necessary consequence of indiscriminate shooting. The excitement incidental to the first "go" at a herd of great stags of which I have spoken wears off very quickly, and soon you recognize the necessity of shooting only those with first-class antlers worth the endless trouble and bother of transportation. Bright as the moonlight is, it is nevertheless very hard to tell the size of heads; and the four or five Wapiti I have rolled over on such occasions, have invariably turned out to be smaller than I anticipated when I shot them.

CHAPTER VI.

CAMPS ON THE TRAIL OF THE BIGHORN.

Sporting trophies—Newness of the landscape—*Mauvaises terres*—
The Bighorn at home—Size and weight—Fremont and De Saussure—Peculiarities of the Bighorn—My big ram—How I lost
my measuring-tape—Sheep-eater Indians—Scab.

FROM my earliest youth the breezy heights of the Alps have been my favourite playground. Before I entered the teens it was my boyish ambition to roam for days at a time in Alpine regions on or above Timberline; at first attended by a keeper, but soon, at my pressing request, trusted to my own faculties to find my way out of the sundry little scrapes into which my youthful ardour for sport was apt to lead me. Later on, days extended into weeks—not always of sunny summer and clear autumn, but frequently of frosty winter weather, which sent fierce snowstorms whirling around the peaks and passes I used to haunt. The reader, who will, perhaps, excuse these very irrelevant reminiscences, can therefore imagine that I visited the uplands of the Rockies with expectations by no means very modest. The one or two specimens of Bighorn I had seen in European collections, and especially some heads friends brought from the American wilds, had roused in me the wish to "go and do likewise" (N.B., if possible, better); for, in truth, there is no more covetous being than the articled apprentice to the craft of venery, and decidedly there is no sight more apt to send him over Oceans and across Continents than such trophies as the majestic horns of a really good ram, or the huge branching antlers of a fine Wapiti head. The former affords, of all others in the West, to the sportsman fond of old-fashioned stalking, and not over-easily fatigued by longish and often fruitless climbs on the weirdly-formed *mauvaises terres* peaks, by far the most interesting sport.

To prevent further interruption to my tale of the Bighorn-chase, let me in this place say a few words on the main characteristics of his home. I have called the West outrageously new. Its newness is by no means confined to men, manners, and cities; there is something decidedly new also about that portion of the mountain scenery of the Rockies called bad-lands.

The bold rock escarpments and cliffs, in places quite as jagged as any we have in Europe, the fissures, cliffs, and canyons—the latter of unrivalled depth—one and all betray a nakedness that somehow is irreconcilable with old age. The absence of all the beautiful mosses and lichens, features which that defiler of Nature, M. Taine, in a loathsome simile, calls vegetable ulcers and leprous spots, deprive the mountains of the West of that picturesque look of hoary age so peculiar to those of most other Continents.

Nature seems to destroy and to reconstruct at a much faster rate in the New than in the Old World. Landslips seem to be ever at work in despoiling slopes of the greensward; and before a new coat of vegetation can spring up, and thus hide the mountain's glaring nakedness, a repetition of the disaster again wrecks the scene. The extremes of heat and cold, liable, as I have said, to vary as much as from eighty to ninety degrees in the course of day and night, and the remarkable dryness of the atmosphere, chip the rocks and fray the outline of the cliffs with an energetic aggressiveness well in keeping with the power which distinguishes natural as well as human forces in the West.

Where bad-lands, or *mauvaises terres*—the name given to them by the old Canadian *coureurs de bois*—occur, the whole country, often many thousands of square miles in extent, lacks the upper crust of vegetation, which seems to have been carried off by some great flood, and left only ruins behind it. Not only is the general aspect one of utter decay, but the very outlines of these singular geological formations have about them a resemblance to great architectural works that have fallen to pieces. But this, the reader will exclaim, is surely contradicting the newness of the landscape with which I introduced these remarks. Ruins are, however, not necessarily the result of age. Nowhere does the traveller come across so many signs of deplorable decay as just in the West. He can see entire "cities," erected a few years back, and inhabited by several thousands of eager miners, totally deserted and slowly crumbling to ruin, the playthings of gales and dry-rot. In his wanderings through the remoter portions of the country he will frequently come upon abandoned log-dwellings, but a few months before the home of families, and now a sad picture of desolation. In like manner must we judge of the ruins of Nature,

A MAUVAISES TERRES PEAK.

nowhere more strikingly presented than in the badlands. The lifeless waste is not the work of immeasurable eternity, but the result of geologic changes of comparatively recent origin.

Geologists tell us that notwithstanding their altitude vast inland seas occupied the present site of bad-lands.[1] The spires, pinnacles, towers, or more compact chains, standing either isolated or in semi-detached masses, are the remains of the once more or less level bottom of the lakes, water having carved them by erosion into their present shape, which, to make a very homely comparison, one might liken to the channelled surface of a walnut kernel. In a country where scientific exploration dates back for not more than fifteen or twenty years, it is next to impossible to mark the stride of Nature's revolutions. In one or two instances, however, we are enabled to ascertain details concerning the mysterious drying up of lakes, and the changed aspect of bad-land formation. Thus, it is known that the country along the upper valley of the Mississippi and Red River of the North has either risen or dried up. The water level of lakes within forty miles of St. Paul has sunk six feet in twenty-five years, and men are living who knew hunters who at one time canoed over portions of the Red River Valley, which is 350 miles long, and from 70 to 100 in width.[2]

The levels of all lakes in the West, including the great

[1] King, in his "Sierras," page 185, says: "During the cretaceous and tertiary periods, the entire basin from the Rocky Mountains to the Blue Mountains of Oregon was a fresh-water lake." Professor A. Geikie gives a very lucid description of bad-lands, in *Macmillan*, July, 1881, which is well worth reading. See Appendix.

[2] Report of the Commissioners of the Royal Agricultural Interests Commission, who visited the United States in 1879.

Salt Lake, in Utah, are known to be sinking; and to mention the entire disappearance of a lake within the past five-and-twenty years, the instance of the Market Lake, in Idaho, can be quoted. Lying in the Snake River Valley, it was visited by a Government expedition, under Lieutenant Mullan, in 1854. It was then a large and beautiful sheet of water, twelve or fourteen miles in length. Its site is now a dry sandy depression. The Chimney Rock, a high isolated shaft of bad-land formation, in Central Wyoming, standing close to the old emigrant trail, and thus coming under the notice of early travellers, was measured in Fremont's time, *i.e.* nearly forty years ago, and has since that period decreased, so I am told by good authority, close upon 100 feet. When I passed it in 1879, the detritus constantly crumbling from its walls had accumulated in great heaps round its base.

In colouring, also, Western scenery exhibits a certain crudeness, the reverse of mellow age. A bird's-eye view of " bad-land " reminds one of early pictorial attempts of primitive races, who, when depicting works of nature, were in the habit of first drawing, in uncouth outline, the diagrams of what they intended to represent, and then filling them in with colours quite arbitrarily chosen. The compositions were not only void of all principles of perspective and chiaroscuro, but also lacked the primary condition of all ideal art—the harmony of tints. A broad vista of such verdureless bad-land "buttes" or peaks, lighted up by the intensely searching achromatic sunlight peculiar to these regions, where the glaring brilliancy of day is unrelieved by shadow or nebulous *half-distances*, leaves on one's mind the impression of bizarre crudeness. Wherever we glance we see the stratified bands of successive layers of differently coloured conglomerates, some of clay-like, others of pumice-like consistency. Here stands one great isolated crag, five or six hundred feet in height. The next pinnacle of equally fantastic shape is half a mile off, yet it is easy to see that every one of the six or eight various bands of disintegrating rock, or the seams of oxides, silicates, sulphates, or carbonates which are very plainly visible on the precipitous faces of both, exactly correspond with each other, and that in both the black, the brown, the pea-green, the purple, and the vermilion streaks follow each other with the same regularity. These bands being of different homogeneity offer not precisely the same resistance to the denuding effects of rain and frost, and hence narrow shelves are formed, that run generally horizontally, but always parallel to each other across the precipitous face of the peak or hill. Generally these ledges are not wider than a few feet; while in other places they will be broad, and rise tier-like from the bottom. On these platforms there is a very scanty growth of grass —so scanty indeed as to be hardly perceptible to the eye, but they are, nevertheless, the favourite dwelling-places of our quarry, the Bighorn. Here, too, the stalker has a good chance of approaching them unobserved; he must, however, to be able to undertake this, possess a clear head, and not know what giddiness is; for often the ledges are very narrow, and the height of the precipice stupendous. Many an enjoyable creep of an hour or two have I ventured, and many a pleasant family still-life scene have I watched in close proximity, to be finally rudely disturbed, if the paterfamilias happened to have good horns, by the crack of my Express. In such localities it was not infrequently quite impossible to save any of the meat, for often it was as much as I could do to saw off the horns, and, tying a short cord to them, drag them behind me as I crept back to safer ground.

But enough of this preamble, let us now speak of the reality—the bold and majestic ram, standing motionless on yonder giddy shelf, showing in perfect repose the classic outline of his noble head against the blue of the Rocky Mountain sky, as if cut in cameo fashion by the deft hand of a Grecian sculptor. With his sturdy, massive body, his thick-set limbs firmly planted on the protruding ledge, looking so dangerously fragile in comparison to its load, his small head carried high, as if the heavy horns were a mere feather's weight, he looks the emblem, not of agility, as does the chamois, but of proud endurance. Of all game that calls the Rocky Mountains, peculiar and characteristic as their natural features are, its home, he is the truest type of their grand solitude and barren vastness.

The Bighorn (*Ovis Montana*), also called *Grosse Corne, Cimarrón*, or Mountain Sheep, is closely related to the monster of his species, the Nyan Argali, or Ovis Ammon, the most famous game of Thibet. He is slightly smaller, but the horns are very much of the same formation, curve, and monstrous size. In build, coat, and habitat the Bighorn resembles the European ibex, perhaps, more than any other animal, the chief exterior difference being, as is perhaps hardly necessary to say, the shape of the horns, which in the former are curved, sometimes like those of a domestic ram, only on a greatly magnified scale.

Of few North American game animals does one meet, beyond the ocean with more conflicting accounts as to its habitat, and round none does there rest such a halo of romance and exaggeration. Not only is the Bighorn often confounded with the mountain goat, but many authors, from the earliest to the most recent, who are not experienced "gunners," delight in promulgating fabulous stories respecting it.

The horns of the largest animals are of stupendous girth, and weigh as much as forty pounds. I was fortunate enough to bag, among the seventy or eighty Bighorn I got, an uncommonly fine ram, each of his horns girthing nineteen inches at the base. It is, or rather was—for I lost this grand trophy by fire—one of the finest heads killed by European sportsmen, at least to judge from the measurements given by numerous reliable veterans, none of whom, so far as I know, shot any exceeding eighteen and a half inches.[3]

On another occasion I saw, and for twelve days followed, an old monster ram, whose horns were, if my eyes and glass did not deceive me very greatly, even larger than those of my master ram. Very severe weather made further pursuit impossible; but, as I intend to look him up again in his desolate home, I may, if luck stands by me, finally succeed in bagging that wonderful pair—incomparably the largest I saw, and most probably ever shall see. He had been seen before on several occasions by hunters and trappers, two of whom I happened to meet, while a sound "three-dayer" confined us to our dug-out, at the base of the mountain chain which sheltered this patriarch. Not knowing that he had been the centre of my ambition for the last fortnight, they very soon opened on the wonderful dimensions of this beast's horns, affirming, with the typical Western love of romance, that they actually dragged on the ground, assuring me they had often seen the marks of the

[3] See Appendix: Bighorn.

horns on the snow on both sides of the animal's tracks. An attempt to outcap this was the only way of effectually silencing these lovers of tall talk ; so, turning to my companion, who was sitting at my side in front of the fire, I said, "Port, don't you think that must be the very same Bighorn that we tracked ? you know, the big one that had sleigh runners tied to his horns, and a little wooden wheel on each of his hind legs? I suppose the snow had got too deep for him." The twinkle in my companion's eye told me *that* would do ; and so it did, for I was no more bothered by romanceful hunters' stories.

But to return to the quarry. The weight of a good five-year-old ram hardly exceeds 280 pounds or 300 pounds (Audubon mentions the weight of one as being 344-pounds), though you will often hear of 450-pounders, statements which of course lack the authority of an Audubon. Amongst the wonderful stories of the Bighorn that are current, the most absurd is that of their pitching themselves headlong down precipices, striking the sharp rocks with their horns, and thereby breaking their fall. Fremont (the great explorer) is alas! one of the first to start this ridiculous rumour in the account of his travels (1842), when describing the "mountain goat," as he calls the Bighorn. He says that "the use of those huge horns seems to be to protect the animal's head in pitching down precipices to avoid pursuing wolves." How history does repeat herself! De Saussure, whose career has many points of similarity with that of Fremont, says of the Swiss chamois, that "when pressed by foes, or driven to places from which they cannot escape, they will hang themselves to the rocks by the crook of their horns, and thus perish." Mr. Rufus Sage, and all the rest of countless authors on the great West, follow suit, and I am sorry to say even an Englishman fell into this trap, repeating in his lately published work on Western travel this wondrous fable, mentioning as a proof the scaled and dented appearance of the horns.

I have never seen any large herds of Bighorn, about fifty or sixty being the most, notwithstanding the numerous stories afloat of bands of four or five hundred. The average number in a herd is very much less; from six to ten or twelve being the most usual. Their rutting season is in November, and then the old rams, which keep aloof from the does and younger males for the rest of the year, come down from their solitudes and take the leadership of their family herd—a habit precisely similar to that of the ibex. The herd at this time of the year consists generally of three or four does with their young ones, now already half-grown, and a couple of two or three-year-old rams. The old ram will during this period be leader, watch, and guard; herein again imitating the male ibex, who, in distinction to chamois—which have one and the same doe as leader all the year round—assumes the duty of the female and acts in that character during the rutting season. As I often used to watch herds for hours at a time, I became well acquainted with their peculiarities. One of the strangest is the friendly relationship existing between them and the mountain magpie—about the only bird you see or hear on the timberless barren mountains, which are the favourite home of the Bighorn. Small flocks of ten or fifteen birds will settle down on the backs of the grazing bighorns, and begin to pick away very busily at the minute larvæ that infest the scrubby coat, two birds often being engaged on the same animal. I had never heard of this before, but subsequently found that the so-called moose bird—a carrion bird, the size of a thrush—does precisely the same to the moose, ridding him of a species of tick.

Bighorn are, with one exception only, at no time to be found elsewhere but on the roughest and most forbidding rock formation. That one exception occurs after rutting time, when the rams, in very poor condition, will wander from their crags to the level plain land, where the rich bunch grass helps to recuperate their strength. Especially if snow has fallen on the higher ground will they be found feeding, sometimes as much as a mile from the base of the next mountain chain. I often saw, in the month of December, small bands grazing in this manner; but so watchful are they on these occasions—an old doe being constantly on guard duty on the most prominent knoll—that it is most difficult to approach them within shot.

Once, by a piece of singularly good luck, I was enabled to "run" Bighorn on horseback, killing my ram with the six-shooter. Easy as this is with buffalo, elk, antelope, and even deer, it is, on account of the habits of the mountain game, a very rare instance of good fortune. Let me narrate how it happened:—

On a fine December morning, the air delightfully crisp and invigoratingly light, I was skirting, on the look-out for game, a high sugarloaf-shaped "bluff," rising precipitously from the perfectly level highland plateau across which we had been already travelling for two or three days. Peering cautiously round a sharp-profiled rocky buttress, I discovered, some 400 yards away, lying in the pleasantly warm sunshine, a small band of Bighorn. Dismounting, I ascended the rocks to a point of view from where I could overlook the *terrain*, and soon had formed my plan of operation. The Bighorn, who had not seen me, were grouped about nine hundred or a thousand yards from the main rocks, evidently their home—a perfectly level stretch of *mauvaises terres* intervening between them and the crags. Leaving all superfluous kit and my rifle at the base of the rock, I mounted my pony—no other than the fast Bessie mare—and made ready for a dash, which, as I had but 600 to their 900 yards, promised to be successful. Gripping my heavy Colt revolver,[*] whose shooting qualities I had brought, by experiments in the way of lightening the pull and changing the sights, as well as by constant practice, to a fair state of perfection, and taking my mare well in hand, I galloped out from behind the big rocks that had hidden me. The first few yards brought me into full view of my game, who, dashing up and gazing for one second at the unwonted apparition, made, as I had anticipated, straight for the rocks. The race was a most exciting one. There was one fair head in the lot; so, singling him out, I was close behind him when still about forty yards from the precipitously rising slope, where if he once got he would have been secure from further molestation. He did reach it, but with three ·45-calibre bullets out of my six shots in him, and these, though they did not bring him down on the spot, made him bite the dust before he had ascended 100 yards. Rolling down the steep slope, the

---

[*] I do not usually carry a revolver, it being a most useless and cumbersome utensil for game; but, in this instance, I happened to have one about me, as it was a short time after the last Ute outbreak (1879); and though the site of the war was a considerable distance off, small bands of the Utes had been horse-lifting in the neighbourhood.

fine ram was lying dead at my feet, all within ten minutes of my first sighting him. I was not a little pleased with my success, and, next to those of my first *ovis*, the horns, though not over-heavy, are the most prized in my little collection.

The coat of the Bighorn is a dusky grey, varying in shade in different individuals; the hair is coarse, crisp, and short, bearing a very great resemblance to that of the European ibex, not only in texture and colour, but also in the fine woolly undergrowth which in winter protects the animal against the great cold. At first the tyro finds it very difficult to see Bighorn, as the colour of their coat is in strange uniformity with the tint of the rock. Absurd as it sounds, I once shot, and frequently saw, reddish Bighorns, the dust of their native rock—blood-red as some of the so fantastically varied formations of the Rockies are—having given the coat a tint similar to its own.

Bighorn are very cunning animals; they will let the sportsman pass them a few paces off and not budge, and, when he has turned his back, rise and make off. Of this I very frequently convinced myself, till finally I got into the habit of filling my right pocket with pebbles, and throwing one or two wherever they could possibly be hidden under overhanging rocks or other shelter; my trouble being rewarded on several occasions by thus starting small bands of eight or ten heads, giving me capital opportunity to select the best. Their tenacity of life is very great. On two occasions I shot old rams too far back, my Express tearing big holes, visible at a considerable distance off; snow was on the ground, and had it been any other animal we must have got them, for our camp-dog, though not regularly trained to it, followed up fresh tracks remarkably well. On both occasions we spent a whole day vainly trying to get our victim, who carried good horns. Leading us circuits up and down endless and very steep slopes, they got away on both occasions by returning like the hare to the spot where they were put up, and from thence keeping to their old spoor, they finally left it where the ground was most broken and no snow, by one huge leap, down steep rocks, where their spoor was soon lost.

My largest head, measuring when killed, as I have mentioned, nineteen inches, rewarded a long, but perhaps the most interesting, stalk of my second expedition. The range the ram inhabited had been hunted previously by English sportsmen, and it was owing to this circumstance that I heard of the existence of this uncommonly large one, who had hitherto outdodged his pursuers. The mountains were a mass of bad-land crags, of the most fantastic shape, with very little timber about them; the time, the latter part of November, and about six inches of snow covering the less precipitous slopes. My trapper, engaged with cayotes, had pitched camp in a sheltered grove of cotton-woods that skirted the banks of a little stream. An old "dug-out," inhabited by him some years before, offered, when cleared of rubbish and the fireplace newly set, a capital retreat; in fact, it was the snuggest camp I remember on that trip. Game, especially the graceful Mule-deer, was plentiful about us, but it did not take me long to perceive that they had benefited by their previous intercourse with white men, for they were shy, and evinced little of that innocent curiosity which unhunted game in those regions not unfrequently betray.

A buffalo-robe behind my saddle, my rücksack and saddle-bags filled with spare ammunition, bread, and a frying-pan, and Boreas, the slow but sure-footed one, with the writer on his back, left camp for a two-days' stalk. I was determined to do my level best with the big ram, of whose existence I had received authentic information; but the chief difficulty, of course, was to find my game in the gulches, canyons, and gloomy "pockets" of an extensive ridge. Fortunately, it was rutting-time, and the rams were now with the smaller fry, moving at this period over more ground than is their wont at other times. I discovered, in the course of the first forenoon, three or four different bands; but my glass, and a stalk more or less protracted, bringing me in close proximity to them, showed me that my would-be prize was not among them. In the afternoon I was sitting on a prominent buttress of rock, examining the surrounding ground, all of the most broken and weirdly-shaped nature, when I discovered, some eight or nine hundred yards from me, a band. With my glass I saw they were on the move, grazing slowly along towards my resting-place. The wind being in my teeth, and the ground very unfavourable for an advance, I resolved to wait at the base of the crag for the approach of the Bighorn. *Ventre à terre*, I lay for more than an hour behind a stunted sagebrush about fifteen or eighteen inches high; but no Bighorn appeared on my limited horizon. I was just about to rise, and had already let down the hammers of my Express, when, looking up, I saw, about twenty-five yards off, a monster head, staring in the most deliberate manner at the bush behind which I was now fairly a-tremble with buck fever; for one glance at the huge horns, curving in graceful one-and-a-quarter turn, was sufficient to tell me I had the patriarch before me.

The ram could not see me, but something or other must have roused his suspicion, for there he stood, his head just showing over the rocks, calmly staring towards me. The dense brush, through which I had made a peep-hole, seemed to grow scantier and smaller as minute after minute passed and the same rigid gaze was fixed upon me. My rifle, lying muzzle downwards, was at my side, perfectly useless, however, under the ram's suspicious scrutiny. How long this continued, I know not; to me it seemed hours. A second and a third head—one of a doe, the other of a smaller ram—had showed up; but evidently their senses were less keen than that of their leader, for they both withdrew, and a few minutes later I saw the herd, some forty in number, slowly file up a narrow ledge leading to yet higher ground. The sun was going down when the big ram began his tantalizing game, and now dusk was fast approaching, and I was thinking seriously of jumping up and taking my chance at a running shot, when the apparition vanished as suddenly and noiselessly as it had appeared. This faculty of stealing away, over ground where it would seem impossible to move one step without starting stones and making a noise, I had previously observed, but never in such a high degree. At such moments the heavy animal seems to step with the velvety paws of a panther, and not a pebble rattles or a stone is displaced.

The utter silence that reigned over the whole dreary, weirdly-grand landscape became, now that the nervous strain had ceased, more oppressive. What to do next was the question. The prize was too great to tempt any rashness. Out of three possibilities I knew not which had occurred. The ram, still on the watch, could either be behind the rocks that had hidden his approach, or he could have followed the band, or, finally, he might have gone quite another course down the steep slope, where he would be lost to me in the dense timber of a deep gulch. Already it was too dark to shoot over a hundred yards with any certainty, and the rapid fall of night usual in those latitudes would make all shooting impossible before ten minutes had elapsed. From the very first I had given up all hope of returning to where I had left Boreas and my buffalo robe; so, as lying out was inevitable, I decided not to move that evening, but to stop where I was. Cautiously creeping down from my post of vantage, I found between two big rocks a sort of cavity, where, sheltered from the wind, I resolved to pass the night. A warm jersey, a pair of warm gloves, a small flask of whiskey, and a juicy elk tongue, with some bread—the two latter my "iron store"—all carried in my rücksack, enabled me to pass the long hours of that night without enduring any very exceptional hardships; and I had ample time to compare the Old World past with the New World present, to review the pleasures of two November nights spent both at an altitude of at least 10,000 feet, the one on a bleak range of the Rocky Mountains, the other in a cavern in the Tyrolese Alps, in which, some years before, a chamois-stalking fix had imprisoned me.

I was right glad when break of day finally enabled me to stretch my cramped limbs. Substituting moccasins for my heavy hobnailed shoes, I was before long on the creep again. My first move was to ascertain if the ram was still in close proximity, and, having a lively remembrance of that long stern gaze, I preferred to ascend the crag from whence I had first observed the Bighorns, rather than trust myself to the more convenient, but also more exposed, hiding-place behind the sagebrush. A close examination of the ground proved resultless; the ram was gone. Descending again, I made for the spot where he had appeared to me the previous evening. The snow lay in patches, and after a little trouble I managed to strike his tracks, which at once showed me that he had made for the higher ground. A toilsome ascent over the amazingly rough ground, covered as far as the eye could reach with huge blocks of rock, most of them bigger than a log shanty, thrown pell-mell together, parted by great cavernous chasms, fifteen to twenty feet deep, and too broad for me to leap them, obliged me to make great *détours*— while the nimbler game had traversed them with ease—and brought me finally to the ledge where I had last seen the band. Here the snow was in better condition for tracking, and I soon detected among numerous others the tracks of my ram, unmistakable on account of their size. The spoor was "clean," showing, by the absence of little drifted crumbs of snow and ice, that it was but very recently made. The wind was rapidly rising, and the cold had numbed my fingers, notwithstanding my warm sheepskin gloves, for the weather was evidently changing for the worse, and a "cold spell" threatening. A long and very cold creep along the ledge brought me in about half an hour to a gap of some five or six feet in breadth. The Bighorn had leaped it with ease, but to human skill it proved an insurmountable obstacle; for not only was the ledge in this place hardly broader than two feet, but the precipice at my side was some hundred feet in depth, and the wind too high to make one's footing very sure. Crouching back on my heels, I managed to turn, and retraced my hand-and-knee steps to the old starting-point, without having seen a living sign of my game.

Knowing that Bighorn at this season feed very long in the morning, I determined to try a low level, where the grass, so scanty that one hardly saw it, seemed a little more plentiful. Again a ledge was the only means of weathering the huge buttress of rock which shut out the view. This time it was broader, and ran right round the whole face of the precipice. In an hour I had gained the extremity, and, peering over the ledge, discovered the band directly below me, grazing at the foot of the precipice, among a belt of low and stunted cedars. Lying on a rock, slightly ahead of the rest, was my ram, his head turned away from me, looking downwards. The distance was comparatively short, but the very high wind, blowing right across the course of the bullet, made the shot nevertheless a riskful one. Crouching back, I took my time, examining the lay of the ground, which proved to me that, without making a *détour* of several hours, during which the band would most probably move away, I could not possibly get closer. Cautiously pushing my rifle forward, I prepared to chance the shot. To my left barrel, shooting a solid ball—in high wind much preferable to the lighter Express bullet—devolved the honour of bagging this royal head, which it did most effectually, by breaking his backbone and piercing his body from the centre of the back to the foreshoulder. Instead of huddling together and gazing terror-stricken in the direction of the shot—as Bighorns which have not been hunted most usually do—the whole band dispersed very rapidly; so quick were their movements, in fact, that I had hardly time to get in my second shot at a yearling whom I wanted for immediate consumption, no warm food having passed my lips since I left camp. I missed him, however, the bullet tearing off a fragment of stone, which must have struck him, for he made a most comical goatlike side-jump.

Impatient as I was to get down to my prize, I could not do so without making a considerable round, so I found it expedient to go back where trustworthy Boreas had been hobbled, in close proximity to a water-hole and good grazing. After three hours of hard work, I had brought him round to the base of the chain, and, leaving him there, ascended again to where the Bighorn lay. He was a glorious old fellow, and with my tape I measured and re-measured the horns for at least ten minutes. Few such heads are to be got, and the accident which subsequently deprived me of it destroyed a grand trophy of which I was exceedingly proud. After cooking and devouring the liver, I prepared to return home. Descending, the *Rücksack* came into requisition, for the head of a Bighorn is not only very heavy, but most awkward to carry, especially if any climbing, requiring the use of the hands, too, has to be done. Two extra straps round chest and waist, holding the head in the position most convenient and least dangerous for the bearer in case of falls, are essential helps on such occasions. It was growing dark when finally I was on my way home, Boreas picking his steps with wonderful surefootedness along the tortuous rock-strewn bottoms of deep gloomy canyons, through which our road lay. Long had the bright stars been shining, and the "dipper" was beginning to slant, when finally a welcoming neigh of Boreas's favourite mate sounded through the frost-laden mist of night, and a few minutes later the fire, lighting up in picturesque brightness the interior of our primitive "dug out" home, no less than the genial voices of my companions, and the affectionate greeting of our faithful dog, ended one of my most interesting stalks after Bighorn.

Speaking of measuring horns reminds me of a ludicrous misadventure defrauding me of a very fair head. I had sighted a lonely old ram roaming on some ugly *mauvaise terres* ground, rendering a stalk very ticklish work. A little perseverance, however, overcame the obstacle, and late in the afternoon I got my shot. The ram fell as if struck by lightning, a fortunate circumstance, as he was standing on a very narrow ledge, overhanging a lofty precipice. The slightest struggle would have sent him headlong down the abyss, a fall which would have smashed his horns to splinters.

When, by crawling along the narrow ledge, the only possible approach, I got to my quarry, he seemed as dead as a stone. Where he lay his body occupied the whole width of the ledge, his legs stretching over the narrow cornice of rock, while his hind-quarters lay towards me. Elated with my success, I was hotly eager to know the size of the head; so, whipping out my tape-measure, and not noticing anything else, I stretched over the body, and using both hands, had succeeded in encircling one of the massive horns with the ribbon, when I suddenly felt myself heaved up; and, before I had time to regain a kneeling position, the ram was on his legs, flinging me back like a feather. Luckily, he threw me so that I kept my equilibruim, a very slight sideways jerk would have sent me to kingdom come. My rifle I had left behind, at the place I had shot from; and my knife I, of course, could not use, owing to the rapidity of the whole thing, and the precarious nature of the ground. The ram stood for half a minute, as if paralyzed, and then, with a rapid and very peculiar motion of his body, which I had never noticed before, made off along the ledge, my measuring-tape fluttering in a loose coil round his right horn. It would seem I had, in trapper parlance, "creased" the ram, and hence his instantaneous fall, and equally rapid "up and away" movement.

What at first annoyed me most was the loss of the tape, as it was the only one in our "outfit," and I had frequent use for it. How to replace it was a puzzle, for in making another I had no standard inch or foot-rule to go by. At last a "happy thought" struck me. My rifle barrels were, as I knew, exactly twenty-eight inches long, so nothing was easier than to turn them into standard inches of the realm, and, with this aid, manufacture out of the binding of my coat a new tape, which, on returning to civilized lands, months afterwards, I found to be quite correct.

The *mauvaises terres* formation is often very favourable (or rather unfavourable) for a wholesale slaughter of these animals, especially if two or three tried hunters circumvent them from different sides, rendering impossible all escape from the narrow belt of rock, or small basin shut in by perpendicular walls. As their hides make the best buckskin, a party of Indians or half-breeds, will slay—if favoured by luck—a whole band; and even white hunters will occasionally be carried away to this extent. As, however, no game I am acquainted with so readily takes to heart the lessons taught it by its human pursuers, opportunities to butcher are rare, and only possible in very out-of-the-way nooks, where Indians have never hunted. On the contrary, however, it has often astonished me, how close to frontier settlements Bighorn will roam in winter, if they are not hunted or disturbed. I know, for instance, one place in Wyoming—an isolated chain of bad-land peaks, not more than 7000 feet over sea-level, and only twelve miles from a settlement of importance, where, in December and January, Bighorn (no large heads) can be killed with certainty.

An acquaintance, whom I happened to meet on the Union Pacific Express, on his return journey round the World, and to whom I disclosed the secret, sacrificed only three days, and, braving the Arctic cold, bagged his Bighorn in that time. But this is an exceptional case; for usually it takes weeks, if not months, of travel to get to the autumn quarters of Bighorn, many shooting-parties I have heard of spending months in the mountains without even seeing the tracks of one. In summer, Bighorn are very hard to find, at least in those portions of the West I know; indeed from observations made during my last trip they seem to migrate during the hot months of the year to the highest and most inaccessible peaks. To judge from my experience, they descend to the badlands, their favourite autumn, winter, and spring ground, in September or October, after the first heavy snowstorm.

In the Wind River chain there existed up to quite recent times, a very interesting and very little-known community of Indians, known as the "Sheepeaters."[5] They lived very

---

[5] One hears, frequently, very wonderful tales about these Sheepeaters; one "authority" affirming that they hybernated like bear, their "winter sleep" lasting through the winter. So far as I can learn, they lived only in the Wind River and Gros Ventre country.

high up on the great mountain Backbone, and their miserable dwellings, across which I frequently stumbled, prove that they constantly lived on or above Timberline, thus making the only known exception to the rule that the Indians of North America are anything but mountaineers. They had no horses, and were the poorest of the poor. They subsisted, so I was informed by a half-breed, whose squaw was a daughter of this tribe, on deer and Bighorn, following the game in late autumn to the lower pasturages. They were very expert stalkers. They belonged to the great Snake Indian tribe, but had their own chief, and had nothing in common with their Plains brethren, who, born in the saddle, deem it most derogatory to walk a single unnecessary step. Sheepeaters' "teeppees," or lodges, are without exception the most miserable human dwellings I ever saw; and, considering their very great altitude, consisting of loosely piled-up stones, and lean-to roof of slender pine trunks, their inmates, wretchedly clad as they undoubtedly were, must have suffered intense cold. In this chain they are occasionally found 800 or 1000 feet over Timberline. In some instances they must have carried the logs forming the roof up amazingly steep slopes. One hut I found on a nameless peak, also far above Timberline.[6] The majority were, however, just on the outskirts of timber vegetation, and here I have counted as many as fourteen very big skulls

---

[6] Mr. Langford, one of Professor Hayden's Government exploration party, who ascended the Great Teton, found on the very summit of an adjacent peak, at a height considerably over 13,000 feet, a circular enclosure six feet in diameter, composed of granite slabs, set up endwise, and about five feet in height, very similar to one I discovered at an altitude 2000 feet lower.

of Bighorn, lying about in a space not larger than a medium-sized room. To judge from this evidence, these Indians hunted only the very largest of the species. There are no Sheepeaters left. One of the last authentic records of them is furnished, I believe, in Captain Jones's report, to which we have already referred, a Sheepeater acting as guide extricated him and his companions from the great forests, where he had got lost. A few of the last *bucks* of the tribe returned, so I was told, to their original tribe, and became "reservation" Indians, but I learn that they have all died. Let us hope that their famous quarry will long survive them.

One of the most singular experiences in my whole acquaintance with this noble game was the conclusive discovery that they are subject to scab. I had heard of it before, but my trapper, as well as several equally experienced mountaineers, never having come across this disease in Bighorn, ridiculed the idea. As it turned out, I was destined to become convinced of its truth in a most unpleasant manner. I had determined to send the whole carcass of a good specimen to Europe, and, in fact, had, before starting out, made the necessary arrangements with the Express Company of the Union Pacific, and with the agents of a large Transatlantic line of steamers, who were to berth the rare guest in the ice-hole on board ship; and hence I had every hope of its reaching the Old World in a good condition. Our means of transportation being limited and already overtaxed by my collection of horns, I resolved on my return to civilization to wait till the last opportunity where Bighorn could be got. This was a day or two's ride from an Union Pacific station—a small Western townlet, where I intended to take the cars back to New York. December was far advanced, and the weather just then very severe, the thermometer being down to 25° and 30° below zero, and a gale blowing the whole time, making our camp, which was in the ruin of a log cabin, roof and one side missing, a very cold and uncomfortable one. Bighorn there were plenty, as the numerous tracks in the snow showed, so I hoped to be able to kill my ram in the course of the next day or two. But chance, which had dealt so kindly with me the previous four or five months—it was on my second trip—now forsook me. On the second day of our stay, a very bad three-day snowstorm—to which a mail-rider, who had stopped with us the first night, fell victim, having been surprised by it on a bleak, entirely shelterless, alkaline desert—began, and only on the fourth day was it possible for me to stir out. The wind blew a *blizzard, i.e.* a hurricane, before which even log shanties were not safe, and continued so for the next eight days, long after it had stopped snowing.

Stalking under such circumstances on the bleak mountain sides was decidedly cold work; but my heart was set on it, and I was determined to succeed. Had the hardships not been so great, the comical sides of my daily hunts would have counterbalanced much that was disagreeable, for ludicrous it certainly must have appeared to a looker-on to see me muffled up in a shaggy buffalo coat, wolfskins wrapped round my knees, creeping for hours at a time along the ledges and craggy heights of the peaks, the wind in exposed parts being so high that upright walking was not only quite impossible, but most dangerous; finally, to get up to a band of my game as close often as thirty yards, for evidently they felt convinced that none but a maniac would molest them under prevailing circumstances, and then miss them, as happened to me once, twice—nay, six or seven times successively. My favourite Express, out of condition by some hard knocks received in tumbles with my horse, shot, I was well aware, no longer true; but the chief cause of my non-success was, I fancy, the high wind.

At last, on the tenth day, I spotted a larger band, six or seven hundred yards off, snugly ensconced on a projecting ledge, where they were sheltered as much as possible from the wind. It was terribly cold, and the effort of keeping my eyes open made the tears course down my cheeks, to turn into ice on their way; and what with the dreadful wind and my trembling hands, I was an unconscionable time about getting a better view of the band with my glass. When at last, resting both elbows on a ledge, and lying flat on the snow, I was successful, I was pleased by the discovery of a fine six or seven-year-old ram among the band. The opportunity was a good one, and this time I was successful—at least so far as to bring down my quarry, whom I managed to approach unobserved to within twenty yards. In high glee I crept up to the Bighorn, still struggling in the last agonies of death. I had already been somewhat mystified by observing a patch of something detach itself as my bullet struck him; but what was my astonishment to find on getting up to him, that the whole coat was one mass of scab of the worst kind, the skin actually hanging in patches round the shoulders. The poor animal was a mere skeleton, and no doubt would not have survived many weeks. I stuck my knife into him, and found what flesh there was of a dark blue tinge, and of course entirely useless. I was so disgusted with my bad luck that I did not even secure the fine horns, but returned to our camp earlier than usual in no pleasant mood.

Next day, Port—who, accustomed as he was to "dog-garned freaks" on my part, had nevertheless, I am afraid, given up all hope of seeing my scattered senses return—and I made a pack camp, *i.e.* only taking one horse, with blankets and some food, leaving the bulk in charge of the boy, to the next range, fifteen miles off; and there on the first day we killed a very fair specimen, untouched by the fatal disease, to which most of the Bighorn on the other chain will probably have fallen victims by this time. It is an undisputed fact, that to the Indians this disease among their game was previous to the invasion of white men entirely unknown.

CHAPTER VII.

CAMPS ON TIMBERLINE.

On the summit of the Great Divide—A snow hurricane—Our fix—That pot of beans—Its effect—Finding the horses—Grand views—Fine weather—Walking on gold—How *not* to make soap—In dense timber—Difficulties of getting through.

OUR first acquaintance with the very summit of the great Continental backbone was a most agreeable one. We reached it on August 27th. The weather was superb—fine warm sunny days; cold nights, when, after an honest day's exercise, it was the essence of luxury to get under our snug buffalo robes spread over a thick layer of springy pine boughs for a glorious night's rest. The atmosphere laden with sparkling oxygen, no less than the pleasure of having successfully surmounted manifold little hardships, and upon which we now looked back with the satisfaction of a schoolboy recalling the experience of those bad five minutes in the headmaster's study, put a very contented air upon our worldly affairs.

It was glorious to roam about on this great broad ridge-pole of North America—now catching glimpses of the Southern slopes, then again of the great barren peaks of the Sierra Soshoné to the North of us, which we had quite recently left, glad to exchange the bizarre volcanic wilderness of that region for the beautifully-timbered slopes of the main watershed on the Big Wind River Mountains. The first two days we camped at the lowest point on the range, where an old Indian trail crosses it[1] at an altitude of 9800 feet. But we were all too restless to stop long where everything was of the pleasantest. The long chain had to be explored, to the left and to the right of us. So, two days later, camp was struck, and, as trapper parlance has it, we "pulled out" for yet higher regions.

We passed Timberline, and got on a bleak ridge, by which we hoped to reach another portion of the mountains, where, on the preceding day, from a high peak I had espied a beautiful " bunch " of little lakelets nestling under the beetling cliffs of one of the highest mountains of the chain. While following this barren ridge, when we were at an altitude of at least 11,000 feet, and from whence the whole vast extent of mountain country on both sides could be viewed as from the roof of the highest house in a town, we made the first acquaintance of a "real up-and-down Main Divide snow hurricane;" and though it was only (as our almanack—my diary, where careful track of days was kept—informed me) the 29th August, we had ears, noses, and fingers frostbitten, and ran a pretty "square" chance, as Port acknowledged, of getting "rubbed out like so many darned cayotes." It was an unpleasant experience, and as it will show the great extremes and amazing suddenness of changes to which the climate at these altitudes is liable, I may briefly sketch it.

[1] Trails cross this range only at two points, eighty-five miles apart.

The day had been unusually wind-still, and a peculiar tinge of the sky had made us remark that it was just as well to get as soon as possible to the end of this barren backbone, where we could again gain the uppermost level of timber. But good and wise as our intentions were, they vanished very suddenly at the sight of a big she-grizzly with two cubs, whom I discovered quietly feeding half a mile off. Hobbles were clapped on to the feet of two of the packhorses, who were all left feeding on the short Alpine herbage, while we, after a brief consultation, scampered off as fast as our horses would take us, in pursuit of the "bar." It was an exciting but, shameful to say, fruitless hour's chase. All three, though very severely wounded, got off, for we had to open fire, on account of the barren ground, at considerable distance; and instead of charging, as we had expected they would, they "sloped," the rest of our shots being put in in a more random way.

When the chase commenced the sky was still bright, and it was so warm that we were riding in our shirt sleeves, notwithstanding that large patches of snow covered the steep Northern slope below us. When the chase was finished and we had again sobered down to everyday calmness, we found an astonishing change had occurred. The wind was howling, and the sky had assumed a most threatening look, an aspect of such savageness as I have rarely if ever seen. We had no goal in particular in view, and would have gone into camp there and then had we been near water and wood; but timber was below us, and not a vestige of friendly creek or lake to be seen. Half an hour later the storm was upon us. The wind had rapidly increased to a hurricane, and the large flakes of snow drove before it with an incredible force; happily it was not hail, for, I am convinced had it been, the terrified animals would have stampeded there and then. As it was, we had our hands full to keep them from doing so. The storm came from the North-West; and as of course there was no possibility of getting the animals to face it, even had we been able or inclined to undertake such an ordeal ourselves, we were driven before it, as it happened, in the direction we were intending to go. The storm was rougher on us than on the horses, for we were still in our shirt sleeves; and as there was no chance of halting the train and getting out coats and gloves—even had we been able to undo the pack ropes, that, first soaked through, had speedily turned into icy knots, which fingers even less benumbed than ours could not have untied—we had to proceed as we were. It was a critical hour that we passed driving before this snow hurricane. Our lives depended upon preventing a stampede, for once parted from our horses, and thus from the means of getting under some shelter and into warmer clothes, there would have been little doubt that the whole outfit would have been "rubbed out," as effectually as any ever had been in consequence of a similar fix. With the "kitchen pony" on the line, Port tried to lead the others, while we three guarded the flanks and rear. The snow came down in such dense masses, driving horizontally before the gale, that it had got quite dark. Often Port at the head of the little band of horses, twenty yards off, was perfectly invisible to me, who rode in the rear. We were all getting perfectly benumbed with the cold, for the wind had turned into icy blasts. Boreas proved himself a jewel, following, when my hands refused to hold the bridle any longer, and were vainly prospecting for warm places about my body, the pressure of my knee, and behaving himself generally as a most intelligent old horse when any of the frightened pack-horses would make a frantic dash to one side, obliging the one nearest to follow at full speed and head the "break away" back. The wind seemed to grow colder every minute: everything about our persons turned into ice. Our scanty clothing was stiff, the rifles were coated with it, our hair and beards wore miniature icicles; everything, in fact, under the influence of the hyperborean wind, had turned to gelid rigidity.

How long that ride lasted none of us ever knew, and it was subsequently a frequent theme of amicable dispute. It was not quite "eternity less five minutes," and neither "all what a stem-winder [2] could do to record it," as Edd and Henry said: but probably it was an hour and a half—an hour on the ridge, the remainder on the slopes—till we camped. The first intimation of the latter was Port's: "Boys, I have struck water, and wood can't be far." It was a little bit of a trickling creek, and of the wood nothing as yet was visible. A halt was called, and amid the raging snowstorm we unpacked, by doing in one or two cases of refractory knots, what a Western man will only do in the direst extremity, namely, cut the lash ropes, for a "lash" with a knot in it is next to worthless, and we had hardly any spare ones with us. But none of us were in the humour to reprove the others for these outrages, for as poor Henry, whose shirt was especially *thin* in many places, expressed himself, he "felt half gone up, and the other half was frozen." So down the "packs" came with incredible speed, and soon the snowy ground

[2] Remontoire watches are called stem-winders in America.

was littered with our household goods. The horses were our chief anxiety. We could not possibly tie them up or picket them, and we had only two pair of hobbles in the outfit. So, trusting as usual to luck, and hoping that they would not leave Wyoming by the shortest route, but rather seek the shelter of the nearest forest, we put the shackles on the two fattest, who were best able to withstand the cold with less freedom of movement, and turned them out. They were off in a second, the hobbled ones following with ominous rapidity. Every one of us as two days afterwards we acknowledged to each other, thought, as we saw them gallop off, that we had seen the last of "them thar horses;" for under such circumstances animals will roam off for fifty and sixty miles; but at the time we all kept our impressions to ourselves, for none of us were, as the Western man expresses it, given to "borrow trouble."

Sacrificing one of the three sailcloth bedcovers, which were very large and waterproof, we got all the bedding and the "dry" packs under cover. The wind was far too high for us to raise the tent, even had our frost-benumbed hands been capable of accomplishing this. So, while two held the corners of the sail-cover, the other two got underneath, and in a kneeling position got at the "Saratogas" containing our spare clothes, and then, with the snow driving in on all sides, we stripped and got dry clothes and thick coats on our backs. Then only, while so engaged, were mutual remarks made, that noses and ears "looked cheesy," or in other words were frost-bitten; so when the change of toilette had been effected, and we were returning the kind offices of the first who "sat down" the dressing-room, we gave those troublesome facial members sound rubbings of snow. With shaggy buffalo coats, warm gloves, and thick overall trousers on us, the aspect of things improved considerably. Night was fast closing in, and there was no time to be lost in looking for wood. Following for some little time the tracks of the horses, whose instinct to find shelter in such cases is the very best guide, we presently came to the conclusion that we "didn't want a fire after all," or, in other words, that even did we find wood it would be impossible to make a fire in the high wind in the entirely shelterless position our camp was in. With grim sneers at each other we agreed that this bright thought might have struck us before. On getting back to camp—not the easiest task, for the snow hurricane had not abated, and it was impossible to see further than ten or fifteen yards—three of us again held down the dressing-room, while Henry, the slimmest, crawled in and spread our robes, which, rolled up, had not got very wet. Two loaves of bread of the morning's baking, which most fortunately had not been eaten at the mid-day meal, were divided and taken to bed to be eaten at warmer leisure, while a good pull at *the* keg—it is on such occasions that spirits are really welcome—comforted the inner man. While Henry was "bed making" we contrived to fasten down the protecting sailcloth, by heaping all the saddles, pack-saddles, traps, and other such like weights, on the side exposed to the wind, and by using the pickaxe as an anchor. When everything was ready we crept into the narrow space, just sufficient to hold us and our rifles sardine-fashion, and after divesting ourselves of the outer garments, which had again become snow-drenched, we were soon snug and warm under the four or five buffalo robes and odd blankets; while the two most miserable-looking dogs you ever saw found a warm corner at our feet, where, notwithstanding the grateful shelter, they continued to shiver for an unconscionable long time; for, as Port said, poor brutes they had to dry their shirts on their own backs.

Notwithstanding the singular surroundings, we passed quite a comfortable night, far more so than many I have spent in the uplands of the Old or New World; though it reminded me of one in particular, a cool December night I once passed on the floor of a deserted Alpine châlet, where not even hay was to be found, wedged in between two other shivering lumps of clay, the whole three covered by the heavy door of the hut, the only cover we could find, and which at least protected us against the snow that whirled about the partly roofless tenement.

It was broad daylight when we awoke. Not having a serviceable watch, we were, when sun and stars were invisible, as on this occasion, in pleasant uncertainty as to the flight of time. The wind had gone down, but the snow was falling fast; and when at last after a deal of mutual recriminations and courageous talk one of us had the moral fortitude to creep out of the snug lair, and peep out from underneath the tarpaulin, which lay heavy on us, it was found that snow lay already to considerable depth, and probably would be half a foot more by the evening, for there were no signs that the weather was "letting up." We were very comfortable where we were. The pickaxe and shovel set on end served as miniature tentpoles, preventing the soaked canvas bedraggling our robes, and giving us breathing, and even smoking space. Had it not been for our inner persons the day would have passed not so disagreeably, though on account of the confined nature all evolutions, such as turning from one side to another, had to be done *en masse* at the word of command, and our lower extremities were getting somewhat cramped from the dead weight of the two dogs, who were constantly being turned over to the neighbours' feet. But, as I have hinted, hunger was the boss; and presently hints began to be loosely thrown round that somebody *had* to get up. My proposal to keep the bed warm against their return was received with cynical applause, and unpleasant allusions that if I did that they would eat against my feeling hungry—which sally seemed to them far more witty than it did to me.

Nobody stirred; for an hour or so the assuaging effect of tobacco wrestled with that self-winding monster housed below our belts; but it was only for a time. Then conversation took a more businesslike and less desperately witty turn. The contents of the kitchen pack was passed in mental survey. This review revealed the fact that there was a large pot full of beans, the last of the lot we got a month ago at the fort. These beans, housed in their iron pot, closed with a well-fitting lid, had been in a semi-boiled condition for the last four or five days; for, as everybody knows who has ever tried to boil beans in the West, and particularly at high altitudes, it takes "a week to boil them, a fortnight to chew them, and eternity to digest them." Our beans had been simmering over half a dozen fires, and still Henry, who had their management, adjudged them as unfit to eat, describing their hardness as making them fatal weapons in the hands of one who "kin heave a rock."[3] After this we relapsed into silence, each busy with his own thoughts and with his own hunger. Mine took flight—

[3] The Western "boy" never says "throw a stone," but "throw," or "heave, a rock."

the former, alas! not the latter—to more summerly regions. It was strange to think that on this blessed 30th of August, while we were being slowly snowed up on the very top of the highest range in the Northern Rocky Mountains, friends were probably enjoying delightful dips in the tepid waters of Longbranch or Newport, or even Coney Island, awakening the germ of a healthy lunch appetite—the very thought of which artificial means of building up one of your sluggish but civilized hungers bringing a sneer of superiority to my lips. Edd, who for a Western boy had a pronounced romantic vein in his composition, disturbed my cogitations by asking me if I knew who was the author of "Snow, the beautiful snow." He had once read it, and thought the writer of it "a coon as was mad afore he was born." Port, and even Henry, had "heerd tell" of this depraved maniac, and indulged in typical Western humour at his expense. According to them no torture of the Spanish Inquisition seemed adequate to punish that misguided genius for giving immortality to such idiotic sentiments. One of the proposed chastisements, decidedly the most original, was to make "the dog-garned ink-slinging word-stringer boil that pot of beans till they were soft, and do it in his shirt-tail; and make him swear on a stack of a certain book never to tell no one how long it took him"—a fate that, under the circumstances, seemed to me the essence of inhuman cruelty. Not so, however, to Henry, whose mind had a leaning towards the Indian's love for inventing exquisite tortures, for he added, "And, boys, by the jumping Moses, we'd make him sit in the snow and watch us eat them when they *ar'* soft."

Whether it was the irresistible suggestiveness of the

word "eat," or whether the whole tone of conversation was becoming unbearably funny, I know not, but blankets and robes were suddenly thrown back, and after huddling on their extra clothing, my three companions made a start. The querry, "Coming along, boss?" made by Port, was tersely answered, "No, I'll stay." "You'll stay with the beans, you mean," equivocated he, who had rightly guessed certain dark hints thrown out by me.

And I did stay with them; for while the men in the waning afternoon light were absent hunting for wood, finally returning to camp after more than half an hour's absence, each dragging behind him a dead tree, and after many ineffectual attempts, at last succeeded in lighting a fire, getting thoroughly soaked in doing so, I had inspected the bean-pot to some purpose. There is truth, I found, in the Western saying, "Beans is pison if you ain't 'forking' (riding) a bucking cayuse," that being about the only extraneous aid to digestion by which their very self-asserting deadweight can be subdued; and this I speedily began to realize. Like a straining vessel with a shifting cargo labouring heavily in the troughs of the Atlantic, I tossed that blessed cargo of pebbles from side to side, and soon the bed seemed too small to hold the beans and me. It got worse, when presently the men, their appetites appeased by half-cooked venison and half-baked dough, returned to their quarters.

When the 31st of August dawned, it was generally agreed that I had passed a restless night, that they had passed a restless night, and that decidedly the beans had, too, experienced a rough time.

The forenoon was a dreary repetition of the preceding day, only that snow lay now up to our knees. Towards noon, however, it began to clear, and the change for the better was as rapid as, two days before, it had been the other way. The snow was shovelled aside, the tent raised, and we all started to look for the horses. Hunting for strayed horses is a profound science, and life-long experience had, of course, made the men wonderful experts at it. If they were anywhere in the country we would recover them; and we did, for though the search that afternoon was unsuccessful, Port tracked them the following day to a glade in the forest comparatively close—not more than three or four miles off.

A breeze had in the meanwhile sprung up whirling the snow about, rendering the atmosphere very thick, and not allowing us to see further than a couple of hundred yards or so. But it gradually subsided; the sun burst out, and in the latter part of the afternoon we had balmy autumn weather and sublime winter scenery, disclosing to us our surroundings. But where were we? Not fifty yards from the very summit of the ridge! While the first trees grew a good many hundred feet below us, proving that while in the latter part of our wanderings before pitching camp we had imagined we were descending a gentle slope, we had kept on a level with the place when the storm first struck us; indeed, if anything our camp was the higher of the two spots. The dead trees discovered by the men during the snowstorm when looking for wood, were the remains of a few advanced but stricken scouts of the main forest that lay below them. Only on ascending the insignificant slope did it strike us on what elevated spot we had weathered this summerly snow hurricane, for from it we saw both slopes of the giant range; and the dome-shaped summit of a great peak looked a mere high hill as in comparatively gentle slopes it rose from the main backbone.

Two days after our release from snowy bondage, you could have seen me ascending the 800 or 1000 feet of the mountain near which we found ourselves camped. The sun shines warm and bright, and the air seems keener and lighter than ever. From the top an immensely vast landscape is to be seen. Standing at my horse's side and leaning over his back, using the saddle as a desk, I sketch in brief myrioramic outline the landscape, for the peak is, on account of its isolated position, a remarkably favourable point of view. Towards the north-west I can descry the steam from the nearest Yellowstone geyser, eighty or ninety miles off, rising over a lower range of mountains. That is all I can see of the Yellowstone region, for immediately in front of me, trending Eastwards, there lies a vast sea of broken country, savagely hacked and torn by a maze of huge fissures and gloomy canyon-like valleys, from which rise an infinity of strangely-formed peaks and pinnacles. It is the weird Sierra Soshoné—a great ocean, as Captain Jones says, of *purgatorial* wave-work, having the appearance as if God's wrath had rested longer on this sublime chaos than on most other spots. There is little timber about it, save on the lower slopes, thereby increasing the forbidding look of this upheaved sea. Far away, eighty miles from our point of view, we see rising from a broad *mauvaises terres* table-land a well-known trapper landmark, the fantastic-shaped cone called Crowheart Buttes, a mountain of grim history. On its height, a natural fortress impregnable as no other natural formation I know of, some years ago eight Crow Indian warriors, deserted by their comrades, retreated before an overwhelming force of Sioux foes. The latter, unable to get at them, drew a cordon of watch-fires round their enemies' retreat, and starved them out. On scaling the hill and finding them dead, the red-skinned fiends tore out the hearts of the brave eight, and devoured them there and then.

The three rivers whose headwaters take their rise on the slopes of the mountain I am on, are destined to be the three greatest rivers of the West, the smallest of which has a course of over 2000 miles, and drains 300,000 square miles of country. One—the Big Wind River,[4] the chief confluent of the Upper Missouri—flows into the Atlantic; the Grosventre[5] joins its waters with those of the world-renowned Columbia, increasing the volume of the Northern Pacific Ocean; while the Green River, or Colorado, sends its waters into the Gulf of California. Such is the maze of creeks, silvery little streaks peeping forth from the green sea of forest, that it is quite impossible to tell the ultimate goal of any one in particular, without following its course for many miles.

There are spots on the Divide where the sources of two creeks—one flowing to the Atlantic, the other to the Pacific—are within rifle-shot of each other; and on several occasions the morning's coffee was made from Atlantic and Pacific water, not more than 200 yards separating the springs. In a day's travel in these regions you "fill your boots" again and again with both waters; for often you have, while following the craggy

---

[4] It changes its name, and flows as the Bighorn into the Yellowstone.

[5] One of the headwaters of the Snake.

course of a creek, to ford it seven or eight times in half that number of hours.

Indeed, I know of one, from an hydrographical standpoint most interesting spot, where within an area of one square mile there are actually three creeks, each flowing into one or the other of the three great river systems; while from a small lake on the very top of the ridge leading to the summit of Union Peak, there were, when I visited it in 1880, two outlets, one at each end, both forming trickling creeks; the one flowing down the Eastern slope being Atlantic, the other Pacific water—an instance, if not unique, though certainly of rare occurrence in potamology.

Our vision is very extended: in the few places where intervening mountain chains do not obstruct the view the diameter of the circle we overlook is scarcely less than 400 miles, perhaps more. To-day the country we see is decidedly the most secluded portion of the Rockies, for in those portions of the landscape over which our vision is unrestricted there is not a single white-man's settlement, and probably there were not more than half-a-dozen human beings, aside of Indians, abiding in it.

As far as the eye can reach in a westerly direction—and in this atmosphere it will range over an amazing extent—vast forests greet the eye, from which at Timberline the giants of the chain, with their snowy entourage, rear their heads. There are no very boldly-shaped peaks among them. All are massive and huge as were they aware that they form the great backbone of the continental watershed. The highest of all, Fremont's Peak, is eighty miles off.[6]

There is a very singular feature to be noticed on the very

[6] The latest surveys have " moved " this peak to a point considerably north of its site on the first maps of 1873.

summit of this watershed. For twenty miles on either side of our camp the slopes were covered by loose stones and gravel, known to miners as "ocean wash." Of the inseparable companion of the adventurous frontiersman, the gold-pan,[7] we had two examples with us, and they proved what had been told to us before, that we were walking on gold. Of the hundreds of pans my men "washed out," none contained less than five or six, and a good many as much as twenty "colours," or fine flakes of the precious metal. Water in sufficient quantity handy, this forty-mile stretch would yield untold riches—which, alas, in the absence of that *sine quâ non*, must remain where they are, some 11,000 feet over the busy bustling ant-hill, lapped by water that once dashed in unbroken rollers over these stupendous heights. Undoubtedly the whole district will be, in not too long a time, a great mining camp; but unlike a small one, that some years ago dug up, blasted, and washed a hillock we passed some time before, its members will probably not fall victims to the redskins' scalping-knives, as did the twenty odd old Forty-niners whose unwise intrepidity resulted in the loss of their hair—and lives. A few burnt logs, and a rusty gun-barrel or two, are all that remain of Ragtown, which is said to have been the most elevated mining camp of the day.

[7] Though this very simple utensil has been described hundreds of times, it is generally supposed to be a more elaborate machine. It is a flat bowl-shaped pan, remotely resembling a barber's dish, some eighteen inches in diameter. It must be held just right, and shaken in such a manner, by a half rotary, half rocking motion, that the water it contains, besides the sand (which is replenished every half minute or so), shall drift away all the loose worthless stuff, and let the gold stay behind. The knack is to agitate the whole panful of water, and "dirt" so as to allow the heavy gold to sink to the bottom.

For nearly seven weeks the weather was all that could be desired; each day seemed lovelier than the last; confirming the pleasant experience I had made the previous year, when from August to December we were travelling over less elevated ground, and not a single drop of rain fell, with the exception of two short though very terrific thunderstorms. This absence of moisture is a very enjoyable feature, for it seems as if no exposure could injure your health. For myself I have never felt so well as when undergoing fairly rough hardships in the way of great cold and snow, while in autumn weather and bright winter days it is literally a pleasure to live.[8] In the latter half of September two short snowstorms surprised us—one in a sufficiently awkward position, for we had temporarily lost our way in an upland stretch of exceptionally dense timber, compelling us to camp there and then without any regard to the question of water, for fear our frightened horses—alarmed by the roar of the wind through the timber, and the frequent fall of dead trees, which come down with a startling report—should stampede and get lost; for it is surprising how rapidly you lose sight of a straying horse in dense forest, and once lost to your view the chances are that in the vast woods the animal will remain so. As the position was sheltered we picketed the whole lot, and thirty-six hours afterwards were again on the way. On the day that we were snowbound in this

---

[8] According to the most reliable observations, which tally with my own experience, there are in Wyoming and Montana, on an average, from 290 to 310 perfectly fine sunny days per annum. Rather a contrast to the 178 days on which rain falls, and the 106 sunless or cloudy days (in an average of twenty-three years) in the valley of the Thames! See Appendix.

place a ludicrous camp incident occurred to me, which raised general hilarity. We were running very short of soap, chiefly owing to the fact that some of our original stock was *câched*, together with some spare flour, at a point we could not reach in less than a week's time. I decided therefore to manufacture some of that most necessary article, and was rather proud of the chance of showing the men that while they could and did teach me a lot of useful domestic arts, I would have an opportunity of teaching *them* something. My introduction, "You just watch and see me make soap; its easy enough," was hardly needed, for they were all attention. So, while the snowstorm raged and the wind howled, I began my manipulation. But, as the sequel will show, the old adage that a little—in this instance a very little—knowledge is worse than none, proved true. I fancied that I remembered to have once been taught that soap was made of tallow, lye, and lime; but being neither a chemist nor a geologist, I committed the grave error of supposing that the alkaline earth of the usual bad-land formation, containing a large percentage of soda or alkali, would act as a substitute for lime. After filling the camp kettle with lye of wood ashes, concentrated by several hours boiling, I began to mix it in the gold-pan with some elk tallow and alkaline earth, using my hands for this purpose. To my surprise the result was a sticky, tar-like, greasy, black mess, of the consistency of thick glue—in fact, anything but soap; and when I finally gave up the attempt, I found to my horror that the black stuff coating my hands resisted all attempts to remove it. I tried every conceivable means to get it off, parboiling them in steaming water, rubbing them with gunpowder, salt, pitch from the trees, earth, ashes, steeping them till I could bear it no longer in the hot lye; but everything failed to remove the infernal tarry stuff from my hands. Even half a pint of precious whiskey was wasted in my vain endeavour to subdue the "boss's soap," as of course it at once was nicknamed. The men laughed till tears coursed down their cheeks; and I threatened to try some of *them*, if they did not desist. Finally, just as I was getting fiercely desperate, a sudden thought —as the sequel will show, decidedly not a soapsud-den thought—crossed my brain; it was to use "saleratus," which we used instead of yeast powder for baking bread. Henry put a lot in the washhand basin—for of course, I could not touch anything while my hands were in the state they were in—and when it had dissolved in the hot water which he poured on the white powder, I proceeded to steep them in it. It made matters not better, but worse. There was a distinct "fiz" on immersion; and some wretched chemical process must have been enacted, for the stuff had concentrated itself to the consistency of melted indiarubber. For hours I sat in a most helpless manner on a snowbank, nursing my hands. They had the appearance of having been steeped in a pitcher of tar; and as the men, not without some truth remarked, " that soap *had* indeed *gone back on* the boss and funeralized him in the most all-fired deci-sivest manner;" while the idiotic young Henry, *à propos* of my *taking root* on that snowbank, began telling that old story of a frontier maiden, who at a dance remained for a long time partnerless, and when finally some kind being did ask her for a turn, she electrified him by her "Yes, sir-ree, for I've sot and sot and sot till I have about tuk root." Fortunately I was among Americans, so I was spared the infliction of choice doggerel, where *Tears* and *Pears*, and *Soap* and *Hoap* (Western spelling) were impressed. To cut short a long day's misery—I had to sacrifice one of the two pairs of winter gloves I had with me, and draw them on, so as at least to be able to eat, and use my hands for the most necessary purposes.

The next day I cut them off; and as the stuff had got dry, I managed with a blunt skinning-knife to scrape off the worst part, leaving my skin raw and sore; but it took months to remove the last traces, indeed, not till I reached the Fort, and steeped them in some anti-soap-generating acid. It was altogether one of the few incidents that refused to yield a bright or useful side, except perhaps the one that it showed how *not* to make soap.

In the stretches of dense timber the difficulties of travel were often of the most perplexing character; and the two axes, handled in turns on those occasions, came in for constant exercise. Here my trophies in the shape of Wapiti antlers gave us endless trouble, for their length—exceeding six feet, including the skull bone—made a path of at least that width imperative, for the horns could of course only be roped down crossways on the horses' backs.

Often we would get for hours helplessly *corralled* in a "windfall," into which, not unlike a maze, it was easier to enter than to find your way out. Here human patience was frequently sorely tested by brute perversity, for on such occasions the animals delighted in exhibiting all the *meanness* that was in them.

In places the forests grew on steep slopes full of abrupt gullies and gorges, where some wonderful climbing up and slithering down of the horses was to be seen. On one such occasion I saw old John perform a roll, or rather fall, down a steep slope that really approached the marvellous, not only because he was not instantly killed, but also on account that not a single tine of the two pair of huge Wapiti heads of which his load consisted, was injured. I have seen a good many wonderful performances of Western horses, many of which, were I to relate them, would be put down as "travellers' tales," but this special feat beat everything of the kind.

The "kitchen pony"—the steadiest of the lot, bearing the *batterie de cuisine*—is, of course, the one of whom most care is taken, indeed usually he is the only one that is led, the rest following. In parties such as ours he occupies the position of the cook in the travelling train of medieval lords. Mishap to him is the most serious thing that can befall the party; and our anxiety on the occurrence of a stampede to know whether the "kitchen pony" was among the fugitives, reminded me of Brillat-Savarin's excellent story of an Italian prince, who, when travelling over dangerous paths to his country-house, was accompanied by his Sicilian cook, a master of his art. At a dangerous point of the road, the prince, riding at the head of his long cavalcade, heard a shriek and the splash of a body falling into the torrent far below. With a face white with terror he pulled up, and looking back, exclaimed, "The cook! the cook! Holy Virgin, the cook!" "No, your excellency," cried a voice from the rear; "it is Don Prosdocimo!" The prince heaved a sigh of profound relief. "Ah, only the chaplain!" said he. "Heaven be thanked!"

Speaking of vast forests, it would be natural that I should also revert to getting lost in them. Few incidents of travel in strange countries have been treated with such fantastical sensationalism as being lost. Let them be ever so exaggerated, they certainly do not speak well for the superiority of our civilization. Neither the rough and ignorant trapper nor the primitive Indian ever gets lost. Either may lose their way, and be obliged to make unpleasant shifts for a night; but one never hears of their falling victims to such amazingly over-wrought terror as, it would appear, paralyzes the educated traveller. In ninety-nine cases out of a hundred he has to thank nothing else but his own quite uncalled-for nervousness for the fix he has got into. The trapper or the Indian, when he loses his way in a fog or snowstorm, or at night, says, *Indian no lost; Indian here; wigwam lost:* and speedily acts upon this supposition by doing what is most sensible, namely, to await daylight, or the lifting of the fog, or the cessation of the storm, on or near the spot where he first became aware of the disagreeable fact that he has missed his way.

Some people seem to have no eye at all for natural landmarks. They see a peak one day, and the next they fail to recognize it. They ford rivers, and presently forget—if they ever did know—which way the water flowed. The sun and the stars are to them meaningless luminaries; and they are weeks or months in the wilderness before they realize the signification of a watershed, or have noticed the direction from which the breeze blows. To such persons, of course, the plight appears decidedly more perplexing than to others who have paid a little attention to these rudimentary principles of woodcraft. But why even they should allow themselves to become a prey to fanciful deadly perils, is somewhat puzzling.

Nothing is so exhausting as fright or terror; and if the traveller bears in mind *never* to be without the means of making a fire, there is really nothing very terrifying in stopping out a night. It will probably be cold work, and as likely as not, hungry work; but that, under all but the most exceptional cases, in the depth of winter, will be the worst that can befall him.

On several occasions localities were pointed out to me where sportsmen had got lost; and more unlikely places for a man to manage this I could not well fancy. The frontiersman is a sharp critic of such weaknesses; and I have heard some unkind remarks made by them on this score.

CHAPTER VIII.

CAMPS IN THE TETON BASIN.

A mythical Trapper's Paradise—Its locality—The Great Teton Peak—Its sublimity—The sportsman in the eyes of the frontiersman—Fishing notes, by a non-fisherman—Pleasant fishing—An unexpected meeting—Wintering in the Basin—Partial ascent of the Teton—A night ramble—Scenery, its peculiarities.

THERE are few spots in the Western mountain lands around which there hangs so much frontier romance as about "Jackson's Hole," the trapper name for the Teton Basin. Few camp-fires in the wilds beyond the Missouri fail to thaw out of "oldest men" tales of that famous locality. When an unprecedented trapping feat has to be located, that mountain-girt Eden will be chosen by the narrator. If an impossible Indian fight has to be fathered on to some quiet and out-of-the-way nook, the "bad man" who tells you the story will make "Jackson's Hole" the bloody battlefield. If a great mining yarn goes the round, dealing with creeks paved with nuggets of gold, but to which somehow the first discoverer never could retrace his steps, the prospector invariably chooses for its site the Teton Basin. When I first became acquainted with the Land of the West, I had Teton Basin on the brain. Everybody seemed to have been there, or was going to visit it. And from the stories I heard, I soon came to the conclusion that it was, undoubtedly, an insufficiently-wonderful camp-fireside tale about that region that called down upon the narrator, a beginner in Western Troubadouring, the deserved and well-known reprimand, "Young man, young man, ain't you ashamed to talk so, when there are older liars on the ground?"

All kinds of great hunters made me their confidant, and poured into my ears their personal experiences—how they had gone to the Teton Basin "dead broke," and returned with gold dust leaking out of their torn boots, and thirty horses doing their level best to pack all the beaver pelts along. "Jackson's Hole" soon became, in my eyes, a sort of beatified "home for destitute trappers." And to judge by the numbers who had been there, the place was apparently of good size to hold all the old mountaineers domiciled in it—and what was strangest, apparently for no other earthly reason than for the pleasure of living in the Teton Basin; for of course, with legions of the best fur-hunters after them, the poor beavers had vanished to haunts less favoured by those old, old—nay, the oldest trappers of the country, men who trapped the *Câche la Poudre* when Fremont was yet sucking his thumbs in the idleness of babyhood.

I well remember how puzzled I was on my first accidental meeting with Port—whom, as he was pointed out to me as one of the best trappers of the country, I was rather surprised to meet 500 miles away from that spot—my stock question to all old trappers, "When are you going back to the Teton Basin?" received the startling answer, "Never been there; and I kinder reckon few white men have." At the time I thought that was the very first "up-and-down" lie told me since crossing the Missouri; but somehow, as time went by, and the brilliant Paris green that coated my composition came off in big patches, I came to the conclusion that it was about the very first truth I had stumbled on.

In the subsequent two expeditions with him through other portions of the Rocky Mountains, bringing me into camp-fireside contact with many would-be " old men of the mountains," my notebook gradually became filled with *reliable information* on different routes to that sequestered spot—and I certainly never knew a place have so many "*best* ways to get there." Singular to say, when, on our third and present outing, we made it our goal, the nearer we got to the spot the fewer grew the travellers who had spent either their youth, or their prime, or their old age in that trapper's paradise; and when finally, in July, 1880, we passed Fort Washakie, the nearest post and the nearest human habitation to it; we found that there was actually not a single person there who knew the way to it, or who had ever been there.[1] An absent scout was said to have actually once visited it; but he was away, and for the rest of the 180 or 200 miles across the Great Divide we were our own Teton Basin discoverers.

A few words will suffice to indicate its locality. South-West of the Yellowstone Park, it lies on the boundary of Wyoming and Idaho, between the Teton Range and the Grosventre Mountains.[2] Up to 1881 it was very difficult of access, being enclosed on all sides by mountain ranges that were very little known, and could only be crossed at certain points, over which led Indian trails known only to a very few white men. But the wonderful tales of the quite exceptional natural beauty of the spot, circulated by

---

[1] A positive fact.   [2] See Appendix.

the few who had visited it on their lonesome fur-hunting expeditions, had taken root, and spread in the remarkable manner already indicated. Up to 1879 only large, well-armed expeditions (the one Government Exploration Party, under the renowned Professor Hayden, had touched it in 1872), or trappers who, by taking Indian wives, had become Indianized, could venture to enter that country, for the two Indian tribes—the Nez Percés and Bannacks—whose hunting-grounds it was, were then very hostile. The Indian war of 1878 cleared them out, and when we visited the basin in 1880, we had the whole country to ourselves. With two exceptions, I saw not a single white man from the end of July to the end of November, and for three months of that period saw also no Indians. To-day access is made easier, for the narrow-gauge Montana line, branching off Northward at Ogden, passes Fort Hall, from whence Jackson's Hole can be reached from the West in seven or eight days' travel over Indian trails.

We reached the confines of the Basin on a beautiful September morning. Debouching very suddenly from a deep canyon, to a high knoll overlooking the whole of it, we happened to strike the most favourable point from whence to view the mountain-girt paradise spread out before us.

At our feet lay the perfectly level expanse, about eight or ten miles broad, and five-and-twenty in length. Traversing the basin lengthwise, we saw the curves of the Snake River—its waters of a beautiful beryl green, and apparently as we viewed it, from a distance of five or six miles, of glassy smoothness—winding its way through groves of stately old cottonwood-trees. A month or two before, the Snake had inundated the whole Basin, and the grass that had sprung up retained its bright green tint, giving the whole picture the air of a splendid trimly-kept old park. Beyond the river the eye espied several little lakes, nestling in forest-girt seclusion under the beetling cliffs of the boldest-shaped mountain I am acquainted with, *i.e.* the Grand Teton Peak,[3] rising in one great sweep from an amazingly serrated chain of aiguille-like crags sharply outlined against the heavens, and shutting in one entire half of the basin,—the other semicircular enclosure being the mountain range on which we stood. It was the most sublime scenery I have ever seen.

Many of the Colorado mountains are called the Matterhorns of America—with about as much justification as the more diminutive Ben Nevis, or Snowdon, merits that name. With the Teton it is, however, different; for it makes, so far as I know, the only and very brilliant exception to the usual dome-like formation of the Rockies. In shape it is very like the Swiss master-peak; but inasmuch as the Western rival rises in one majestic sweep of 7000 feet from this natural park, to an altitude all but the same (13,800 feet), I would, in this instance, in point of sublimity give the palm to the New World.

Pursuing the hardly perceptible Indian trail (we came

---

[3] The Government Exploration party who visited, in 1872, the Teton Basin, and of whom three or four members ascended the great peak, re-christened it Mount Hayden, in honour of the well-known *savant* and indefatigable leader of the Territorial Exploration Expeditions. Though no peak in the United States is more worthy to carry that distinguished name, it seems a pity—considering that hundreds of great mountains are still nameless—to rob the master peak of its famous old name, the exact translation of its Indian appellation. The shape of the Teton is particularly striking when approaching it from the East, as we did.

along the Grosventre Creek) which zigzagged down the
steep slope, we soon reached the level bottom of the Basin,
and shortly before sundown made, in one of the extensive groves on the banks of the Snake, what, without
exception was the most strikingly beautiful camp of
my various trips. The immediate surroundings were of
idyl-like charm. From the smooth sward, fresh, and
singularly free of all rubbish, rose straight and massive
the stately cottonwoods, their trunks of a silvery sheen,
while festoons of creepers connected garland-like, often
at great altitude, the upper branches of the trees that
formed the grove. Immediately in front of us glided the
broad river, its glassy surface broken here and there by a
minute swirling eddy. Right at the bank it was ten or
twelve feet deep; and great salmon trout, each spot
discernible, hovered under the abrupt rootwork bank.
Not a sound was audible, not a sign of living being was
visible. The river was not broader than sixty yards, and
trees as large as the ones that surrounded us dotted the
opposite bank. Over this mass of brilliant verdure rose
the Titanic Teton; and did we not know that two miles
of level ground intervened between us and the base, the
clearness of the Western mountain air is so deceptive that
the great Peak seemed to grow right out of the opposite
grove. Bend your neck as far as you would, still your
gaze seemed incapable of reaching the needle-shaped
summit, and—similar to the old Californian miner, who
when he first saw El Capitano, in the Yosemite, said it
took two looks to get squarely to the top of the peak,
with a chalk-line to mark off on the cliffs how far his first
had got—the real sublimity of its height impressed itself
only after the second or third look, notwithstanding that

Nature came to our aid by substituting a narrow belt of snow-fields half way up the mountain for the old Californian's chalk-mark.

For once, as we all stood crowding the bank, feasting our eyes on the scene, I wished myself alone, to do homage to what I then, and still, consider the most striking landscape the eye of a painter ever dreamt of, by half an hour's examination more in keeping with the wonderful stillness which cast a further charm over it. For once, too, two of the unimpressionable Western characters round me gave vent to appreciative exclamations; the third, however, young Henry—a hopelessly matter-of-fact being—turned sublimity into ridicule, by his "Darn the mountains! Look at those beaver dams yonder." Alas! I have given up all hope to teach that young mind to admire; and I believe that were he suddenly introduced into Olympus, the only feeling that would move him would be expressed in a terse "Doggarn it, if I ain't forgotten the traps and the pison."

The following morning we crossed the Snake at one of the upper rapids,[4] where two of us, and several of the horses, got sound duckings, and the dogs and one colt were swept down stream, amid considerable commotion, for quite a quarter of a mile. An hour's ride across the level brought us to the banks of one of the two larger lakes I have spoken of, and where, as the sequel will show, I had some unique fishing.

Let me say a few words on the topic of old Walton's gentle art in the Rockies.

The light in which the Express-wielding Englishman,

---

[4] Deep rivers are best crossed where there are shallows or rapids, if they are not deeper than will allow footing to the horses.

in quest of sport in the Far West, appears to the frontiersman, the rough-and-ready resident of those equally rough-and-ready regions, is sufficiently quizzical to establish in their eyes our national claim to something more than oddity. Still more incomprehensible to the Western "boy" is, however, the Englishman who visits those districts for fishing, or, to use names by which that art is known to him, for *lining, poling, bug-hooking*, and a series of other equally unflattering designations. Most English shooting parties visiting the United States for sport take back with them trophies of the chase, more or less numerous according to the means of transportation employed by them while out in the wilds. These heads, horns, and skins are at least something tangible; and though the question frequently asked of me, "How much them ar' hides and headgear be worth over in the old parts," proved to me that it would be useless to try to dispel the deeply rooted suspicion that my much-treasured bear skins, wapiti, and bighorn heads were intended for vulgar sale and mart; they are nevertheless "something that shows," something that in another world and among another people may possibly be worth a certain, if limited, number of dollars.

Much worse does the fisherman fare who visits the semi-civilized home of those intensely practical roving forerunners of civilization. The fisherman, poor fellow, has nothing more tangible to take back to his home than pleasant recollections and an astonishingly big score, both about balancing each other for utter valuelessness in the frontiersman's eyes, both betraying, in his opinion, about the same degree of lunacy in a mild shape. No sane man, argues the free but dollar-hunting citizen of Uncle Sam's empire, rich enough to pay for the men, horses, and stores of the outfit, could possibly act so strangely; leave his " tony " house, discard the luxuries of civilization—" turning his back on whiskey," is his own expressive phrase for similar conduct—put up with all the discomforts and hardships of camp life, which to him have of course long lost all charms; and all this—after travelling five or six thousand miles, and spending enough money to start a silver-mine—for what? To stand all day in water knee-deep and " line " fish!

So thinks the Western man while he gladly pockets the guide's fee, or the hire for the horses and mules that have carried you and your belongings to the scene of your big bags. His quizzical gaze rests upon your elaborate fishing-tackle; the five-guinea rod, or spy-glass pole, as I have heard it called, is to him as wonderful an instrument as your parchment book of flies, the pride of your art, is of mysterious use and purpose. Landing net, reel, and all the numerous etceteras usually to be found hovering about the person of Walton's disciples, are not less puzzling to him; and when finally he sees you issue forth from your tent, arrayed in all the brand-new finery of your West-end outfitter, his mouth puckers up more than usually as he squirts from it a stream of tobacco juice. He will not say much, for the Western man is apt to keep his impressions to himself; but he will think all the more. *His* fishing has been done in a different style. A change of diet becoming desirable, his ponderously heavy Sharp's rifle or the keen axe—its shape and make a *chef-d'œuvre* of practicalness—is laid or flung aside, while the next patch of willows furnishes him with a rod, not as long or as straight as yours, but strong enough to handle a five-pound trout, or a lazier salmon of twice that weight. His line will not break—of that we can be assured, for it is a very cable among lines, being fine-cut buckstring (cut from Indian-tanned buckhides); while the hook, fastened to one end by a knot nearly as big as a pea, is of home manufacture, old horseshoe nails, well hammered, being favourites for the purpose. For bait, the Western fisherman is never at a loss; if a "bug"—all insects go by that name, grasshoppers and crickets being favourites—cannot be found, a piece of raw meat, the iris of the last deer he killed, or a minnow will do. If the time of day be propitious, the sky clear, and no ripple on the water (these conditions I have found to be of the greatest moment), the native angler will land in half an hour as many trout as he can conveniently carry. If bugs are scarce, he will cut thin long slices from the first fish he catches, the glittering scales being, after insect bait, the most deadly for the finny tribe. Often have I watched such fishing on lake, river, and creek. The gigantic hook, duly "spiked" with an equally huge green or black " hopper "—both so large that I once wagered (and won) I could pick off the bait with my rifle at a distance of thirty steps—splashes down into the circling eddy, and often before it has time to reach the bottom a two-pounder will be testing the strength of the buckskin line, which, if the " pole " does not give way, would hold a fish ten times his weight.

I am no fisherman;[5] in fact all the trout I had ever

---

[5] With very few exceptions, good trout fishing can only be had on the Pacific slopes of the main chain of the Rocky Mountains; though I have frequently heard of English fishing parties visiting the different parks in Colorado, where, as I am told by one who knows, compara-

caught up to that period could be easily stowed away in the pockets of my shooting-coat; so before I write any further, and betray my ignorance on some vital point, as I assuredly should, I am desirous of impressing this fact upon the reader.

When leaving Europe I found that a light fishing-rod that had been knocking about my gun-room, unused for years, could be crammed into one of my rifle cases; and passing down Oxford Street on the day preceding my departure, I favoured the owner of one of the many fishing-tackle-making emporiums in that thoroughfare with a general order to put up ten shillings' worth of line and trout fly hooks. This personage, more astonished I suppose at the nature than pleased by the meagre extent of my patronage, did so in the most business-like (*i.e.* prompt) manner, never deigning to lose a further word upon such a customer.

I was glad of it at the time, for had he asked me any one of the ninety-nine questions regarding details—which I believe are necessary to define the exact nature of the fly you want—he would have been no doubt shocked beyond measure by the extent of my ignorance. Subsequent events, however, made me regret my carelessness in the selection of the tackle; for my very first day's fishing demonstrated to me in the most convincing manner that in my unskilful hands the line was far too light, the flies useless, and the hooks themselves hardly strong enough to hold a half pound trout. At a rough calculation that day's fishing cost me nine shillings and elevenpence worth

tively poor sport rewards the traveller. Twenty-four hours' railway journey further West would enable them to get some of the finest trout fishing that can be had.

of tackle ; for at the termination I found myself minus most of my hooks, the greater part of my line, and the two top pieces (the spare one being one) of my rod snapped in two ; and of the countless fish that had risen to my bait, none landed but the very smallest. Fort Washakie, the last human habitation we had passed, was 180 or 200 miles east of us; and where to get a fresh supply of line and hook nearer than that post, I knew not.

Game just then was very scarce ; the Bighorn were still high up on the mountains, and Wapiti had not yet come into the Basin, so that we had been out of meat for one or two days ; and the long faces of my men when, on my return to camp from my first day's fishing, I informed them that I had sacrificed nearly all my hooks and part of my rod, put a hungry aspect on the matter, our "grub outfit" being then of the very lightest description. My pocket tool-box—a very essential commodity, as I found out, without which nobody ought to travel in those regions—had unfortunately been *câched* with some extra stores and the tent a week or so before, and hence we could not metamorphose horseshoe nails, of which we had some few with us, into fishhooks. But the instinct of practical self-help, so strongly developed by Western travel, came to the rescue, and by the end of a couple of hours' work, aided by the bright light of a huge camp-fire, we had completed three very deadly instruments. One was a landing net made of the top of a young pine-tree bent into a hoop, with an old flour sack laced to it with buckstring, half-a-dozen holes being cut in the canvas to let out the water. This was a triumph in itself; but what will the reader, who is probably an expert fisherman of long experience, say when he hears of the other two ? I had just six hooks left, and the broken top pieces of my rod (I must plead ignorance of the technical name of the component parts of a rod) furnished the necessary thin thread wire to make two hooks out of the six, by fastening three together, their points diverging grapnel fashion. The torn pieces of line were carefully twisted into a stout hawser, the strength of which we tested by fastening it to the collar of a Newfoundland pup, and lifting him clear from the ground.

The next day was a warm balmy September morning—not a cloud was to be seen in the sky of Alpine blueness. I returned to the same spot on the banks of the lake—the scene of the wholesale robbery of hooks on the preceding day, and on my way thither filled a small tin canister with "bugs" in the shape of remarkably lively crickets, of large size and jet black colour, that could be found in thousands on the open barrens. In an hour I had landed about forty pounds of trout, mostly fish about two pounds in weight. All the larger fish—and I must have had at least three times the number on or near my hook—broke away; while the very large ones—of which I saw quite a number, and some of which must have scaled six pounds or seven pounds—snapped up the bait *en passant* in the most dexterous manner.

My favourite spot for the sport was, as I have said, at the outlet of one of the lakes (Jennie's Lake it is called on the latest Government Survey map), and the time an hour or so before sunset, when, after a long day on the rocks and in the dense timber, I would have returned to my old horse and got on my way back to camp. Highly fantastical, not to say demented, must I have appeared to an Old World angler, as, wading old Boreas into the water where creek and lake joined till it reached to within a foot or so of the saddle, he would stand perfectly motionless till I had filled the two capacious Stalker's bags slung one on each side of him with the speckled beauties.[6] Sitting well back in the saddle, with both legs dangling down on the same side, my rifle slung over my back—the landing net when not in use hung on one of my steed's ears, the only handy place for it—I plied my grapnel with never-failing success. Fish after fish, with hardly a quarter of a minute between, would gobble up the bait, generally still alive, and if the fish was not of large dimensions, would be jerked out of the water, and safely ensconced in the folds of the flour sack.

As I have said, I usually began fishing "an hour by sun"—the trapper expression for an hour before sunset—and, with only one exception, I succeeded in filling the two bags with twenty-five pounds or so of fish (while proper tackle would have accomplished it in a quarter of an hour or twenty minutes) before the long shadows of the tall pine-trees growing down to within two or three feet of the water's edge would fall across the smooth, glassy surface of the tranquil mountain tarn. The sun once off the water, the fish would vanish as if by word of

---

[6] Speaking of receptacles to place fish in, one can often, if not provided with sufficiently large bags, be placed in a dilemma concerning means of transportation. An experience in Port's life gives a useful hint. He once was fishing in the Columbia; and when it was time to return to camp, he found that the empty flour-sacks, wherein to carry his fish, had been lost from his saddle, and nothing whatever at hand to take their place. But Port is a Western man; so, divesting himself of his nether garments, he tied up the legs at the bottom and filled the whole with his fish, fastening the top in a similar manner; and seating the fish-filled unmentionables on his horse, in front of him, he brought his take safely into camp.

command, and I do not remember to have caught a single fish in that lake after sundown. Resuming my usual seat in the saddle—a signal well understood by trusty Boreas, and with a yelp of delight from the young Newfoundland, who, intensely interested in the whole proceedings, would sit, all attention, on the bank fifteen or twenty yards off, restrained only by my word from keeping up constant communication between me and the shore—I would turn my horse's head campward. Once, and only once, did serious disaster threaten me—it was when a more than commonly vigorous two-pounder snapped the threefold gut. But luck stood by me, and the second throw with my spare grapnel landed the very criminal, the hook still in his jaws.

Has the reader ever eaten salmon trout (for I believe this is the proper name of the fish I caught in the Teton Basin) fried in bear fat, with a bit of beaver's tail simmering alongside the pink mess? If he has not, I venture to say he knows not what makes a right royal dish.

Three times a day did six big frying-pans full appear on our primitive greensward dinner-table, and never did fish taste nicer, and never did four men and two dogs eat more of them. Hardly credible as it sounds, thirty pounds a day was hardly sufficient to feed our six hungry mouths; and when, towards the end of my short stay in the Basin, great economy in flour became imperative, forty pounds vanished in a similar wonderfully speedy manner.

Two ludicrous little incidents happened to me in the Teton Basin; and though I took, to use Western parlance, a *back-seat* in both, I shall narrate them. The first one occurred in this way: I had filled an old tin to the brim with hopper-bugs, and was crossing the outflow of the lake, seated, or rather crouching, on Boreas's back, with legs tucked under me so as not to get them wet; when right in the centre of the stream, with the water up to the saddle, my steed took it into his head to come to a dead halt. My impressive "Git up!" was in vain, and considering my ill-balanced position, and that my hands were filled with the "pole," landing-net, rifle, and bug-tin, while the reins were hanging knotted over his neck, it was not the easiest thing to enforce these words by more active measures. Just below me was a large deep pool, and as Boreas had a wonderful faculty of doing the most unexpected things when left to his own free-will, I dreaded a dousing in the limpid depth at my side. Tucking my rifle under my left arm, clutching the rest of my outfit in the same hand, and the landing-net in my teeth, I began to belabour his plump back with the thing most handy, *i.e.* the bug-tin. One whack, two whacks, and with a click out flew the bottom of the canister, and for the next second it rained black bugs. Nearly all, of course, fell into the rapid-flowing stream, and the next instant were whirling for a brief second over the surface of the limpid pool. That moment, reader, I saw more fish than I had ever seen before or ever will see again.

The other little mishap was quite as ludicrous. I must mention that these bugs are lively animals. They jump, dodge about, and creep out of your way with astonishing rapidity, and the only manner I could stalk them successfully was to throw my limp felt hat at them with sufficient force to stun without squashing them. Even this requires some quickness and undivided attention. Well, one or two days preceding the above incident, I was out on my usual preliminary bug stalk; and going along with bent form, now hitting, then again missing, my plump game, my whole attention being fixed upon my occupation, I reached a clump of dense service-berry bushes. I had just delivered a successful throw, and was about to stoop to gather in the prize, when out of the bushes, as if growing from the earth, there rose—a grizzly. Rearing up on his hind legs, as they invariably do on being surprised, he stood, his head and half-opened jaws a foot and a half or two feet over my six foot of humanity, and hardly more than a yard between gigantic him and pigmy me. The reader will believe me when I say he looked the biggest grizzly I ever saw, or want to see, so close. It would be difficult to say who was the more astonished of the two, but I know very well who was the most frightened. My heart seemed all of a sudden to be in two places; for had I not felt a big lump of it in my throat, I could have sworn it was leaking out at a big rent in the toes of my moccasins.

Now grizzly shooting is a fine healthy sport—I know none I am fonder of; but there ought to be neighbouring trees to facilitate *centralization to the rear*, and above all I must be handling my old "trail stopper"—and that moment I was here on a treeless barren, *en face* with one I " was not looking for," or " had not lost;" and yonder, 100 yards off, lay that famous old rifle—Boreas in the distance putting some spare ground between him and that noxious intruder. Fortunately the Old Uncle of the Rockies had more than probably never had anything to do with human béings, for I saw very plainly that he was more puzzled as to my identity than I was regarding his. His small, pig eyes were not very ferocious-looking, and first one, then the other, ear would move; expressing, as I interpreted it, more impatience than ill-feeling. I do not exactly remember who first moved, but I do recollect that on looking back *over my shoulder* I saw the old gentleman actually running away from me! On regaining possession of my rifle, which on this quite exceptional occasion I had allowed to get beyond my reach, as it interfered with my " buggings," I felt considerably braver, and spent the rest of the day in a vain endeavour to resume our acquaintance-ship on more satisfactory terms. But the old gentleman evidently thought he had frightened me sufficiently, and so kept out of my way.

This is not the only bear story I could tell, but as none have the slightest claim either to originality or sensational adventure, I will not weary the reader's patience with what has been told so often, namely, that grizzlies want no fooling.

A very cursory examination of Jackson's Hole ripened in us the determination of wintering in the basin, notwith-standing that we were quite alive to the fact that once a passage over the Main Divide was made impassable by the deep snows of winter,[7] (we had twice to cross the great backbone at altitudes over ten and nearly eleven thousand feet,) escape from the basin was impossible for eight months, till the following July or August, for the two great rivers we had to cross are, on account of the melting snows, quite impassable during the spring. It was very fortunate that ultimately we were prevented executing this plan. I

---

[7] There is a considerably lower pass, if you approach from the north. As we were not at all acquainted with these densely timbered districts, it would have been most unwise for us to risk getting lost, with the snowstorms of winter threatening us. Very different are they to those of autumn.

subsequently heard, too, from a trapper—the only human being who, so far as I could learn, had ever wintered in it—that owing to the sheltered position, enclosed on all sides by high mountains, and the altitude of the Basin itself (nearly 7000 feet), the snow remains lying, and is not blown off, as on the equally elevated plains, by the high winds. He told me—and I have every reason to believe him, for we found sufficient evidences that snow lies there very deep—that for three months the roof of his log cabin was flush with the white pall, and that he fed his three pack animals with elk meat, and bark of the cottonwood-trees boiled to a pulp.[8]

We stayed for ten days in the Basin, and probably would have remained another fortnight had not a great forest fire, raging in the timbered regions north of us, the smoke of which we had seen for a week, threatened to invade the Basin, obliged us to leave it—with the intention, however, of returning a month or six weeks later. As it turned out this was not to be; and our winter palace, the site of which was duly selected, and the way to it blazed by me on the trees of the forest that shut it in, is yet to be built. Most annoying was one of the consequences entailed by the fire, namely, that I was prevented ascending quite to the summit of the great Peak. On one of my expeditions after the mythical mountain goats—which I can assure sportsmen are *not* to be found on the Teton Range, though on a chain about 120 miles north of it

---

[8] Dutch George—the name of this old pelt-hunter—was, as he always is, quite alone; and when finally the snow on the mountains melted, the creeks and rivers were so high that he was imprisoned in his mountain-girt basin till the end of July. He had left the last settlement in the preceding September, and had not seen a single human being, not even an Indian, for more than ten months.

they *have* been killed—I got within 1000 or 1100 feet of the top; but the distance to the summit from our camp was too great to go and return in one day, and as no horses could be got further up than our camp, I decided to let the men help me to convey the necessary food, robes, &c., wherewith to pass a night or two close up to the summit. The men just then were very busy, and I unfortunately delayed the expedition from day to day, till the fire, running before a north-westerly breeze, and approaching us very rapidly, though yet several miles off, obliged us to leave the Basin by the way we had reached it. From the point which I reached on the main Peak, and from the top of a minor aiguille which I ascended, I could see what remained of the main ascent. Indeed had it not been so late that day, or had I been provided with some covering for the night, I would have proceeded there and then. And very sorry I am I did not, even without covering; the night I would have had to pass on the rocks would not have been the first in such a position. The remaining portion, as I had every chance to observe, was fairly easy for anybody trained to Alpine, and especially rock work. Many a second class peak in the Dolomites, though of lesser altitude, presents much graver obstacles than those that I saw on the uppermost portion of the Teton—the very formation of rock speaking for an easy ascent, while the snow was nowhere of exceptional steepness, and withal in perfect condition. In this respect I was rather disappointed, for the very bold outline of the whole mountain led me to expect a first class climb,[9] though in point of distance the clearness of the air led me to underestimate it.

[9] See Appendix.

One of the chief difficulties in exploring the Teton Range, are the immensely deep canyons that cut up the chain in detached blocks. The water in many cases has worn them down to the level of the basin, and they are often so narrow that you come upon them with startling abruptness, and look down yawning gorges two and three thousand feet deep, and at the top only half that width. They are undoubtedly finer than anything we have in the Alps.

While in the Teton Basin we had a full moon, and if the reader cares to entrust himself to such a moonstruck individual, I shall ask him to accompany me on a quiet, after-supper stroll in the beauteous calm of night. Of the many nocturnal rambles I have enjoyed in the Rockies, the one in question stands out in pleasant relief, for the surroundings were exceptionally picturesque.

Our camp, pitched on a great spur of the Teton Range, two or three thousand feet over the basin, commands an expansive view, and even the bright light of a huge post-prandial camp-fire can hardly outvie the brightness of night. About us there are half a dozen veteran spruce, so gnarled and weather-beaten as to resemble that grand tree of the Tyrol, the arve, its branches festooned with wavy tresses of the grizzly "beard of the Alps." Supper, the pleasantest meal of the day, is over. The usual camp-fire conversation, dealing with recent events in our primitive travel, and mainly centring on sporting subjects, of late represented by my sorely disillusioned hopes of finding moose or mountain goats on the Teton Range—for the mountains were pictured to us by persons to whom even Port gave credence as harbouring great numbers of both species—has duly seasoned the meal.

We have lingered longer than commonly over it, and as usual Henry has neglected to put the camp-kettle with the dish-washing water on the fire, so that when finally it is remembered, and the much-travelled pot is placed near the blaze, the circumstance is seized as a welcome excuse to lengthen that luxurious after-dinner *dolce far niente*, while another outrageously Western story, another hearty laugh, enliven our comfortable repose. A glance at the "dipper," for some months our only watch, for the two with which the outfit started have long been invalided, warns me that it is time to set out, for the constellation slants to nine o'clock, and there is half an hour's walk to the sight of my, or rather our, stalk. I say "stalk," for such a moonstruck ramble as we intend to take would seem the height of ridiculous sentimentality to the men, whose natures—good and fine fellows as they are—are of the genuine frontier stamp, *i.e.* up and down practical and unimpressionable. To save appearances, it is therefore advisable to let on such occasions a stalk serve as an excuse for prolonged absence at strange hours.

The rifle is taken as a matter of habit, for here you never let, or ought to let, it get beyond your arm's reach. You sleep with it under your saddle pillow; when you fish, it is slung over your back; and in the same way that in many of the missionary churches in frontier-country the men stroll into church their rifle in their hand, you would, so accustomed do you get to handling your shooting-irons, very likely in a similar case do precisely the same, or only discover what you are about to do, as you are passing the doorstep. Not that I think there would be any special harm about it—certainly no more than there is in frantically gripping a tightly-rolled umbrella in the bellicose "Who are you?" sort of fashion which distinguishes many a brave son of Albion, as with squared shoulders he strides into some peaceful Midlandshire church at home.

So, with the old "trail stopper" over our shoulder, we stroll forth. A rise in the ground presently shuts out all view of camp, but 100 yards further on we again catch sight of the bright pile, and the dark shadowy forms hovering about it. To the uninitiated they would appear to be engaged in some mysterious heathen rite, for while one is kneeling on the ground with his face to the fire, his hands pressed to his breast, moving to and fro in silent incantation; another is lying on his back, with one leg held up high in the air; and the third is cutting mad capers in front of the blaze. We know better; there is nothing at all mystical about it. The first is drying a tin campplate he has just washed, by pressing it against his body and rubbing it with the cloth, much as had he a mild pain below his belt; the second is testing the strength of his evening's handiwork, a new bridle, plaited of long strips of elkskin; while the third has very probably burnt his fingers when reaching for the camp-kettle standing near the fire.

We follow the slope, dotted with great boulders, leading us to a lower level, and presently reach a buttress of rock, from which *en passant* we see the Teton Basin stretched out at our feet—one or two little lakelets, and the silvery coils of the great river traversing the valley, reflecting the rays of the moon. We see the whole vast slope of the Teton chain on which we are; for the spur juts far out, enabling us to view not only the mountains opposite, but also those that overshadow us. We see where great profound canyons cut down in the massive range, and form gorge-like fissures of extraordinary abruptness and depth.

Yonder dark streak, a few hundred feet over our heads, is Timberline. In gentle curves it follows the spurs and the smaller ravines that scar and fissure the face of the great chain. Beyond the plainly-marked band, much of the rock is mantled by a pall of glistening white, from which, in one great glorious sweep, rises a huge black tooth, boldly outlined against the grey blue of the nocturnal heavens. It is, as I need hardly say, the Grand Teton.

The outline of the landscape is of entirely Alpine character. Only in details does it differ. In daytime the searching glare of a brilliant sun, cloudless skies, and a crystal atmosphere, give it a tinge of crude disharmony. Peaks do not float in the air, for, so to speak, there is no air that we can see or feel. The absence of moisture in the atmosphere, while it affords vision far greater play than in other mountainous landscape, is practically achromatic. The bold buttresses and pinnacles, their snow, their shadowy ravines, their gloomy canyons, are displayed with tantalizing precision and uncompromising hardness. There is no tender play of colour, no harmonious perspective blending the near and the far. There are no great banks of airy silver-streaked billows to give depth to the picture, and to cast fairy shadows upon the mountain slopes; while the wondrous play of shifting light and shade caused by these fugitive exhalations—effects dear to the lover of European Alpine scenery—is sadly wanting. By moonlight these features of landscape beauty are no longer lacking. In autumn, when the days are warm and the nights very cold, filmy vapour not unfrequently rises after dark. The summits of the mountains rear their glittering heads from gauzy clouds of it, while the subdued and silvery light of the brilliant moon is chary of invading the gorges and ravines. There is light, there is shade, there is tender perspective. The stark rocks and austerely colourless backgrounds are lost in mysterious half-distances, and an air of tranquil, romantic beauty is cast over scenery, which at other times chills you by its raw vastness.

In viewing spacious panoramic landscape in America, one generally finds that the eye rarely encounters specific points about it that leave a lasting impression. When on some future occasion one endeavours to reconstruct the picture, it is far more puzzling than had it been European Alpine scenery. The picturesque details about the latter, far more numerous and far more varied, can somehow, much more easily be remembered.

We proceed on our stroll. Not the whole great mountain side is clothed in its primeval garb. In an hour's stroll we notice at least five or six more or less extensive expanses of timber, every one of different age. Fire, caused by lightning, and windfalls, avalanches, and hurricanes have all been at work, and all have left their distinctive mark. We pass grassy slopes, dotted here and there with very old trees, gnarled and weatherbeaten, and not a few of crippled shape, which in days long past were spared by the snow avalanche that started from the heights above and swept away their brethren, leaving on its course Cyclopean boulders strewn about on the glade, and now as deeply imbedded in the soil as had they always been there. Our walk has brought us to the foot of walls of rock of vast height, for here the main chain falls off in one great precipice. Skirting along their base through occasional groves of spruce pines, we presently reach the mouth of one of the canyons. Striking through the mountains at a right angle, it has cut the chain very nearly in two, and its perpendicular sides are quite 2000 feet in height. A small stream, ludicrously insignificant in comparison with the great gorge its waters have made for themselves, issues from the buttressed gateway. A colony of beaver, who generations ago made this spot their home, have, by building dams across the stream a few hundred yards lower down, turned a couple of acres of ground right at the mouth of the gorge into a beaver-meadow—a perfectly level expanse of velvety turf, as smooth and silken, and as brilliantly green, as some favoured lawn at home. We are standing a yard or two from the open space, in the deep shadow of some pines which encircle it on all sides save those where the abruptly-rising cliffs bound it. The glade-like beaver-meadow is flooded by the broad mellow moonbeams that stream through the gigantic portals of the gorge as though it were an arched window in some ruined old abbey. On the glade move about a small band of Wapiti, the stags whistling their weird Æolian music, the hinds and their more than half-grown progeny feasting on the juicy "aftermath" that invariably grows on the rich alluvial soil of these beaver-meadows, grasses that in hue and texture are very unlike the rank herbage commonly to be found in elevated mountain regions. We stretch ourselves under the sweeping boughs of a great pine, and from there watch the family life, the occasional angry thrusts delivered by indignant master-stags in chastisement of some impudent youngster who has dared to approach his hinds. Stags ramble off into the forest, and stags come—now approaching within ten yards of our hiding-place, then gradually fading away into luminous "Waldesduft," the poetic German name for the shrouding vapours of the forest. Not thirty yards from us there lie close together, two big antlers, shed probably last season, but already blanched to chalk-like whiteness. One of the stags, wandering idly over the glade, presently comes up to them, and the lordly animal, for some reason or other displeased by these relics of his race, lowers his head, and catching up on his brow-tines one of the branching horns, weighing probably twenty pounds, tosses it like a feather, sending it crashing into the pine covert twenty yards off.[1] The second horn he does not touch; he has shown what he can do. Except the quaint call of him and his fellows—sounds for which there is little cause, for the fair ones they are so jealously guarding evince no intention of evading their masters' endearments—save this, absolute stillness hushes the scene. The moon has topped the great chain, and no other light but that streaming through the vast rock-bound gateway of the gorge reaches the spot. Never did forest scene breath more entrancing peacefulness. As we look up at the great orb, it seems as if she had shone from that spot for millions of years, and would continue for time evermore to touch up with silvery sheen the little glade and the group of stately animals dispersed over it. But, alas! what a rude awakening awaits that family of Wapiti! Where, less than two years ago, the nearest human habitation was ten or eleven days' ride off—longer than it takes the traveller from the Old

---

[1] It is the only time I have seen Wapiti do this.

World to reach the New one—there will be, or perhaps there is already, a mining town, and Texas or Oregon steers will roam where, from time eternal, was the home of our antlered friends and of our favourites the indefatigable constructors of dams and beaver-meadows, while the ubiquitous cow-puncher or stock-raiser, who is turning the vast West into one huge cattle-yard, to the utter extermination of game, will replace the lonesome old "stags," who with their Indian squaws passed many a profitable trapping season in this beautiful mountain retreat.

CHAPTER IX.

THE BEAVER AND HIS CAMP.

The bank and dam beaver—Their dwellings—The beaver's intelligence—Beaver timber—Trappers and their craft—Indians indifferent trappers—Beaver towns, their aspect—Influences of the beaver upon the topography of the country.

THE trappers of the North-West define two species of beaver, distinguished from each other not so much by any individual characteristic as rather by the nature of their dwelling-places. They are the "bank" and the "dam" beaver. The former live in excavated caverns or nests in the banks of large and swift-flowing rivers, where the current is too strong, and the spring rise too considerable, to allow them to build dams. The entrance to their subterranean dwelling-places is effected by means of long burrow-like channels from three to eight feet in length, starting upwards, so that, though the ingress hole be four or five feet under the surface, the nest itself is above water level, and perfectly dry.

The "dam beaver" lives, as the name indicates, in dams, or carefully built houses, generally of a round and somewhat conical shape, two and three families occupying frequently different tiers in one and the same house, which,

I understand, is never the case with the other variety. Of the dozens of "bank beavers" the men I was with dug out, they never found more than one "set," or family, occupying the warmly padded nest.

The houses of dam beavers are not difficult to examine, for they are above ground, and five or ten minutes' careful work will usually suffice to lay open the neat inside of the "wood pile" structure. The number of inmates, as well as the size of these houses, varies considerably. Regarding the former point, my personal observation is numerically far behind that of other travellers. I have never seen, or had actual proof of, more than eight beaver living in the same tenement—a number far exceeded by others. The greatest number authentically recorded is, I believe, instanced by Hearne, in his narrative of exploration in the Hudson's Bay country, nearly a century ago, where he relates that the Indians of his party killed twelve old beaver and twenty-five young and half-grown ones out of one house, and he adds, it was found on examination that several others had escaped. The house was a very large one, and had nearly a dozen apartments under one roof, which, with two exceptions, had no communication with each other, except by water, and were probably occupied by separate families.

Not so easy is it to examine the dwellings of bank beaver, for during summer and autumn the entrance is several feet under water, and the nest itself can only be reached by digging down in trapper fashion—a process not conducive to a closer examination of the dwelling. In winter, however, when even the swiftest and most rebellious mountain torrents are laid in icy bands—at a period, too, when the water level is generally at its very lowest—the entrance hole is not infrequently half or entirely over the ice; and on such occasions, if the burrow is short and perfectly straight, the explorer is able to squeeze himself two or three feet up the passage, till, by the light of his candle held in front of him, a glimpse can be caught of the inside of the nest. Old dog beaver seem to care far less for the comfortable padding of their dwellings than do family beaver. On several occasions have I thus surprised solitary old males in their winter abodes, the frightened tenant, unable to escape, crouching in the furthest extremity of his bare and cold cavern, and eyeing me with his small and not particularly expressive eyes.

The beaver is one of those animals whose instinct and intelligence have been most discussed among naturalists. Cuvier, it is well known, used to demonstrate by a series of experiments with a beaver taken when quite young and artificially suckled, that the admirable industry and intelligent appreciation of certain laws of nature evinced by the works of beavers spring from a blind mechanical force—pure instinct, unrelieved by the higher faculty. Cuvier fed his young prisoner with branches of willow, of which it ate all the bark, cutting up the peeled stems into pieces, piling them up in a corner of the cage as building material. He then provided it with earth, pebbles, and tree branches; they were all used by the beaver in the manner peculiar to his species. "This," argues Cuvier, "was blind instinct; no good could result from the trouble which it gave itself, for it needed no house." Buffon's argument, that solitary though free beavers do not know how to construct dams, is refuted by Cuvier's young prisoner, who constructed and built his dams and dykes. With very few animals is it apparently so difficult to draw the line between instinct and intelligence, or rather between instinctive intelligence and reflective intelligence, as in the beaver's case? Intelligence is, as we know, deliberative, conditional, modifiable, and is the result of observation and preceding experience. The story of Mr. Broderip's pet beaver who manifested his building instincts by dragging together warming pans, sweeping-brushes, boots, and sticks, and piling them together crosswise, is, as we have authentic facts before us, a typical instance of this difficulty.

The use of the beaver's tail as a trowel for plastering down their mud constructions has been frequently doubted, and the very isolated instances in which I found the marks of the scale-covered tail on dams or houses can hardly prove the contrary. More frequently have I found "prints" of the tail on the slimy, mud-covered slides, for when in repose the tail lies flat on the ground. When at work gnawing down trees, the beaver seems to prop himself on his tail, though not to the extent pictures drawn by inventive pencils would pretend.

If you surprise a beaver in deep water, he will commonly duck under, with a loud slap of his broad tail on the water. Indians and half-breeds believe this to be a well understood sign to alarm their comrades; but from the build of the animal, and the fact that he only makes this noise when in deep water, I am inclined to believe that it is a movement tending to expedite his disappearance.

Another very popular myth endows the beaver's tail with a further use, namely, as a medium for carrying sand and mud. Major Campion, in his "On the Frontier," a work published a few years ago, says,—

"Nature has provided the beaver with a natural, flexible trowel—his tail—and he uses it as such, making a mortar by puddling the earth of the banks of the stream, carrying it on his tail to where it is required, and then with it spreading and plastering the prepared mud just as a mason would apply his mortar with his trowel. Authority worthy of high respect says this is not so, is physically impossible; but many times I have seen the unmistakable print of the beaver's tail on his mud-mortar."

As far as my experience goes, I certainly have to differ from this opinion, for I have never seen anything of the kind; and I should say that a glance at the beaver's extremely short forelegs, and at his anatomical construction, makes it at once patent that it is quite impossible for him to place anything on his tail, aside of the further impossibility of carrying such sand or mud on it, were he indeed capable of twisting his body into the contortions implied by the writer. Of the very numerous fabulous stories of the beaver's activity, this is, I expect, one of the newest, for I have not found it in any of the older natural history works so much given to shed round the beaver's devoted head a halo of more than human intelligence.

Even Indian lore, the history of untutored and barbarian aborigines, gives the beaver prominence for intelligence among animal creation. Indeed, according to one source, this tail business would seem to be actual truth. I am alluding to Power's most interesting but very little known work on the Indian Aborigines of California. In it the author relates a myth of the creation of man and woman by the animals of the forest, which is or was prevalent among the Miwok tribe. In it the following passage occurs: "After the cayote had spoken, the beaver said he never heard such twaddle and nonsense in his life. No tail, indeed! He would make a man with a broad flat tail, so he could haul mud and sand on it."

Incredible as it sounds, there are people who believe that beaver climb trees—a belief based on the fact that you frequently find the marks of their teeth high up on the trunks or stumps of trees, which they have gnawed down, of such height as would apparently furnish incontestable proof of this circumstance. Rational examination at once shows us that such gnawing has been done in late autumn or early spring, when deep and crusted snow covered the ground, by the help of which beaver could gnaw trees eight feet or ten feet up the trunk. A similar instance is afforded by the height of beaver dams. Naturalists of past days claimed that beaver knew exactly how high creeks and streams inhabited by them would run when the spring freshets swelled their volume, basing their argument upon the circumstance that beaver dams were invariably neither too high nor too low, but always of just sufficient altitude to allow the water to lap the topmost edge of their dyke. Nothing is easier to explain, if we remember that at the time these freshets occur the beaver is in the prime of his activity, and the proper level of his dam can be sustained very easily by tearing away or adding to its height—a circumstance borne out by the fact that you will find the uppermost portion of dams consist of timber shorn of its bark, the remains of the winter provender used for this practical purpose.

Beaver are persecuted by man with a persistency from which few if any other animals have to suffer. Unfortunately man's preposterous selfishness comes into play, and two-thirds of the trappers do not scruple to trap out a creek or a lake as completely as possible. This is a very unwise policy; for beaver, if left undisturbed, multiply rapidly, one single pair repopulating a whole mountain stream in a decade. Beaver, moreover, are not very shy animals; they do not shun man's neighbourhood, as long as his hand is not turned against them. They often build in close vicinity to ranches and frontier settlements. As their work is chiefly done at night, they are not liable to be disturbed, and it is by no means unusual to find fresh beaver dams, and other signs of their presence, where the baying of watchdogs and the shout of the lusty cowboys are heard day by day.

That well-known, and I believe perfectly authentic, instance of Missouri beaver repeatedly building up a culvert through a railway embankment, made to drain off the water from a pond inhabited by them, is a striking proof of their sagacity; for when the workmen persisted every other day in destroying the dam built by them during two nights to stop up the culvert, and so prevent their home pond being laid dry, they decided, with human intelligence, to build up the culvert no longer near the entrance, where their work could so easily be broken down, but to close the channel right in the centre of the drain, which was some forty feet in length, well out of reach of the long poles used by the men to poke down their work. Here, then, was a beaver family actually at work with express trains thundering over their heads.

Naturalists maintain that beaver observe no particular method in building their dykes. While not venturing to dispute this authoritative opinion, I would desire to mention a curious and instructive instance which assuredly proves a certain amount of method. It was related to me quite recently by an Englishman, a well-known civil engineer in California, of large experience in all matters appertaining to the irrigation of land. A large English company had bought up a vast tract of land, bordered by the sea, in one of the centre counties of California. The land was considered perfectly valueless, the company proposing to make good grass-land of it by erecting sea dykes and damming a swift river, so that fresh water became available for irrigation. It was only after the purchase was concluded that it was found the whole surrounding country was peat, which not only floated in water, but seemed of far too little substance wherewith to erect dams. Timber and stones were alike distant, and the transportation wholly out of the question. At this critical juncture, when the company's purchase capital appeared irretrievably lost, my informant was consulted. His opinion could not be different from that of the other engineers employed by the company, and the undertaking was about to be given up. He was riding homewards, following the course of the stream, when, some miles higher up its course, he came upon some men engaged in beaver trapping. Stopping at their camp for that night, he learnt from his hosts that numerous beaver were to be found in the stream, and questioning them a little closer, he was told that they built their dams of peat. Examining next morning some beaver work, he found that the men had spoken the truth, and that dams of considerable strength, jutting out into the swift current, were constructed solely of peat. From the trappers he then learnt what means these animals employed to make this substance retain a submerged position. It was by gradually pushing out their dams into deep water, building them much higher over the surface of the water than they usually do with earth or timber, so that, while the weight of the unsubmerged peat kept the foundation work in its place, the angle of the "bulkhead," where it was swept by the current, was of the requisite steepness. Twelve hours' examination made my informant very confident of ultimate success. He began his work amid the sneers of his incredulous fellow-engineers, and by strictly keeping to the constructive plan of the beaver he succeeded, and better than he had ever hoped, in making the whole undertaking such a great success that several companies have since been started with the same object. He told me that the chief dam was 130 feet in width, and the locks by which the reservoir water was controlled, of sufficient capacity to float a small steamer; and all were made of peat only.

The teeth of the beaver, at least the four incisors or gnawers, are, as is well known, remarkable instances of the kind provisions made by nature. They are provided with an outer coating of excessively hard orange-coloured enamel, the core being of a much softer substance. The constant gnawing wears this latter down first, leaving the harder coating to form a gouge-like edge of amazing sharpness. A constant growth at the roots keeps up the length of the teeth, a circumstance which in isolated cases has caused death. For a beaver deprived of one of his incisors (they break them very frequently gnawing at the steel traps in which they are caught), and the absence of any check to the growth of the corresponding incisor, results in an abnormal growth which very soon makes it impossible for the animal to feed. I found one old beaver skull with an incisor five inches long. From the shape of it, I should judge that the animal could hardly open its mouth—a fate which befell once a pet squirrel, obliging me to have it killed.

There are very numerous traits in the beaver's activity that appear incompatible with the argument that only blind instinct moves the little workers. To watch two beavers at work gnawing down a big cottonwood-tree, three feet and a half in circumference—each worker keeping strictly to his side, the incision being made with perfect, one might say mathematical accuracy, so as to bring the tree in its final plunge to the very spot they want it, athwart a creek, or, as an additional protection to their dam, a foot or two on the upper side of it, where the danger from the swift current is greatest, is a sight which will probably convince even the most unbelieving. An experiment made on several different occasions by me tells its own tale.

Coming, in the course of my rambles, upon quite fresh beaver work, say a moderately big cottonwood-tree five or six inches in diameter, standing on a slope, and partially cut through by them, I would put my shoulder to it, and, if possible, break it down, so that it fell up the slope in a direction opposite to that which the beaver evidently intended. Visiting the spot the next day, or two days afterwards, the tree was invariably lugged round, with the top downhill or athwart the little creek, the foundation work probably of a new dam.

Many a huge camp fire have we kept up day and night with old "beaver timber"—logs cut in lengths from twelve inches to twenty inches, and generally from six inches to fifteen inches in diameter. This beaver timber at first puzzled me a good deal; apparently much too large for feed sticks, and too short and thick for building purposes, I failed to find a reasonable explanation for it; the only one that presented itself to me, namely, that the logs were the result of naughty-boy beavers of the destructive age of thirteen or fourteen, eager to sharpen their teeth, seemed too absurd. None of the trappers I interrogated on this matter could assign a reason, for they had never given the question a thought; so I set about to discover it for myself by dint of careful watching. The first thing I did was to make mental notes regarding the condition of the ground in those places where beaver timber was found; for its distribution was singularly uncertain, some localities abounding with it, while along other creeks where beavers lived we could find not a trace of it for days and weeks. I soon discovered that these short thick logs occurred only along creeks having level banks, where nature failed to aid their transportation by providing more or less steeply-inclined planes to roll down the trunks of trees. In fact I found them to occur mostly where no large trees grew close to the creek the home of the sturdy woodcutters, and where patches of dense shrub and cottonwoods flourished at some little distance from the waterside.

Soon after making this discovery I passed a very bright October moonlight night, watching, as I often did, for a grizzly, in a copse of this description. I was perched in the fork of a good-sized, leafless cottonwood, at the base of which lay the carcass of a white-tail deer, the bait intended to attract bruin, and near which, a day or two before, he had first *câched* and then devoured a similar *bonne bouche*, provided for him by my rifle. With my hand-axe I had made myself a comfortable seat, carefully concealing the shining barrels of my rifle—a very necessary, but often neglected precaution, where wary beasts of prey, never more wary than when approaching a *câche* or a bait, are concerned. The calm, glorious evening had long merged into the peaceful tranquillity of a moonlight landscape, my pocket literature enabling me to while away the time, when a noise of breaking twigs attracted my attention, and made me "grab" the Express concealed under my coat. The disturbance, however, was not caused by my expected bear, but by old friends, a tardy family of beavers, about to begin, somewhat later than usual, their nocturnal "cutting." On this occasion, and only on this one, have I watched the production of these logs, which, with the bark left on, were cut from trees previously gnawed down, the entire trunk being far too heavy for the beaver to move or turn on level ground, while the single pieces could be pushed along with perfect ease.

It was an interesting sight to watch the old *pater familias* set to work on a previously felled trunk, soon followed by several more youthful labourers, scions probably of the diligent foreman of the works. With amazing energy their sharp, ever-keen gnawing tools plied through the wood, the shavings in width corresponding to the breadth of the gouge-shaped edge of their teeth, now and again jerked aside with a comic vicious-looking toss of the bullet-shaped head. Unfortunately, not having a watch, I was unable to time the speed with which the logs were cut. I should say that half an hour amply covered the period occupied in cutting one log of about ten inches in diameter. While standing trees are gnawed round the circumference from nine inches to fifteen inches from the ground, the deepest cutting being done on the side towards which the tree is to fall, felled trunks too heavy to turn over offer more difficulties, the greater portion of the gnawing having to be done from the uppermost side; hence also it is easy to know, by the surface of the cut, whether a tree has been worked on while standing, or when prostrated on the ground. These logs supply, I am inclined to think, a twofold want; for not only is the bark welcome winter provender, but their bulky nature makes them good building material wherewith to dam up the base of a dyke. I have found them in many instances built up in the lower submerged part of big dams torn down by ruthless trapper hands, and where, in the original condition of the dyke, they could not be seen.[1]

While all, or very nearly all, old beaver-timber is peeled, most of it betrays, when found on dry land, its having been once submerged for a considerable period. The fact that the logs are found on dry ground, often some distance from the next creek, is easily explained, if we remember that the high water of spring time uproots many a beaver dam, drifting the logs, and also smaller building material, all over the surrounding level stretches of country. The few isolated instances of beaver timber with the bark on, and which had never been exposed to water, are, as I had occasion to see on my last trip, the result of cutting down felled trees to a certain length, so

[1] One of Professor Hayden's scientific assistants in the Second Survey party of the Territories has published in the *American Naturalist* some interesting notes on beavers. The beaver timber-logs of which I have just spoken seemed to have puzzled him, though he makes a happy guess at their use when he says, "They are probably prepared with the intention of filling up chinks in the walls of dams," no actual proof of this, however, being furnished by the writer.

as just to span the creek or fit the outlet of a pool, for which desirable end the trunks were originally gnawed down.

Beavers live chiefly on the bark of their favourite trees, at least during the open season. But it is unquestionable that they subsist also on wood, it having been found on dissection that their stomachs were filled with lignine with no perceptible remains of bark, and the contents of the cæcum disclosing the same fact, the digestive process simply removing the saccharine from the wood. The frequent absence of chips at the foot of trees freshly gnawed by beavers speaks also for this fact.

Regarding the altitude at which beavers live, it seems wholly governed by the presence of their favourite trees and shrubs. In the Big Wind River Mountains I found families peopling some of the small lakes at an altitude of over 9000 or 10,000 feet. Many of the lakes, however, had no willows or asps about them, and there also no beavers would be. I was unable to determine whether beavers remained at such extreme heights during the long winter months, or whether they migrated down the creeks into the bigger valleys 2000 or 3000 feet lower. Trappers appear to favour the latter theory. That beavers winter at 8000 or 9000 feet over sea level is an undisputed fact, of which I convinced myself personally, for I found them inhabiting their snug houses at that altitude in the month of December.

Autumn brings a full complement of work for our little workers. The winter house or the nest in the bank has to be repaired—the first replastered with mud, which on becoming hard shields the inmates effectually against the attacks of hungry wolves; the latter padded with moss. Then the winter provender has to be collected in the shape of feed-sticks—pieces of cottonwood, willow, or ash saplings, from nine to twelve inches in length, of which the bark is the favourite food. These are stacked up under water, generally at the foot of the nearest dam, or in the case of bank beaver are taken right into their subterranean caverns. Some of the old-bachelor beavers, who, not unlike very old stags or bull buffaloes, stray from their fellows, and go roaming about the country, seem strangely improvident concerning their winter supplies.

Most trappers believe implicitly in their victims' proficiency as weather clerks; if beavers collect their feed-sticks early, winter is close at hand, and *vice versâ*. On the two occasions when I have been able to watch this, it certainly turned out correct.

Beaver, in countries where their favourite quaking-asp and cottonwood-trees flourish, very rarely touch the resinous evergreens of the forest, whether for feeding or for building purposes. In one or two localities I found cedar-trees of medium growth gnawed down; but it was impossible to tell whether they had done this in the extremities of hunger or simply to clear their path. Never having come upon fresh cedar cuttings, I cannot account for it with any degree of certainty.

In Oregon, however, the animal appears to evince a less marked partiality. Dr. Newberry, in his "Zoology of Oregon," states that in the Cascade Mountains, in that Territory (a range not visited by me), "whole groves of young pine-trees are cut down within a few inches of the ground, and carried off bodily. . . . . The largest stump I noticed was a spruce pine twelve inches in diameter." There is a possibility that the evergreen trees observed by Dr. Newberry were cut down by the beavers to obtain the nutritious mosses, which grow upon certain species of evergreen trees in Oregon in great profusion. This vegetable parasite is collected by the Indians, and cooked or baked in much the same way they prepare their "kamash," a sort of moss glue being thus obtained, which is said to be both palatable and nutritious. Certain it is that while beaver on the Atlantic slopes of the Rocky Mountains and the Eastern lake districts never touch evergreen trees, those on the Pacific slope apparently sometimes make an exception. Most of the trappers of experience whom I took occasion to interrogate concerning Oregon beaver, told me that occasionally they came across instances of spruce, tamarack, or any other resinous evergreen, showing beaver signs. Dr. Newberry's experience may have been exceptional.

Beavers migrate, and for two reasons, dearth of the willow brush and cottonwood-trees, which are their means of subsistence, and constant persecution on the part of man. They go down stream till they strike the main river, and then, moving up or down its course, make for another tributary creek.

In Canada, I understand, trappers subdivide beavers into lake and stream beaver; but in the northern portions of the Rocky Mountains of the United States this does not hold good, as creek or river beaver will migrate to lakes and *vice versâ*.

One hears and reads a good deal about trappers and their craft; but the details of their art—how, when, and where their quarry is caught—are less known, for not only are fur hunters generally uneducated men, who in their isolated lives have long forgotten—if they ever knew it—

how to wield a pen; but they are also governed by extreme jealousy respecting what they fondly imagine to be the secrets of their craft.

Beaver trapping is by no means an easy craft to learn, and to be moderately successful long experience and sharp eyes are essential. The first thing to be done on reaching trapping ground is to discover "slides"—*i.e.* the places where beaver pass up and down the banks of the river, lake, or creek in quest of food or building material. Keen and practised eyes will detect slides more readily, for they are often well-worn passage ways. The same beaver will rarely use more than two slides, though often half a dozen or more will scramble up and down the same slippery pathway. "Runways," another technical expression, are the places where beavers pass over their dams, usually where they are lowest.

The traps in general use are the Newhouse No. 4 steel trap with plain, blunt fangs, and weighing from $2\frac{1}{2}$lbs. to $3\frac{1}{4}$lbs., according to the length of chain. The springs are very powerful, closing with amazing force, and requiring some practice to open them. Ordinarily they are set in the water at the foot of the slide, or now and again at either end of a runway. Before setting, the trapper must make sure the slide is not an old one; a brief examination will suffice to settle that point. The trapper, protected by his high indiarubber boots, then wades into the water, not unfrequently up to his chest, if the banks are at all steep. A stake two or three feet in length, cut from the young pine-tree, is then driven firmly into the bank, under water-line, care being taken that the cut surface of the wood is masked by a dab of mud or a piece of bark. To this stake, a couple of inches in diameter, the chain of the trap is then fastened, making it impossible for the beaver to drag the trap away—mere child's play for the very powerful animal were it not for this precaution. Then the trap is set, that is, opened and placed in such a manner on or near the bottom of the slide, nine or ten inches under water, so that the beaver, going or returning over it, is apt to strike the trigger plate with one of his feet—if possible, one of the hind ones; the trap itself is concealed by mud or leaves. Now comes the nicest part of the undertaking, the question of "medicine" or scent, the purpose of which is to attract any stray beaver wandering up and down stream by placing a minute particle of a strongly smelling substance on or near the slide. Some few trappers never make use of scent, but by far the greater number are fanatical believers in one or other of the hundred and one different "medicines." With the exception of those that apply only beaver-scent—that is, the contents of the beaver's oil or musk bag (or castoreum), a yellow butter-like matter of a very peculiar odour—the choice of artificial medicine is a matter of great controversy among the fraternity; and it is highly amusing to listen to the high-flown praise the gnarled old "stags" will bestow upon their own peculiar mixture, the recipe of which they treasure as *the* secret of their craft. A reliable pelt hunter once told me that the Fur Company trapper, an old veteran, with whom, many years before, he passed his trapper apprenticeship, would not divulge the recipe of the compound he used till his dying day, notwithstanding that they lived and trapped together in the far-off wilderness of the Oregon and Montana forests for six long years. Finally, mortally wounded by an Indian arrow, he revealed, while lying on the ground gasping for breath, the grand secret of his life to his faithful partner.

Assafœtida, oil of aniseed, and other pungent essential oils, are not usually subjects to which hang romantic tales; but this story of life and death proved the contrary.

I was not a little amused when, on returning to civilization from my second trip, several old veteran trappers, entrusted me, in whispered confidence, with certain never-to-be-revealed secrets, namely, the names of such drugs for their medicine they could not obtain in the frontier settlements, which they begged me to send them from Chicago or New York—a sufficiently overwhelming token of confidence to make an old man of me in the conscientious endeavour to keep the secrets. I am not transgressing my trust if I mention that they were of the most varied nature, some of the commonest being oil of aniseed, of amber, of cassia, of cloves, of fennel seed, of thyme, and oil of rhodium.

After using the trap, great care has to be taken that every article, twig, or stake touched by the hand is carefully washed off with water, which is done most effectually by dashing some over it. Beaver have exceedingly keen scenting powers, and would not think of passing over a slide near which a trapper has been at work who failed to observe that precaution.

The traps are always set in the early evening, an hour or so before dusk, the majority of beavers being caught in the early hours of the following morning. A trapper's camp is an early-rising one, breakfast being generally eaten at dawn, for it is essential to visit the traps as soon as possible, as beavers have a knack of getting away in an astonishing manner if left too long between the fangs of the trap. If caught by one of their front legs, they will gnaw it off, just above the fangs; or what happens as often, they are drowned in their vain endeavours to rid themselves of the trap by getting entangled in the chain; or, if the water is very deep, they are liable to get submerged in such a position that the latter holds them down. On an average, I should say about one-third of the beavers caught are found alive in the traps when the trapper gets to them. Say twenty traps are set, it is considered good work if six beavers are caught, as many traps will have been sprung without retaining the victim, and the rest will not have been touched.

Beavers are rarely trapped in summer, on account of the inferior quality of the pelt, the latter half of October being generally considered the opening of the season, though at higher altitudes, where winter may be said to commence in September, the pelt will be much earlier in prime condition, the animals shedding their winter coat very late, and "rehairing" very early. There are numerous tricks for increasing the weight of the skins; for, as they are all bought by the pound—the present price in New York being about $2, or 8s. per pound, a big skin weighing, or, as the trapper will say, "hefting," a little over two pounds—it is an object with many an unscrupulous man to get together as many pounds as he can. A very general dodge, which ruins the skins, is to strew a cupful or so of fine sand made red-hot over the fresh skin; each minute particle sinks right into the hide, and as it dries, these artificial pores close up, and the fraud is only discovered when the pelt comes under the furrier's knife. A more innocent trick is to rub cold sand into the skin while yet wet; this does not impair its market value. But also the trappers are subjected to ruses on the part of the trade. To mention only one, it is a common stratagem to "rig up" the fur market in summer, the great fur-buying houses in the Atlantic seaboard cities sending out circulars to their Western correspondents in which prices of all pelts are put at advanced rates, fifty or more per cent. over the last spring values. The news that beaver has "riz" spreads like wildfire, and trappers set out on their dreary and dangerous winter's occupation in the lonely wilderness with redoubled zeal, only to find on their return to the frontier settlements in the following April or May that prices have gone back to lower rates than ever. Thus the old story of grindstone and knife repeats itself.

It must not be supposed that a daily catch of six beavers is an ordinary one. To be able to score that number for any length of time, the most out-of-the-way places have to be sought, and then even the trapper risks finding not a single good "ground," earlier birds having picked up the crumbs. To reach such secluded beaver grounds, weeks and months pass in autumn or winter travel through districts where, even in the height of summer, the difficulties are often overwhelming. Or, again, say the goal is finally reached, the hardships of an Arctic winter face the lonely trapper. While on the Plains and among the foothills of the Rocky Mountains very high winds prevail, which sweep off the snow, this is not the case in the higher Alpine forest regions, where snow lies deep and very long.

The Indians of the United States—at least those of Wyoming, Colorado, Idaho, and Montana—are very indifferent trappers. The half-breeds, on the contrary, are deadly enemies of the beaver tribe, for they combine the 'cuteness of the white man and the dogged perseverance and primitive style of living of their mothers' race. They will winter in regions where but very few even of the amazingly hardy trappers will venture to remain; and, moreover, as they have generally a little party of squaws and young bucks with them, they reap all the advantages of skilful and gratuitous labour in the skinning and preparing of the pelt. Not a few white trappers are married to squaws; but while their wives' kith and kin will not willingly accompany the paleface, they would do so very readily were the man a half-breed. Not a few trapper " outfits " I met or heard of were composed of both elements, say one white man and a half-breed, with a couple of willing female slaves. These, as a rule, are perhaps the most successful, and I have heard of very large takes, making the business a really profitable one, were it not that the trappers, both whites and natives, are usually terribly cheated when exchanging their peltry for provisions. The Government post traders and Indian agents at the remote little Indian forts, pushed far in advance of other white settlements, make a 250 per cent. profit in buying up beaver skins (they usually allow $1 or 4s. worth of provisions, which cost them perhaps little more than half) and sending them direct to wholesale house in New York, where they fetch from 8s. to 10s.

In the old days of the fur traders the beaver skin was the unit of computation in buying or trading. Provisions, ammunition, and blankets were bought with beaver skins, and horses and squaw wives were traded for them. A thirty-skin wife was an average article. Considering that the working of the peltry, the tanning and softening, fell always to the lot of these unfortunate female slaves, it was in past days no unusual occurrence for one wife to work up skins wherewith, in good Mormon fashion, a new wife was to be traded. Among some few North-Western Indian tribes this monetary standard still prevails; but, generally speaking, money or buckskins (deer-hides) have taken its place in intertribal dealing.

The market value of beaver pelt is liable to considerable variations, and the trade subdivides this species of fur into eight or ten different categories.

In travelling with trappers through their favourite mountain retreats, the most secluded spots left on this vast continent, you very frequently come upon sad scenes of havoc, where beaver have been completely trapped out—or what is perhaps more correct, very nearly annihilated by trappers, the few remaining ones, probably crippled by the traps, leaving their hitherto peaceful homes to seek elsewhere security from man's persecution. I well remember a cluster of small lakes in the Wind River Mountains that presented a woeful picture of desolation. Half-breed trappers had discovered the very secluded dams the previous season, and had made an enormous bag, trapping right from one camp 173 beaver, the inmates of the tarns, which had probably never before been visited by human beings. Traversing the vast and very nearly impenetrable tracts of forest that surround the lakelets, I happened to stumble upon unmistakable signs of human travel through the woods. Following these signs, now as my guide a blazed trunk, then a tree felled to clear the way for pack animals the cut surface showing the clean work of white men's or half-breeds'[2] axes, and not the chop of Indians—I finally, after half a day's ramble, came upon the goal of my predecessors, six or seven small lakes nestling under an isolated towering mass of rock, and so securely screened by dense timber, and an inner belt of cottonwood-trees and willows, that you might have passed five-and-twenty yards from their banks without ever suspecting the presence of a lake. It was the *beau idéal* of a trapper's camp; a small clearing made by their axes was still dotted with skeleton remains of "wickey-ups" bower tents—I might describe them—and strewn about in great number lay birch or willow saplings bent into rings about two feet in diameter, whereupon the beaver skins had been stretched while drying. The pools had evidently once been one single lake, but the beaver, by ingenious dykes, had divided it into six or seven smaller sheets of water, lying tier-like, one slightly raised over the other. The nearest to the spring supplying the water was, of course, the highest, about eight or ten feet being the difference between its water level and that of the lowest, miniature cascades and channel-like timber floats connecting the different lakelets. These channels for timber are very ingeniously laid-out contrivances, from three to five feet in width, and from two to four feet in depth; they are intended for floating larger pieces of wood from place to place, especially where the previously-constructed dykes render the transportation of trunks a difficult or impossible job for the little workers.

[2] An Indian, be he ever so handy at other things, never learns the use of the axe as white men do. He invariably notches the tree in a most unsightly manner; here a chop, there a cut, but never the clean, even handiwork of civilized man. Half-breeds, with the "white" blood infused into their veins, learn also the use of the axe.

On one side of the pools the ground rose at a steep angle to a slight eminence, the slopes of which were covered by cottonwoods and quaking asps (asp-trees), some of considerable girth. Down this declivity the beaver had made regular timber shoots, showing very plainly that many generations of the indefatigable little workers had dragged or "shot" their building materials down the well-worn grooves in the soil. A glance at the numerous neatly-trimmed stumps that dotted the hill-side, many over four feet in circumference, gave a further proof of the wonderful activity of this beaver town's population. I do not remember ever seeing a more complete colony, with bigger dykes or better planned accessories, one and all evincing, to a very striking degree, perfect knowledge of the principles of hydrostatics.

At the head of the topmost lake, and surrounding the spring, lay a beautiful stretch of what is known as beaver meadow, caused by the gradual accumulation of alluvial matter in the basin formed by the first dyke of the "town." Some 150 yards in length, and half that width, it was covered with a close and even carpet of fine grass, forming a charming contrast to the sage green of the cottonwoods, here and there touched up with autumn hues, and the uniform dark sombre green of the silent pine forest in the background. It was altogether a picture not easily forgotten—beautiful but sad.

The half-breed trappers, whom I happened to meet some weeks afterwards, had worked like Vandals. Not only was there not a single beaver left, but several of the large dams dividing the lakelets from each other had been ruthlessly torn down by them in their efforts to recover lost traps; for if beaver can manage to loosen the stake to which the trap in which they are caught is chained, they will walk it off, dragging it after them to their subterranean houses in the dams. Traps are very valuable in the wilderness; for though you can buy them by the dozen for something like eighty shillings in Western towns, they are of course worth five or ten times that in the wilds. The water-level had of course been lowered considerably where the dams had been torn down, so that the lower portion of the dykes became visible. There were two or three of forty and fifty yards in length, about seven feet high, and at the base at least four feet in breadth—massive structures, wonderfully planned and built. In several places willow roots had been used by the beaver, and during the past summer they had made shoots a foot or two in length, giving the solid dyke a very singular appearance. In one of these saplings, larger than the rest, a bird had built its nest; but the inmates were long flown, and the shoot with the nest was swaying gently to and fro in the evening breeze. The melancholy silence of American Alpine forests lay over the whole scene. It was too late to return that day to my camp, so I picketed my old horse in the opening, and after a frugal supper watched the sun go down on this desolated beaver town. Not a sound was to be heard, nor was a solitary living thing visible; and so profound was the death-gloom that hung over the spot, that even the roaring fire that I presently lit, in front of which I stretched myself on my saddle blankets, failed to chase away the melancholy mood of Nature and man.

As I lay there, my head comfortably propped up on my saddle, smoking my pipe, and idly watching the lights and shadows of my fire dancing with weird effects on the dark wall of rock frowning overhead, the fate of this devastated home of sturdy little animals—nothing left but ruins to represent what but a short twelvemonth before was the picture of wonderful animal activity, of brute intelligence of the highest order—made the ruthlessly desecrating work of man seem doubly vile.

Beaver have left far more lasting and useful monuments of their laborious activity on the surface of the country than the aboriginal inhabitants.

Whole valleys are refertilized by them, the process being far quicker than one might suppose. Tersely rendered, it is as follows :—Given, a stream traversing a small valley, with rocky ground, on which grow only occasional cottonwoods; a colony of beaver on taking possession of it will soon make it into meadow-land. The grove of trees furthest down the stream is first tackled. When autumn comes few of them are left to rear their heads. They have been gnawed down, their trunks cut into logs, which form the foundation of an amazingly strong and massive dam stretched across the stream where it is narrowest, forming on the upper side a profound pool, as deep as the dam is high. If the supply of wood lasts, consecutive dams will be built up stream, from thirty to a hundred yards apart, so that finally, in the course of twenty or thirty years, there will be no running water left. I have passed many such streams, when for miles you will pass beaver dam upon beaver dam. Time comes when the supply of wood is exhausted, or from other causes a migration of the indefatigable workers occurs. If no exceptional freshet or waterspout sweep them away, the dams soon become part of the soil. Earth and vegetable matter gradually accumulate, and the beaver-ponds, no longer cleared of rubbish by their constructors, slowly silt up, turning first into marshy expanses, and then gradually into firm perfectly level meadow-land of the richest alluvial soil, on which flourishes sod of a beautifully close and silken texture, rivalling the famous glacier meadows in the sierras, which, according to King, presumably occupy the site of glacier lakes.

CHAPTER X.

WINTER CAMPS AND INDIAN CAMPS.

Life in a dug-out—Our Indian neighbours—Hunting *dead* deer—Our relations—A precipitate return—An Indian episode—A reservation—Two misunderstandings—The Indian languages—Parting with my men—A cold drive—Civilization—Relapsing into semi-savagery: its benefits.

ONCE or twice in these pages mention has been made of *dug-outs*. I happen to write these lines in one of these subterranean abodes, so the information I have to give comes from the first hand. To give the reader an idea of the construction and *mise-en-scene* of a *dug-out*, let him imagine a big Cheshire cheese divided in halves, the two surfaces of the cut moved slightly apart to represent the perpendicular loam banks of a nameless creek. In one of the walls, at its base, cut a square hole, not quite as high as it is long and broad. In front of this opening pile up bread crumbs in lieu of stones plastered with mud, leaving but a small aperture by which to creep in and out; and the reader will have before him a faithful miniature model of a *dug-out*.

It will be seen that, while its construction is simple, its space, some ten by nine feet, is somewhat confined to house four men, two dogs, a dozen or more saddles and pack-saddles, the stores, sundry shooting-irons, two dozen beaver traps, bales of fur, and trifles too numerous to mention, all of which have to find shelter in this Rocky Mountain Welbeck Abbey, where the famous large Gothic hall, the great dining-room, the ball-room, the drawing-room, the riding-school, the miles of subterranean passages, and the rest of its wonders, are all thrown into one, and sight-seeing can be done without moving from your robe bed or gunpowder-keg seat. For the reader must not forget that this narrow space is at once sitting-room, bedchamber, kitchen, harness, and gunroom; that the beds, consisting of bear and buffalo skins, have to be spread where the tablecloth, a waterproof sheet, was laid; that the hole in the doorway, where the smoke ought to go out, is continually getting blocked by snow, and hence that a recumbent position is, as long as the fire burns, the only one where you do no more than cry and cough, the more being death from suffocation. He can picture to himself the amenities of life while a snowstorm is raging without, and probably consider my invitation to "creep in" (I cannot say "walk in") the height of presumption. But Western manners, while hearty and full of welcome to the stranger, are lacking in patrician polish; so make yourself at home, and take a seat—or rather, stretch yourself with smoking-room *abandon* on yonder pile of fur robes; for the only chair-like article in our dwelling, the powder keg, is occupied by a busy author, plying his pen in front of a novel species of camp writing-table, made of the horns of a wapiti, the end prongs stuck in the ground, and a piece of dry, raw hide stretched across the middle tines, in lieu of the green-baize-covered and blotting-pad-supplied article. Our electric

Brush-light is furnished by a "devil," a shallow, iron basin filled with elk tallow, with a rope-end as wick.

An eight days' heavy snow hurricane is a very stern truth-teller, and makes us for the moment forget that our habitation's chief merits—warmth in winter and coolness in summer—are amply counterbalanced by its failings, its uncommonly annoying dust-producing qualities, and such minor disadvantages as the fact that it is hardly ever clear of the smoke produced by the open fire in the centre of the floor, and that, on account of its smallness, it is apt to crowd the "outfit."

It is the latter half of November, and the locality a canyon in the unexplored Sierra Soshoné; altitude 8000 feet; surroundings, a white pall that covers peak and forest, lake and gulch; thermometer 35° below zero Fahr.; distance to the next white man's habitation, 105 miles; date of the newest newspaper, September 2. For nearly half a year our eyes have not feasted on a civilized female face; last news from the outside world, 95° Fahr. in the shade in New York.

It would be idle to describe how all the outfit found room in this box-like home. It is not the first or the second time, but perhaps by the experience of a dozen trials, that you and your men succeed in getting everything into it. To store the flour sacks where no driving snow can get at them; to pile the saddles and the bales of valuable beaver, otter, and grey wolves' skins upon each other without their toppling over; to put your coffee and sugar where the ever-falling dust from your loam roof cannot find them; to hang up the wet garments and soaking saddle blankets where they are least in the way; to find room for the cooking-utensils and the water-bucket; to discover a snug corner for the dogs; and, finally, to plan out space enough for yourself and the men to move about in—this, and a lot more, can only be learnt by long experience, no easier to acquire and no less useful than the knack of making a dug-out with but one spade and one pick, with the ground frozen to the consistency of lead, and a snowstorm just setting in preceded by an intensely cold wind freezing out of the shivering snow-soaked mortals almost the last vital spark. If you still add that the "boss" or master is afflicted with *cacoëthes scribendi,* or, as his buffalo-coated companions put it, "is kinder partial to ink-slinging"—the *raison d'être* of aforesaid stag's-head writing-table, and the somewhat riskful position of the powder keg, containing more than sufficient to send the whole shebang with Jack-in-the-box-like effect to kingdom come—the public will appreciate, I am of course vain enough to suppose, the value of lines penned, as these are, under such peculiar circumstances and among not less peculiar surroundings, and jotted down not with an ordinary pen, but with the self-trimmed quill of a big eagle, and with ink made not as other mortals' is, but of vermilion *paint* diluted with water.

Outside the *dug-out,* if you dare put your nose out of the entrance hole, which is covered curtain-like by an elk-skin, the snow hurricane is howling, and from the gaunt giant cottonwood-trees that line the creek, massive branches are dismally rattling down. How lucky we are; how fortunate we must consider ourselves in our warm dug-out, sheltered from snow and cold! Look yonder at that patch of leafless willows, behind which our poor horses are huddled together, their heads low, and their flanks gaunt with hunger. Poor faithful brutes, they have had of late some terribly rough times—long marches through deep snow, heavy packs, and little food; for the winter in these regions set in unprecedently early, and with unprecedented vigour. With snow two feet deep, and continual storms such as none of my men had ever before experienced, the sun-dried buffalo grass could not be got at very easily by the patiently-pawing animals; in fact, many a night have the poor beasts passed huddled together behind sheltering rocks or bunches of willow, not daring to stir out into the open where the scanty grass grew. More than surprising is the wonderful stamina of these animals. Reared in the country, they have never seen the inside of a stable, and know not what grain is. The cold has, therefore, to be of the very severest to prevent them seeking their wonted pasturage. I was out the preceding winter, travelling with the same horses and two of the men; but though in the opinion of Westerners the winter of 1879-80 was a bad one, it could not compare with the extremes of that following. November, especially the latter part of the month, was particularly severe; and on six different occasions did the mercury congeal in my thermometer, which it does only at 71° of frost. At that time, too, we had no warm *dug-out*, and not even a tent, to shelter us, but had to "sleep out," with nothing but our robes and sail-cloth bed covers to protect us against the exceptional inclemencies of the weather; for though we had a tent with us part of the time, the gales sweeping over the barren highlands through which we were then travelling were far too severe to allow us to put it up; while, if the hurricane did moderate, we were generally so dead beat when at a late hour we pitched our camp, that nothing but the most imperative necessity could summon us to activity. To shovel snow for hours at a time, or to wield the heavy axe in relays, breaking trails through the dense expanse of dead timber, where trunks, fortunately of no very great size, lie thick across and over each other, is a time-robbing and most fatiguing job.

As I have said, an "eight-dayer" was raging outside, and we were beginning to doubt very strongly whether the majority of our horses could live through the ordeal. Poor things! we had nothing to give them. Flour was running very low with us, and that was about all we did have, save some sugar and coffee.

Quite close to us there was camped a large hunting-party of Soshonés, who, in small batches of five or six *bucks*, were in the habit of dropping in on friendly visits. We were on the best of terms, for since they had discovered that it was easier to hunt dead deer than live ones, I had saved them a lot of precious Sharp and Winchester repeating-rifle ammunition. When I shot anything they knew they were welcome to the most of the meat, and to what they were particularly anxious to secure, namely, "buckskin," which with them, dressed in different manners, is quite as essential as linen, cotton fabrics, and leather are to more civilized people. The Indians of the United States as a rule are very indifferent shots with the rifle, and to see three or four *bucks* hunting, or rather running, Wapiti or Mule-deer is a very ludicrous sight, disillusioning all one's romantic notions about Indian Nimrodship. With the bow and arrow it was something else; there was no report—in which, it must be mentioned, they all take a boyish delight—and of course they had to approach game much closer, and do it in a very stealthy manner.

I never heard so much shooting and saw so little hitting as I did in the month we were right among these perfectly wild Indians. Often I have counted fifteen shots to one poor deer; and there would be more shouting and waving of arms, and riding at full split up and down the most amazingly steep slopes, than would supply an evening's entertainment at a circus. We had got to the place a day or two before the Indians, and found great herds of Wapiti and Mule-deer roaming over the isolated highlands. Wherever one looked there was game. A fortnight afterwards I was actually a whole day vainly endeavouring to replenish our larder. Then the storm and cold "snap" came, and for a week it was anything but pleasant to stir out. Through stress of weather game was pressed down from higher and more exposed regions, so that when we could again pursue our various duties and pleasures there was a fresh supply of buckskin.

Some of the Indians were great fun. I remember particularly one or two, *i.e.* Old Secundum, a podgy old pasha, with as wonderful an assortment of squaws and papooses, ponies and dogs, bits of civilized finery of the most outlandish nature, and Indian curios, as you could wish to meet. He was a vain old Indian, and one of our best customers for *paint;* and moreover, he had been bitten by the white man's love for trading. Day after day the old dog would come slouching down to our *dug-out,* and after a friendly "how how" sit down at our camp fireside, and give us an amicable grin all round. Then the heavy blanket that shrouded the portly form of the old gentleman would be unfolded, and there would be produced some article for "heap trade." He would proceed to inform us that the "man with the split body" (that being my name with the Indians) had "heap paint,"[1] but "Secundum had heap beaver skin," and so the trade would commence. When his few English words failed him, and our Soshoné gave out, and finger-talk provided no aid, then would commence the tug of the trade, and many a hearty laugh on our part and a stoical grin on his would enliven the dreary hours.

They were all well-behaved Indians—some, it is true, more so than others. Thus, for instance, a few of the *bucks* made a practice of coming regularly at meal times, the coffee, of which they are passionately fond, being the main attraction. But most of them would just peep in, and if they saw that we were at our dinner they would wait outside till we had done. In the eyes of my men, who were poisoning wolves, they were, however, arrant thieves, for they habitually followed their tracks and picked up the poisoned bait, using it for their own purposes in another part of the country. There were a great many wolves, the common as well as the far larger and more valuable grey or silver species, about; hence long "strings" of poison [2] would be laid by the men; but generally by the following morning they had all mysteriously disappeared,

---

[1] *Heap*, signifying much, is one of the few English words nearly all Indians know. I once heard of a ludicrous application. Walking up to where one of the commanding officers, with his wife—a very stout lady—was standing, a reservation Indian addressed them, with the usual greeting: "How how," and presently, without any further introduction, remarked, pointing pointblank at the lady: "That *heap heap* squaw!"

[2] There are two ways of using poison (strychnine); either to poison a whole carcass, or to take a number of medium-sized chunks of meat, poison each, and while riding along, drop piece after piece about a hundred yards between each. This latter is called stringing poison.

and no victims were to be seen. Watching the men as they laid it, it was easy enough for the Indians to follow, and remove the bait to other places which they alone knew.

Speaking of poison, I may as well here mention, that under circumstances it proves a more profitable, and always a more useful occupation, than trapping. Wolves do an enormous amount of damage to game; indeed, the big grey wolf is quite a formidable fellow to look at (weighing fifty and sixty pounds), though it never troubles human beings. In frontier country nearer civilization, they commit great ravages among the calves, so that all the Territorial legislatures pay head-money for wolves, varying from three to six shillings. In Wyoming it was then four shillings ($1); and as the skin besides is worth, of the common wolf four shillings, and of the grey twelve shillings, a big haul of wolf-skins is quite as profitable a catch as trapping beaver, which is a far more uncertain business. In the different Territories the head-money used to be paid not on the same, but on different trophies. Thus in Wyoming the right fore-paw had to be produced; in Colorado, the scalp with the two ears; in others the left fore-paw, and formerly also the tail. Stories are told of unscrupulous old trappers who got head-money twice or three times over on one animal, by presenting the scalp in one, the paw in the other, and the tail in the third Territory, or by turning the left front-paw into a right front-paw, by dexterously skinning it and transferring the "dewclaw," or false claw, from the right to the left side, and then drawing the skin again over it, effectually hiding, particularly in a dried condition, all traces of the doctoring. Where wolves are "thick," *i.e.* where there are many, both methods of applying the strychnine are employed. Now and again more than a dozen wolves (the men once got sixteen) will be found round one carcass. Death, particularly if the stomach is empty, which is mostly the case, is very rapid. On moonlight nights I have on one or two occasions watched the action of the poison. It is as rapid as strangulation, hence on the whole is less cruel than shooting, for there are no wounded and crippled to die a lingering death.

Indians—to return to them again—are very curious, and my Express rifle was an object of great interest, affording us vast amusement on the two or three occasions that I let them try it, for by a little artifice I managed it so that both barrels went off simultaneously, producing an immense recoil sufficient to knock down a grizzly;[3] and to see a stoical straight-backed old *buck* sent a clean summersault backward was too ludicrous a sight, and only to be likened to a pompous old alderman, clothed in a breech clout, and an old blanket tightly drawn about his back, shrouding, but not hiding his well-developed form, suddenly turning head over heels. As the victim picked himself up—entirely ignorant, of course, of the trick—with all the inbred seriousness of his race he would pronounce the Express, the "heap boss gun of the man with the split body to be big medicine." A similar notable reputation for "big medicine" I once gained by administering to a

---

[3] Both triggers could be set to hair triggers, and by firing one barrel while the other was set, the concussion would make it go off too, the lightness of the rifle and the double charge of about eleven drachms, or about 310 grains of powder, producing an overwhelmingly formidable recoil. Through inadvertence I tried it on myself once or twice, and it knocked me clean out of my saddle, much to the astonishment of Boreas.

very livery-looking Arrappahoe a gigantic dose of six pills.

Another Soshoné, a good-looking young *buck,* called "Powder in the Hand" by his comrades, though he had another quite unpronounceable Indian name, managed to fool us in good style. He had served on a short Indian campaign as assistant scout to some troops, and had learnt English, not only to understand it, but to speak it. When we first saw him he shook his head in the usual fashion when I addressed him in English, letting it appear as if he understood not a single word of it. For a fortnight he had been constantly coming round to us, generally when there was some trade or other on, and on one or two occasions I noticed that secret signs passed between him and his companion, whoever it happened to be, and that always on these occasions the little trade between the men and the Indians was a stiff one, convincing me that he understood English. A little catch I prepared for him proved successful, and "Powder in the hand" was found to be quite a scholar. Indians are very apt to hide their knowledge of English if they think it can serve them; and caution in this respect under certain circumstances is very advisable.

Indian philosophy is of a primitive, though not unpractical character. It consists, so far as his daily life is concerned, in the dogma of, *I want it,* or *I don't want it.* If he wants a thing he will do his best, give almost his all, risk his own skin, and tell the greatest lies, to acquire it. If he is short of ammunition when setting out on his "fall," or winter hunt, he will trade a handsome Indian-worked buffalo robe, worth at least 3*l.*, for cartridges worth as many sixpences. When he comes back from his hunt, a cupful of coffee or sugar will often obtain the same trade. A horse worth 10*l.*, which at the beginning of the hunt he would not give you for three times that amount of money in the most cherished articles of trade, he will give you for less than a tenth on his return. This is the main reason why Indians, who often own a number of valuable horses, never seem to accumulate wealth in kind. Though the word *nomadic* Indian is, with one or two exceptions, a grossly misapplied term for the Aborigines of North America, this getting rid, at a ruinous loss, of anything and everything when they no longer have immediate use for it, and paying exorbitantly for what, at the moment, they may happen to want, is yet a characteristic of all nomadic races, and is opposed to all principles of mature civilization.

While among the Soshonés, old Secundum brought us rather unpleasant news, namely, that the neighbouring tribe of Arrappahoes were on the war-path—news which one of his *bucks* had brought him, and which seemed to be confirmed by the fact of a party of Crow Indians having passed us a short time before on their way to Black-Coal, the Arrappahoe chief, with some fresh Sioux scalps as an intertribal offering to secure the co-operation of him and his tribe. As our course to the nearest Fort, the only way to get out of the mountain wilderness we were in, lay for nearly a hundred miles through the Arrappahoe hunting country, the outlook was not the very pleasantest. The truth, however, was not as bad as the alarm, though it precipitated our return. On the tenth day, after the most trying short journey that I ever remember, we at last sighted the snowed-up Fort Washakie, which we had left the preceding July, when the thermometer was up in the nineties. The cold was very great, quite equal to that of the Arctic regions; worse still was the wind, requiring constant care to prevent frostbite. And as at the time we had no tent, and simply slept on and under our buffalo robes on the snow, the hardships of that trip were, quite in consequence of the unprecedented cold and storms, of an unusual kind.

To one incident of these ten days I would desire to refer, as showing the Indian character and the incredibly miserable position of the squaws, upon which so many writers have dilated. We were within a day or two's travel of the Fort, and late at night, after a perishingly cold ride, reached the banks of the Big Wind River, at one of the few fords, intending to cross it as best we could the following morning. We were saddling up our wretched, emaciated horses at an early hour of the terribly cold morning—during the night the mercury had congealed in my thermometer, so that there must have been, at the least, seventy-one degrees of frost, and the dismal aspect of the snow-clad unutterably dreary bad-land scenery needed not the fine powdery snow driving before the wind to make it peculiarly depressing—when an Indian with his squaw, driving before them some ten or twelve miserably thin horses, packed with their usual *lares et penates*, passed us, and proceeded to cross the river. As we thought it likely that they knew the exact spot of the ford, I went to watch them take the water.

It was about as nasty a crossing as ever I saw. The Wind River is at all times a very dangerous stream, for its great fall and the vast volume of water that fills it in early summer, change the bed from year to

T

year—nay, from month to month. Where you were able to ford in September, you will find in October deep water and most dangerous under-currents or quicksands. Now, though it was at the lowest, the ice had raised fresh obstacles. Fancy a river as broad as the Thames at Hampton Court running in the centre as swift as a mill sluice, so rapid that even the Arctic cold could not subdue it, while on both sides, where it ran slower, ice to a thickness of at least eighteen inches or two feet had been formed. Standing on the brink of this bank of solid ice you had before you the gurgling, rushing, dark green current, in the shape of a gulf some forty yards in width, without the slightest clue as to its depth. It was, under the circumstances, as uninviting a plunge on this terribly cold day as could well be imagined. The squaw, a good-looking young creature, was ahead, astride of a pony, while the *buck* was in the rear, "whooping" the animals along at a fast pace. In her arms, suspended by a broad band, she held a miserable morsel of humanity, wrapped in a wolf skin; it was a baby, apparently only a week or two old.[4] On getting on to the firm ice she slackened up, proceeding at a walk, for it was very slippery. On getting close to the brink of the yawning gulf of water she evidently began to be afraid, and pulling up her pony, looked back at her lord and master with a pleading look—quite merited by the aspect of the river in front of her, gurgling and splashing past her with great velocity. But there was little chivalry or mercy in the stolid-faced Arrappahoe *buck*. Without saying a word, he simply

---

[4] Quite young babies are held in the arms, for obvious reasons, while when they are a few months old they are strapped to a small board and carried by the mothers on their backs.

stretched out his arm in a commanding field-marshal-like gesture, and the wretched woman knew she had to proceed. Laying her punishing "quirt" or whip about her shrinking pony, she forced him to plunge from the ice step into the current. But the water was deeper than she expected, and the horse turned a summersault and was swept away by the rushing water. The wretched woman had, of course, lost her seat, and though she had still hold of the reins, there was every chance of her getting drowned. With a yell the *buck* had run his horse at full speed (it was unshod of course, as all Indian ponies are) along the ice bank, and long before I could reach the bend of the river, where I fancied I could aid her, he was there, and amid a volley of Arrappahoe helped the squaw out—by this time she had let go of the reins—and taking her up on his own horse, plunged again into the river, and in two or three minutes had got across safely. On reaching the opposite bank, she slid down from the horse; while he, apparently far more anxious about the pony than on her account, galloped down the stream, and finally managed to get out the struggling horse at a point where there was no ice to speak of on the pebble-strewn bank. The whole thing was over in seven or eight minutes, but it was sufficiently long to turn the poor woman, who was fondling the screaming baby, into a column of ice, and by the time the rest of the ponies were got across by the buck, the folds of the heavy blanket—her only clothing except a buckskin under-garment—were frozen so stiff as to impede her movements when she remounted her pony to proceed to some brushwood, where rising smoke soon showed that the miserable creature was drying or changing her blanket toilet.

When, three or four hours later—for we were more cautious in selecting a ford, though the water even then came up to our saddles—we passed the place where the Indians had halted, they had already left, I suppose not much the worse for that bath with the thermometer down to fifty degrees of frost. Frederick the Great's dictum, *Il faut traiter son corps en canaille*, is, as we have seen, very generally acted upon by these hardy tribes of the North-West.

On reaching the fort—the first habitation I had seen for five months—we were hailed, by those who knew that we still were out, as risen from the dead.

I have been so often asked what an Indian "reservation" is, that I fancy a very brief explanation of this term will be useful. A reservation is a vast tract of country "given" to, *i.e.* secured by solemn treaty to, one or more tribes. On this land whites are *supposed* not to mine, or settle, or build houses, or hunt or trap game. There are laws to this effect; but as the land is a perfect wilderness, and the boundaries are on paper or on maps, and those papers or maps are securely locked up in the Indian Office at Washington, and as, finally, there is nobody deputed to see to the enforcement of this law, the military forces not being used for this purpose, nothing but the fear of a sudden Indian rising can restrain the white man, be he mining prospector, rancheman, hunter, or trapper, from encroaching upon the red man's property leading—for frontiersmen like some risk—to reprisals and counter-reprisals. This, together with the concomitant results of nefarious cheating on the part of white man generally, is, in broad outline, the usual cause of the frequent Indian wars—a topic upon which very nearly all authors on the West have theorized. With the reader's permission I will make an exception.

The Washakie (or Soshoné, or Snake Indian) reservation is as large as a good-sized kingdom. The Agency, where reside the few Government officials whose business it is to look after the Indians, and carry out the stipulations of the treaty in the way of distributing blankets, flour, &c., among the tribe, is in the centre, protected by the Fort; and well may it be protected, at least among the few remaining wild tribes, for the residents are usually the first to fall victims to a sudden outbreak. Only the year before, at the next reservation, that of the Utes, the whole Agency was murdered, and the females carried off. The reservation I am speaking of is shared by the two tribes—the Soshonés and the Arrappahoes. The former have long been a very peaceful tribe, chiefly owing, it must be mentioned, to the sage advice of their old chief—the famous Washakie, in appearance one of the most characteristic patriarchal braves of the old school. Since 1863, when the tribe experienced a severe "whipping" at the hands of the troops, white man has not been injured by them. The Arrappahoes, on the contrary, with whom they are not on the best of terms, are to-day, next to the Appaches of the South, the most unsettled and dangerous of the Redskins. Only the year before, my party had been made aware of this in an unpleasant manner. However, this time, owing to several circumstances, we remained on good "how how" terms with the young *bucks*, who, as a rule, are the most eager to go out a' harvesting glory and solitary white men's hair.

The greater part of the year only a small portion of the two tribes, mostly the old and decrepit, are near the

Agency, their skin or canvas teeppees or tentlike wigwams dotting the broad mountain-girt Plain surrounding the Agency.

Owing to the severity of the weather we found on reaching Washakie the greater portion of the Indians camped in the immediate neighbourhood; among them *Black Coal*,[5] the Arrappahoe chief, with a portion of his tribe, just in from their fall or winter hunt, brought to an early termination by the exceptional cold.

Many of the younger *bucks* had, however, absented themselves on French leave, and were now supposed to be engaged in a miniature war of their own, though nothing certain was known. Having a lot of *paint* left, and wanting some Indian trifles to take home with me, I had my presence announced to *Black Coal*, and received a polite *invite* to his big teeppee or wigwam. I knew him from a former occasion, but was curious to see him in his chieftain's home. The Arrappahoe language is the most difficult of all Indian tongues; indeed, it is said that two Arrappahoes cannot perfectly understand each other in the dark—that is, without the aid of finger talk, or language of signs common to nearly all Indians of North America, and of which all genuine trappers understand the rudiments. *Black Coal*—whose name is derived from the circumstance that after a sanguinary victory over the Utes, when he lost two or three fingers and received other wounds, he, in commemoration, wallowed naked in the hot ashes of the enemy's camp fires until he was black as coal—is not only an uncommonly intelligent Indian, but a remarkably jealous

[5] One of *Harper's* for 1881 (either March or April), contained an able account of this tribe, and had some capital and exceptionally good likenesses of Black Coal and other subchiefs.

one. The morals of his tribe are, in strong contrast to those of the Soshoné, notoriously bad. The squaws when quite young are not quite as repulsive-looking as Indian females generally are, and one or two I saw were swarthy beauties with piercing black eyes—a feature which marks also the men in an unusually prominent manner. There is a peculiar steel-blue glitter about the piercing and sloe-black eyes of Arrappahoes that gives them an uncommonly unpleasant and ferocious look, quite wicked enough without the fire of war and murder lighting them up. I met several young *bucks* who possessed this steely glitter to such a degree that it acted on me like a snake-charmer's glance. I could not take my eyes off theirs.

Black Coal received me in the usual stoical Indian fashion. He was alone in the big chief's teeppee with two of his favourite squaws—very superior personages. When he saw my parcel of *paints* his face became more lively. I had opened the waterproof covering, displaying the Seidlitz-powder-shaped papers of vermilion; and evidently the temptation was too great, for he suddenly reached over, took up several, and put them into the pocket of his chieftain's coat—an old soldier's cape. Now to allow this would have been madness, for if ever a white man lets a wild Indian possess himself of the proverbial finger, he is very apt to want not only the hand, but also the body of the finger's owner, diffidence being a word the sense of which is quite unknown to the Indian. Therefore had I permitted this barefaced annexation to go unchallenged, I might have passed a bad quarter of an hour at Mr. Black Coal's hands. Understanding English very fairly, I soon convinced him, chiefly, I am inclined to think, by placing my cocked Colt in my lap—we were sitting on mats round the fire on the floor in the centre of the wigwam—that the paint *had* to be returned. Presently it was. Then the trade I had come for commenced, and in exchange for a lot of little trifles of Indian workmanship I got rid of all my *paints* but two. After our little misunderstanding at the commencement of the interview, I did not wish to appear shabby; so just before rising to leave I threw the remaining two *paints* into the laps of the two squaws sitting opposite to me, who with eager eyes had followed every movement, for I suppose their feminine vanity had never been gratified with the sight of so many *paints*, which are as highly prized by them as by their lords. This act, done in the thoughtless heedlessness of the moment, might easily have cost me very dear, for I could not have given the chief deadlier insult than by thus impugning the good fame of his queenly squaws, the simple ethics of the Indian comprehending no other solution of my act than one to which the common squaws of the tribe were constantly subjected.[6] With one bound he was on his legs, and I am convinced, had not my revolver happened to be still lying at my side, his clutch would have been at my throat the next instant. As it was, he raised himself to his full height, his eyes glistening with anger, and stretching his right arm out in the most imperious manner, he pointed with it to the entrance, and exclaimed, with unmistakable force, "Go!" And I went. Outside when the full ludicrousness of the situation burst upon me, I enjoyed a good laugh—but it was after I had put myself beyond Winchester rifle range.

[6] The presence of several hundred soldiers, mostly unmarried men, in the Fort, contributed, as is generally the case, to the exceedingly bad state of morality among the Arrappahoes.

That day was fated to be one of misunderstandings. While strolling through the reservation, where the news of a *paint* Crœsus had spread, bringing me into contact with other Arrappahoes who were desirous of trading, my attention was drawn to a huge old Indian warrior. Of very commanding presence, unusually tall, and of corresponding physical development, he was more like what fancy generally leads one to suppose the Indians à la Cooper to be, than any specimen I had ever seen. He was an under chief—I forget his name—and, to judge from the very numerous scars of arrow, knife, and bullet on his body and limbs, he had seen a vast deal of fighting. He was a particularly fierce-looking old Arrappahoe; his eagle nose, one of the distinguishing features of his tribe, the ghastly streaks of bright vermilion on his face, and that deadly steely glisten in his eyes, gave his physiognomy a look that would probably haunt a nervous person. I had exchanged civilities with this old fellow, and he was now finishing the stump of my cigar, when I was tempted to enter upon a more extended conversation, carried on in the sign language, at which I am no great proficient. The old fellow's chin was distinguished by a few hairs that started from his massive under-jaw in a very desultory hog-bristly fashion. Struck with this—Indians have, as I need hardly say, no beards—I was desirous to know the cause of this phenomenon. It was not an easy phrase to frame in the sign manual language, and unfortunately instead of saying, as I afterwards learnt, " How has it come to pass that the bravest of the brave, the man of all men, the dearest friend I have among the ' good hearts,' [7]

---

[7] The Arrappahoes call themselves " The Good Hearts," a meaning which is designated by touching the left breast. Every tribe has its

has grown such a flowing beard?" (if I remember rightly, I counted seventeen bristles)—instead of this, I say, I sign-talked "that his face was like a young maiden's, and his heart that of an old squaw"—about the most mortally offensive affront I could have offered him. Flinging the cigar stump, the pipe of peace, aside, he started up, and if ever business shone in a man's eye, it was in that Indian's. Very fortunately for me, I was on this occasion not alone, for just previously a young Arrappahoe, whom we had met out hunting, and whose good will I had secured by a few little presents, had joined me. I left him to explain matters, and vowed I would henceforth confine myself to such sign manuals as I was perfectly sure of—a piece of advice I would humbly offer also to others.

Of the languages of the North American Indians little is known, but of quite late years several men of science have devoted a good deal of attention to this subject. Foremost among them stand the names of the indefatigable Powell, Trumbull, Colonel Gibbs, and other philologists. The perusal of their most interesting works filled-in many puzzling voids in my own far more modest acquaintance with the subject. Confining myself to a most brief epitome of the most striking facts, I shall first dwell on the self-interpreting definition of all Indian names.

Mills defines a proper name to be a mere mark put upon an individual or a place, and of which it is the characteristic property to be *destitute of meaning*. As has been pointed out, we call a man Williams or Robinson

own Indian name; thus the Soshonés are known as "Long Hairs," and if you want to express this name, you pass both your hands from the ears down to the breast, as if passing the long plaited tresses worn by that tribe through your hands.

just as we put a number on a policeman's collar or turn the personality of an hotel visitor into No. 99 or 999.

Indian names, on the contrary, *describe* the locality, sometimes *topographically* or *historically*, or indicate one of the *natural products* or *peculiarities* of the place.

While one tribe calls the beaver " the animal that fells trees," another terms it " the beast that puts its head out of the water," while a third has it as " the sharp-toothed swimmer." The Utes call the bear, " the seizer," or " the hugger." The Senecas speak of *North* as the place " where the sun never goes."

Thus *horse*, which in our language tells us nothing about the animal it names, is expressed by names indicating " the beast that carries on his back a living burden," or the " creature whose hoofs are all solid," or the " wonderful domestic animal introduced by white man." Colonel Gibbs[8] gives some interesting instances of the analysis of numerals in the Indian language often resembling those of the Eskimo, who express, for instance, *twenty* by *one man, i.e.* all fingers and toes. Regarding concrete nouns, the Indian languages are even more definite in their expression. The Indian never kneels; so when Elliot translates *kneeling* (Mark i. 40), the word which he was compelled to form fills a line, and numbers eleven syllables; which again, to render into English require for its accurate interpretation eight or ten English words.

In the Indian languages economy of speech is not practised, though we must not mistake economy of utterance for economy of thought; the first has to do with the

---

[8] "Instructions for research relative to the Ethnology and Philology of America, prepared by the Smithsonian Institute."

phonetic constitution of words, the latter with the development of sentences.

Mr. Powell gives an instance in the Ponca language. If one of this tribe wants to say that a man killed a rabbit, he would have to express himself thus:—The man, he, one animate (not dead) standing (in the nominative case) purposely killed by shooting an arrow, the rabbit, he, the one, animate, sitting (in the objective case).

In some Indian languages there are certain words used for the names of children given them in the order of their birth, so that the child's name indicates this order.

One of the most singular features, says Mr. Powell, of the Indian languages, is the fact that the verb often includes within itself subject, direct object, qualifier and relation-idea—or in other words, that the Indian verbs include within themselves meanings which in English are expressed by adverbs and adverbial phrases and clauses. Thus the verb *to go* may be represented by a word signifying *go home,* or by another *go from home,* or *to go on foot,* or *to go up a river,* or still another, *to go in a canoe.*

In the Eastern, or Atlantic regions, nearly all the geographical names have become strangely mutilated, and, as Mr. Trumbull remarks, in view of "the Indian polysyntheses, with their frequent gutturals and nasals, it is hardly possible to be different. The river *Swatara* becomes: 'Sweet Arrow,' the *Popoagie:* 'Proposure,' the *Potopaco:* 'Port Tobacco.' *Nama' anki* (the place for fish) passes through 'Namurack,' 'Namalake,' and finally becomes: 'May Luck.' *Moskitu-anke* (grass-land) is metamorphosed into: 'Mosquito Hawk.' The Canadian Jay, better known as 'Whiskey Jack,' derives its origin from *Ouishcatcha*." Sometimes, as is remarked in the same Report, Etymology overreaches itself by regarding an aboriginal name as the corrupt form of a foreign one. Thus the *Maskalongé*, or 'great long nose' of the St. Lawrence river, has been reputed of French origin—*masque élongé*; and ' *Sagackomi*,' the Indian name for a substitute for tobacco, has been derived from *sac-à-commis*, on account of the Hudson's Bay officers carrying it in bags for smoking, as Sir John Richardson believed (Arctic Exped. ii. 303). "It was left for the ingenuity of a Westminster Reviewer to discover that barbecue (a wooden frame or grille for roasting meat) might be a corruption of the French *barbe à queue, i.e.* ' from snout to tail '—a suggestion which, it appears, has found favour with lexicographers."

There is a wonderful multiplicity of distinct languages and subordinate dialects among the Indian tribes. Thus among the Snake Indians, of which tribe the Soshonés are a branch, seven perfectly different languages are spoken. Under these circumstances the sign manuals fill a decided want. Somehow its interpreting meanings are known throughout the West; and I am informed by persons who have been among the Appaches, in the extreme south of the States, that the signs used by them are the same as are understood by the Flatheads in the northernmost portions of the country, 2000 miles intervening between them. The syntactic and descriptive construction of all Indian languages facilitates, of course, communication by sign manual. It is possible to describe by signs a certain place as the spot " where near big caves the elk shed their horns and the rocks are red," a locality which we, perhaps, would call " Clark's Fork," or " Carson Basin."

The weather continuing excessively severe, and our horses, notwithstanding their loads, consisting mostly of my antlers and heads, had been reduced to a minimum—obliging me with much heartburning to throw aside many grand trophies—being at the last stage of emaciation, I decided, two days after leaving Fort Washakie, to bring our trip to a temporary termination. While the men were to proceed to their winter-quarters to await my return, I availed myself of the mail sleigh conveying despatches and mail from the fort to the nearest U.P. station, 155 miles south of us, from whence I intended to proceed to Salt Lake City, there to await more favourable weather to take up my interrupted journey with them into the Colorado River country. But the winter of 1880-1 was one that knocked on the head all my plans, for not only was my little pack-train rendered entirely *hors de combat*, several of the horses having perished, but even had they been fresh animals they could not have crossed the snow-hurricane-swept 250 miles of bad-land country intervening between their home and the head canyons of the river I desired to visit, and of which I shall have to speak in the next chapter.

I had an intensely cold sleigh-ride before me, across two great barren passes, one of them 10,000 feet above the sea, and on the whole I had every reason to congratulate myself that the journey from the Fort to the railway took me only five days (in summer it is covered in thirty-six hours). In all my experience of sleigh-driving, to me the pleasantest manner of travel, they certainly occupy a prominent place. Severe snowstorms had snowed up the two regular mail sleighs, obliging the drivers to cut loose the horses and abandon them, they themselves escaping in both cases in a badly frostbitten condition, from which

I heard the one never recovered. My own journey had therefore to be performed in a very primitive vehicle, knocked together in a forenoon. The driver and I sat but a few inches over the snow (where it was beaten down) on a platform consisting of a few packing-case boards nailed across the runners, the mail sack as a seat, and several buffalo robes to cover us. While crossing drifts, great billows of powdery snow would close over us. The drivers changed twice a day, while fresh horses were put in every twelve or fifteen miles, the miserable log shanties where the relays were stabled being—except two mining settlements, then completely snowed up—the only human habitation we passed on the whole weary hundred and fifty-five mile drive. The cold on these elevated steppes was of that dangerous kind that benumbed before one had an idea of its doing so. Added to the sixty or seventy degrees of frost, a high wind did its best to increase our sufferings; and as on the bleak mountain ridges we had to cross about Timberline snowdrifts thirty feet high would be formed by the hurricane in a quarter of an hour, there was also something of a risk; the high mail forfeits, and consequently good pay of the drivers, being the only reason that the mail service was not stopped altogether. The drivers on these terribly exposed routes are invariably good men; and the way the one who took me across the highest of the two passes managed to find his way in the blinding snowstorm, night falling fast, and nothing whatever to guide the horses or the driver, was very creditable. While I was crouching close up to him, my head covered by buffalo robes; he, poor fellow, with only a veil over his face, had to expose not only that but also his hands for seven hours. Now and again, when in his dry tone he would exclaim, "Boss, I guess my nose is friz (frostbitten) doggarned near off my face," I would relieve him, and let him occupy himself rubbing his nose and cheeks with snow under the shelter of the robes, while I took the ribbons. But notwithstanding I imagined myself fairly inured to cold, and I had two pair of gloves on my hands, the outer one of warm fur, half an hour's exposure made them so stiff that, however unwilling, I was forced to relinquish the reins. When finally, at midnight, we drew up at the log shanty where we passed the night, the 70 odd degrees of frost which the thermometer was then marking seemed more like 700. We were both frostbitten, and I shall carry mementoes of that and of the following day's cold about with me for my life.

The driver who took me the last stage of my journey into X—— was an amusing fellow. For all I know, the former ones might have been that too, but it was far too cold for them to show it or for me to find it out; but as the thermometer had "struck the twenties," and an Arctic-looking sun was doing its best to make things look brighter, conversation, helped on by an ample allowance of whiskey, cropped up apace. A mile or so outside of the city we crossed a small, shallow gulch, spanned by a rude bridge consisting of two cross-beams and seven or eight transversely-laid trees, the construction of which at the utmost could have cost six or seven dollars. Hardly were we on it, when down came the whole affair, and we were landed in some drifted snow at the bottom of the gully. As for me, it was the eleventh or twelfth upset on the drive; but inasmuch as, owing to the narrowness of the gulch, the horses very nearly came to lie upon us, it was the most unpleasant one of the lot. My driver took it even more stoically than I did, and jocularly remarked, "For a $700 bridge it oughter (ought to have) stood an extra cuss's heft (weight)!" We were indeed approaching civilization! for the structure which had given way under us had really cost the "city" that sum, owing, as I need hardly say, to gross jobbery. We had both escaped without the slightest injury—a circumstance which did not seem to please Joe, for, according to him, if you had any friends among the "bosses as were running the town, there was hefty money in that thar bridge" in the way of damages for a black eye or contused nose; and when we finally got our vehicle up the bank and found it whole, not a board or nail missing, it was in Joe's eyes "Just like his darned luck; might have got a hundred dollars out of the county."

A quarter of an hour later we rattled through the snow-imprisoned "city" of X——, and I was back in civilization.

The following was a bright December day; to me it seemed quite summerly, for the settlement lay very sheltered, and much lower than the steppes over which I had been travelling.

My cane-bottomed chair, tipped back at an angle; a pile of letters, and a bigger one of newspapers—the accumulation of four or five months[9]—lying on a chair near me; I was sitting on the platform in front of a certain

---

[9] Intending visitors to the West, it may be useful for them to know, should bear in mind, when ordering their letters to be forwarded, that a United States post-office regulation obliges the postmasters, if not instructed to the contrary, to return all letters that have remained unclaimed at their offices for thirty days, to the Chief Office at Washington, to be thence forwarded back to the senders.

railway hotel. So far as a warm bath, the barber, and civilized clothes could accomplish the metamorphosis, I was again a white man. But it was, at best, only a partial and outward change. Though the natives were walking about with cold-pinched faces, wrapped in furs, the heat of the rooms in the hotel seemed as unbearable to me as the ordinary costume of mankind appeared ludicrously elaborate, and, after the loose, though tattered and stained flannel and buckskin wardrobe, most uncomfortably confining. I felt as awkward and gawky as a schoolboy does the first time he appears in a swallow-tail coat. My shirt cuffs seemed too long, or too short; and having increased more than a stone in weight, there was just cause for my wriggling my head about, trying to ease the tight fit of a stand-up collar. Altogether I felt myself unpleasantly conspicuous; and the nameless tortures experienced by a man "walking out" a new suit of clothes for the first time, beset me. My linen looked uncommonly white, and contrasted with the chestnut tint of my face and neck. And why on earth did the passers-by stare so at me? I finally detected that it was for the very good reason that they could not quite understand why I sat sunning myself on that bitterly cold winter's day, in front of the hotel—a circumstance the editor of the local paper deemed, as I afterwards heard, sufficiently eccentric to furnish an item for his broad-sheet.

I was awaiting the West-bound express (it was on the Union Pacific line), but as the trains, in consequence of the unprecedented snowstorms, were running, not hours but whole days late—there is only one train each way every twenty-four hours on the great trans-Continental line—I had to wait thirty hours at X——.

While still busy with my correspondence the East-bound train, that four days previously had started from California, arrived. It was the first train that had been able to get thus far for the last forty-two hours, and the huge structure, drawn by two locomotives, as it slowly drew up at the station looked as if it had been to the North Pole regions and had burrowed its way through mountains of snow. Huge icicles festooned the outside of the cars, and big drifts of snow had accumulated on the platforms in front of the doors. The three or four palace-cars were well filled, for the train bore also the passengers and mails of the preceding one, which got snowed-up East of the Sierras. Dinner was awaiting them, and a motley, shivering crowd bustled into the ample dining-room of the hotel. It was of the usual cosmopolitan character: a couple of Japanese bigwigs on their way to join their Embassy, a few Chinese, jovial Californian millionaires, successful mining men who were going East in quest of "a good time." Frenchmen, Germans, and Italians, thronged past dainty waxen-complexioned Americaines, carefully muffled up in furs and wraps, as they stepped from the overheated interiors of the cars.

Over the crowd towered three tall young Englishmen, who, less in a hurry than the rest, stalked through the throng in a leisurely manner, with their hands stuck deep in the pockets of their loose shooting-coats. They were the first English faces I had seen for more than half a year. How familiar they seemed to me; how unmistakably English the long stride, the low laugh when they caught sight of the black gong-belabouring demon at the door of the hotel! Like the Pitcairn Islanders, who are so anxious to talk to a stranger that before he has time to ask how they are, they will say "Quite well, thank you," I wished to jump up and shake hands. But they were entire strangers to me, and I had to be satisfied with as close an examination of the exterior of my countrymen as could be crammed into a fleeting moment. None but those who have been in a similar position can know how your critical glance rests on the rough shooting-coat, on the broad-soled Glengarry stalking-shoes; and the question, *Who made that Tweed suit or those boots?* becomes one of moment. If the minute though unmistakable signs of workmanship convince you that the article in question is of London make, a smile of recognition mantles on your face. It does not take so much, after all, to bring out the mellow sides of human nature! Six months of a lonely life far from countrymen's faces will suffice to metamorphose the angry scowl, called up by your discovering that the man tripping up the Club-steps in front of you wears unmentionables of precisely the same pattern as yours, into a beaming smile of welcome.

While the passengers were dining, a gang of men was set to work to free the train of its load of ice and snow. In twenty minutes shovels and brooms had cleared off the white shroud, and the magnificent palace-cars shone forth in all their pristine grandeur of plate glass, polished metal, highly varnished wood, the outside shell of a luxurious velvet, mahogany, and silver-mounted interior. What a crass contrast did not the flimsy mushroom "city" of matchboard houses, uncouthly new, grotesquely tasteless, afford, as it lay there snow-buried and hurricane-swept in a desolate gorge on the great desert steppes 6000 feet over the sea, hardly more than ten years back the home of the cayote wolf and of the rattler. Two strips of steel had not only built the houses, but raised the desert sand-dune-girt hollow to the dignity of a wayside station on the great iron route circumnavigating the globe.

Slow and stately the two great massive monsters and their load glided out from the station; and as I watched the train swiftly disappear in the gathering gloom of the winter's afternoon, which sunk dull and grey on the unpicturesque and unreal scene before and around me, the mighty force of man's most wonderful invention came back to me with redoubled impressiveness. My backwood philosophising was presently disturbed by the courteous station-master, with whom I had struck up a cigar friendship. *He* looked upon steam and its power in a more practical light. "Big money on board that train, sir; 'r'kon not a cent less than twenty millions in dust, bones, and flesh." That "dust" meant gold dust or bullion, I knew; but "bones and flesh" were a mystery to me, which was presently cleared up without my being obliged to resort to questions, by being informed that Mr. C——, a very wealthy New Yorker, had *defuncted* in San Francisco, and his body was being "shipped home;" while three noted but live San Francisco millionaires were speeding eastwards—"filling the bill consisting of dust four, bones five, and flesh eleven millions."

As I take a short retrospective glance at those first days back in civilization, let the latter be even that of the Walkerhouse Hotel at Salt Lake City—than which, however, I know worse places—I become more and more convinced of the usefulness of man now and again returning to a savage state. Quite aside of its rejuvenescent effects, which, on returning to your fellow beings, endow the vapid pleasures of civilized existence with the attractions the tuck-shop had for you when still a schoolboy—though not unlike the sixth-form prefect whose recently donned *toga virilis* obliges him to eat his cake with the air with which we now take a Podophyllin pill—aside, I say, of all this, there are some downright practical results to be recorded by the traveller on his return from the wilds.

The trite old saying, *No man is a hero to his valet de chambre*, is never more true than in the West, where the valet has necessarily very multifarious duties, and uncomfortably many opportunities of making himself intimately acquainted with his master's vileness of temper and other unflattering characteristics. If the valet is worth his salt, he will, as the daily exigencies of a very rough life afford him ever-recurring chances, push himself into the confidence of his lord, till finally the robustly practical underling is boss of the city-worn swell—of course only metaphorically speaking, for I need hardly say I am here referring to the case of master and valet being personified in one and the same individual.

By turning temporarily a semi-savage you realize how civilization was gradually built up. As you look at the copper-coloured aborigines of North America, whose customs withal remind you of those of the Scythians as described by Herodotus, and you detect that the skin garments in which they are wrapt are fastened around them by precisely the same primitive thongs that hold together similar garments in which John the Baptist is clothed in Carlo Crivelli's great altarpiece painted more than four centuries ago, your inductive acumen notes that the red man has not yet reached that stage which makes pockets a necessity. Presently you discover, at the further expenditure of your ingenuity, that these self-same pockets of which for many centuries our race has made use, are, in reality, nothing but the savage's bags sewn on to the garments of our maturer understanding.

Lord Dunraven, in one of his most attractively-written papers on the West, very truly remarks, "it is the clothes that make the man," at least the man with whom our civilization has made us acquainted—"that the gentility of most men is contained in their shirt collars." Nothing will prove this more indisputably than a temporary relapse to semi-savagery in the wilds of the West, for it will show you that your hunter or your guide, or the next best cowboy, can under equalizing circumstances look decidedly more the gentleman than you, who have taken to a wild life only temporarily.

Of the more practically useful results let me mention, that while in your wild life you learn to do and to go without the most essential necessaries of your former luxurious existence, you realize how inflated are man's daily wants. When that valet of yours has once got the whip hand, or, to use a Westernism, has got the "bulge" of you, it will amuse you to observe how, as your journey extends from day to day, that *too much of a job* grows more frequent; and finally, when you do pull yourself up at the more than commonly outrageous neglect of some lifelong habit, you smile at your hero, and place a mark of approbation against Montesquieu's maxim, that what you can do yourself, *you* will do best.

CHAPTER XI.

CAMPS IN THE CANYONS OF THE COLORADO RIVER.

History of the Colorado and its exploration—First white explorers—Their perils—Our expedition—First view of the *Flaming Gorge*—A winter day in the Canyons—Grand surroundings—Horseshoe Canyon—Geological speculations.

UNLIKE the other great natural wonders of the North American continent, the Niagara Falls, the Yosemite Valley, the Yellowstone Park, the great Kentucky Caves—one and all the scene of a revolting trade in the charms of nature—there is yet left one in the Far West grander than the rest, which happily is not likely ever to become the vested property of a gang of 'cute Yankee guides, touts, and that ilk. I mean the famous canyons formed by the Colorado River. To-day these wonderful gorges, occupying at intervals more than 1000 miles of the course of the Colorado, and formed by walls which in some places reach a height of 6200 feet, are undoubtedly by far the deepest and the longest known; and, in view of certain signs in the geological formation of the as yet perfectly unexplored portions of the Himalayas, it is not likely, so authorities affirm, that the only locality where this American natural wonder might find a match can boast of fissures of as great or greater profundity.

Before I speak of a visit of exploration I paid to these canyons at a somewhat unusual season, namely, in midwinter, I would desire to revert shortly to the chief events in the recent history of this most interesting river. The Government of the United States, displaying a characteristic energy in the scientific exploration of the Western Territories—recognizing from the first the important influence of such work upon the early development of the mineral and other riches of these vast domains—made the thorough exploration of the Colorado River the subject of one of its most interesting official reports. These documents, displaying to an uncommon degree painstaking zeal and deep scientific research, are, as is well known, models of their kind, and have long become standard works of high scientific value. The one I would specially refer to is practically in two parts, the first for a general, the second for a scientific public ; while the copious and remarkably truthful illustrations, mostly from photographs, bring some of the wonderful sights in a lifelike manner before the reader.

Captain, now Major, J. W. Powell, who compiled the first portion of the report, was the leader of the four Government expeditions that explored the Colorado River country in the years 1869, 1870, 1871, and 1872. And to him and his men belong the honour of being the first human beings, at least in our times, who passed alive through the whole length of the canyons. Considering that the interior of most of the gloomy gorges was entirely unknown, that Indian and trapper tales teeming with horrors far eclipsing those of Dante's "Inferno" had woven round them a halo of unknown peril, the feat was decidedly a remarkable one. Once within the stupendous rocky gates of the first canyon, the bold explorers embarked in light boats which had been transported across 1500 miles of desert, well knowing that return would be impossible, and that to escape on foot was next to being so, and would only be feasible at certain places few and far apart. Carried along by the strong current of the stream, they passed many weeks in the wonderful labyrinth of gorges, hemmed in by walls often 5000 or 6000 feet high, never sure that the next hour might not be their last; for cataracts or whirlpools might engulf them, or rapids wreck their boats, leaving them, even if they did escape with their lives, to die a lingering death by starvation— a fate of which report furnished several instances. It was generally believed, too, that the river, like many others in America, was lost underground for several hundred miles, while other accounts told of great falls, whose roaring could be heard on the distant mountain summits.

Altogether, the first expedition which, on May 27, 1869, started from Green River City in four boats, with provisions for six months, was one to which was attached more than usual interest, more than usual peril.

A glance at the map of the North American Continent shows us that the Colorado is one of the longest rivers in the West, its course being over 2000 miles in length. It drains some 300,000 square miles; and few rivers have more eventful or diversified courses, none offer richer fields for scientific research. The Colorado, bearing in its upper course another name, *i.e.* Green River, a circumstance occurring very frequently in the West, has its source, as we have heard, on the Western slopes of the Big Wind River Mountains. After flowing for about 100 miles through vast stretches of Alpine forest, which few white men have ever penetrated, it soon leaves the upper mountain region, to commence its southerly course across the treeless foothills of the Rocky Mountains, over the arid wastes of the Plains, through the dreaded badlands of Wyoming and Utah, where the Union Pacific line crosses it, till it reaches the first canyon on the boundaries of the State of Colorado. Here begins the most wonderful portion of its course. For more than 1000 miles the waters have cut, at shorter or longer intervals, deep gorges, varying in length all the way, from a mile or two to two hundred and seventeen, that being the extent of the longest canyon. Their character, owing to a great variety of geological reasons, differs much in general aspect. While some are excessively narrow fissures, and from 1200 to 6200 feet in depth, others exhibit on a most gigantic scale various types of formation, brought about, one and all, by erosion, or, as we might call it, the carving-out power of water. The whole country of the Colorado, as Powell remarks, is a history of the war of the elements, to beat back the encroaching advances of land upon ocean depths.[1]

After leaving the last canyon the river reaches the hot, arid Plains of Arizona and New Mexico, and enters upon the last third of its course, its level but little above the Pacific, till, finally, the limpid mountain waters, long

---

[1] As I am no geologist, and hence am not a partisan of either the great *Camps* of erosionists and their opponents, I simply quote the words of the two chief authorities who have recorded their views in Powell's report.

metamorphosed into turbid mud-stained floods, empty into the Gulf of California.

The mouth of the Colorado has been known for two and a half centuries. Fernando Alarcon discovered it A.D. 1539, when, sent by the Viceroy of Spain, he explored the Gulf of California. The first ascent from the mouth up to the commencement of the canyons—about 620 miles in length, the only portion of the river that is navigable— was made not twenty-five years back (1858) by a Lieutenant Ives, who explored, for the Government, the lower Colorado. He reached by boat a point some eighty miles below the Grand Canyon, and being unable to proceed farther in his craft, he organized a land expedition, by which means he and his companions caught sight, from above, of the stupendous abyss of the great gorge, at the bottom of which ran the Colorado, a sight " which rooted them to the ground in profound wonderment." Three or four years before, the upper canyons had been the scene of a remarkable exploit. It was a descent attempted by two prospectors (gold-seekers) who had penetrated into the then still perfectly unknown regions of South-Eastern Utah, where they had been attacked by Indians. Taking refuge in one of the uppermost canyons of the river which happened to be in close vicinity, these two men, White and Strobe by name, rather than attempt a retreat through country beset by Indians, where worse than death awaited them, constructed a raft of such wood and timber as they could get hold of, and with a very short allowance of provisions dared the unknown dangers of a descent through the canyon. Four days after entering the head canyon, while descending a rapid, the raft was upset, Strobe drowned, and all provisions, blankets, and arms lost.

White, who had clung to the raft, managed to right it, and continued his journey alone, amid great peril from rapids and whirlpools, hemmed in by the huge walls of some of the deepest canyons of the river. Ten days more it took him to reach a creek in the formation of continuous gorges, and here he found a few miserable adobe huts, tenanted by half-breed Mexicans. White during the ten days had eaten food but once, and then only some fruit pods and leaves he had gathered from bushes growing along the bank. Report mentions that he escaped on this occasion with his life, but, like many others of his brother prospectors, was killed the following year by his old foes.

In 1855 a similar attempt was made under like circumstances, but by a numerically larger party. They were also wrecked, and with the exception of one Ashley and another man, all were drowned, Captain Powell discovering fourteen years later some of the remains of the wreck and provisions. Ashley's name will not be forgotten, for Powell, when christening the various hitherto nameless rapids and canyons, named the spot where the party of bold prospectors came to grief Ashley Falls.

But the Government expedition also met with many disastrous adventures, for, although the reported disappearance of the river and the rumoured presence of high falls were found to be mythical, yet the many rapids were of a highly dangerous nature, entailing constant portages, several shipwrecks, the entire loss of one boat and its load, the partial loss of the contents of the other three, and the depriving the explorers of a great portion of their stores, provisions, and instruments.

But now, after these lengthy introductory remarks, let me speak of my own visit to the upper canyons; and though my expedition was framed on a far more modest scale, and I saw but a portion of the wonders of the canyons, I yet hope—considering that, so far as I know, absolutely nothing has ever been published in England concerning this wonderful gorge land—that my notes may prove of passing interest. The reader has learnt that the exceptional severity of the winter prevented the execution of my original plan of following the course of the Green or Colorado River, after leaving the Big Wind River and Sierra Soshoné country. The expected and usual spell of fine winter weather about January was that year conspicuous by its absence, and I had to give up all idea of carrying out my plans in the way I had intended.

What otherwise could not have been accomplished, the kind assistance and exceedingly-appreciated hospitality of Captain Y——, of the Scouts, at Fort Bridger,[2] enabled me to undertake. About the middle of February, 1881, two English friends and myself started from Salt Lake City for the Fort, where everything was in readiness for the expedition. So the following day a small caravan, consisting of two or three huge waggons, a small detachment of troopers, and some other camp-followers, altogether quite a formidable party, "pulled out" for Henry's Fork, a tributary of the Colorado, joining it just before the first canyon. After a weary journey over the bleak and desolate regions of the *mauvaises terres*, where heavy snowfalls played our little party many awkward tricks, obliging us on several occasions to break roads with the

---

[2] Fort Bridger has only recently (in 1880) been re-occupied by United States troops, on account of the Ute Indian outbreak in 1879, and the unsettled state of the country since. Previous to that it was for a couple of years unoccupied by the military.

snow-shovel and pickaxe, we reached, on the fourth day from our starting-point, the banks of the Colorado.

I must pause here to explain to the reader the reason why, contrary to all preceding explorations of the river and canyons, I chose the depth of a very severe winter to accomplish my object. Hitherto, the canyons had been visited only in boats during the summer season; but as I was quite unable to provide such craft—a time-robbing and very expensive undertaking in the wilderness—I based my plans upon the supposition that the river would be ice-bound, and I would then be enabled to thread my way through the canyons in a novel and expeditious manner. As such a thing had never been done before, at least as far as I could learn, and as the country through which the Colorado forms its chief canyons is entirely unpopulated and barren, I had no information whatever to go by as to whether such a proceeding were possible. My conjectures turned out, however, to be correct, for even the rapid current of the mountain stream could not resist the intense and long-continued cold.

The first canyon is formed by the river breaking through the Unitah Range, one of the few branch chains of the Rocky Mountains running in a transverse direction, *i.e.* from East to West, at a point where it rises to elevations of nearly 14,000 feet.

Right at the head of this canyon, and at the foot of the very precipitous mountains, there is a stretch of meadow land. Here, isolated from the world, three old trappers, after turning squaw men, *i.e.* marrying Indian wives, had taken to raise their cattle in a patriarchal fashion, and their primitive log cabins and Indian lodges dotted the plain. From them, to my joy, I learnt that also within the canyons, as far at least as one of them from curiosity had ventured to penetrate, the river was frozen. This was indeed good news, for, while I was sure that outside the canyons, where the river was comparatively shallow and broad, the ice would bear any weight, I was very doubtful of a similar state of things within the gorges, where the channel was considerably narrowed, the depth much greater, and the current naturally stronger, thus defying, as I previously feared, even Arctic cold to lay it in bonds.

Close to the head canyon we pitched a permanent camp, where our waggon and extra stores could be left, while we made independent expeditions, hampered only with the most essential portion of our camping utensils, into the rock-arched gorges of the famous stream. The morning following our arrival was to witness our first introduction to the canyons. It was a bright, crisp, wind-still winter's morning, and at 8 a.m. when, after the usual *contretemps* in the saddling of fractious horses and packing of unwilling mules, we left camp, the thermometer marked in the shade one degree below zero. The vast, marvellously grotesque landscape of the bad-lands through which we had been travelling, and to which we were now about to bid good-bye, lay before us with a snow-endowed brilliancy painful to the eye; and when soon afterwards the sun topped the jagged ridge overhead, and the uniform pall of snow over which we were moving was lit up with refulgent brightness also unbearable to the eye, we had to halt in order to take those primitive but effective precautions against snow-blindness which are afforded by dabbing the face round the eye with a coat of gunpowder moistened with water. In due time we reached the enormous portals of the head canyon, the famous Flaming Gorge

A RAPID IN THE COLORADO CANYONS.

—so-called from the flaming orange and pink hue of the rocks confining it. A glorious sight burst on our eyes on turning the sharp corner of the nearest buttress, and for the first time entrusting ourselves to the ice of the river. In solemn gloomy stillness the marvellous gorge lay before us, and though the cliffs on both sides were not sheer precipices, but rather built up in terraced steps of gigantic magnitude, the wonderful colouring of the rocks gave the whole a weirdly beautiful charm. So narrow was the chasm, so close did the huge buttresses of rock, forming the portal between which we were standing, approach each other, that a very few steps into the interior, where a bend in the river occurs, sufficed to let the narrow entrance disappear entirely. The cliffs at this spot are not so much remarkable for their height (Major Powell's measurement of them gives them a sheer altitude of 1200 feet), as for their grotesque formation and colour. It was about noon, and the sun, just climbing over the knifeback eastern ridge, cast slanting rays into the gloom and stillness of the gorge, lighting up with a glorious halo of vapoury light the bizarre array of pinnacles, turrets, and bold fantastic carvings imitating architectural forms, and suggesting rude but weird statuary, which lined the escarpment on the top of the Western cliffs.

Before us lay a long vista of rock-hemmed river, far more like a broad, smooth Alpine road through a gigantic mountain defile than the emerald-tinted, smoothly-gliding Colorado of summer-time. A thin layer of snow covered the ice to a depth of an inch, while outside, on the plains and on the mountains, the snowy pall was at least eighteen inches deep. We were strung out in a long line some eight or nine men, and twice that number of horses and pack-animals), and so impressive was the scene that for some time we proceeded in silence, each busy with his own thoughts. Five hundred yards from the portals was a grove of gaunt, leafless cottonwoods, the last trees deserving that name for many miles. I easily recognized in this spot the last camping-place of Major Powell before entering the canyons, then still quite unknown to them. As I picked my steps through the grove, where old signs of human presence apparently proved the correctness of my discovery, I could vividly picture to myself the thoughts that must have moved the breasts of the bold explorers as, on the eventful morning of May 30, 1869, they pushed off in their boats, having before them about as intensely exciting a journey, as full of unknown dangers, as human mind can picture to itself.

Warned by white man and by Indian, who foretold certain destruction, the little party must have left the spot with mingled feelings of keen anxiety and hope. An Indian chief, whom Powell had previously consulted respecting the possibility of passing through the canyons, had described to him an attempt made by some of his tribe to run the canyon in boats. "The rocks," he said, holding his hands above his head, his arms vertical, and looking between them to heaven, "the rocks h-e-a-p, h-e-a-p high; the water go h-oo-wough, h-oo wough; water-pony (boat) h-e-a-p-buck; water catch 'em; no see 'em Injuns any more! No see 'em squaw any more! No see 'em papoose (babies) any more!"

Very soon we came to the first rapids, the object of intense anxiety to Powell, for the waters plunged madly down among great rocks, and it was their first experience with the dangers of the canyon. Now everything was bound in icy fetters, though one could see, by the very uneven nature of the surface, and by the huge blocks of ice that lay scattered about—evidently cast up before the whole was frozen over—that it cost the king of winter a very severe effort to subdue the unruly element. The rapids are not long, but there is an interesting feature connected with them, which I found repeated in most of the lower canyons.

At the bottom of the rapid, where, as is to be supposed, the current is very strong, we observed a big green patch, and on approaching found it to be an open space in the ice. Standing on the brink of the hole, the latter about eight or ten feet square, you could see the green waters bubble and whirl beneath you; and a stick of wood which I held down was swept away with great velocity. The hole, as could be seen from the hundreds of foot-tracks of game leading to and from it, was evidently a water-hole, kept open, I fancy, chiefly by the agency of beavers, whose numerous tracks, forming regular paths, had already attracted my attention. Whether this and other holes of like description were caused, to a certain extent, by warm springs, the action of the whirling waters, or whether exclusively the work of animals, I am unable to say. In the course of my subsequent exploration I certainly found that frequently these open spaces occurred at the foot of rapids. The ice was of prodigious thickness—between eighteen inches and two feet—and, when free from snow, of a beautiful green, a hue imparted to it of course by the colour of the water beneath. Now and again there would be a loud report, and a broad crack would run across the icy highway, caused, I presume, by a sinking of the water-level after the freezing of the river, leaving a minute hollow space beneath our pavement. Harmless in itself, it frightened the horses and mules very considerably. The first two canyons are short—half a mile and a mile, perhaps—and after each the river broadens considerably, while the banks decrease in height and steepness. Our goal for the first day was an old log cabin, erected, I believe, years before by Ashley, when trapping for beaver a mile or so up the first tributary creek we came to, and to which our ranchemen friends had advised us to direct our steps. We reached the solitary spot towards evening by making what in local parlance is called a "cut off" across an intervening ridge of mountains. Here, close to the deeper canyons, we found a most desirable locality to pitch camp for a thorough exploration of the whole country. The log cabin, a mere crumbling wreck, was of greater value as a fuel-producing than as a shelter-giving asylum. My companions being more interested with other features of the country than with the canyons, I was left a good deal to myself when exploring, in the course of several days, for mile upon mile, the beauties of the Horseshoe, the Kingfisher, the Swallow, and Red Canyons.

Perhaps the most remarkable of the upper canyons is the Horseshoe, a name given to it by Powell, on account of its likeness to the letter U, the upright lines being much elongated. Prior to reaching the canyon, the river crosses a comparatively level stretch of highland, when suddenly, instead of pursuing its course across the flat, where nothing obstructs its course, it turns sharply to the left, and, at a right angle to its previous direction, enters the mountains, cutting for itself a channel 1800 or 2000 feet in depth. After proceeding for more than a mile towards the very heart of the chain, it wheels back, and, after a curve, makes a straight cut towards the level land it left, at a point not half a mile from the one where it quits the mountains. I am told that a like instance is unknown to topographers, and to me it certainly seemed a most perplexing exhibition of Nature's arbitrary power.[3]

It was a beautiful winter's day when I explored this and the following canyons. Alone, with some necessaries packed on my Indian pony, I threaded my way through the gorges. The walls rapidly increase in height, but the eye, unaccustomed to measure their altitudes, hardly detects the difference between 2000 and 3000 feet or more. In some places the channel is very narrow, so that the winterly sun, excepting about half an hour at mid-day, remained invisible. It had snowed during the night, and a thin film of snow that had reached this depth covered the ice, enabling me to track the numerous beavers, and also a bear, who had been tempted from his winter lair by the warm bright day. Of the latter, however, I did not catch sight, for he left the main canyon by a side creek, and it was impossible to follow him. With the beavers, however, it was different, for I scared up two old "dogs" (male beaver), and in the rock-bound canyon, in the absence of water-holes, no other escape was left to them but a rapid flight on the ice, affording me the rare chance of watching their movements outside their proper element. Clumsy and heavy as the animal seems on land, the rapidity of its movements when on "the jump" are doubly wonderful. The second one offered too tempting a chance for a shot; but, before I had time to get my Express from the horn

---

[3] I since hear that, although not on such a grand scale, the abrupt and acute cuts in the bed of the Zambesi above the Victoria Falls, afford an almost equally wonderful instance of this apparent freak of nature.

of my saddle—my pony, used to this kind of independent work, was quietly following me, with the reins hanging knotted over his neck—a series of most grotesque leaps of very flat trajectory had taken it nearly 200 yards off, so that when I did fire the miss was a clean one, the race being left to the fugitive beaver and my ricocheting bullet, while the echo, of appalling intensity, and of duration never before heard by me, went rolling and crashing backwards and forwards through the gorge, breaking with rude violence the silence of eternity.

Beavers and a couple of large eagles, who soared at great height over the river, were the only living things I encountered in this and the other main canyons. Of Bighorn, the ibex of the Rockies, of which Major Powell, in his summer explorations, saw numbers when the formation of the walls was such as to leave them a footing, I discovered none till, towards the end of my stay in this part of the country, I one day saw an old ram in a side canyon. He had a good head, and his meat would have been a very welcome change in the camp diet, but the nature of the ground precluded the possibility of approach. The last I saw of him was on the very top of the canyon walls, where, clearly outlined against the sky, he occupied a protruding ledge overlooking, and actually overhanging, the giddy depth of the gorge below him. Here he stood for a long time watching, I presume, with contemptuous glance, the movements of the designful pigmy who dared to invade his realm. I have no doubt that in summer, when the cool shade of the canyons offers an irresistible attraction, Bighorn are very plentiful. In the centre of the next canyon after the Horseshoe I found a broad, open space, in this instance caused evidently by one or more warm springs. The gorge was here very narrow—sixty yards, perhaps, intervening between the opposite walls, which rose perpendicularly from the ice. The open space, where you could see the green water rushing swiftly along, and in beautiful contrast to the snowy pall around it, very nearly took up the whole breadth, leaving a narrow band of ice not more than ten feet wide on either side. Being somewhat doubtful if the ice would carry me and my horse, I reversed the order of precedence, my pony taking the *pas*, which he did with a cautious diffidence by no means usual with Indian-bred "cayuses." A slight cracking—at the moment, however, of uncomfortable import — was all that happened, and we got across this and another similar spot in safety.

Close to the mouth of this short, and, as I believe, as yet nameless canyon, a picturesque tributary "creek" flows into the Colorado. Its waters have riven a stupendous fissure in the mighty walls of the main canyon, which here widens out very considerably, forming a gigantic amphitheatre of the grandest beauty. Right at the mouth of the creek, formed, I presume, by the rocky *débris* washed down by its waters, there is what Powell calls a "canyon park." Fancy a patch, some 200 acres in extent, of comparatively level garden-land dotted with graceful groves of trees—pine and cottonwood predominating—swept on three sides by a curving reach of the river, the whole shut in by stupendous walls 2000 feet high, through which, to the right and left, open gigantic portals, showing on one side vistas of mountain highlands with stretches of cedar forests, on the other, the gloomy depth of another gorge. In summer, when vegetation lends further charm to it, this scene must be of surpassing beauty, and the name which Powell has given it—Kingfisher Park, from the number of those beautiful birds he found playing about—is one happily chosen. The emerald-green of the water, the darker hue of the foliage, the far-away blue of the heaven, and the streaks of crimson and vermilion that ran across the vast walls in startling confusion—what palette but that of Nature could reproduce more harmonious tones?

So impressed was I with the grandeur of this spot, that a day or two later I revisited it at night, when the fitful rays of a bright moon shed their weird charm over it. The mellow beams starting through one of the stupendous portals, lighting up only portions of the amphitheatre, cast long shadows of the jagged and pinnacled brow of the cliff, and of the serrated buttresses forming the gateway, over the white pall on the river. The majestic silence, the twinkling stars overhead, the quiet of Eternity that seemed to rest over all, combined to make it one of the most singularly impressive night-scenes I have ever enjoyed.

Four or five miles below this canyon I passed Beehive Point, a dome-shaped buttress of rock, on the bare face and sides of which little cells have been excavated by the action of the water. In these pits thousands of the beautiful American cliff-swallows (*Petrochilidon lunifrons*), whose compact villages clinging to the steep faces of rocks I had noticed in most parts of the uplands, have built their nests, thus giving the whole the appearance of a colossal beehive, though the swarm of bees to which Powell, who gave it this name, likened the fleetly-winged army, existed of course, at this season of the year only in my imagination. Opposite this point another of the numerous amphitheatre-shaped widenings of the canyon occurs. Here, a little lower again, the walls attain a height of some 1500 feet, consisting of gigantic steps of sandstone, each with a face of naked red rock and a glacis clothed with the stunted growth of gnarled cedars, fringed by a belt of snow, giving the whole a quaintly stratified appearance; bands of red, green, and white following each other at regular intervals. A day or two later I visited the lower canyons, beginning with the gorge rendered memorable by the Ashley Falls. The river here is very narrow, the right wall vertical for many hundred feet, and then sloping off; the left towering to a great height. At the foot of the latter there is a huge mass of *débris*, a portion of which has evidently fallen into the river. Indeed, one or two gigantic boulders occupy the centre of the channel, and here the waters (so Powell says) tumble down about twelve feet, and are broken again by the smaller rocks into a rapid below. The very confused mass of slabs of ice, rent into hundreds of different shapes, which lay in piles about, and the partly open, partly closed condition of the river at this point, made it difficult to recognize the falls from Powell's description, and it was nearly impossible to make a correct estimate of the height. By keeping to one side, and striking the river again immediately beneath the cascade, I avoided passing over them—a feat that would have been impossible for my horse.

On the same day I ascended the walls of the canyon at a point close to the place where Powell reports having done the same. The climb was a stiff one, but by leading him carefully, I even got my very sure-footed pony, who climbed like a cat, up the excessively precipitous slope. On reaching the top I found that the landscape had lost a good deal of its *mauvaises terres* character. There were a number of tiny valleys, each containing separate patches, some very extensive, of stately pines, reminding me much of Alpine scenery. In summer the country must be exceedingly beautiful, in rare contrast to the arid stretches north and south of it; and Powell gives a charming description of it. Now it seemed the chosen retreat of great numbers of the graceful Muledeer. In the course of an afternoon's ramble I roughly counted over 600. They ran in small bands of forty or fifty head. It was just the time they shed their horns, and several bucks I scared up ran off with only one antler on their heads. In the far distance I also detected with my glass a band of Wapiti, who were feeding on a high table-land. Round the high sandstone "buttes" that cropped up in every direction, I also found many signs of Bighorn, though I saw none in the flesh during the hour or two that I stopped there. In summer I should say there must be great numbers, for the country, wholly Alpine in its character, is well suited to Bighorn. The altitude of the country is very high, scarcely below 7000 feet. I was rather surprised at the presence of so much game in the dead of winter; but I suppose the wreath of high peaks that surrounds this collection of natural parks shelter it from the high winds which animals dread more than snow. Powell, who visited this portion on two or three occasions, speaks of the country as being full of every kind of game—grizzlies, wolverines, and mountain lions included. Red Canyon, which I only explored at the beginning, is twenty-five miles long. An expedition on foot across a high range took me to a point from whence I saw the mouth. It was, however, impossible to get down, as the sides were more or less sheer precipices, 2500 feet in height.

The following day I managed, by going a little further, to find a place where a person who is not giddy could get down. A scramble, in which I sacrificed an essential portion of my unmentionables, brought me back to the gloomy depth. It was my last day in the canyons of the Colorado, and, much to my regret, I had to turn my back on the unseen wonders of the Lodore, the Marble, and the other great canyons, to which I was comparatively so close. Our provisions were already running very low, and, besides this, Captain Y—— had to return to Fort Bridger with the escort. But so attracted was I by what I had seen of these wonderful gorges, and also by some of the features of the surrounding country, that I hope to revisit them at an early date, and penetrate their whole length, for I know of no more enjoyable manner of spending a summer, combining the best of sport with the pleasures incidental to boat travel of such a novel character.[4] But far greater than the rest must be the attractions of the Grand Canyon, where all the various features of the dozens of preceding gorges are repeated on a yet grander scale. Powell, when writing of the morning when they started into the Grand Canyon, says, in his grapic way, "We are three quarters of a mile in the depth of the earth. We have an unknown distance yet to run, an unknown river yet to explore. What falls there are we

---

[4] The boats used by Powell were built by a Chicago builder. I should certainly say that this would be the most expedient for a similar expedition. In any case there ought to be two boats, one lighter than the other, to act as pioneer boat, a proceeding imperatively necessary in many places.

know not, what rocks beset the channel, what walls rise over the river we know not. With some eagerness, with some anxiety, and some misgiving, we enter the vast canyon, and are carried along by the swift water through walls which rise from its very edge." The first half-hour they made six miles, but soon low falls and bad rapids retarded their progress, and a bad wreckage was avoided by a mere wonder. A thunderstorm overtook them in the depth of the canyon, and three days afterwards one of the boats went over a fall, but the man who was in it was saved. The Grand Canyon is by far the longest, and also the last. It lies in three Territories—Utah, Nevada, and Arizona, the latter Territory being distinguished by the most weirdly bizarre formation that can be seen in any portion of the globe. The illustration I append gives one but a faint idea of the reality. At its mouth, where the Rio Virgen flows into the Colorado, there is a small settlement, Callville, up to which from its mouth the main stream is navigable. Here, on August 31, 1869, the first exploration ended. Three months and seven days were the adventurous travellers going through the gorges, a journey as keenly interesting as any our much-travelled-over globe affords.

Another interesting feature of the lower canyons, especially the Marble and Grand, are the remains of human habitations which belonged to an extinct race, enjoying a far higher degree of civilization than the present inhabitants of the desert country around—*i.e.* roving tribes of Navajo Indians. The first house of these cliff-dwellers discovered by Powell was on a narrow shelf of rock about 200 feet over the water, on the face of the wall. The building was once probably three stories high,

MAUVAISES TERRES COUNTRY IN THE LOWER COURSE OF THE COLORADO.

Page 316.

the lowest story is yet almost intact, while the second is much broken down. The walls are of stone laid in mortar with much regularity. Round the house on the face of the cliff were numerous rude etchings and hieroglyphics. Fifteen miles below a second group of these buildings was discovered, and here a " kiva," or underground chamber in which religious ceremonies were performed, was found in good condition. The approach to these dwellings seems to have been by ladders or narrow stairways cut into the rock by hand. They usually occupy the most inaccessible cliffs, and are provided with other means of natural defence against the incursions of enemies. For the probable origin of these canyon cliff-dwellings we have to go back to the Sixteenth Century, to the time of the first settlement of Mexico by the Spanish. Many expeditions were sent, though none of them returned, into the Far Western country now comprised in Arizona and New Mexico by the greedy European conquerors, who evinced a monstrous lust for gold and an energetic partiality for saving souls. Powell mentions one of these heathen hieroglyphic designs. On one side of the picture there is a lake, and near by stands a priest pouring water on the head of a native, on the other side an Indian with a rope round his throat: lines run from these two groups to a central figure, a man with a beard and in full Spanish dress. The interpretation given to it by Powell is: "Be baptized as this saved heathen; or be hanged as that damned one."

In view of the manifold as yet very hastily, if at all, examined objects of prominent interest, it is somewhat singular that more than a decade has been allowed to pass without a repetition of Powell's trip.[5]

[5] If my feeble attempt to do justice to a most enticing subject has,

A word or two before I close must be devoted to the questions anent some topographical points. I have said that the Colorado offers an exceptionally rich field for geological research. To a person studying the physical geography of the country without a knowledge of its geology, it would seem very strange that the river should cut through vast chains of mountains, when, apparently, it might have passed around them, on one side or the other, where the mountains are but hills, existing valleys offering ready channels. The first explanation suggesting itself is, that it followed previously formed fissures through the different ranges. But this, the modern school of geologists tells us, would be incorrect, for proofs are abundant that the river cut its own channel, that the canyons are so-called gorges of erosion. If, again, we ask, why did not the stream avoid these huge obstructions altogether, rather than pass through them? the answer is, that the river was there before the mountains were formed; not before the rocks of which the mountains are composed were deposited, but before the formations were, to quote Major Powell, "folded so as to make mountain ranges.

Professor Newberry, who first examined this region, in his report on the geology of the country, observes, concerning the creation of the great gorges: "Having constantly this question in mind, and examining with all possible care the structure of the great canyons which we entered, I everywhere found evidence of the *exclusive* action of water in their formation. The opposite sides of even the deepest chasms showed perfect correspondence of stratification, and nowhere displacement," and this would of

by chance, instilled the requisite spirit of adventure into any of my readers, I shall be glad to communicate with him or them.

course prove other natural forces not to have been at work. Professor Hall has advanced some interesting speculations concerning the future of the Colorado river canyons. As is known, he maintains that in the future of the Niagara Falls there will come a time when the great fall can no longer be maintained by the undermining of the limestone buttress from which it leaps, and that it will be replaced by a rapid, a stage in which two of the most interesting canyons of the Colorado, namely, Grand and Marble, are at present. In these two gorges a descent of 1600 feet is accomplished within a comparatively short distance entirely by rapids, where formerly, probably, more or less, extensive cataracts took their place. The incidental discovery made by Powell during his expedition, namely, that, in canyons through soft strata, the river ran invariably much smoother and quicker than in those of hard rock, seems to bear out this speculation.

CHAPTER XII.

CAMPS IN COWBOYLAND.

> The stock-raising business in the West—Its aspect and history—How it was conducted, and how it is now managed—Different manners of starting into it—On trail—Round-up—The Cowboy's life—What a man most needs—Hospitality of the West.

As the stock-raising business in the West is deservedly attracting a good deal of attention among the more adventurous class of our educated young men, I am tempted to dwell with some detail on its chief features. The stockman's life out West is one offering certain attractive inducements to the English character; for not only does his vocation bring with it an infinite amount of exercise on the bright breezy Plains, in a temperate zone, in the most delightfully bracing climate in the world, but it is a life where manly sport is an ever-present element. The cowboy and his horse are one. The interest he takes in his equine friends is not of the vicious nature to which our national attachment to the equine race has been degraded in our own land; it is healthier in all respects. If the young settler goes far enough West, shooting of the best kind can be combined with the duties of his life. Wapiti and Bighorn are often either a day's or a two days' ride, and an encounter with the dreaded grizzly roaming freely over the uplands, will test his nerves. It is a rough life; indeed, coming straight from his English club existence, it will at first, perhaps, repel him. But the roughness has its good sides, a short experience generally sufficing to weed out the effeminate and unmanly. With the exception of Australia, which I do not know, I opine that in no country will the traveller see, in the most out-of-the-way nooks and corners, such happy faces, such sterling manliness, as among stockmen in districts where they are often several months without seeing a human being.

Even much further East, in Iowa and other central states, where civilization has long subdued wild nature, we find some very happy types of small English colonies. Thus, to give a well-known instance, we have the Le Mars Colony in Iowa. "St. Kames," the able correspondent of the *Field*, has given a pleasant picture of it. With much truth, he likens the sight to a metropolitan picnic in a provincial town. The streets are filled with English ladies, and English gentlemen, and English children, and English babies. The young fellows have about them the unmistakable hall-mark of the public schools, the universities, the services; and the hard work that is performed bears more the air of pleasurable picnic roughing-it than genuine toil. No caste is lost by the young man who, dissatisfied with the slower returns of farming, engages in any of the numerous occupations—we should call them trades—of a new colony. The auctioneer, the butcher, the livery-stable keeper, provided they are recognized by society at Le Mars as gentlemen, are not considered to degrade their good old names by such experiments in new enterprise, and continue on the footing of gentlemen with the young farmers. You see the heir-apparent to an old English earldom mowing, assisted by the two sons of a viscount; you can watch the brother of an earl feeding the thrashing-machine. The happy sunburnt faces of the well set-up, strong-backed, young Britishers are pleasant features in the rich, agricultural landscape. If you would see the English character to its full advantage, hie from Pall Mall and St. James's Street to some Colorado ranche or Kansas farm. There, in not a few instances, you will find the survival of what has gained England her grand repute—sterling manliness and uncompromising honesty. But forewarned is in this case forearmed. Let not the young emigrant expect to find in the Western farmer or stock-raiser men of the English prototype. There are no broad-skirted coats, buff-leggings, ruddy, beef-fed exteriors; no rural farmhouses, with thatched roof and creepers trailing over the front of the cosy-looking dwelling. The men and their houses you will see in the West will be in pronounced contrast to such home impressions; but as they have been described hundreds of times, I need not say more about them. Of the many difficulties which beset the path of the young Britisher, none will be so formidable as those consequent upon the necessary unlearning of his British idiosyncrasies, and as long as he manages to do this without pecuniary losses he is fortunate.

There is a deal of wisdom given in the reported advice of an old settler to an Englishman who was about to send his son to America. "Can you trust me?" says the settler. "Yes," said the father, "we know you long enough to do that." "Then trust me with the capital you intend giving your son, and I will dispose of it to his best advantage."

The father hands him notes to the amount of 2000*l*. The settler strikes a match, and proceeds to set fire to the notes. The irate and astonished parent extinguishes the flames and demands an explanation. He gets it by the settler telling him that he *was* about to dispose of the son's capital to his best advantage ; that the money would be wasted before the youth would begin to work for himself; and that by burning the notes much valuable time would be saved in his son's life.

Before I proceed to enter upon the details of the ranche business in the trans-Missourian West, I must mention that what I say of its rough sides only holds good for the new sections of the country. In not a few of the large Colorado cattle-ranches you will find yourself surrounded by luxuries of every kind. But as this is not a region where a new comer is likely to start on " his own hook," I have purposely confined myself to the rough sides of the picture.

Accustomed as we are to large figures when examining statistics relating to the domestic or foreign economy of the United States, the vast surplus of the two last years' harvests in that country,[1] no less than England's very rapidly increasing cattle trade with the United States, have of late served to bring before us in more than usually startling manner the dangers threatening our agriculturists by the nearly unlimited food-producing capacities of America.

Of special interest, under the prevailing circumstances, is the question of raising cattle on the free

---

[1] I am writing of 1879-80. The figures I mention can be considered trustworthy, for they were furnished to me by the Chief of the Bureau of Statistics at Washington.

public lands of Western Territories; and recently published accounts of a perfectly trustworthy nature, no less than the results of the personal investigations of the Royal Agricultural Interests Commission, only enhance it; for they prove beyond doubt that stock-raising under such very favourable circumstances as exist in some of the North-Western districts of the Union has a great future before it.

If we examine the origin of Western stock-raising, we find that, like so many other institutions in the United States, it took its first start while the country was yet in the throes of its last great war. Texas at that time was still a much-neglected territory—a safe refuge for fugitives from justice, disguised with long beards, quaint aliases, and broad sombreros. This immense expanse, consisting mainly of prairies—Texas has 274,356 square miles, or more than France, Portugal, Belgium, and Switzerland combined—was the home of enormous herds of semi-wild cattle of a very inferior breed, "all horns and tails," as the frontiersman said of them. Their wild eyes and wide-spreading horns were in keeping with their forbidding, raw-boned, ungainly aspect, and fierce tempers. There were millions of them. In 1860 the tax returns, of course considerably under-estimated, showed 2,733,267 head of cattle, and 172,243 working oxen, in Texas; and not a few of the astonishingly lazy and ignorant rancheros—mostly of Spanish or Mexican origin—could boast of herds exceeding 50,000 head, and some few, if accounts are true, owned as many as 100,000. They were, however, of little pecuniary benefit to their owners; the absence of any market and foreign demand on the part of Northern neighbours made them very nearly as valueless as were at the same period the countless "beef" on the rolling pampas of South America.²

Towards the close of the great national struggle, when meat, cereals, and, in fact, every kind of food, rose in the Northern States to hitherto unknown prices, some venturesome Government contractors tried the experiment of driving small herds of these cattle from Texas to the Northern armies. In the beginning only small " bunches " of two or three hundred travelled that weary journey over the subsequently so historic trails leading from their prairie homes to Missouri and other Eastern states. The profits were enormous, for steers could in those good days be bought for about 25s., and sold at the end of their two or three months' overland journey for 7l.; they were, in in fact, so large that the secret soon oozed out, and men with larger capital, and unfettered by Government contracts, "started in," and for a year or two—till at last the astoundingly easy-going rancheros of Texas found out the increased value of their stock—profits remained as high. Gradually they were cut down finer; for rapidly as money is made, and incomparably higher as are the profits attainable by a successful speculation in the States than in slower and surer-going Europe, the fact that a man could double or quadruple his capital in four months, running no very great risks, allured great numbers of Eastern men to embark their own and their friends' money in stock-driving operations. This was, it must be remem-

---

² In 1879 the United States contained more than 33,000,000 head of cattle; and as 12,000,000 were milch cows, the increase of the country's stock, after all home and foreign consumption is covered, can hardly be estimated at less than a million and a half per annum : under the circumstances startling figures.

bered, long before cattle or meat export to Europe had taken root; hence it was but natural that soon, with increased numbers of drivers, competition decreased the profits—first to 75 or 100 per cent., and then gradually even to lower rates. In the eyes of the men who had first started, the business was soon played out. Not so, however, was the inventive American genius. Hitherto the cattle business was simple, that of a drover buying stock in a cheap market and selling it with a good profit in Northern towns. What was easier, asked the keen-eyed speculator, than to do as the now millionaire Texan cattle kings did, let nature work for you? Yonder lay the vast stretches of the so-called American Desert, ranging from the Mississippi, in those days the Western boundary of civilization, to the Sierra Nevadas—a track 1500 miles long and 2000 wide—on the Eastern confines of which the new Territories of Kansas, Arkansas, and Nebraska were just then constituting themselves, with that rapidity peculiar to the migratory Yankee, to whom the making of laws and building of towns is a natural occupation. While tens of thousands of half-crazed mining emigrants were crossing the Plains, pushing Westwards to the new gold countries, many more, belonging as a rule to a far better and thriftier class of Eastern-raised folk, were crowding into the new Territories, with the intention of settling down as farmers. What wonder that Horace Greeley's precious advice, "Go West, young man," was also applied to the bovine race? Very speedily the new settlers awoke to the vast profits of stock-raising, in countries where not only land but also grazing costs nothing, and where the incidental expenses of a farm are, to European ideas, exceptionally low.

Soon a regular trade in Texas cattle was started, and great numbers of the shaggy Texas steers were driven North, over " trails " that soon became famous in Western history. Cities sprang up along the route, whose entire existence depended upon the business. Their character was the "worst of the worst." To give an instance, the history of Ellsworth may be mentioned. This town, built in a fortnight, was soon a recognized centre. It was most favourably situated 250 miles from the Missouri border, and, rapid as success is in those regions, it had soon outstripped its competitors. Mixing with "cowmen," as all cattle-raisers are generally termed out West, you will even now hear of the wondrously reckless life in that mushroom "stock" town. The profits were so enormous, wages so high, and money so plentiful, that bagnios and gambling-hells out of number, each owned by some municipal official, sprang up, and life was as "cheap" as in a mining camp of the worst class. To give a typical instance of the speedy manner by which Western towns are apt to "regulate" themselves, it may be mentioned that, after having passed resolutions stigmatizing the conduct of the municipal government of Ellsworth, the "cowboys" one night rose, and quietly shot the mayor, the police magistrate, the city marshal, the chief of police, and six policemen, besides one or two minor officials who took part with their superiors. After a three-days' state of siege, during which the boys held the town, and shot at every head that showed itself out of window or door, order was restored. Since then—similar to most other like instances of self-purged settlements—Ellsworth is a model of order and quiet.

Raising cattle on the free public land of the Great West

can be done at the absurdly low rate of from 4s. to 5s. per head; for when once the ranche or dwelling is built, an affair that need not cost more than 60*l*. to 100*l*., and your provisions and horses bought, there remains absolutely no other expense to be provided for but the wages of the stockmen or "cowboys," each of whom, for his 6*l*. monthly pay, will, when on the range, take care of 1000 head of cattle. Fortunately for the farmers of Europe, the frontier rancheman—probably hundreds of miles from the next railway station, and the latter again 1000 or 1500 miles from his great market, Chicago—is handicapped by the enormous expense of the transport of his "beeves." Mr. Dun, the author of an interesting paper on cattle-raising, states that the cost of transit from the slopes of the Rocky Mountains to Liverpool is not less than 8*l*. per head, which adds quite $2\frac{1}{2}d.$ a pound to the *dead* weight of each steer.[3]

But to return to the growth of stock-raising. A further very great impulse was given to it by the building of the Pacific Railroad, which was begun sixteen years ago. As more emigrants from the East continued to pour in, land became valuable, and the cattlemen began to move Westwards to new districts, where their herds could graze free of expense on the Plains.

Colorado next became the goal of the West-bound stock-raisers, and at the present day that vast State—it became such in 1876, and hence is called the Centennial

---

[3] From statements I heard I should have put this at even a higher figure, for the freight rates of the Union Pacific are, as there is no competition, enormous. According to the report of the Royal Commission, the cost appears a little higher, namely, from 9*l*. to 10*l*. per ox.

State—with its 105,000 square miles, and a population under 200,000 souls, is, in the eyes of stock-raisers, practically speaking already "full;" that is, all land available for this purpose, with the necessary water frontage on a creek or river, is now occupied. To-day, Wyoming, Montana, Idaho, and New Mexico, no less than the extreme Western portions of Texas, are the most desirable countries in which to "locate" a cattle ranche.

Since 1875 the profits have been greatly reduced, by the increase of freight rates and decrease of Chicago prices for meat. The first shows a rise of quite 100 per cent. since 1878. Before that year the car holding twenty-one animals cost $50 (from the Plains to Chicago or St. Louis). Of late the charge is $110. Live-meat prices in either of these places have decreased quite 25 per cent. Nevertheless, the profits, as the Royal Commissioners say, are still fully 33 per cent. per annum if the rancheman has no bad luck, such as severe winters, &c.

In the same way that most Americans with difficulty realize the conditions of tenure in England, and invariably discover, when finally they have mastered the details of entailed ownership, a strong incentive in it to "skin" the land—a proceeding arising necessarily, as they think, from the absence of those selfish motives to improve it—in the same way, I repeat, does land tenure in the Union puzzle us.[4]

To Old World ears it sounds strange to be told that you or I, reader, can to-day start for any of the three or four

---

[4] I am speaking here of legitimate land holdings; for, as everybody knows, the lobby system in the United States Houses of Legislature has opened the doors to "land-grabbers," who work their little game on a very vast scale.

last-named Territories, pick out a good "range," or district for grazing, as yet unoccupied, drive on to it a herd of 10,000 cattle, select a suitable spot near to a convenient creek, and there build our ranche or farmhouse, fence in 50 or 100 acres for hay land, and, in fact make ourselves entirely at home, disporting ourselves as virtual owners of the land—without paying one penny for it, or outstepping any Territorial or United States statute, or doing what is not perfectly lawful. There is no trouble about title-deeds, surveyors, or lawyers; possession is nine points of the law, sturdy defence of your *property* being the tenth. No man has the "right by law" to prevent another man driving as many head of cattle as he chooses on to his range; but here local cattle laws come in. As in every mining camp, ranchemen have their own statutes unanimously agreed upon and tacitly obeyed by every member. The stranger who would intrude his own herd on a range already full, would, after receiving one or two friendly warnings to "move on," be made acquainted with that peculiarly Western process of being "bounced." But this occurs very rarely indeed.

Very naturally this state of things, existing only in socalled "unsurveyed" districts, can only continue so long as the supply of Plains available for grazing purposes lasts. Huge as Uncle Sam's possessions available for cattle ranges are, they are nevertheless approaching exhaustion; and, indeed, it would be difficult to imagine *what* possibly could resist the energetic onslaughts of his speculative children, pressing Westward with unabating impetuosity. A spirit well epitomized in the saying "If hell lay in the West, they would cross heaven to reach it," which has even found place in the Report of the Royal Commissioners on Agricultural Interests—certainly the last place where one would expect such unparliamentary phraseology. This as yet unexhausted supply makes contentions among frontier settlers respecting land very rare ; for, unlike the mining claim-jumper, landsharks find it not worth while risking life in enforcing their fictitious claims of ownership, when, perhaps, twenty or thirty miles farther up the valley, land as good for their purpose awaits them.

To make American land tenure, not only in the West but also in the East, more intelligible to the reader, let me recapitulate broadly the most prominent features of the law on this subject.

The whole of the United States[5] must for this purpose be divided into two categories—the surveyed and unsurveyed. To the former belong, of course, all the Eastern States, also Kansas, Nebraska, Colorado, and some few other portions of the "Great West." California I leave quite aside, as, for Europe, only its vast mineral and wheat-growing resources come into play—at least as long as the Great Pacific Railroad is not compelled by wholesale competition to lower its exorbitant freight rates. To the "unsurveyed" belong, broadly speaking, Montana, Wyoming, Idaho, portions of Oregon, Washington Territory, New Mexico, and Arizona—the latter, on account of its sterile soil is, I understand, of little value for stock-raising,—here ownership rests with the first comer, until at a future period the Territory is surveyed by Government officials, and the land mapped out and divided into districts, each coming under a Government district official. Those that

---

[5] With the exception of the State of Texas, where it is State property, land in the United States is the property of the Federal Government.

have "located" previous to this period are left in undisputed possession, provided they have improved the land—that is, either cultivated it, fence it in, or, as would be in the case of stock-raisers, have cattle of their own grazing on it. A nominal fee secures to the settler a Government title. In Montana and Wyoming cattlemen consider that each head of cattle would require from fifteen to twenty-five acres if the land was enclosed. This gives one some idea of the requisite extent of a range for a large herd.

The "squatter's right," in contradistinction to "pre-emption," which latter is the taking possession of unsurveyed land by building on it, or improving it, comes into play in the case of unoccupied but surveyed land. By it, every adult who shows that he intends to live on the land himself, acquiring it for that purpose only, and not for speculating, is entitled to 160 acres; or if the land comes under the denomination of desert land, under which head the Great Plains generally are placed, to 620 acres; for this surveyed land Government charges the settler 5s. per acre (the 620 acres of desert land being considered, in point of payment, equal to 160 acres of good soil) distributed in certain proportions over five years, thus enabling the poorest to found a home. Of course, unoccupied land can be bought to any extent for ready money from Government, but naturally this occurs rarely, as by moving farther West, land, as we have seen, can be had for nothing. If the settler, occupying soil by squatter's right, has grown-up sons, they in their turn can benefit by the same Act; the intention of Government being the high cultivation of small expanses, rather than the careless or only partial improvement of larger tracts. These are the broad outlines upon which rests land tenure in the United

States. The principle of demand and supply, which governs the mercantile intercourse of civilized people, comes into play beyond the Mississippi very much in the same way. Out West laws make themselves, but not a day before the want of them is felt. And in the same way, as long as the supply of land exceeds the demand, that commodity, in an unimproved state, will be valueless, or very nearly so.

If we compare the Northern Territories with the Southern, with the intention of examining their adaptability for stock-raising, and their several advantages and disadvantages as fields for English immigration, we at once strike at the only great source of danger for such enterprises, namely, the climate. The greater part of Wyoming, Montana, and Idaho, all of which are traversed by the numerous branching chains of the Rocky Mountains, are four, five, and the first-mentioned six and seven thousand feet over the sea, exposed to very severe winters. The Southern Territories, such as New Mexico, Western Texas, and those few portions of Southern Colorado still unoccupied, are equally liable to suffer from the other extreme—great summer heats, producing every few years prolonged droughts; for it must be remembered that the climate is a far drier one than that of Europe, and the supply of water all along the slopes of the Rocky Mountains exceedingly scanty—a fact which must be attributed to the absence of rain, sandy soil, and to the barren surface of the mountains, shedding moisture far more rapidly than in timbered countries. Besides these climatic risks, the Western stock-raiser has to chance another danger, which, though it has not yet made its presence felt, could with one cruel blow wreck the fortune of thousands;

and this is the cattle plague—pleuro-pneumonia, and the rest of these terrible scourges—up to now unknown west of the Missouri. To what this immunity is to be ascribed—whether to the dryness of the climate, the constant equality of the feed, to some medicinal quality of either herbage or water, or to a lucky chance—is unknown; as is also how long the happy exemption may last. The consequences of disease once gaining a foothold on the vast expanse of the Plains, stretching from the frontier of Canada to the Gulf of Mexico, and from the Sierra Madre to the great Mississippi, are perfectly frightful to contemplate. Hardly one of the 15,000,000 of cattle, which on a moderate estimate range wholly unrestrained over this tract, could escape contagion. It would be one terrible leap from wealth to bankruptcy. As no stock, save the bulls for breeding purposes, is imported from the East, or from countries where pleuro-pneumonia has ever been prevalent, it is obvious that the chief danger of importing contagion rests with the introduction of breeding stock. This danger is of late impressing itself upon stock-holders all over the West. Congress has been appealed to with the view of establishing commissions composed of veterinary surgeons and experienced stockmen, in order, first of all, to exercise proper vigilance on the Eastern frontiers—a sanitary line very easy to control, as all bulls are brought West by one or the other of three great lines, and the Missouri is a natural frontier drawn by nature—and secondly, should, notwithstanding all precautions, the disease make its appearance, to empower them to destroy immediately all animals that have, or possibly could have, come into contact with the diseased stock. Congress evinces, however, for problems of this kind, not only very little interest, but suffers from a chronic state of poverty when matters of national welfare like these come upon the tapis. That inbred happy-go-lucky trusting to fortune, which is strongly represented in the individual's character, is also represented in the Parliament. The chances are, too, that if such a Board of Supervision were created, it would, like the Indian question and other questionably conducted public matters, fall immediately into the hands of a ring—putting wealth into the pockets of a few, to the utter ruin possibly of a whole community, should the Board's active services become necessary. Very little reliance can, therefore, be placed on Government help. More likely does it seem that the whole body of Western stockmen will arrive at some arrangement among themselves; for, like making laws and building houses, ready self-help becomes second nature among a frontier population.

It must not be supposed, however, that Western cattle are wholly exempt from the ills of their flesh. In Texas there is a peculiar disease known as Texas fever, and very nearly all adult cattle of an improved stamp imported into Texas for breeding purposes, take it and die. Texas-bred stock, however, very rarely suffer from it, but, strange to say, they appear to be able to infect other cattle with a form of disease hardly ever showing in themselves, so that at certain times of the year, when droves of Texas "beeves" are driven northwards, other cattle crossing the trail are smitten with the Texas fever, and die by thousands. The report of the Royal Commissioners speaks of it as a very mysterious disease.

Most visitors when first they see the great Plains of

Western North America are grievously disappointed. The Missouri once passed, the verdant green, the most prominent feature of our own pastoral landscape, vanishes totally, and the traveller on the great Trans-Continental Railway will see for upwards of 1000 miles hardly a tree; and his eyes, accustomed to our home grass-land, will be painfully struck by the arid, waterless, and verdureless aspect of the country. If he travels across this vast district late in summer or in autumn, it will seem totally destitute of grass; for the blades, or rather bunches, of buffalo grass, of such singularly nourishing properties, have long been dried up and cured by summer heat. Instead of rotting away and losing every atom of strength, as European grasses do if they are not cut in time, they retain all their most valuable qualities; in fact, it is generally maintained that this self-cured hay, as we might term it, is more nutritious for cattle than fresh grass, which, as in the case of green clover-feed for horses, fills, but does not nourish. However this may be, it is certain that all the various kinds of cattle imported from the east, south, and west flourish on it. A herd of 5000 head will feed the year round and grow fat on a stretch of arid-looking table-land, where an English farmer, if he saw it in autumn, would vow there was not sufficient grazing for his children's donkey. There are, of course, different degrees in the quality of grazing-land; some are very much superior to others, and these latter are generally to be found in the neighbourhood of great ranges of mountains.

If we examine the natural features of the Great Plains, we find that, with very few exceptions no part of them will feed nearly as many cattle, sheep, or horses to the square mile as land will in the Eastern States or in Europe; but the almost limitless area counterbalances this. The grasses of the Plains are not kept strictly apart, and are called somewhat indiscriminately gama, buffalo, or bunch-grass. One kind grows about six inches high, the other is smaller. Their growth, beginning about the first of May, continues to the end of July, when the dry season commences; they then dry up, and are cured by the sun; and as the frosts, let them be ever so hard, do not seem to penetrate to the roots, or else do not harm them, they retain their full strength for the whole winter. It is interesting to note that the virtues of this self-cured hay were discovered comparatively quite recently—viz., during the building of the Pacific Railway, not twenty years ago, when some draught-oxen were lost one autumn, and, much to the surprise of the owner, were found the following spring quite fat and healthy. Nature has provided in many ways for her children; for not only can stock find ready shelter under the bluffs, and in the many small valleys and glens called pockets and gulches, and under the clusters of hardy cedars and spreading cottonwood-trees which almost serve the purpose of barns and stables, but the hurricanes which prevail after every snowstorm clear the slopes in a marvellously short time from the snowy pall, driving it together in banks, and filling up depressions in the ground. Rarely does the dry and flour-like snow crust over, a process which for cattle means starvation if warm weather does not soon follow.

The snowstorms in Wyoming, Idaho, and Montana are usually very severe indeed; they generally last three days with unabated fury, the thermometer going down to 55 or 60 degrees of frost. In the Western vernacular they are known as "blizzards." It is specially the so-called "breaking-up" storm which is dreaded by ranchemen. It is the last, coming about March or the first half of April; and not only is it the severest of all, but it finds cattle less able to withstand its fury, and go without food for three or four days, exposed to great cold and Arctic winds.

Losses in severe winters are often very great. Where sheep are raised, as, for instance, in Colorado and some districts in Wyoming, whole flocks of four or five thousand head perish in one night; and one case is related, when the breaking-up storm came as late as May, that two men lost in four hours over 10,000. Of cattle, no such extreme instances have to be chronicled, though in some places ranchemen lost, in the winters of 1871-72, and 1880-81, the two severest ever known, half their herds. But experience has taught stockmen many lessons, particularly in the choice of their range, respecting which they were formerly very much more careless. The presence of the ravines and bluffs so peculiar to the Rocky Mountain formation, is as essential as water and grass; and men starting now prefer to go 100 or 200 miles farther from the railway, and have a sheltered range, than risk heavy losses and be nearer the point from whence they "ship"[6] their produce.

Notwithstanding that cattle, no less than sheep, are able to obtain their own subsistence all the year round, the avocation of stock-growing, as we shall see, is attended during part of the year with no little care and labour. During the summer, autumn, and winter, the cattle roam

[6] The term "ship" is commonly used in America for "send by rail."

at will over the Plains, and different herds, or parts thereof, mingle together, and perhaps wander for long distances from their home range. Very frequently single heads, separated most likely from their herd in a stampede, are found two or three hundred miles away. To collect these stragglers and to take a census, no less than to pick out the beeves for market, the annual "round-up" is held. At this period, falling in June and July, the whole country is searched, and the cattle appertaining to a district are driven together in one vast herd, from whence the different ranchemen separate their own cattle, easily recognizable by the brand. After a mutual exchange of strayed ones, each owner takes his herd back to their home range, and after branding the calves, turns them out loose, not to see them again till "round-up" next year.

For each district, embracing many hundred square miles, and from ten to twenty ranches, a captain—generally one of the old settlers well acquainted with the country—is chosen. Under him work the cowboys from the different ranches, numbering often seventy or more men, and 200 or more horses, for each cowboy has at least three spare mounts with him on these occasions. The whole country, so large that it will take them two or three months to work it over, is laid out in daily rides. If there is a large stream in the district, the watercourse is followed; the country for twenty or thirty miles on both sides being carefully searched by the mounted cowboys, who, all working under one head, develop great aptitude for their laborious work. They are in the saddle for at least sixteen hours every day, and most of the time on the "lope," or canter, chasing and collecting the semi-wild cattle, till at last, often long after dark, they bring in, driving before them, the stock found that day.

If the range, as very frequently is the case, be a mountainous one (there are many in Wyoming seven and eight thousand feet over the sea, in the heart, one might say, of the Rocky Mountains), the search for cattle is far more difficult than on level or undulating prairie-land. Among the rough and steep chains of mountain full of "draws," "pockets," and gulches,—generally densely timbered at the bottom—the search is anything but easy. A cow or small bunch of cattle overlooked on one round-up, is, however, not necessarily lost; for generally they will turn up on that or some neighbouring range during the next year's round-up. Wyoming ranchemen have told me that often they accidentally pitch upon cattle they missed four or five years before; while on such occasions the original cow will make her appearance with quite a little family of unbranded steers, yearlings, and calves. These "foundlings" are often appropriated by others than the rightful owners, the branding iron covering in this instance a multitude of sins. Considering how broken is the ground, and of what huge dimensions is each range, it speaks well for the cowboy's powers that the losses from straying amount, under proper care, to not more than one or two per cent. per annum. The total percentage of losses incurred from stress of weather, droughts, &c., varies considerably. More than half of the owners or managers of the ranges (about 100) I visited, declared that five per cent. in average years will amply cover; others maintained seven, and a few even thought ten per cent. The round-up is a busy time for man and horse on frontier ranches. It is a period affording pleasant change to the cowboy, who the rest of the year is buried on his isolated ranche, often months without seeing a white man, and years frequently pass before the glance of a woman's gown makes his heart flutter. There is a wonderful amount of animated life, light-hearted merriment, and vigorous and healthful rivalry about one of these round-ups. They begin with a substantial breakfast, at which often a whole steer, divided among the different messes, is used; the rising sun sees the tall, lithe-figured, and bronze-faced cowboys, their spurs jingling, their legs encased in leather 'shaps, the heavy six-shooter and cartridge-belt girt round the waist, leap into the saddle, man and horse equally eager for the exciting chase. With the snake-like lariat swinging round his head with that peculiar hissing sound so terrifying to the chased, the mettlesome little broncho, urged by a shout from the easy "lope," a cradle-motioned sort of canter—a pace kept up by cow ponies for hours at a time—into a sharp gallop, the whole company, like Lützow's "wilde verwegene Jagd," disperses over the boundless plains or the mountain-girt highland, each man making straight for his post, only to return, driving before him the cattle he and his comrades have found, when dark renders further search impossible. These, if it is an open country, will often be as many as 200 to the man; if broken, and full of pockets and draws, or densely timbered ravines, perhaps not more than ten or fifteen. Cowboys learn to track animals as Indians do game, and I was often amused to watch from some elevated spot a "field" of cowboys at work. Here you will see a couple dismounted and leading their ponies, following some faint tracks on the hard gravelly soil which, till softer ground is reached, or other indisputable stock signs discovered, might prove those of elk or (unshod) Indian ponies. Generally, water betrays cattle; for let them be ever so far from it, or carefully screened from discovery in dense timber, they must at least once every twenty-four hours repair to the next creek or water-hole, when their tracks are easily discernable. Yonder we perceive two of the daring riders pursuing a small "bunch" of frisky young bulls stampeding down a steep slope, tails raised high, evidently frightened at the unusual sight of man, and the pursuers at full gallop tearing down the hill at more than break-neck pace, endeavouring to head them off; man and horse apparently oblivious of the steepness of the grade, and the many treacherous gopher-holes that dot it. They are all wonderful riders, and on these occasions they strive to out-do each other. I saw one spill on a steep hillside, occasioned by a prairie-dog hole, into which the horse put one of its forelegs; and from motives of curiosity I measured the distance the rider was sent spinning, and found that between the gopher-hole and the spot where the man's shoulder touched ground first was twenty-seven feet less three inches. The man was only slightly stunned, and amid the laughter of his companions, who never show any mercy on such occasions, picked himself up, and pulling his six-shooter, forthwith shot the disabled "broncho."

While on the round-up, the cattle found each day are collected, and during the night half of the men are on guard keeping them together. Finally, after four or five weeks' hard work the whole country is thoroughly searched, and the herd, now numbering many thousands, is ready for the "cutting out," performed with an incredible dash by the cowboys. Each man singling out the cows with the brand of his ranche on them—about seventy-five per cent. of which are followed by as yet unbranded calves—dashes into the herd. Their wonderfully sagacious and well-trained ponies, now running at full speed, now turning and dodging like flashes, anticipating each move of the frightened mother-cow in her vain endeavour to find security where the herd is most densely packed, seem to enter into the spirit of the sport as keenly as the light-hearted rider, who, now swinging in his right hand his raw-hide lariat or lasso, prepares for the throw, The whirling rope, circling in black rings round his head, is launched forth; the loop drops with unerring aim round the calf's head; the horse stops the same instant, throws himself back, and with one frantic plunge the calf is down, to be dragged the next minute to the fireside, where the brand is applied. Equally easily is the strong steer thrown, for in the hands of the trained cowboy the lariat is a dangerous tool. The loop about the neck, or over one or both hind legs, about the body, or over one foreleg—at the will of the masterful hand—and the powerful bull lies prostrate and helpless on the ground in an incredibly short space of time. When all the calves have been branded, ownerless "mavricks" brought in, and any disputes arising respecting the ownership of these waifs settled, the "beeves" or steers for the market are selected by each rancheman and driven off to the nearest Union Pacific railway (U.P.) station, where they are "shipped" to Chicago. Ranchemen in a small way frequently club together, and make up one party to drive their beeves thereto *en masse*.

Monotonously lonely as are their lives for the rest of the year, buried in their isolated ranche, where the advent of strangers is an unlooked-for and rare event, the round-up is for the laughter-loving though hard-worked cowboy a merry period; for his perilous vocation then gives him the best of chances to exhibit his daring feats on horseback, to indulge in attractive rivalry respecting the fleetness of his several "cayuses" or ponies, the unerring aim of his lariat and revolver; and finally, is not the camp fireside nightly the scene of the vast story-telling powers inherent in the true cowboy, especially if he be of Texas grit and grain?

I have already mentioned, that after the branding the cattle are turned out on the range, there to remain unguarded and unwatched during the winter months. The same is done with the horses, or at least with the majority, only a few head being reserved for use, stabled in a log shanty near the ranche, where, during the severest weather they are fed on the scanty supply of hay collected on hay bottoms during autumn, and at other times are turned out to graze close by.

Cowboys can be divided into two classes—one hailing from the Lone Star State, Texas; the other, recruited either from Eastern States, chiefly Missouri, or from the Pacific slopes, Oregon contributing no mean number of Webfoots, who are so called from the long winter rains in that colony. The Texans are, as far as true cowboyship goes, unrivalled: the best riders, hardy, and born to the business, the only drawback being their wild reputation. The others are less able but more orderly men. The bad name of Texans arises mostly from their excitable tempers, and the fact that they are often "on the shoot,"—that is, somewhat free in the use of their revolvers.

If we come to the practical issues of the question, the first point to be settled by the intending rancheman, when once he has chosen his range, is what cattle to purchase. There are three great sources from which countless herds are annually drafted: Texas, Utah, and Oregon. The first mentioned was, as we have heard, originally the only stock country. The two last have entered the competing lists very recently, thereby giving us another proof of the enormous productive capacities of the Great West. Thirty-five years ago, when Oregon was a perfect wilderness, and Utah not yet in existence, there was not a head of stock in those regions, save the few which each settler family brought with them from the East; half, if not more, of the number they started with usually succumbing to the hardships of over-driving and the want of good food and water on the inhospitable and endless desert. Cattle-driving, as a speculation, was then and for a long time to come unheard of, so none brought more than they could conveniently drive; and old guides have stated to me that the average number was decidedly under ten to each family of emigrants. These bovine immigrants in the meanwhile have multiplied in the green valleys of Oregon at an enormous rate; and now there are hundreds of thousands where, thirty, and even twenty years ago, there were not hundreds. Curious to say, the progeny of the original ancestors are now being driven in vast herds back Eastwards, over the very same old Mormon road which fifteen or twenty years ago their grandsires had travelled on their way to their new Western homes.

To return to the choice of stock. The general public voice declares the Oregon and Utah breed to be far superior to Texas cattle; and while the earlier ranchemen in Colorado, Wyoming, and Montana had only the latter, the Oregon cows driven to the two last-mentioned Territories in 1879 outnumbered Texas stock at least three or four times.[7] At first it was greatly doubted whether cattle raised on the Pacific slopes, and especially in the damp, moderately warm climate of Oregon, could possibly stand a Wyoming or Montana winter with its terribly severe snowstorms. Experience, however, has established not only that Oregon stock can withstand great climatic hardships, but also that they flourish on Wyoming soil. As both Utah and Oregon cattle fetch comparatively much higher prices in Chicago and other great markets, those breeds are now the prime favourites; and, as a natural consequence of the vastly increased demands, cows in Oregon have risen quite seventy-five per cent. in value within the last four or five years.

The choice of your stock decided, there are three different ways of getting it. You can first of all buy it on "the range," and this is the quickest, and, if you exercise due caution, fairly sure, but withal the most expensive way. The cattle are bought so many head, "more or less;" but as taking the census and the control over vast herds belonging to a number of different owners, roaming at large over large tracts of country, is naturally not easy, and only possible at the round-up, this mode leaves a good many openings for sharp-witted "cussédness," to which the newly arrived "tenderfoot" very frequently

---

[7] Twelve years ago these Territories imported about 800,000 head of Texas cattle annually; while 250,000 is the number now.

falls victim. The second way, and for newly arrived settlers by far that most to be preferred, is to make contracts with any of the large and responsible drovers for a number of cattle of a certain breed and age, about seventy-five per cent. of the cows to have calves, the stock to be delivered at a specified time at your ranche, you stipulating a heavy forfeit (often as large as 3000*l.* or 4000*l.*) in case of non-fulfilment of contract, and having the option of rejecting animals not perfectly healthy or according to agreement. Generally a year, however, elapses ere you receive your herd; for, say you sign contracts in Wyoming in autumn, the cattle will be bought in Oregon by the driver in early spring, and the whole summer will pass ere the herd reaches Wyoming. The third, and originally the only way of procuring your stock, is to go yourself to Texas or Oregon, buy your cattle there from different owners, and start with them for your distant home as soon as the warm May sun has turned the vast Plains an emerald green. The process of driving cattle is called "riding on trail," one of the most laborious and dreary undertakings imaginable, of which we shall have to speak a little farther on. This, though the cheapest, is for "tenderfeet" the most risky mode of purchasing stock.

There are to-day two different ways of conducting the stock business out West. The one is to buy young steers, keep them two years on your range, and sell them as four-year-olds to market. Per head the increase in value varies between $10 and $15 (2*l.* to 3*l.*); thus enabling the rancheman very nearly to double his capital in that short space of time, provided his losses do not exceed five per cent.

The other manner is to *raise* stock, buying Texas, Oregon, or Utah cows, and the necessary number of Eastern, bulls of a good breed. This, if from the first you make up your mind not to sell a single animal for the first three years, is in the end far more profitable than the mere "feeding-up" of stock. Formerly fewer men went into it, on account of the larger capital required to keep the concern going for the first three years with no incoming funds; but the last few years have brought, as the large profits of the business became better known in the East, larger capital, and now it is the favourite with men, tempted to go West, by the very fair chance of making a fortune in six or eight years.

In an account added in the Appendix, I furnish detailed estimates, based upon the most trustworthy authorities, examined by me personally, of the increase of cattle in a certain number of years, and the profits accruing to the stockman. I placed the amount invested at the outset at 10,000*l.*, and proved that the profits at the end of three years amounted to 8800*l*. This, with fair luck, and losses taken at five per cent. each year consecutively. Of course the rate of increase grows considerably larger in subsequent years, as seventy-five per cent. of all cows have calves annually; at least this is the generally accepted percentage in Wyoming and Montana, some few putting it as high as eighty, others seventy per cent.

The whole subject of stock-raising on the Western Plains is attracting very general and deserved attention in the Eastern cities, and numbers of young men of good family start, or are started annually by their friends, the capital invested varying frem 2000*l*. to 20,000*l*. But even with a smaller start money can be made; and not a few of the independent stockmen I met, sprung from the lowest social rank, were rapidly trebling their $3000 or $4000. Others, recruited from the middle classes of the States, had two or three years ago been railway conductors, hotel-keepers, Western merchants, petty civil servants, and, quite a number, trappers and Indian scouts.

A considerable number of the former (trappers) had served as guides to rich English sportsmen, on their shooting tours in the Rocky Mountains, and had been started by them with a few thousand dollars. I have heard of some half-dozen gentlemen in England who are reported to draw fifteen and twenty per cent. interest from the capital they advanced to their former camp-fireside companions.

In the United States, where "tall" talk is so common, the numerous accounts that have been published of late of Western stock-raising all exhibit this national failing. Of the dozens I have had occasion to peruse, all were more or less overcoloured. The profits, according to them, were more like those of the old-day Texas cattle-trade than the actual truth, namely, from thirty to thirty-five per cent. per annum on the average of three or four years, and about forty per cent. on the average of seven years. They would be considerably greater (as the stock after the fourth and fifth year increases at a startling rate) were it not necessary to take into account the chance of one very bad winter out of seven, when the losses much exceed the five per cent.

Nothing will give a better picture of a stockman's fortune in those wild regions than a sketch from life. Let us select Mr. Iliff, one of the best known cattlemen of Colorado and Wyoming, recently deceased. Mr. Iliff was one of the many thousands who, in the great Pike Peak's Gold excitement in 1859, crossed with frenzied energy the Great American Desert—as the vast tract of desert-like land intervening between the Mississippi and Colorado was then still called. Unlike the majority of his brethren—who after a short spell of fruitless work awoke to the stern reality that gold could not be picked up in panfuls, and either returned home, or pushed still farther West towards California, founding on their way that fabulously rich silver state Nevada—Iliff remained on the spot, threw shovel, pan, and rocker aside, and settled down to cultivate a small patch of ground near Denver, then a city of less than 100 miserable shanties, and peopled with the roughest of the rough; for the numerous "hanging bees" which cleared off the most desperate element in subsequent years had then not yet been introduced. Iliff was not over fond of those dark sides of frontier life, and being himself "not on the shoot," decided to move North. "Moving" was, and is, a very simple affair in the West. Iliff, perfectly destitute when he came to Denver from the mines, had managed to save sufficient in the one season of his residence in that town, where the "garden truck"—vegetables—raised by him found a very ready market, to buy a pony and some few provisions, and a rifle. Loading them on his horse, he turned his back on lively Denver and his primitive "dug-out," his home for the last six months. He reached the Northern Californian (Mormon) emigrant road, about 160 miles North of his late home in autumn, and at once set to work to build himself a log shanty, which he completed before the worst weather of winter could surprise him. He had, so he stated in later years, only a few dollars in his pocket, a small cask of whiskey, and a little store of tobacco. With these he hoped to trade with the Mormons, and other emigrants passing over that weary road in the season, who were often as many as 100 per diem, while in winter he was months without seeing a civilized being—the pony express, and later the stage, then passing on the "Southern road," much to the south of his location.

With the emigrants, generally as poor as himself, he bartered his whiskey, tobacco, and other necessaries of life, which he gradually managed to "lay in," taking in exchange cattle, of which all Western-bound emigrants took with them as large a number as their means would allow, for not only did they furnish them with milk in the totally uninhabited regions through which they journeyed for five and six weary months, but they were at the same time the most valuable stock-in-trade of the new settlers in their distant homes. Many of the Eastern raised cattle, however, accustomed to other feed and plenty of water, succumbed to the bovine hardships of the trip; and so Iliff drove many a good bargain, giving for a broken-down cow or a tottering steer—mere walking raw-boned ghosts of their former selves—a pound or so of tobacco or a few glasses of precious whiskey, which seemed the very elixir of life to the parched emigrants by the time they reached Iliff's store, already two or three months on the road. Some miles from his shanty he had discovered, amid some sheltering but very broken hill country, a very oasis in the alkaline desert, a considerable tract of good hay-land, with an ever-flowing creek traversing it.

To this place he drove his purchases, and the nutritious bunch grass and total rest, so strange to their weary limbs of late, soon fattened them up to their pristine condition. Iliff showed in this predilection for cattle a singular foresight ; for, as the end proved, the dollars so invested accumulated at a rate before which even the twenty and thirty per cent. per annum which Western banks in those days gave for ready cash deposits were as nothing; and, moreover, it was storing up money in perhaps the only safe way. The Plains from the Rocky Mountains to the Eastern portions of Nebraska and the Missouri were, as everybody will remember, overrun by hostile Indians, and the scene of countless massacres.

Iliff's shanty was twice burnt over his head by the red men, he escaping each time with nought but his life. Cattle in those days had, in the eyes of the wandering Indians, unlike horses and everything else white men possessed, no value ; hence he found on his return to his desolated home that his bovine riches, grazing quietly in the hills fifteen or twenty miles from the road, had not been tampered with by the white man's enemy, who, still happy possessors of matchless hunting-grounds, held beef in utter contempt as " squaw's game." For ten years Iliff, like so many other venturesome spirits, braved the perils of the Plains; and, in 1869, the first locomotive that passed over the Union Pacific Railroad, in close proximity to his ranche, found him a rich man. Not only had he found a splendid market for his beef in the numberless railroad camps while the road was building, but, while formerly he had no human habitation nearer than seventy miles, Cheyenne, a city of 10,000 inhabitants, had sprung up, so to say, over-night not ten miles from his home.

His range, on the frontier of Wyoming and Colorado, extended already, in 1872, from Julesburgh to Greeley, a distance of more than 150 miles, and about 100 miles broad, on which were grazing for years 40,000 head of cattle, representing 160,000*l*., all belonging to the man who scarce fifteen years before had driven the first stake of his shanty.

What is most instructive about such a career is, that Iliff had in no way to thank luck for his success. His losses were often very great; thus in the exceptionally severe and long winter of 1871-2, cattle to the value of 25,000*l*. starved, and above 21,000*l*. were spent by him in spring to find strayed animals, some of which, in the agony of a slow death by hunger, had strayed 400 miles in search of food, part of his herds being finally recovered in two different States and four different Territories.

While thousands of his former mining comrades had returned to their Eastern homes half-starved desperadoes, and hundreds had found a lonely grave in the mountains of Colorado, and a few—a very few, alas!—had been favoured by luck and had found great riches, to be squandered again in the most incredibly reckless manner, he had pursued his course with singular perseverance, and besides leaving his heirs millionaires, had enjoyed for the last seven years of his life, from his cattle, quite apart from other speculations, an income of upwards of 25,000*l*. per annum.

The first cattle ranche in Colorado was that of Colonel J. D. Henderson, who, starting from Kansas in the spring of 1859, bound for the gold-mines at Pike's Peak, was one of the first to realize that raising cattle was more profitable than gulch gold-mining. He had taken out with him on a waggon a stock of groceries and a few barrels of whiskey. His first trade with a band of Ute Indians secured him, for two barrels of the precious liquor, a large island in the Platte River, below Denver. A stout and roomy log hut and cattle corrals were built with the aid of the Indian squaws, who, while their noble lords were lying around, made helplessly drunk by their "trade," helped to drag the logs from the nearest forest; and very soon Henderson Island became a favourite rendezvous and stopping-place for the Mountain-bound gold-diggers and emigrants. In 1861 Henderson had already 2000 head of cattle, and trade was brisk. Whiskey, sold in drinks at 2s. each, returning 5l. per gallon; while a cow could often be bought for a fifth of that sum.

The wonderfully rapid growth of ranching in Colorado —which only became a State five years ago—is proved by the fact that in 1871 only 145,916 head of cattle were assessed for taxation, while six years later, 483,278 were returned, the present number being estimated between 900,000 and 950,000.[8] In 1877, 80,000, in 1878, 88,000 beeves were "shipped," mostly to Chicago; while the home demand of Colorado in the latter year accounted for quite 20,000. Thus in one year the sale of 108,000 beef steers realized for the new state (at 5l. per head) considerably over half a million sterling.

"Riding on trail," to which I have already referred, is an undertaking requiring on the part of the leader great experience, the intuitive natural talent of the trapper skilled in "Plains craft," and the astute genius of a commander

[8] In sheep the increase has been even more rapid, for while ten years ago Colorado had less than 20,000, it had in 1880 2,000,000. These latter figures I obtain from Mr. Fosset's work on Colorado, published last year.

—adroit, firm, determined, of quick eye, and versed in the mysteries of Plainscraft. From the chief cattle centres in Texas it takes from four to six months, from Oregon not much less, of constant travel to reach North-Western Wyoming. Great mountain ranges have to be crossed; vast stretches of dreary, absolutely barren Plains to be covered; rivers full of dangerous quicksands, in which whole herds have been known to perish, and streams subject to the most terrifically sudden freshets, to be forded; long expanses of barren, ashy-hued, alkaline desert-land, where for forty or fifty miles not a drop of precious water is to be found, to be traversed; and all this, with two, three, or four thousand semi-wild shaggy cattle, straight from their pathless home, unaccustomed to the sight of human beings, and only too easily startled into a frenzied stampede, resulting in general disaster. All this, through countries where Indians, if not actually hostile, are—or rather were —always ready for a haul, and where Nature herself, in the shape of violent thunderstorms and early snowstorms, seems to delight in wrecking the fortunes of the adventurous frontiersman.

Let us examine the "outfit" of a party riding on trail, say with a herd of 4000 cattle. It consists of the captain and six or eight cowboys, a large waggon with tarpaulin cover to hold provisions and bedding, a boy cook, and a bunch of cow-ponies, numbering from forty to sixty head, which, if the start is made from Texas, can be bought there for about 2*l*. 10*s*., and sold at their destination for quite double their original cost. As the ponies will be wanted at the ranche, they are usually not sold at the termination of the journey. Not infrequently one or two hundred are driven along with the cattle as a speculation, the cowboys making a purse covering the purchase and the extra hire of a man to attend them.

Until very recently, the journey was generally made in company with two or three similar outfits; for the countries through which runs the well-known old Texas trail (now of classic name, about which there clings a terribly sanguinary history of bloodshed and war) was infested with hostile Indians, and the equally dangerous and even more cruel Mexican border ruffians. Larger numbers afforded greater security. Every man was a walking arsenal. Over his saddle-bow was slung, in trapper fashion, a Winchester repeater; the two long, ever-present Colts at his right and left hip, his long raw-hide lariat looped to his California-rigged saddle, a very clumsy-looking and heavy contrivance, necessarily so, however, for the strain of a powerful bull making frantic efforts to loosen himself from the fatal loop must be withstood, and hence every particle of the saddle must be of the strongest.

Hardly credible stories are told of the fate of many an "outfit" that passed over the Texas trail eight or ten years ago. One quite authentic one may suffice: The party in question, consisting of forty-odd men and nearly 13,000 head of cattle, starting some 150 miles south-west of San Antonio, reached North Colorado after an exceptionally disastrous journey, so decimated by stampedes, losses in a fatal quicksand, Indian and Mexican surprises, and fatal shooting affrays among themselves, that only nine men and little over 5000 head were left. Now-a-days some of these risks have ceased to exist, and an "outfit on trail" will rarely consist of more than 4000 head. The revolver, snowstorms, and stampedes are, however, still serious stumbling-blocks—especially the former, if part of the crew are recruited from the detested "greasers," viz., half-breeds, or a mixture of the native Indian and imported Spaniard. Between these and the "whites," as Americans of pure blood insist upon being called, an instinctive hatred has always existed, and will for ever exist ; for, apart from race antipathy, the curious marital relations of the two people, both impulsively hot-headed and of a jealous disposition, must always prove a source of trouble.

Thunderstorms, though by no means frequent are a source of danger in summer, are very terrifying to wild cattle. On the approach of one of these violent outbursts the whole force is ordered on duty. The spare horses—of which each man has always three, and often as many as eight or ten—are carefully fed and tethered, and the herd is "rounded up," that is, collected in as small a space as possible, while the whole force continues to ride round the densely-massed herd. Like horses, cattle derive courage from the close proximity of man. The thunder peals, and the vivid lightning flashes with amazing brilliancy, as with lowered head the herd eagerly watches the slow steady pace of the cow ponies, and no doubt derives from it a comforting sense of protection. Sometimes, however, a wild steer will be unable to control his terror, and will make a dash through a convenient opening. The crisis is at hand, for the example will surely be followed, and in two minutes the whole herd of 4000 head will have broken through the line of horsemen and be away, one surging, bellowing mass of terrified beasts. As an American writer on the origin of these panics very correctly remarks, stampedes may arise from any cause. Sometimes an inexperienced cowboy may startle the herd by an unusual shout. Sometimes the war-whoop of Indians may alarm it. Sometimes a stampede may result from some uncommon sight, which, frightening the leaders, will take off the whole herd. Fancy a pitch-dark night, a pouring torrent of rain, the ground not only entirely strange to the men, but very broken and full of dangerously steep watercourses and hollows, and you will have a picture of cowboy duty. *Coûte qui coûte*, they must head off the leaders. Once fairly off, they will stampede twenty, thirty, and even forty miles at a stretch, and many bunches will stray from the main herd. Not alone the reckless rider, rushing headlong at breakneck pace over dangerous ground in dense darkness, but also the horses—small insignificant beasts, but matchless for hardy endurance and willingness—are perfectly aware how much depends upon their showing speed on that night, if it kills them. Unused until the last moment remain the heavy cowhide "quirt" or whip and the powerful spurs, with jingling rowels the size of five-shilling pieces. Urged on by a shout, the boys speed alongside the terrified steers until they manage to reach the leaders, and finally swinging round, and fearless of horns, they press back the bellowing brutes until they turn them. All the men pursuing the same manœuvre, the headlong rush is at last checked, and the leaders, panting and lashing their sides with their tails, are brought to a stand, and the whole herd is again rounded up. The run has taken them far out of their road—led them, may be, into close proximity of hostile Indians, or crafty "greaser" marauders; and when finally dawn breaks, new dangers may await the small contingent, who, as is often the case, do not leave their saddles, save to change horses, for thirty-six hours at a stretch. I once witnessed a stampede under similar circumstances, and a more strangely exciting scene I have never seen. That comparatively few fatal accidents occur must solely be ascribed to the matchless riding of the men, and the wonderful sagacity and unsurpassable sure-footedness of the trained cow-pony. All night long, through rain or fiercely driving snow, the watch continues, and when morning comes a census is taken. Then only the men find how many head have strayed, and some of them are at once despatched on fresh horses to find the lost ones. Single animals on such occasions have been known to stray 100 miles, and, to find them, vast tracts of country have to be searched. Generally, all are found; but now and again small bunches disappear, to turn up on an entirely different range as "mavricks," *i.e.* the name given to all unbranded animals, which are the prizes of the owner of the range, or of the herd with which they have got mixed up.

Speaking of brands, there are two, the road and the permanent brand. The first is not always used, and consists in a superficial branding of a certain mark, owned and registered by the person driving the cattle. The permanent brand is applied in the usual manner with hot irons, that makes it impossible to be obliterated. Two or three letters, or some sign, are chosen for the brand, generally placed on the left hip in six-inch letters. Once registered, the mark belongs to the rancheman, who, if he has been long in the business, owns often four or five different brands, having brought up herds on ranges which, of course, were already provided with one. The term "mavrick" is one long in use, and is said to be derived from the name of one of the first large cattle-drivers, who, while on trail, was surprised on a mountain pass, 10,000 feet over the sea, by a heavy snowstorm, and lost his entire herd, consisting of many thousand head, by a stampede exceptionally disastrous, for he recovered only a small portion months afterwards. Another story has it that the term comes from "Mauvric," an old Frenchman in Texas, who is said to have added largely to his worldly stores by a systematic abstraction of these waifs and strays. But this last version does not receive much credence, as cattle-thieves, like road-agents, horse-rogues, and claim-jumpers generally, get "rubbed out" in an uncomfortably speedy manner, long before the ordinary run of mortals have time to make a lasting name for themselves.

The long, fatiguing journey of many months, scanty feed on the trail, and overwork, reduce the poor horses, half broken at best, to a terrible state of emaciation. At such times you will see them stand about with drooping head, mere gaunt spectres of their selves, and possessing hardly sufficient strength to feed; and worst of all, the winter with its heavy three-days snowstorms and fierce cold is at hand, and no shelter except the sparsely-timbered ravines of the next mountain range to protect them. It is really wonderful that these animals, whose lot is far worse than that of the carefully driven cattle—equally accustomed to a warm climate as they are—manage to survive a winter in these latitudes; and yet, if you happen to see them again in June, you would be more than astonished at their first-class condition. Plump and full of spirits, they seem different animals.

The herd and the dust-begrimed weary men, after their

long summer's journey, at last arrive at their future home. Work of a different kind begins then: the ranche, the house, and the "corral" have to be built; a stock of hay for the horses, if such is procurable, laid in; the cattle branded, and then carefully distributed over the range—here 1000 head; there, twenty miles farther, 500; and so on till the whole herd is "turned out." Not always, however, is the long journey accomplished in one season; unforeseen obstacles—early snowstorms and other causes—may have delayed them on the road, obliging the party to "lay over" the winter. This they do by stopping at the first unoccupied grazing-land they reach. A temporary ranche is erected, the waggon with a couple of men is despatched to the next settlement, often 100 miles off, to fetch provisions for the winter, and there they remain till spring, when the "cow-camp" is broken up, and the party proceed towards their destination—eighteen months and more intervening, in such cases, between the day the owner set out on his voyage to purchase his cattle and the day they reach their future home.

The permanent ranche building is often only a little better than the temporary one—formed of logs, the interstices filled with a mixture of mud and sand, making the inside (one chamber, with a fireplace in one corner, and two or three bunks along one of the walls) fairly weather-tight. The door moving on raw-hide hinges, is made of packing-case boards, and one small window cut into the logs. And yet you will find very contented beings in these miserable dwellings. Plenty of vigorous exercise, a life-giving air, and the absence of the vitiating pleasures of civilization, go a long way in making the lot of these jovial, light-hearted cowboys by no means an unenviable one.

The social features of stock-raising are as peculiar as the natural ones; and if we follow the steps of the more adventurous ranchemen, pushing Westwards, edging the red man from his happy hunting-grounds, replacing the buffalo and elk with domestic kine, we read also a piece of frontier history.

The peopling of a new Territory is an interesting study. We see the tide of emigration, called forth by the discovery of gold, sweep over the land; a period of crazy speculation and lawless ruffianism ensues, only to end in another Westward start for new fields, leaving behind a small residuum—the "colour of the gold-washer's pan," or, in other words, the less adventurous but more industrious and thrifty, and hence a valuable portion of the emigratory horde—as the founders of a new community.

For the last ten years the ranchemen have played a very prominent part in the peopling of new countries, and generally of those which, by their elevation or poorness of soil, could not be turned to any other use. Not a few of Western cities subsist on the stock business; and portions of Wyoming and Montana would no doubt be still the dreary uninhabited steppe deserts they were a decade ago, were it not for the stock-breeder.

There are a good many false notions abroad respecting the general character of Western men. Of the old-time gold-digger we have a series of unpleasantly faithful pictures in the writings of certain clever American authors; but it would be a great mistake to apply their mould to all others, and especially to stockmen, who, as a rule, I found to be a thrifty, energetic, and very hospitable class. Strangers, and particularly Englishmen, will be struck by this last feature—all the more welcome in those uncivilized regions, inhabited in our fancy by a race of desperadoes, whose only law is the revolver, whose only god is whiskey, and whose one prayer is foul-mouthed blasphemy. This, however, is not so; though naturally—as in all new countries where society is jumbled together of the most heterogeneous elements; where one neighbour is a gentleman by birth and education, an Oxford undergraduate or a Yale College student, whose love for a roving life has led him to exchange a luxurious existence for one of activity and adventure in the West; the other, as a strange contrast, a rough, uncouth Western-raised "boy," an old prospector, or even a desperado, who, after a quarter of a century's adventure in the wilds of Arizona, New Mexico, or Texas, has now settled down to steady work on his ranche—the English settler will for some time sadly miss the social laws which govern the intercourse of different classes in the old world. At first he will not like the independence of the cowboy under him, who by look and manner will let him know that the question who is the better man of the two has long been settled in his own mind. His hands will itch when some saucy "Do it yourself" is the only answer he receives to some order concerning a matter not quite within the scope of his "help's" duties. In time he will get accustomed to the ways and manners of the country; and if there is no false pride about him, the good points of the English character, to which none are more keenly alive than the Western men, will have gained him not only the good-will but the devoted attachment of the free-handed boys!

To speak of my own experience, I may mention that often, cold, hungry, and weary, I rode up to an isolated cattle-ranche, bespeaking a meal and shelter for the night.

The best of everything would be offered. Hay, always scarce in those regions, would be given to my horse, and the snuggest corner, the warmest blankets be forced upon me. Many times have I extended my visit for two or three days, and yet not a penny would my hosts accept on parting. To this I would fain tag a word of warning to Englishmen intending to settle as cowboys. It is "to do as others do." That marked feature of America, social equality, which, while it has often a way of expressing itself in a very extravagant and disagreeable fashion, is undoubtedly a main factor in the unusually rapid growth of the Great West, must never be forgotten by the English settler. A man out West is a man, and let him be the poorest cowboy he will assert his right of perfect equality with the best of the land, betraying a stubbornness it is vain and unwise to combat. This is an old truth, and numberless writers have expatiated upon it. In connexion with the cattle-business, it is, however, of tenfold importance; in no vocation is popularity more essential than in this, for let a man receive once the name of being moved by unsociable pride, and there will not be a man in the country who, while he otherwise would gladly share his last pipe of tobacco or cup of coffee with him, will not then be ready and willing to spite or injure him. In no business is a man so dependent upon his neighbours, so open to petty annoyances, and so helplessly exposed to vindictive injury to his property, as in stock-raising out West.[9]

[9] For more detailed information, see Appendix.

CHAPTER XIII.

REMINISCENCES OF THE WEST.

" It is not wealth, nor birth, nor state;
But get up and git, that makes man great."
A Bard of the Rockies.

THE traveller is often asked for "first impressions" of foreign lands he has visited. The West grows a rich harvest of this fruit, and there are people who never stop gorging their minds with the luscious firstlings of frontier humour. For mine—to speak of really the first genuine impression—I have to thank a far more familiar and harmless incident than any of the typical Western scenes —the audacious "road-agent," or grimly-grotesque "hanging-bee," or any of the hundreds of such-like *événements* that are wont most to impress the new comer; I got mine, namely, from nothing more or less awful than a squealing baby.

There was nothing very peculiar about the appearance of this baby. Not over-burdened with garments, it was strapped in Indian fashion to a board about two feet long and one foot broad. The board and the baby were leaning against the log wall of a frontier shanty on its shady side. There was nobody near; and as I had heard a good deal about the 'cute dodges employed by Westerners when "pre-empting" new locations, the letter of the land-laws obliging them to mark possession by some visible and unmistakable "squatter's sign," I imagined this possibly might be a new way of demonstrating ownership to would-be "claim-jumpers," always ready to pounce upon unprotected property. The baby seemed very happy; its little arms were free, and kept up constant movement —the only sign of life on the arid, dusty plains that surrounded the miserable sod-roofed shanty with oppressive vastness. Urging my horse a little closer, I remarked that some strings were dangling about the baby's neck, and that one was tied to the big toe of one of the rosy little feet of the infant. I was puzzled. Dismounting from my tired "sawbuck," I proceeded to examine the arrangement in tape. The child was complacently sucking at a bit of raw pork, about the size of a large walnut, tied to one end of the string, while the other was fastened, as I have said, to the little foot, a second piece of twine, knotted to the board over its head, prevented the piece of meat falling to the ground, should the child loosen its clutch. Nine men out of ten would, I fancy, have immediately detected the connecting link between the toe and the pork I was, however, the tenth, for at that time you could not have seen anywhere a more brilliant specimen of the genus "tenderfoot" than I was. So what wonder that even that baby began to wax wrath at the density of my perception, and with the typical Western love of displaying the greatness of the "biggest country in the world, sir," it forthwith proceeded to give me that first genuine impression of which I have spoken. Its face suddenly got very red, then bluish its eyes filled with tears, and its little arms beat the air with frantic energy. It gradually dawned upon me that the baby might be choking; at least, had a grown-up person evinced such symptoms, I certainly would have commenced thumping him on the back. My native cautiousness stood a sore trial, for I had heard that to tamper with a man's land-claim was an offence visited by "shooting on sight." But nevertheless that baby acted its part in such a life-like manner that, had not at that moment the mother made her appearance, I think I should have risked rendering assistance.

"That baby is choking, ma'am," I cried.

"No he ain't, and he can't," replied she, tersely and, for her, truly, for at this instant the infantile legs also began to work—one kick, two kicks, and there on the bib lay the obstruction, the piece of pork, jerked from the baby-throat by the judiciously applied string, to the judiciously kicking little leg. I was vastly relieved, but also vastly impressed.

"Ain't you ever seen this a'fore, mister?" queried the woman—as true a specimen of the lady of the Rocky Mountains—a survival, not of the most beautiful, but certainly of the fittest as ever I have had the pleasure of meeting.

To my quavering "No—o—o" she answered, "Then kind o' remembrance it; mayhaps yer wife won't go back on it;" and noticing a smile on my face she added, "but I reckon you ain't married any how; wa'al, it'll keep, you bet." And keep I hope it will, for others as well as for me. If there is anything that could possibly tempt the most mysogynistic old bachelor to enter a more blissful condition, it would, I should say, be the hope of by-

and-by rigging up such an arrangement in strings, and seeing it work in his own nursery.

Several years have passed since that day. I have seen, to speak metaphorically, that baby in a hundred different guises, all displaying the keenness of Western intellect, and from sheer habit it has become with me a sort of standard wherewith to gauge novel and striking instances of the three great qualities of Western men—self-help, self-confidence, and adaptability.

But our picture of the frontiersman would hardly be complete were we to leave unnoticed another feature of the West, namely, its humour. Much has been written about American wit, and in the preceding pages I have essayed to give some of its spontaneous emanations as were wont to crop up on my little travels—genuine frontiersmen my companions. Lincoln said the grim grotesqueness and extravagance of American humour were its most striking feature. In the West it is all-pervading; from cradle to the death-bed, through sickness and adversity, it cheers the Western man. Removed from civilization, we see it in its happiest, most unlaboured garb, dramatizing dry facts into flesh and blood. The lingo of the West, so rich in happily-coined words, stands in close connexion with it. A late clever author on Americanisms,[1] says they are a fair representation of the Western world, which has been created on a larger scale, which in its turn grows faster, works harder, achieves more than any other land on earth has done. Slightly toned down, there is a good deal of truth in what he says. No doubt the language of the West *is* an intensified and strangely impulsive speech, just as the

---

[1] Dr. De Vere.

life's blood of the whole West throbs with a faster pulse and courses with fuller vigour through all its veins.

In the West *good stories* are rife, and to the stranger nothing is more puzzling than to tell their real age. In the phenomenal complexity of social organism in frontier country, a genuinely healthy *good story* never dies, and even such unwholesome ones as, for instance, Greeley's coaching horror, will evince in the naturally salubrious atmosphere of the Plains and mountains an amazing tenacity of life.

You hear a *good story*, and as it is the first time, you enjoy it. You go your way, and, if you are lucky, you travel from Kansas to San Francisco, and fate permits you to grow one week older before you hear it for a second time; but hear it again you shall, let you wander whither you will. It will be told you perhaps while sitting at your camp-fire on the arid Plains of New Mexico or while cantering along at the side of an Oregon "Webfoot;" you possibly have to lend your ear to it in the depth of a Nevada silver-mine, half a mile under the earth, or on the top of the Great Divide of the Rocky Mountains, three or four miles over the earth. The first six words suffice to put you on the track of it, let it be ever so cleverly adapted to entirely different circumstances, let the narrator make ever so "personally conducted" a story of it, you immediately recognize the good old tale you heard the first time in Chicago, San Antonio, or Sacramento, till finally sheer practice enables you to *point* them as easily as were their trails marked in the fashion of the Miook Indians in California, who used to drag the carcass of a defunct "fragrance pedlar," *i.e.* skunk, along the intricate paths through the forests, so as to enable their friends to follow them guided by their noses.

Some *good stories* take their origin in the Eastern Cities, but by the time they reach the Territories they are Westernized. The Coroner's *good story* is an instructive instance of the adaptability of some of the Eastern tales to Western life. I have traced its origin to facts which occurred in New York A.D. 1879. In that year, as I see from a leading New York daily paper now lying before me, reporting the proceedings,[2] a famous case of bogus inquests was unearthed. Coroner D—— was the ingenious official, and in the course of the law proceedings it was proved that this gentleman, whose domain was Staten Island, near New York, where numerous cases of *found drowned* are the rule, had hit upon the ingenious plan of anchoring a corpse in a quiet cove of the sea, and holding inquest at will on him. When discovered, nine Coroner's inquests had sat on this one SPECIALLY RESERVED corps, each putting a shabby nine dollars into his pocket. The idea was one that "took." Cases of anchored corpses were heard of all over the Union. Inland cities that had no rivers or lakes handy, had always townwater reservoirs to fall back on. Everything gets old very quickly in America, and by the time California had gripped the idea, it had assumed very mature form, though only a few short weeks had elapsed since Coroner D——'s preliminary examination in New York, a fact which the following conversation between a Californian official and a San Francisco Judge, as reported by a 'Frisco paper will prove :—

"'The fact of it is,' said old Dr. Potts, the Los Angelos

[2] The *World*, June, 1879.

Coroner, the other day, as he strolled through the morgue with Judge Van Snyder, 'the fact of it is, that these San Francisco coroners don't really understand how to work up their business for all its worth, and make it boom as it were.'

"'What do you mean?' said the Judge, somewhat horrified.

"'Why, they don't know how to really run a corpse for all the coin that is in it. They don't handle 'em scientifically, so to speak. Now we do that sort of thing better down our way.'

"'Do, eh?'

"'Yes. For instance, there was a Chinaman killed by smoking opium a few months ago, out in the suburbs of our town, and of course I was around there and had sworn in a jury before the cadaver got cold, and what with summoning witnesses, taking testimony, &c., before night I had a bill against the county for $96.50.'

"'More than the Chinaman was worth, I should think," said the Judge.

"'But wait. I opened the grave in the county burial-ground the same night, rushed the corpse down to the laboratory and had it embalmed, and all ready for emergencies. Well, about three nights after that they had a free fight out at the Digger Indian encampment, and so I had the Celestial pigtail cut short, a few feathers twisted in it, and hid him in a bush out that way. Of course it was discovered pretty soon, and reported; and as the jury couldn't agree as to the particular tribe of Indians the deceased belonged to, I impannelled another one—nearly double the fees, don't you see?—and gave the papers a rousing good item. It's a way-up plan to keep in with the reporters, by the way.'

"'How much did that make?'

"'Well, I was about $240 ahead on the speculation then, so I waited until a lot of Dago emigrants passed through the town, and the next day one of 'em was found dropped dead on the road of heart-disease—don't you see? Same old corpse, with a big felt hat and rawhide boots, and his pocket full of macaroni. I think I squeezed about $175 more out of the tax payers that time. Well, I kinder let up for about a week after that, and then had the remains doubled up in a packing-box and found among the unclaimed freight down at the railroad station. The papers wrote it up as a " Mysterious Murder Case," and we had a ten days' examination. Lem'me see, I think it was $445.50 the whole thing panned out before we were through that time. What do you think of that?'

"'Why, it's the most extraordinary—'

"'Why, that's nothing, my dear sir, nothing. I haven't got half through with that Chinaman yet. When I left home I just kinder wedged him in among the top branches of a tree in the woods just out of town, dressed in a suit of complete black with an old telescope in his coat-tail pocket, and a pair of big green spectacles on his nose. Catch the idea, don't you?'

"'Can't say I do.'

"'Why, that's the aeronaut dodge, don't you see? Unknown scientific party, fallen out of a balloon. My own design entirely. Splendid, isn't it? The corpse is a little worn by this time, I know; but what are you going to do with such an infernally unhealthy climate as Los Angelos? I expect to send the old lady and the girls to Paris on those remains yet, if I have to wire 'em together to do it. No, my dear sir, depend upon it what those metropolitan coroners lack is push, enterprise, sir, and ingenuity.'

"And the doctor reluctantly stopped poking a defunct stock speculator with his cane, and permitted the Judge to take him out for a drink."

Now for the practical application of the tale.

Four months later an acquaintance of mine, while travelling in the wilds of the West, had the following occurrence happen to him. I give it in his own words.

"On a considerable river we had to cross, notorious for its quicksands, we found, much to the surprise of my men, a newly erected ferry close to a desolate-looking log cabin. The charges written on a board near the cabin were high, and would have amounted to fifteen dollars for my outfit. The river was low, and my men had crossed it several times at a ford they knew half a mile below the ferry. They decided to try the ford. When we got there we found a freshly made grave close to the river bank, and written on a rude wooden cross the following epitaph:—

'Here are drowned and buried Old John, from Texas, and Lame Billy, his brother. N.B.—The ferry is less than half-a-mile up the river.'

"I did not like this, and wanted to prevail on my men to turn back and use the ferry rather than risk the quicksands. But they would not hear of it; they knew, they said, that the ford was perfectly safe—which indeed it proved to be. The whole outfit had crossed except my headman, and when I looked back I saw him, to my astonishment, engaged in digging at the grave. Five minutes sufficed to show that Old John from Texas and Lame Billy his brother had not been old trappers, as in the innocence of my heart I supposed, but two old mules. As the ford was situated on a route frequented by emigrants to Oregon, many of these unfortunates would, no doubt, be frightened to use the ferry. We happened to pitch camp for the night close to the river, in view of the cabin on the other side. We had done supper, when who should make his appearance for an evening chat but the 'cute originator of the grave dodge, the practical ferryman. To listen to my men taking him down was worth millions, though in Western fashion he seemed very proud of his ingenious trick. 'Ever seen that game worked afore?' he asked. 'In course you never have; it's mine; and it pans out boss, you bet, for it runs them emigrant folk right up to the squealing-point. It struck me not long ago, when reading in an old paper of that yar Yankee Coroner who kept a dead man's body anchored in a quiet corner of Staten Island bay. That er' chap ought to have come West; too good by a full hand (poker expression) for them Eastern folk.'"

But I must bring to a close my rambling disquisition on a theme that has yielded, and will yield, food galore, for the master-pens of great humorists. Let me rather make an attempt to picture another feature of frontier life, not so oft described as the equally ephemeral Mining Emporium of the great Silver and Gold Land beyond the Missouri, namely, a pioneer settlement of a half-dozen huts that does not owe its origin to the wild crazy search after precious metals. To what does it, then? the reader will ask. But that is harder to answer; perhaps to a broken axle-tree; to a sick child that finally succumbed to the terrible hardships of emigrant travelling in the ante-railway days—a visitation of

Providence which has hallowed the spot where their only offspring lies buried, and upon which the parents have not the heart to turn their backs;—or, what more frequently occurred, to a *dash* of a band of yelling red fiends, which, while it left them, as a piece of good luck, with their hair on their heads, resulted in their being stranded in the middle of the dreary desert-like Plains, hundreds of miles from the next settlement, without a single horse or oxen left to haul their heavy waggon, laden with their all and everything, on to their yet very distant goal on the Pacific shore. The next water and timber-land is sought ; and a few days' wood-felling and hauling, two pair of strong arms, a brace of energetic wills, and the first hut of the settlement is sod-roofed, and ready for occupation.

A Chinese proverb says woman's heart takes a lot of breaking ; but this could be equally reasonably said of the frontiersman's organ. He is constitutionally a sanguine being—all his surroundings tend to make him that—so that finally when he does strike a "pocket," let it be in precious ore or in the way of surer though not so large gains accruing from any one of the multifarious undertakings this Jack-of-all-trades tackles to, he makes but another one of the thousands of vastly energetic settlers who, not so many years hence, will have connected the rich land of gold and corn—California—with the Missouri, by one unbroken chain of States, towns, and farming or stock-raising land.

The typical pioneer settlement I shall attempt to describe is one of this sort. There are only some eight or ten huts, and its origin was an emigrant's break-down, which three or four years ago stranded the *oldest inhabitant* in that neighbourhood. His few cattle have multiplied at a patriarchally fast rate, and some other emigrants to Oregon have acted upon the old maxim of the bird in the hand, and have let Oregon be Oregon. I visited the spot on two different occasions. The first time (in 1879) I reached the few scattered log-cabins, nestling under the beetling brows of a gorge intersecting a vast upland plateau some 6000 or 7000 feet over the sea, the inhabitants were in the throes of an Indian scare, the Utes had "broken out" 150 miles south, had massacred a lot of troops that had been sent to subdue them, and were now supposed to be on the war-path northwards, ready to do as a kindred tribe had done a year or two before, *i.e.* to sweep the whole country, and butcher the solitary white settlers. I happened to strike the settlement a day or two after the first rumour of the Ute outbreak had reached it. Riding a few miles ahead of our men, who followed with the pack-animals, I reached the cabins some hours before them. The men of the settlement were all away attending to a distant cattle-drive; they had left before the first alarm, and were not expected back for some days yet. The women—there were some eight or nine families—had, on receipt of the first warning, held a council of war, in which it was decided to retire to a small underground "fort"— cellar would describe it better—connected by a subterranean passage with the largest log-cabin of the settlement. It was hastily provisioned; a woman who was in child-bed brought hither, and everybody ready to repair to this last refuge at the first approach of the dreaded foe. My looks, as I rode up to the first shanty, I suppose were not very reassuring. Long absence in the wilds of the mountains had reduced my dress to the last extremity. The skin and venison of a Bighorn I had killed that morning were slung over my saddle, and festooned old Boreas's flanks, while my hands were still red with the blood of my game, as I had passed no water since my morning's kill. Altogether I must have looked, astride of my pony, who was likewise bespattered by blood, a somewhat uncanny character. Not having seen a white man for some time past I was unaware of the Indian news, and hence was quite unprepared for the shrill "Halt!" that stopped me a few yards from the fence surrounding the first log-cabin. On looking at the spot from whence issued the voice, I espied a huge needle-rifle resting on the top bar of the fence. Its business end was pointed at me with unpleasant steadiness, while at the butt end I descried a diminutive bit of humanity in the shape of a boy of eleven or twelve.

"Say, stranger, what the —— —— are you, anyhow? Be you a —— tarnal redskin half-breed, or a white man?" demanded the miniature sentry, who, on the look-out for Indians, wanted to make quite sure ere he let me pass. My laughing answer was followed by his letting down the hammer of his rifle; and standing up under the shadow of his huge old arm, at least a foot and a half taller than himself, disclosing to me a bright-eyed youngster of frontier breed.

"I am the boss in this yer camp," he replied to my query, and taking from his trouser-pocket a roll of plug he made a formidable bite at it. I had arranged to wait for my men at the settlement, so dismounting and tying up my horse, I followed his indication to go into the house, "where mam oughter (ought to be) cooking dinner."

This latter personage, busy with her stove, seemed somewhat taken aback when I stalked into the cabin.

However, she seemed prepared for squalls—a well-filled cartridge-belt girthed her waist, a long six-shooter in its sheath being attached to it, while a Winchester rifle was leaning against the stove ready for immediate action. In ten minutes the loquacious Western lady had informed me of the state of things—had told me in what a perpetual state of fright they had been the last two days; how every soul in the settlement retired every evening to their underground "fort;" and how they longed to have their husbands and sons back again. She seemed delighted to hear that my party would presently follow, and that we had seen no signs of hostile Indians further north. After partaking of dinner, and the boy-sentry being relieved by a neighbour's daughter, I made the round of the cottages under the guidance of the boy-sentry, who turned out to be a very wide-awake little chap, a genuine Western-raised child, more of a man than many a swaggering lout double his age further East; his astonishing flow of bad language and the constant application to his plug being the only drawbacks to a more intimate acquaintance with him.

I visited the cellar "fort," and comforted the sick woman with the news of the reinforcements the settlement had received. Some twelve feet square, with loopholes where the walls, only seven feet high, joined the earthwork roof, it seemed a safe enough place, however insufficient in its dimensions to hold twelve or fifteen human beings. The narrow passage, sloping upwards, some four or five yards long, and only four feet high, connecting this cellar-like excavation with the body of the log shanty, was so arranged that it could be filled up with earth at a moment's notice, while the heavy pile of earth that covered the rafter roof, raising it slightly over the ground, made it difficult, if not impossible, for the Indians to fire the structure.

My men arriving in due time, we pitched camp close to it, and remained there for two days, giving our worn-out cattle a very necessary rest. A part of the male contingent of the settlement returned before we left, and, as was not unnatural, felt very grateful to us for our presence. Some months later, in the depth of winter, a very bad snowstorm compelled the "English outfit," as my party was called in the Western vernacular, to retrace their steps to the same settlement, and there we were obliged by stress of weather to "lay over" for an entire week. During my stay there Thanksgiving Day, the great national fête-day, occurred. Frontiersmen are an eminently hospitable people, and thus I was not astonished to be invited in a hearty manner by the chief personage of the little settlement, the owner of a typical Western "store," or shop containing the necessaries of daily life, such as whiskey, flour, ammunition, beaver gloves, and woollen comforters. He was in the habit of giving on this day a free dinner to all comers, the expenses of the repast, for which a turkey had been provided at the cost of a horseback ride of more than 100 miles to the next town, being covered by the "drinks," sold at the customary rate of a quarter (one shilling) per glass of whiskey.

Though the snowstorm was of the severest, the men from the next cattle-ranches, forty, fifty, and, one or two, seventy miles off, came riding in, often at the risk of their lives, to partake of this friendly meal, attracted by the welcome change in their lonely ranche life. I was myself glad, once again after months of roughing, to sit down—

I was going to say on a chair, but it was a barrel—to a square meal, served on a table.

The inside of the log cabin presented, when I entered it half an hour or so before dinner, a typically Western scene. The only room of which it consisted, besides the store, which was in an adjacent barn-like structure, was filled with chatting and laughing groups of men, all attired in the peculiar, practical, and not unpicturesque frontier dress, in which leather and huge jingling spurs seemed the predominating features. Tall, lithe men, their faces all aglow after their long rides in the storm, their sombrero hats, often shapeless structures of felt, set jauntily on their heads, cartridge-belt and long six-shooter round the waist, they were all busy disposing of their *'fore dinner drinks*. Here was a knot of trappers fresh from the mountains, swapping stories and telling big yarns. A little aside, speaking with my own trapper, I perceived a white-headed old mountaineer, dressed in worn buckskin from head to foot, who, as soon as he saw me, stepped out and gave me right hearty greeting. The old fellow was one of the best-known personages in frontier country, for he had been in the West, at first as a Fur Company trapper, and later on that of an Indian scout, for the last fifty-one years. Port knew him well, and from him I heard a good deal of the taciturn old stag's former life. Married to a half-caste girl of great beauty, the daughter of a well-known scout, his wife eloped with one of the '49 miners; and the story goes that he followed the pair through the West for six years, and finally came up to them on the frontier of Mexico, with the result that shortly there were two people less in the world. He himself never spoke of that event, or indeed, with rare exceptions, of any other in his long veteran life on the

Plains and in the mountains. At the camp-fireside, where only one or two listeners were present, and these were old comrades, his taciturn nature would now and again shake off some of its reserve, and the old man would recount events bearing upon the subject we were happening to discuss. Never by any chance was there about his tales the slightest ring of the wonderful or sensational, and what he told was narrated in such naively truthful manner that its veracity was pleasantly manifest. We had to tell him all the little incidents of our expedition, and give him accurate accounts of the localities visited by us. Now and again he would chip in with some pregnant remark, how in the fall of '45 or in winter of '34 he had trapped that 'er creek, or done some hunting with the Black Snake Sioux, or wintered in a dug-out on some stream we had passed; or how in '62, when the Sioux and Soshoné were " out," he had " a couple o' months scouting of just the liveliest sort with them darned 'Rappahoes (Arrappahoes), the doggarned meanest cusses of redskins ever a white man drew a bead on (shot at)."

Presently dinner—which, in the meanwhile was being prepared by the store-owner's wife, aided by a neighbour's daughter, on the iron cooking-stove occupying one corner of the room—was announced; and the steaming dishes of turkey, haunch of bighorn, potatoes, and " corn," with very grateful coffee as beverage, were placed on the long board, on which were ranged tin plates and cups. All the guests had indulged in a preliminary " fixing up" at the " wash-basin," a battered gold-pan, for frontiersmen are, as a rule, very cleanly people. I recall few occasions that I did not notice the raggedest cowboy before sitting down to his meal first washing his hands in the battered old tin wash-hand basin, and using the "Jerusalem Overtaker"—as he calls the remnant of a tooth-comb, tied with a bit of string to the fragment of a looking-glass, mostly the size of one's hand, fastened to the logs of the cabin. In frontier settlements, when returning from their half-yearly roamings in the wilds, the mining prospector or trapper will usually have a general "overhauling" to do honour to the occasion of again seeing a white woman. He will scrub his face and hands with soap and sand, and torture himself by the application of his whetted skinning knife to the tangled beard of six months' growth, while his sailor's needle and "buckskin" thread are set to work patching any very glaring defects in his deerskin or canvas wardrobe. Many and many a time have I watched, with curiosity mingled with amusement, the behaviour of these uncouth men of the wilderness when in white woman's presence. The rough joke, the threatened oath, the careless fling of some saucy answer to a fellow craftsman, are hushed—stayed as abruptly as could the hand, that in child-like fashion is brought up to the mouth, thrust back the half-uttered jest, or the yet unpronounced name of the Deity. . The Western woman's word is never disputed. Her dignity, *savoir-faire*, and independence make her the master of the most puzzling situations.

An acquaintance once witnessed a scene, which will illustrate the frontier woman's privileges. I will narrate it in his own words :—

"It was at a remote little settlement, consisting of some twenty log cabins, tenanted by burly pistol-girt miners, three or four "baching" (bacheloring) in every hut. Two cabins, however, knew woman's face, the wives of the owners, who were the 'top shelfers' of the little frontier colony. The two husbands, close neighbours had some 'difficulty,' and when I became the inmate of one of the two 'married' huts 'shooting on sight' had been threatened and counterthreatened. The morning following my arrival, while I was sitting in front of the door, the enemy's lady hove in sight, and passing me made her way into the hut, where, while everything from the double-barrelled shot-gun, standing at full cock in the corner, to two Colts in the belt of the owner, was in readiness to receive her spouse, the unexpectedness of *her* "coup" resulted in a grand victory for her. Going up to the unfortunate man, she began to belabour his face and head with the brawny fists of a frontierswoman. The victim, a huge fellow, who could have crushed her with one tap of his sledge-hammer biceps, never raised himself from the chair on which he was seated, but presently remarked, in the drawl of his Eastern home, 'Neow, you'd better skin (leave), or fix for a squar' fight, for she be a coming,' alluding to his own wife, who was approaching the hut. The next day the promised on-sight business did come off, and the man who never raised his finger to stay the summary chastisement inflicted by a woman, shot her husband—the same fate threatening him, only his was the handier of the two guns."

But to return to my Thanksgiving dinner. The two chairs the hut contained were reserved for the two women, the men being seated on barrels and old packing-cases. A merrier or more enjoyable dinner I have not often sat down to; and as I looked round and noted the bright faces all aglow with rude health, and noted the zest and pleasure sparkling in the eyes of at least the younger portion, mostly Texas cowboys, as full of ready wit and fun as they were of dare-devilry, and further remarked what a salutary influence the presence of the two women exercised upon these rough fellows and their conversation, I could not help drawing a favourable comparison with similar incidents under like surroundings in countries claiming a higher degree of civilization. Not an oath or unsuitable word fell on my ears while the women were present.

There were several *characters* present which I either knew personally or had heard about. One, old "Trading Jack," a quaint old mountaineer I had previously met, had, much to the astonishment of the party, failed to put in his appearance. He inhabited an old dug-out, forty miles up the mountains; for, when the settlement increased to half-a-dozen or so of families, the quaint old stag, who had lived his life in lonely seclusion, found the *country got crowded*, and had retired to his dug-out in the mountains. Poor fellow! while we were sitting there discussing the absent one, nearly everybody having a story or two to tell of the eccentric old fellow, he was wrestling with a terrible death, the details of which I heard some months later. He was out setting bear-traps, and while so occupied he was caught by the heavy beam of one of his "falls," which are so set as to come down with great force, either killing the bear outright by breaking his back, or imprisoning him. This heavy log had come down on old Jack, only maiming but not killing him; for when his remains were found some week afterwards, his legs gnawed off by wolves, there were unmistakable signs of his having tried to cut the beam asunder with his knife. How long he remained alive, nobody of course could tell. Thus poor old Trading Jack got "rubbed out." The preceding Thanksgiving Day he had been present, and one of the company told me how the old fellow, who on account of his religious devotion was supposed to have once been a preacher, said grace on that occasion.

'It seems that the entertainer had asked him to do so, and I must mention that this personage, an old miner by profession, had been once blown up in a mine, disfiguring his face and entailing the loss of one hand, which was replaced by an iron hook. "Rising and fumbling with the hilt of his hunting-knife," my neighbour proceeded to tell me, "old Jack began: 'Wa'al, boys, it's kinder mean of that thar man with the one eye, iron-hook paw, and skunk-backed nose to pass the kiards in that 'er fashion; but, boys, I am thar when I am thar, so don't you bark up a wrong tree, and rest for a straddle on that thar blind. This thar is a boss day, and I'm always kinder willin' and ready to remembrance the Old Boss up in hiven, to thank Him for His mighty goodness to us all, when I once gets on His track; so, boys, let's pray, as white men oughter on this thar day.'" This quaintly-worded introduction was probably on a par for grotesquely-expressed religious devotion with the grace itself, which latter my informant had mostly forgotten; remembering only that the old fellow ended it, not with the usual Amen, but with "Yours truly and obediently, Trading Jack."

Of the Western types present, there was one I would desire to introduce to the reader. He sat next to me on my left, and for a long time kept silent, but his notorious "leading subject" was not to be thus subdued. By birth a Prussian, a native of Berlin, he had been leading for the last eight-and-twenty years the precarious life of a prospector, beginning far in the East in Missouri, where he demonstrated to me the largest coal-fields in the world were situated, he had finally reached a point 1500 miles west of where he commenced. He was known as Dutch Cent, the latter being the abbreviation of hundred, which arose from the circumstance that in his long wanderings, it was said, he had with the instinct of a genuine Teuton built, or as the Western phrase has it, located more than 100 homes for himself. A log cabin is very quickly built, and such was the passion of this grey-headed old bachelor for house-building, that wherever he stopped for more than a passing visit he would build himself a house, and then when the fever of prospecting came over him again, pack his blankets, tin cup, and gold-pan on his old mule, the "oller Fritz," and start out for pastures new.

In the course of my wanderings I had come upon several of Cent's cabins, some mere charred ruins, others in a fairly good condition. Another peculiarity was that while in ordinary every-day life you could not have found a more taciturn companion, whiskey opened his heart, but unfortunately only to one single subject, and that of all others—Berlin. To judge by his volubility, when presently he did begin to talk, he must have put himself outside a large dose of "tangle speech." His language was a strange mixture of bad English, with very pronounced German accent and frontier lingo, which happy combination made it at first somewhat difficult to understand the old fellow. Not knowing at the time his penchant for his native city, which I may mention he had not seen for close upon forty years, I innocently answered his question if I had ever visited Berlin in the affirmative, and with that, much to the amusement of the boys, I delivered myself, a self-immolated victim, into his hands. With a tantalizing flow of language, interlarded with even more bad German than usual, he persisted in describing to me the wonders of the "Brandenburg Gate" and the statue of "old Fritz"—Carlyle's hero, Frederic the Great—their position, height, dimensions, aspect, material, cost, all to the very minutest detail were dwelt on. Finally I got tired of my neighbour's home-talk, of his incessant "My Brandenburger Thor" and "My oller Fritz,"[3] so presently with serious face I informed him that neither of these monuments existed any more, "that the Nihilists had blown them up." The old fellow looked at me, and though he probably did not understand what Nihilists meant, he yet seemed to take in the sense of blowing up, for he collapsed into welcome silence, and another glass of whiskey he presently drank sent him at last to sleep.

The weather clearing, I and my men made an early start next morning, and I had proceeded some ten or twelve miles, when to my astonishment old Cent, mounted on a very aged and decrepit animal, came galloping after us. On reaching us, he hardly took time to answer my greeting, but blurted out in anxious tone of voice whether "it was drue de olle Fritz was plow up, dem poys pack at the ranche had dold him I had said so." On my reassuring and telling him it was only a joke, I asked him whether he had come all that long way only for that purpose. "I'd ridden to de end of Greation to hear *dat*," was his answer, and about his voice there was a ring as if he quite meant what he said.

In frontier country now and again little adventures can befall the traveller, though they are much rarer than the

[3] The Berlin idiom, oller, for alt, or old.

literature of the West would lead one to suppose. In my prolonged experience of the West only two such incidents happened to me. Neither would be worth telling, were it not for the very circumstance that during my extended visits to frontier regions they were the *only* two incidents of the typical Western character that came within my personal cognizance.

The one which I propose to relate occurred to me while I was temporarily travelling with a party of cattle-men. We were out of meat, and I had made a light pack-camp to a neighbouring range of steep "buttes," where I hoped to get some antelope; and on my return to our route missed connexion with the men I was with. I had not seen a ranche or a man's face for nearly two days, and the desert-like country seemed totally uninhabited. Striking a creek towards evening, I followed its course, hoping to come across a ranche I had heard the men talk of. There was a cattle-trail along its banks, so I continued my journey after darkness had set in—as I was anxious not to delay the party, and I knew they would have to pass the lonely outpost of civilization I was looking for.

It must have been close upon ten o'clock when my horse gave unmistakable signs of the vicinity of a human habitation, and presently I came upon a beaten trail leading to a miserable shanty, half "adobe," half log, the roof not six feet from the ground, covered with gravel and earth. It was the long-looked-for ranche. All was dark, and not a sign to show the dwelling, if so it deserved to be called, to be inhabited. The door, or rather the apology for one, was made of thin packing-case boards, half an inch between each, so that neither rain nor snow were shut out. Unprovided with either lock or latch, it flew open to my kick.

A loud hallo on my part was answered by a gruff voice inquiring who was there. Half an hour later a cheerful fire was blazing in the hut; my horses were led into the sacred enclosure of the hayrick, and a nice supper of bacon and beans, the best the men had, was being discussed by me. The two cowboys, the inhabitants and owners of the ranche, typical specimens of their class, hospitable, humorous, and full of life, were both Texans, jovial, merry-hearted fellows ; and very soon I was on the best of terms with them.

After supper, when I had told them all the " outside " news, and my tobacco-pouch of ample proportions, no less than the contents of my small whiskey flask, that golden key to cowboy heart, had gone the round, the boys proposed a game of poker "just for fun." Indeed it could not very well be for anything else, for I am very sure my cowboy friends could no more have mustered up five dollars between them than I could.[4] Though, of course, out West among such surroundings I would never play cards for money, I was tempted to enter into the spirit of the thing, and agreed to take a hand. To heighten the fun one of the boys proposed to play for " them thar new boots," pointing with his thumb to the corner of the hut occupied by a low trestlework bench of the rudest construction, on which generally saddles, boots, &c., are piled. I hardly looked round, and neither did I think of inquiring why the elder of the two men wore his left arm in a sling. As a set-off to their new boots I offered to stake a spare gaudily-coloured silk handkerchief that was knocking about one of my saddle-pockets ; and further it was agreed that he

[4] When once out in the wilds, money is not required ; hence it is never carried about on one's person.

who should "clear out" his two antagonists, *i.e.* win all the markers, represented, in the absence of anything else, by matches, each player receiving a full box, was to win the boots and handkerchief. Soon afterwards we were lost in the intricacies of that great American game; "bluff" followed "bluff," and between the deals cow-camp stories were told with that peculiar zest and dry wit so humorous to listen to, and so utterly impossible to do justice to all ludicrous exaggerations of facts on paper. Luck favoured me, and by a final big hand I collected the sum total of the matches on my side of the fire,—we were playing stretched out on our robes, using an empty waterpail as card-table,— and I was pronounced winner of the boots. "Guess you had better take them off at once," remarked one of them; and to my query what he meant, he told me they were on the saddle-rack in the corner.

Desiring to keep up my incognito a little longer by entering into the spirit of the thing, I rose and stepped up to the trestlework frame. A very ragged horse-blanket was spread lengthwise over the rough wooden framework, which was nearly six feet in length. Something, I don't know what, whispered to me, that a "put-up job"—practical joke—was in the air, so I hesitated to remove the cover. The men perceived it, and one of them remarked, "Needn't be sceered, you ain't afeer'd of dead men." Before I could answer, he was at my side, and with one jerk pulled the cover off. I involuntarily recoiled a step or two, for there on the trestle-frame lay a dead man, on his feet, as I presently learnt, the new boots I had won!

"By all what's good, ain't you ever seen a dead man afore?" broke in upon the silence, long before I had recovered from my surprise. "You see we had a little shooting scrape last night, and Loafer Dick got the cold deck; he was ar' always kinder ready with his irons, and just a bit crooked as how he ingineered his aces,[b] and it warn't his fault that the six-shooter missed fire; he just creased Hiram with his second. Hadn't you won them ar' boots, Hiram was a'going to break them in when he rides into town to give himself up. But I reckon his old on's ought'er good enough for *that* job; anyhow were'r off to-morrow, for I've got to go 'long and stack the Bible"—(appear as witness)—"that all was squar' as a new born kid, for, you see, Dick pulled first, he did, and it ain't kinder likely that a cuss 'll stand *that*."

I slept on the hayrick that night, and next morning saw vanquished Loafer Dick laid in his grave. Hiram and his "pard," the former with Dick's boots on his feet, rode off to the city—a collection of log cabins, ninety miles off, where of course the whole case resolved itself into justifiable self-defence.

The bane of new countries is the absence of the restraining and humanizing influence of woman. The older States of the Union have, as the census very clearly demonstrated, a superabundance of what would make "suitable wives for the West." There is a good deal of pathos in the constant reference to a "home" in some far-away eastern or southern states, to which, on a little nearer acquaintance with the hospitable and keen-eyed, though rough men of the frontier, one has to lend one's ear. The poorest log cabin, door and windowless, a tin-cup and plate being about all that reminds one of civilization, has generally about it some little memento of "home." A ghastly "tin-type" portrait of a buxom dame, or of a

[b] Cheated at cards.

young girl, a blurred print of an eastern town cut from
some poorly illustrated paper, if the owner happens to be
a native of a town, tell their own tale.

I once happened to strike a ranche more than usually
remote and unvisited, where the men, two lonely young
"bachers," one a native of Yorkshire, the other a Texan,
had actually during the long summer and autumn months
not only never set eyes upon human being, except Indians,
but had lost, strange to say, reckoning of time, for while
it was the 11th of November, they imagined it was about
the middle or latter part of October, and were complaining
of the early winter. "We don't go much on almanacks,
you see," they said; " but just to know *when* to finish that
last bottle of Christmas-day whiskey, we'll notch off the
days on the door-posts." This they did, each taking one
post, so as to control "the count." One of the men
informed me he had been on three cattle-drives in succession, and had not seen a white woman or had been near
any settlement for two years. The other had ridden to
the next "City" the previous spring for provisions, and their
only visitor since then until our unlooked-for arrival had
been an old trapper. Game abounding in the neighbourhood, I stopped with them a day or two, pitching the
camp in front of their cabin. I was not a little amused,
and often not a little struck by the ideas and impressions
which my intercourse with these two lonely young
"bachers" revealed.

Over the open fireplace in their hut were hung a couple
of spare rifles and revolvers, and below them, nailed to the
logs with old horsehoe nails, were two pictures, one a faded
photograph of an elderly woman of unmistakably English
type, the other a cheap print of San Antonio in Texas.

Over them and connecting the two was nailed a slip evidently cut from the heading of a newspaper, bearing in large type the single word "Home!" The very simplicity of the display was touching, much more so the words of the young recluses when alluding to the aim of their present existence, a speedy return to their own countries as rich men, a goal to be reached, alas! only by the most arduous labour and exposure to ever-present danger. "I'm going to the old country with Jim," said the Texan. "I started for it once before when I had struck a rich ore-pocket, but I didn't get there quite;—I got as far as Newfoundland."

More than twelve months later I happened to ramble close to the vicinity of this same ranche, and curiosity tempted me to ride one afternoon over to their home from our camp, in order to visit the two young fellows. It was long after dark when my tired horse brought me to the isolated cabin more than a hundred miles from the next white settlement. A door, I found, had been hung by rawhide fastening to the upright logs of the entrance, and I also saw that the only window, unglazed of course, was supplied with a shutter made of the same material as the door, *i.e.* packing-case boards. The many chinks between the logs, of which the hut was built, betrayed that the inside was lighted. I pushed open the door, and as I did so, the sight that burst upon my eyes, so different from what I expected, rooted me to the spot. A bright fire was burning in the open fireplace, the source of the illumination, and seated on two empty packing-cases pushed close together, was our Yorkshire friend Jim, and a buxom, fair-haired lass, who in a very bashful manner, was presently introduced to me as "the wife." It was a little picture. The strapping young fellow, his face burnt to a ruddy brown, his shapely lithe form clad in buckskin, the ever-present Colt in his girdle, his legs encased in the long leather *'shaps* of the cowboy, reaching up to the hips, one arm thrown lightly over the shoulder of the woman, while a very lately arrived squalling young frontiersman told its own unspoken story, and required not the young husband's shy nod towards the young Westerner or stumbling explanation to prove that for once a " home," happy and peaceful, had been found on foreign soil. I looked around the log interior; there in one corner was a space screened off by a horse-blanket nailed to the rafters, behind which was spread on mother earth their buffalo-robe nuptial couch, while a tiny looking-glass, some six inches square, hung between the two old pictures, still surmounted by that single plain word in big printer's type. A new tin cup and a couple of bright plates of the same metal had been added to the household goods, but nought else had changed, save that the young fellow's face was brighter, and that I missed his brother "bacher" of the preceding year.

"Said he couldn't stand it, looking on at us two, so he skinned out with the wife's brother as a pard (partner). If the Indians ain't got them, they have got through to Wyoming by this time," was the answer I received to my inquiry after the Texan.

And how, pray, was this happy event brought about? the reader will ask. By a broken waggon-tire, which stranded a small party of emigrants to Oregon,—amongst whom were the present wife and her brother,—on the Plains far from human habitation, for, as must be mentioned, a good many emigrants from the Eastern States, especially those destined for Oregon and Washington Territory, who cannot afford the railway, still follow the example of the first explorers, and spend six or eight months *en route* from the East to the far West, their household goods taken along on waggons, preceded in patriarchal fashion by their little herd of cattle.

My Yorkshire friend and his wife—the latter married to him, as I was duly informed, by a "judge"—seemed outrageously happy, and I remember few more pleasantly-passed evenings than the one I spent in that little isolated habitation. Things were looking well with them. A series of good winters had allowed his herd of a few hundred head of Texas cattle to increase very rapidly, and in five or six years the young couple could "go home" with a fair competency.

Home! What a talismanic word it is! Amid the most desperate company, amid the roughest surroundings, its purity remains undefiled. It is an *open sesame* to the heart of the worst criminal, and its hallowed charm is nowhere more felt than in the vast far-off West. And though its heart-stirring associations are apt to pale for a short crazy span before those of an equally cabalistic word—*gold*—few, very few, Western hearts are dead to its stirring memory, and none are so hardened as not to know moments when, as a grizzly old veteran of the Rockies once quaintly expressed himself, "home is gnawing at their bones."

APPENDIX.

THE WIND RIVER AND SOSHONÉ MOUNTAINS.

THE Territory of Wyoming is a square, containing 100,000 square miles, and its Eastern half forms a small portion of the Great Western Plains (*not* Prairies), into which England could be fitted thirty times, and which, bounded on the East by the Missouri, slope steadily upwards, till finally, at an altitude of about 7000 feet, they merge into the foothills of the Rocky Mountains, which occupy the great square's Westerly half. All this table-land is a treeless barren, portions of which are of a desert-like character, and in earlier days gave the whole strip of country intervening between the Missouri and the Rockies—a belt 800 miles wide—the name of the Great American Desert. As so often remarked, there is no such thing as a *chain* of Rocky Mountains; they are entirely separate ranges, intersected by high table-land passes, often 100 miles and more in width; such as the well-known South Pass, where, at an altitude of 8000 feet, you see not a tree nor a mountain, and, for all you know, might be only eighty feet over the ocean—a circumstance similar in its misnomer to the "pass" at Sherman, where under precisely the same conditions the trans-Continental Union Pacific crosses the Rocky Mountains at an elevation of 8271 feet.

In this Western half of Wyoming there are four great distinct chains, the most Easterly being the Bighorn Mountains, running, as very nearly all the ranges of the Rockies do, from North to South. The largest, longest, highest, and most important is the Big Wind River Range, about 130 miles West of the former. It is one of the principal elevations of the entire mountain system of North America: 120 miles long, from thirty to fifty miles broad, it rises to altitudes of 14,000 feet, amongst them the famous landmark, Fremont's Peak, which can be seen from places 250 miles off. Its Northern end joins a huge triangle-shaped expanse of mountain-land with eminences of a little less altitude: it is the Sierra Soshoné, a sea of peaks, raising an insurmountable barrier to human approach to the famous Yellowstone Country from the South-East. I need hardly mention the well-known fact, that from the North, from the West, and from the North-East the Yellowstone (or National) Park is very easy of approach. In two years probably from now a branch of the Northern Pacific will touch that famous district. Where the Big Wind River Chain meets the Sierra at a sharp angle, there are two passes—"Togwotee" and "Two Ocean," both about 10,000 feet. The former is very little known, for its approaches are through excessively dense forests. All this country is over 9000 feet, and the peaks rise to 12,000 feet.

The Sierra Soshoné, of which I will speak first, is to-day, without exception, the least known of the numerous mountain chains on the Continent. It is more a sea of mountains than a chain, and, speaking quite literally, there are portions of it where it can be said with moral certainty no white or red man has ever set foot. The first Government exploration party who touched the Sierra Sohone was that of Captain Jones, who in 1873 achieved the feat of crossing the Sierra at both its extremities. Captain Raynolds, several years before, at the head of another exploration party, tried to force a passage; but, after losing himself in the dense forest at the foot of the range (notwithstanding his Indian guides), gave up the plan of ever reaching the Yellowstone country from the South across the Sierra Soshoné. Bridger, the most famous scout of his day, who led the party, made the characteristic remark that nobody could get across that mountain barrier unless he had wings, "for," as he said, "a bird cannot fly over it without taking a supply of grub along." Captain Jones proved that it was possible, though at the Westerly extremity, and not at the centre where we forced a passage. It was, however, but partial in so far that we proceeded only to the top of the range, and did not descend the Northern slopes, where the great Yellowstone wonderland lay spread at our feet, and this not because we should have found it impossible, but because I had no desire to turn my back on the promised scenic beauties of the famous Wind River Chain, which at that period I had yet to visit.

Captain Jones, in his exhaustive and interesting report on his expedition of 1873, pronounces the Sierra Soshoné to be the most remarkable mountain system in the entire Rocky Mountains; and from what I saw of it, I am decidedly of the same opinion. The original range, of which, as he says, we find many indications, lies buried beneath an outpouring of lava rock, forming a crust which it is safe to estimate at being from 4000 to 5000 feet in depth. Numerous deep canyons, such as those of the Stinking-water River, show only this volcanic material down to an elevation of 6000 feet in depth. Except the bizarre Washakie Needle, a prominent landmark, and the only mountain in the vast ocean of pinnacles that has received a name, and another nameless one, which I discovered North-West of it, which are of granite, the other hundreds—nay, thousands of peaks and eminences—are of volcanic origin. We penetrated into this range from two sides—from the South and from the East, and more weird mountain scenery than was disclosed to me day after day cannot be imagined. Rugged, as perhaps no other upheaval in the world, the eye wanders in amazement from the turreted and castellated upper surface, to the deep canyons, lined with great caverns, pillars, towers, and steeples, often hundreds of feet in height. Most of the narrow fissure-like gorges have been produced by water-erosion through consecutive strata of various lava conglomerates, to a depth of 1500 and 2000 feet. Captain Jones says:—

"Often it seems quite incredible that these chimney-like columns can remain upright. In the canyon of the North fork of Stinking-water River there is a vertical block of volcanic material fifty feet in length, only *two* feet in breadth, and 500 feet in sheer height, standing alone, at a distance of three or four feet from the North wall of the canyon."

We discovered a comparatively easy pass to the highest ground of this chain by following the East fork of Del Nord Creek, one of the first tributary creeks of the South fork of the West fork of Big Wind River. While exploring the Eastern extremities of the Sierra, the human remains were found of one of the party of nine prospectors who, in the year 1878, were massacred by the Bannocks, and who, it would appear, had succeeded in traversing the Sierra from the head of Big Wind River to the head of Owl Creek, a feat which it can be safely assumed no one before them had accomplished. Captain Reynolds, in his report to the War Department, speaks of the Sierra in the following terms: "Directly across our route lies a basaltic ridge, rising no less than 5000 feet over us, its walls apparently vertical, with no visible pass or even canyon" (this latter is only true for a small portion), and he proceeds to describe the several attempts made by his expedition to traverse them. On referring to my diary, I find we spent over forty days on the Sierra, including the Owl Creek country, *i.e.* from August 10th to August 24th, and from October 21st up to nearly the end of November.

Between the Sierra and the Big Wind River flows the river of the latter name, formed by a multitude of "forks" or headwaters.

The Wind River is for the first 140 miles of its course, till it makes that wonderful bend to the North, a very swift mountain torrent, fordable only during autumn. There is a good Indian trail along it, and another, less plain one, on the first "bench" of its right bank. By taking the lower and easier one the river has to be crossed repeatedly; indeed I remember in one day's ride to have swum it no fewer than five times. On one of these occasions Henry very nearly lost his life by being swept from his saddle and getting entangled in the stirrup.

The Big Wind River Mountains, of which Richardson in his "Wonders of the Yellowstone" (1874), speaks as a snow-clad mountain barrier, which no white man has crossed, are a very famous chain, though not quite as uncrossed as this author would have it appear, for its vast slopes have been for years the favourite haunts of several of the more adventurous trappers who have joined Indian tribes. I doubt, however, if the top of this vast backbone of North America has ever been explored by white men so thoroughly as we had occasion to do. According to my diary we were camped on the "Divide," *i.e.* watershed, the highest points of the chain —nowhere under 9500 or 10,000 feet—from August 27th to September 4th, and from September 15th to October 10th, altogether thirty-three days, the interval being taken up by an expedition to the Teton Basin, on the Pacific slopes of the chain.

Lord Dunraven, in his most fascinating work "The Great Divide," gives that name to regions immediately to the North of it. It is, however, equally merited by the Big Wind River Range. Indeed, considering that the great Colorado heads on the Western slopes of that range, within a walk of the spot where the head tributaries of the Columbia and Yellowstone (Mississipi) rise, I think even a better claim to that title can be advanced by the district under consideration. Lord Dunraven (writing in 1876) speaks of it as not being well known to him, and says it "can be visited only at considerable risk, owing to the restless hostility of the Indians;" and again, when alluding to the possibility of reaching the Yellowstone Basin by a third route, traversing the Soshoné reservation at Camp Brown (now called Fort Washakie), the identical route we followed, he calls it very unsafe, and hence "was compelled to abandon all idea of penetrating to Geyserland (Yellowstone) from the East (or rather, South-East) through mountain passes hitherto untrodden by white man's foot."

Changes have taken place even since those recent days, and the Bannock War of 1878 drove one of the restless Indian tribes into Agency life, and cleared for the moment those districts of immediate danger from Indians. There are three tribes to whose hunting-grounds the districts in question appertain, though none of these tribes penetrate (except while travelling) to the upper altitudes of the ranges. They are the Soshonés, a very peaceable tribe, held in good order by their famous old chief, Washakie, who have not killed a white man for close upon twenty years; the "Crows," or Mountain Crow tribe, a very large and hitherto on the whole peaceable community; and the Arrappahoes, a decidedly dangerous tribe, one of the few remaining ones who are ever ready to take to the war-path. Until they receive a final thrashing from the United States troops the country cannot be pronounced perfectly Indian safe, for their outbreaks are unpreceded by any warnings, and the "strike" is ominously sudden. We saw nothing of Indians or white men while on the Wind River Mountains or in the Teton Basin.

The Map I append comprises the most recent researches of the United States Government surveys, although considerable portions of the country have not yet been explored. My notes enabled me to add some details, especially between Fremont's Peak and Togwotee Pass.

As I correct these proofs I receive news that very probably the Mountain Crow Indians, joined by the Arrappahoes will very shortly make a "strike," *i.e.* enter the war-path against the whites. As both are powerful tribes, persons intending to visit the Wind River or Soshoné country this season had better exercise some judgment, and inform themselves of the danger by inquiries at headquarters.

THE SKUNK.

THE animals indigenous to the Western Plains of North America have, up to very recent times, been supposed to enjoy immunity from rabies. The skunk was the first concerning whom an exception had to be noted.

Baird gives eight species of Skunk as inhabiting North America. *M. mesoleuca*, Whitebacked S. (Mexico); *M. varius*, Longtailed S. (Texas); *M. occidentalis*, California S.; *M mephitica*, Common S. (Western Plains); *M. bicolor*, Striped S. (Southern Texas); *M. mesomelas*, Blackbacked S., Louisiana (?); *M. leuconata* (Mexico); *M. macroura* (Mexico); *M. vittata* (Mexico)—the last three named species being of doubtful character.

The skunk's reputation was never of the fairest. The old Canadian voyageurs called it *Enfant du diable*—child of the Devil; and the discovery made within the last ten years that its bite at certain periods produces hydrophobia, has invested it with further horror, especially as researches have as yet not been able to explain or to account for the epidemic appearance of rabies in skunks.

Science, it is well known, has demonstrated that rabies is the parent disease of hydrophobia; that the latter attacks only the human species, while rabies, quite distinct from it, victimises animals. It is, therefore, erroneous to apply the term hydrophobia to a rabid dog. Sir Thomas Watson, an authority on the subject, further maintains that, while in the canine race rabies can propagate rabies, hydrophobia does not ever produce itself. There would be no hydrophobia were there no rabies; there can be no rabies unless it be communicated by a rabid animal.

It has always been remarked that *rabies canina* breaks out at various epochs with exceptional violence, and then remains dormant for a longer or shorter period. In certain countries it is to the present day perfectly unknown. Thus in Australia and New Zealand no case of rabies is reported to have occurred (up to the year 1872). Greenland and Kamchatka are also entirely free from it, while to other regions this fell disease evinces a special predilection, Algeria being, perhaps, if not the most, at least one of the most, dangerous countries. To the Arabs, as several eminent authorities have shown, it was known long before the French Conquest. One authority, Dr. Roucher, goes, indeed, so far as to maintain that rabies was not imported, but indigenous in Algeria.

The geographical distribution of rabies affords much interesting study. Careful investigation leaves no doubt that the facilities for increased communication with different and hitherto little known quarters of the globe have of late years much extended its area, and, by introducing it into countries where, until recently, it had not been known, has tended to generalize the malady. The case in question is a striking proof of this. Up to the year 1871 the Western Plains had been singularly free from all symptoms of rabies, and in all the accounts of early Plains travel and the settling up of Western Territories we find up to that year not a single instance mentioned of mad dogs or wolves. It is true Western civilization is but of yesterday's creation, but yet portions of the country have been known to explorers and travellers for more than half a century, and the great number of dogs to be found round most camps of the wild tribes of Indians would have opened many channels for a rapid extension of rabies all over the Plains. Medical history shows that, while rabies has frequently followed the introduction of European dogs into new regions, it has also appeared in an epizootic form in countries where it had been previously unknown, the most remarkable instance being, perhaps, one which occurred in Peru in 1803, the appearance of which could not be traced to any foreign source.

From the various authentic sources now at the disposal of the curious, it has become patent that skunks are as liable to epidemic rabies as are wolves, foxes, and dogs; but unlike the latter, which for a long time have been known to be subject to rabies, the first appearance of the disease among skunks in the Eastern States of America is also of very recent origin.

Of the two or three American writers who have made a study of this new disease, termed *rabies mephitica*, the two most prominent occupy very antagonistic platforms. One lends the whole weight of his observations to the opinion that rabies among skunks is an entirely new disease, and hence that the malady caused by inoculation of its venom is not the same hydrophobia as results from the bite of a mad dog. The other argues that the *rabies mephitica* is identical with *rabies canina*, or, in other words, that no such disease as *rabies mephitica* exists, and that the hydrophobic effects of the bite of rabid skunks are precisely the same as those of the bite of a mad dog. A third theory advanced by certain writers (Colonel Dodge, in his work "On the Plains," is one who makes statements to this effect) is that hydrophobia is the natural result to man of skunk bites, meaning that bites inflicted by that animal, whether diseased or healthy, result in hydrophobia. This, I am inclined to think, is a mistaken view, as I know personally of a good many cases of skunk bites that have had no bad effects whatever, my own case being one of dozens that are perfectly authentic.

In the summer (August) of 1871 the first authentic instance of hydrophobia occurred West of the Missouri. It was the result of a bite from a skunk, an injury which hitherto had been considered a comparatively harmless wound, and never known to result in any way seriously to the person bitten. It took place in Colorado, and the sufferer, a buffalo-hunter named Ashby, treated the injury in the then usual way, of taking internally large doses of the only handy medicine, *i.e.* whiskey—a powerful antidote for rattlesnake bites. The arm, however, swelled rapidly, and a feeling of oppression and uneasiness overwhelmed him, so that he finally went to seek the assistance of the nearest medical practitioner, Dr. O. Clark, from whose own mouth I have these details. Ashby had been bitten on the arm while trailing a wounded deer, and the first medical treatment he received was seven days after the infliction of the wound. He rapidly grew worse, and notwithstanding large doses of morphine, his final paroxysms, which took place on the sixth day, introducing death, were terrible to behold. Dr. Clark had never seen a case of hydrophobia before, and, while the symptoms left no room to harbour doubt that the man was suffering from it, the sight of the death agonies made upon him the most lasting impression. Dr. Clark soon afterwards returned to his Eastern home, and has never since had occasion to treat bites of the skunk or any other animal in trans-Missourian countries. This occurred, I believe, in August, and I particularly mention Dr. Clark's testimony, for, so far as I can learn, it was the first case West of the Missouri. In September and October, 1871, several fatal cases were reported, and from that time up to the summer of 1873 hydrophobia caused by skunk bites was a frequent occurrence on the Plains and foothills of the Rocky Mountains. It has since never entirely died out, and every year some few cases of fatal results from skunk bites are reported. But it is very evident that it is no longer of epidemic frequency.

I will here give some of the evidence collected by the two writers to whom reference has already been made. The first to write on the subject was the Rev. Horace Hovey, who is also the theorist claiming to have discovered in *rabies mephitica* a new disease. He remarks, too, that possibly there may be a causative connexion between the inactivity of the anal glands, squirting the nauseous fluid, and the generation of malignant virus in the glands of the mouth—an opinion which his adversary claims to be conclusively proven by certain evidence he brings forward. The Rev. H. Hovey lived in Kansas city, at that time the great centre of the buffalo hunting trade, occupying thousands of men. Within a comparatively short time from the fall (autumn) of 1871, in the summer of the following year, he obtained particulars of forty-one cases of rabies, all proving fatal except one. At that time, it must be remembered, most of the persons bitten were entirely ignorant of the dangerous epidemic, and of the fatal results; and, as bites from skunks had been, since the first settling up of the country, of not infrequent occurrence, there was therefore in the majority of cases, none of the nervous forebodings to which the appearance of hydrophobia in certain cases gives rise. The men bitten were all robust, hale men, who attached but little importance to the scratch of an animal the size of a large cat. In most of the cases Mr. Hovey enumerates (he gives the names of the men, date, and place with all accuracy) the period of incubation varied between ten days and five months; the majority, however, ended with death within the first five-and-twenty days, which in all cases took place amid the most terrible convulsions. This writer maintains that the final frightful struggles of nature to eliminate the poison are more prolonged in *rabies canina* than in *rabies mephitica*. He remarks, too, that no constitutional changes take place in the latter, such as are well known to occur in the former; and equally does the absence of certain nervous symptoms constitute a conspicuous difference between the two species of rabies. In every case, where there was time, the wound healed easily and permanently, and in several instances not even a scar was visible; and in no case that came under his notice was there recrudescence of the wound, as generally follow the bite of other rabid animals. Indeed, there were so few premonitions of any kind that, in most instances, the attending physicians themselves supposed the indisposition to be simple and trivial, until the sudden appearance of convulsions taught them differently.

Dr. Janeway, at one time military surgeon at Fort Hays, is the second authority to which I have made reference. In his introduction to a very painstaking paper, he tells us that he has personally witnessed fifteen fatal cases of hydrophobia, six caused by the bite of skunks, three by wolves, and two by hogs; and hence his testimony is of especial value. In his opinion, the malady produced by the virus of the skunk is simply hydrophobia, and the disease itself is identical with *rabies canina*; and likewise he fails to agree with Mr. Hovey, that mephitic inoculation is certain death. He proceeds to mention in detail numerous fatal cases of skunk bites treated by him, in which the symptoms were precisely similar to those of hydrophobia caused by the bite of dogs, in which the period of incubation varied between thirteen and twenty-four days. He attributes the higher percentage of deaths resulting from skunk bites to the circumstance that the skunk is of nocturnal habits, and attacks at night, and generally bites exposed parts of the sleeper's body, the alæ of the nose, the lobe of the ear, the thumb, or one of the fingers. There is no doubt that clothing, in very many cases, prevents inoculation by removing from the teeth the poisonous saliva; and it is interesting to note that Dr. Janeway's personal experience proves this circumstance very conclusively. At a frontier post (Fort Larned, in Kansas) a mad wolf suddenly sprang upon the officer of the day while he was making his rounds, and bit him on the arm through his clothing. Passing on, he bit a sentinel on post in the wrist, between the sleeve of his coat and his glove, and then sprang upon a woman who was nursing a child near by, and bit her on the shoulder through a thick woollen shawl. All the cases were treated the same. The officer and the woman escaped, but the soldier died of hydrophobia. A European authority, M. Bouley, General Inspector of Veterinary Schools in France, has had similar experience in the matter of bites of rabid dogs. According to him, the documents of investigation furnish ample information respecting the innocuousness of bites, according to the different parts of the body upon which they were inflicted. Out of 73 cases in which the wounds were inflicted upon the hands, 46, and of 32 cases when the face was bitten, 29 resulted fatally; while out of 52 cases when the bite was inflicted on either the arm or lower limbs covered by clothing, only 15 ended with death. Dr. Janeway says, that in all the fatal cases of skunk bite observed by him, the stages of the disease were more or less marked by symptoms of acute melancholy. An indefinite feeling of dread, and a general *malaise* were chiefly prominent, and, as he specially remarks (he is speaking of the years 1871-73, when the epidemic raged), to most of the unfortunates the fearful result of the trivial wound they had received was unknown, and they were unaware of their perilous condition.

The percentage of fatal results of bites from rabid skunks is a very high one—much higher, it would appear, than from all other animals. Sir Thomas Watson states that in this country the number of deaths from hydrophobia varies between 1 in 21 or 25. The saliva of mad wolves is more dangerous than that of dogs. Thus at Troyes, in 1774, of 20 persons bitten by a rabid wolf 9 died; while in another instance 10 deaths out of 17, and in a third case 14 deaths out of 23 persons bitten by a wolf in a similar condition, leave no doubt on this score.

In the United States, racoons also, at rare intervals exhibit rabies, and the well-known instance of the terrible death of the grandfather of the present Duke of Richmond, who, while travelling in Canada, was bitten by a rabid fox, gives colour to Mr. Youatt's opinion that badgers are also subject to rabies. Regarding the possible recovery from the bite of a rabid skunk, all authorities agree that the chances are small. Dr. Janeway, indeed, reports but one, to which I shall presently allude.

It is now a well-authenticated fact that rabid skunks are entirely free from the odour so characteristic of these animals, which could not occur if the secretion was not exhausted. To refer to my own case, this circumstance was fortunately not known to me at the time I was bitten, for it would have greatly added to the unpleasant suspense of not knowing whether the animal was rabid or not; for it so happened that the skunk, after biting my finger while I was lying asleep on the ground (in the foothills of the Rocky Mountains) scampered off without leaving any of his scent.

According to Dr. Janeway, and the testimony of others I questioned on this matter in the course of my several trips on the Plains and in the Rocky Mountains, intense thirst is one of the most prominent signs of hydrophobia from skunk bites; the sound of splashing water, or the sight of it, invariably bringing on the terrible convulsions peculiar to this disease. I heard, however, of several cases where the patient could drink water through a straw from a covered vessel. Dr. Janeway also remarks that morphia and hydrate of choral are frequently, whether applied by hypodermic injection or externally, perfectly effectless.

Among the numerous remedies employed in the treatment of bites of skunks supposed to have been rabid, those recommended by Dr. Janeway appear to me to be the most rational—namely, free use of nitrate of silver. After repeatedly removing the eschar of the wound, he cauterized it so as to promote suppuration. He also gives a most interesting account of a cure, the only one he claims to have performed, effected by him with very copious doses of strychnia, beginning with one-sixteenth of a grain every three hours, gradually increased to the enormous dose of half a grain of that deadly poison, As the man did not die of the drug, which he had taken in quantities sufficient to kill ten men, it shows either that he was inoculated and that the strychnia acted as a tonic to the nervous system, thus enabling it to resist the invasion of the disease; or that he was not inoculated by the virus when bitten, but exhibited a wonderful tolerance for the drug. Dr. Janeway claims that the former of the two was the case, and argues (I think with perfect justification) that, as a companion of his patient, who was bitten by the same skunk and at the same time, died of hydrophobia within ten days, his remedy very probably saved the man's life.

If we let ourselves be tempted to examine a nauseous matter—the fluid ejected by the healthy skunk, and with which rabies, as we have heard, stands in intimate causative relationship—its physiological *rôle* is obvious.

While it is, of course, no longer necessary to refute the vulgar notion once prevalent, that the secretion was that of the kidneys whisked about by the bushy tail, and other unfounded tales not less ridiculous, it is not so generally known that the sole use of the muscular covering enveloping the anal glands, and capable of compressing this reservoir, is to eject the liquid. The teatlike projections have, according to Dr. Parker, one large orifice for a distant jet of the substance, and also a strainer with numerous holes for a near but diffusive jetting of the matter.

As a curiosity may be mentioned the case cited by Audubon, according to whom Professor Joes, of Newhaven, gave three drops a day of the fluid to an asthmatic patient. The invalid was greatly benefited, but he soon was afflicted by the mephitic secretion peculiar to the skunk, and became so highly offensive, both to himself and those near him, that the cure had to be stopped.

Travellers have spread the belief that the instantaneous death of the animal always prevents an escape of the well-known effluvium. This I can by no means share, and as I find my experience in this respect is shared by Dr. Coues, who some years ago published a most exhaustive treatise on North American Mustelidæ, I am emboldened to mention it. I know of no death quick enough to frustrate the ejection. I have very frequently blown skunks' heads off, approaching the muzzle of my six-shooter or express rifle to within two or three inches of their heads—indeed, one or twice they have had the steel between their teeth when I pulled, and in not a single instance has the victim failed to discharge his glands, though very probably it was caused by a spasmodic contraction of the muscles. Some authorities maintain that while in daytime the discharge is invisible, a certain phosphorescence renders the fluid luminous by night. I never noticed this, though perhaps the exceedingly dry air of the Rocky Mountains foothills, to which my acquaintance with the skunk is confined, is a locality not as favourable for the development of the phosphorescent qualities as the more humid atmosphere of Eastern states.

It is interesting to note that, similar to *rabies canina*, the malady to which the skunk is subject does not appear by any means only in hot weather. Thus, September, October, 1871; March, April, May, September, October, 1872, and the Spring months of 1873 furnish the larger proportion of cases both of rabies and hydrophobia.

The spring, summer, and autumn of 1872 witnessed the height of the epidemic out West. Not only were there many rabid skunks, but wolves, foxes, and wild cats seemed similarly affected, and several cases of hydrophobia in consequence of bites of the last-mentioned animals were reported to me when travelling through the regions where the ravages of rabies had been most virulent.

To epitomize for practical purposes the whole subject of skunk-bites, I would lay stress on the following points: If you are bitten, endeavour to ascertain whether the skunk is rabid, which, if you have the chance, can be best done by trying if his anal-glands have ceased to perform their duty. In this case—a very remote one—so long as no new epidemic occurs, I would use a knife very freely in cutting out as soon as possible the flesh or muscles surrounding the surface of the bite, or, if it is a deep bite, make a cone-shaped incision. This, however, I would only do if no clothes or covering protected the part bitten; for with covering the chances of inoculation are very remote indeed. As in all similar cases, the quicker the knife or the cautery is applied, the better the chance of effectual preventative.

BEDS.

THE most practical bed for a tour like mine, where many exigencies have to be taken into consideration, consists of the following articles:—first, and most important of all, is the waggon-sheet cover. This, as its name implies, is a large piece of stout canvas (such as is used for tents is the best), from sixteen to eighteen feet in length, and from eight to ten feet wide, large enough to cover the big freight waggons, and hence to be procured at every outfitting place. This is folded lengthwise, and when the bed is to be made, spread out on the ground. On one half of this long canvas strip are laid buffalo robes or blankets (one robe and two pair of best California blankets suffice for autumn weather), those on which you lie, as well as those with which you cover yourself. Before getting into bed, draw the other half of the sheet over your bed. Being eight or nine feet long, it will not only cover all your bed, but lap over your head. This is an important point, for otherwise the rain or snow would beat down upon your head, or if that is under the blankets, which it most probably will be, soak your blankets. If properly made and laid, your bedding will be thoroughly protected against such unwelcome visitations. In travelling, this canvas sheet, into which all your blankets are rolled, and round which a stout strap is passed, will protect the latter, and makes of the whole a bundle just of the right weight and size for one side of a pack. If the outfit is that of a trapper, and not that of a well-fitted-out shooting-party, a different use is made of the blankets when *en route*. They will be used as saddle-blankets under the pack-saddles. My men habitually did this with their blankets, and when

that disastrous prairie fire reduced our blankets, mine, which hitherto had
escaped that fate, were turned into saddle-blankets during the day, and
used for the bed at night. At first this is not pleasant, as very often you
have no chance to air and dry them before you make up your couch, and
hence will have to put up with a damp bed; or if the thermometer sinks
low, they will be metamorphosed into boards. During that fearful snap of
cold which surprised us last November, it was generally quite impossible
to prevent this, for as soon as the blankets were removed from the steaming
horses they were frozen hard, and one had to be quick to get them spread
out before they turned stiff as sheets of tin. At such times buffalo robes
come in capitally, and with one under you and one over you, and a pile
of "boards" stacked on top, we had nothing to complain of—at least
as long as no snow hurricane was blowing. When that is raging you have
to take refuge to heavy logs of wood, stones, or half-a-dozen pack-
saddles, scientifically distributed over your bed, to keep anything on it.
It has often occurred to me that sleeping-bags, lined with fur and made on
the principle of those in use in the Pyrenees, would be capital things for
men travelling in a more luxurious way than I did. For "roughing it,"
there is, however, nothing like a waggon-sheet, for it can be turned to
various uses. As a windbreak, tied to two trees and weighted down, it is
unrivalled, and in emergencies it will make a capital dog-tent. We
weathered two very bad snowstorms in one rigged up with a few poles and
a waggon-sheet.

THE CLIMATE OF WYOMING AND MONTANA.

FROM Mr. Strahorn's "To the Rockies and Beyond," I take the following
statistics regarding observations made at Fort Benton (Montana) :—

In 1872 there were 305 perfectly fine cloudless days; in 1873, 291;
1874, 277; 1875, 289; 1876, 286; 1877, 300; giving an average of 291
fine days per annum. The average temperature in January for the eight
years beginning 1867 was 20° 2', the greatest extreme cold (presumably
during day-time) being, in 1875, —44° Fahr., and, as the papers reported,
in 1880 (November), —52° Fahr. In Virginia City, 5713 feet over the sea,
the greatest heat in 1877 was 94°, while for six winters the thermometer
never went below —19° Fahr.

Mr. Granville Stuart, well-known as *the* oldest settler of Montana, for
he came there in 1857, has made faithful observations of the climate of
Deer Lodge Valley, in that Territory, which, it may be mentioned, lies on
the same parallel of latitude as Venice, and he has come to the conclusion
that the hard winters seem to come exactly five years apart; but this is

hardly borne out by the fact that the two severest winters he noted in the West were those of 1857-8 and 1880-1. On the former occasion the *mean* temperature for January was 1½° Fahr., or 30½° of frost: 1875 being also a hard winter. The average snowfall for the four winter months for eight years was not more than 24½ inches. With the exception of the severe winters, cattle and sheep owners experienced no losses to speak of. In one respect Montana has the advantage over Western and even Central Wyoming, for being less of a high table-land, there are more sheltering mountain ranges against the very severe blizzards, or winter storms, which in Wyoming rage with a violence nobody who has not lived through one can possibly imagine.

OUTFIT FOR SPORTSMEN.

ARMS.—If the sportsman intends to visit only the Rocky Mountains, a shot-gun will be found an encumbrance. As accidents to rifles are not infrequent, especially in the case of the slender-stocked English Express, the following plan, I found, works very well. Take one double-barrelled ·450 or ·500-Express and one of Bland's Cape rifles (one shot, 12 bore, and one Express-barrel), and have them made, so that the stock and barrels of both arms are interchangeable, thus if you break the stock of your Express you can use the one of the Cape gun, and *vice versâ*. The shot-barrel will come in useful for a change of *grub* in the way of grouse, though, being very tame birds, they can very easily be killed with the rifle by shooting their heads off. The Express rifle should shoot a solid bullet in one barrel. For grizzlies there is nothing like a long cannelured (not patched) missile, though if made very long it will perceptibly increase the recoil. On the whole, I think a ·500-bore better than ·450 for the Rockies.

POWDER.—The American powder is nearly as powerful as our best grades. For Express purposes I have found the coarse-grained *Orange Lightning* brand to answer remarkably well.

CARTRIDGES.—If a longer stay is meditated, it answers much better to take out empty cartridges and reloading tools, and load your *shells* yourself, or let your men do it for you. The solid-drawn straight shells of the National Arms and Ammunition Company at Birmingham are, I have found, decidedly superior to those manufactured by Eley Brothers. The former are more uniform in size, and their cap (containing the anvil) is better than Eley's plain cap. I have had a good many missfires with the latter, and only one with the former.

WADS.—The lubricating wad suitable for hot climates I have found to be worse than useless for the West, as somehow it seems to foul the barrels very quickly, particularly in cold weather. I always use a thick felt ungreased wad over the powder, and on it, when in the cartridge, I place a little fat, such as Elk-tallow, &c. This, I found, gave me the best results, and it allows more powder.

EXPRESS BULLETS ought to be taken with you.

REVOLVER.—If a revolver *must* be taken, then a small ·450-Bulldog is as good a weapon as can be recommended for purposes of self-defence at close range, the disabling powers of this pistol being, on account of its large bore, of fair amount.

A TOOL-BOX, or better, a "tool hold-all" of leather, to be rolled together, is an indispensable article. Messrs. Holtzapfel and Co's., Charing Cross, and the Army and Navy Stores, are good places for this. HUNTING KNIVES, containing a dozen or two of domestic tools, are *not* useful things. If attached to the belt—the only way the cumbersome knife can be carried—they are very liable to be lost. For my part I would recommend a smaller pocket-knife to be carried in the pocket (made of chamois-leather), and a proper skinning-knife worn at the belt. The only place where, so far as I know, these somewhat oddly-shaped tools can be bought in London is at Silver and Co., Cornhill, where they are sold as "Green River Knives,' for 3s., including case.

A CAMP BUCKET is a most useful article. While the bucket itself can be used as water-pail, the rounded lid as washhand basin, the former, when packed, contains the entire hardware crockery—plates, cups, kettles, frying-pans, tea, coffee, sugar, and salt-tins, knives, forks, and spoons, for the entire party. Langton and Sons, King Edward Street, E.C., made me one to my design which worked capitally. Its weight for four people is about 25 lbs., cost 3*l*. to 4*l*. They should be used once or twice on picnics, &c., so that no entering-duty will have to be paid.

"RÜCKSACK," OR STALKER'S BAG is, as I have said, for all sporting purposes a most useful article; also, as I maintain, for carrying spare cartridges, concerning which there was lately a lively controversy in the *Field*. Its three chief points of merit—the easy distribution of all weight carried in it, and the circumstance that when not used it can be stuffed into a coat-pocket, while when required it will hold an entire roe-buck, and being waterproof—place it quite beyond the competition of the old-fashioned game-bag and knapsack, both inventions that for unpracticalness could take prizes. The only place in England, so far as I know, where the stalker's bag can be obtained is at G. Cording's, 125, Regent Street.

CLOTHING.—In late autumn very warm clothes are required. One ought to look more to their windproof than waterproof qualities. Lambswool-lined driving-gloves are capital things, and a so-called Icelander cap (knitted), covering the whole head—a great comfort.

Boots, of course, should be taken from England. Low ankle-boots of the stoutest make are the best. Bedding had better be got out West.

OTHER ARTICLES.—A pair of stout lawn-tennis shoes with the so-called "pyramid" sole (*not* ribbed) will be found most useful. You hardly get used to wear moccasins in less than a month or two, and the lawn-tennis shoe answers the same purpose.

WAPITI.

A FEW remarks concerning the period when the three chief species of Western deer have their horns "cleaned," and in a further degree when they shed them, will perhaps be not unwelcome to sportsmen intending to visit the Western hunting-grounds.

Wapiti shed their horns later than the smaller deer, April being the usual time. Mule-deer shed about the latter half of February. I happened to be last February in a locality where this species had congregated in thousands, offering exceptionally good opportunity to watch the process. Unlike the Wapiti, who shed their antlers simultaneously, or very nearly so, the deer not unfrequently carry one horn much longer than the other; and within a few days towards the end of the month of February I saw a number carrying only one horn. Whitetail, the smallest of the three deer species to be found West, shed about the same time as the mule-deer, though, to speak of my own experience, which is somewhat contrary to that of others, I found that they are later in cleaning than the last-mentioned kind. Two summers ago, about the middle of August, I happened to shoot a buck of each sort on one and the same day; and while the larger one had his antlers perfectly clean, those of the Whitetail were still in velvet.

Wapiti, I find, vary in different years. In 1877 and 1878 they were cleaned quite ten days earlier than in 1879, observations being made in one and the same locality in Wyoming, at an altitude of about 7000 feet. Last summer they were still later, though I must remark that in this instance I was further North, and a good deal higher in altitude.

The shooting of the four bulls on August 13th, 1880, to which I referred in the text, gave me a good opportunity to arrive at some conclusions respecting the reason of the difference. Favoured by the ground, which was, if not covered with snow, of very soft nature, I tracked the four I had killed. Evidently my victims were strangers to each other, and had probably met by accident on the enticingly cool snow. Two bulls which, when I shot them, were closest to me, had come up from the southern slopes, where dense timber and low brushwood, the home of myriads upon myriads of mosquitoes and flies, covered the mountain. The rest— evidently belonging together—the males of which were all in "velvet," had come from the North-West, had crossed the very highest part of the range, quite 12,000 feet in elevation, and had descended a slope some 900 feet in height, which, if not actually a sheer precipice, was the very next thing to it, and which I would have sworn no living creature save a chamois or a mountain goat could descend, least of all an animal handicapped by branching antlers of great size.

This lot had come from their usual homes at that season of the year, a vast stretch of barren highland, situated on the other side of the range, where there were no mosquitoes or flies. Hence I came to the conclusion (possibly a wrong one) that those Wapiti which habitually range in forests where flies are bad, shed the velvet considerably sooner than others which are not bothered by these pests; and, as some years and some localities are much more exposed to these scourges of man and beast, I fancy prolonged experience would establish the fact that in such years, and in such places, Wapiti "clean"—or, as the Western hunters call it "shake," from the motion of the trees against which they rub—from two to three weeks earlier than others.

A few days later I had again occasion to watch Wapiti descending a slope as precipitous as the other one. It was a most interesting sight, and one certainly I never expected to see. They came down very slowly, following a sort of chimney-like gully. In the steepest parts they would sit back on their haunches, and, with their antlers also well thrown back and their front legs thrust forward, half slide, half edge down the amazingly steep declivity. In other places they would step down broadside on, while the last part of the descent was made in one big rush, carrying them far out into the level ground at the foot of the rocks. None of the men had ever seen a similar performance on the part of elk; and when I showed them the first precipice they were so incredulous, that I took them up to where the tracks proved in an incontestable manner the truth of my words.

In another respect the last season was a phenomenal one, namely, in the irregularity of the "whistling" time (rutting season) of Wapiti. It began a fortnight earlier, and lasted quite three weeks longer than usual. I shot my first "whistling" stag on September 4th, and my last on October 25th, though they were still whistling on November 2nd. In connexion with the shedding of horns, Wapiti, it would seem to me, make an exception to most other species of deer that I know, namely, that their horns are nearly always cast within a few yards of each other. I happened to pass last year through a favourite district of Wapiti in shedding time, as was proved by the extraordinary number of antlers that lay about on the barren slopes facing the south, frequented by them in April and May. Many of them were of truly gigantic proportions; one pair, I remember, measured four inches more in length, namely, sixty-eight inches, than the biggest head of my own killing. It was curious to observe how singularly close the two separate horns always lay to each other. Of twenty-six very big pair I counted, only one pair was further apart than forty or fifty yards.

Wapiti die hard. I remember a very big old bull I once opened fire on at a distance of some 250 yards. He was standing looking at me broadside on, when he received my first two bullets. As the distance was somewhat great, and not seeing the slightest sign that I hit him, I gave him, while yet standing perfectly motionless, two more. Port, who happened to be with me at the time, cried "Shoot! shoot! Don't you see you have missed him." I felt sure this was not the case, for I had taken careful aim, and my old "trail stopper" was good for that distance. Before I had time to follow his advice the stag "broke together" precisely in the manner I have described. When we came up to him we found that Port's big hand covered my four bullet-holes. No other deer that I know would act in this manner, but no other stag proper approaches the Wapiti in size. If not well hit he will carry off an enormous amount of lead. I have put as many as fourteen Express ·500-bore bullets into one, and in the end only got him by a mere fluke.

Some authors on the Wapiti have endowed him with trucculent viciousness, maintaining that a wounded Wapiti will charge you. Of this I never came across the slightest evidence. Owing to carelessness I once got a slight prod while I was in the act of severing the spinal cord of a beast at his last gasp. It was only a spasmodic movement. Respecting their fighting propensities among themselves, I frequently witnessed during whistling time battles between old bulls, waged with a deadly fury quite as great as mark the duels between their European brethren. Of some twenty odd good heads I bagged at one period, more than half were damaged, having from one to four tines broken off short. Later on I came across much fe   bulls with damaged antlers—a circumstance not easy to explain. My own experience tends to prove that many bulls injured in fights die subsequently a lingering death. Of the above-mentioned twenty stags, six or seven showed severe wounds, one or two among them being hardly able to stagger along at the time. My bullet delivered them from further misery.

On one occasion my trapper and I were running a band of Wapiti, numbering some four or five hundred, picking out the biggest—which are always the best protected by a surging mass of does and smaller fry. We followed them for five hours, with two or three halts, over the stiffest ground that horses could possibly cross, when a big bull, shot too far back, charged another one, a fierce fight ensuing there and then between the two, who seemed entirely oblivious of our close presence. This "running" a gang, is lively sport, provided you have fresh horses. Up and down precipitous slopes, across ravines and through timber, always at a hand-gallop, one's riding qualities are tested; and one's nerves tingle with life and excitement, so that the risks of broken bones are set at nought. But there is a dark side to this exciting sport; for not only is it hardly worthy of the noble game to shoot them as you would the unwieldy and dull-spirited bison, but as you necessarily wound animals which you never can hope to release from their sufferings. I indulged in it only on two occasions, and I hope never to do so again.

It is a singular fact, that suggests many interesting explanations, that in Germany—the home country of our European deer—and among certain of the mountain tribes of Indians in North America—the two so-called canine teeth of the stag (growing in the upper jaw) are equally much prized.

Among the "Crows" in Montana, fifty pair of ordinary ones used, till quite lately, to purchase a good pony. And in Germany I have made many a sportsman very happy indeed by a pair of Wapiti teeth; my stock being only too soon exhausted.

The big pair of my great stag are no longer together, I had them mounted as pins; and the memory of the grand old fellow is honoured by two august sportsmen who graciously accepted them.

Regarding the comparative weight of antlers, and of the whole stag, my experience, both in Europe and America—*i.e.* with Red Deer and Wapiti—leads me to say that the usual proportion is about 1 : 25, as long as the stag is in good condition. However, after rutting-time the proportion is very much less; in the isolated cases, where I have been able to arrive at the weights, they stood about 1 : 15.

Of all deer, the skin of the Wapiti makes the poorest leather, though the hide, if shot about the end of October, can be made into a pretty rug or robe. It is not uninteresting to note that Lewis and Clarke's famous exploring expedition in the first decade of the present century, when they penetrated to the upper waters of the Missouri, very nearly came to grief owing to the unenduring quality of the Elk hides, of which they had made their only boat, packing in it all their instruments and stores. The boat and its contents were entirely lost, and, as the explorers maintain, only on account of the spongy nature of the material. "Had we used buffalo skins, we undoubtedly would have passed the falls of the Missouri in safety," remark the intrepid explorers in their narrative. Wapiti hides are on this account practically worthless.

It will not be out of place if I here draw attention to the fact, that the problem of the preservation of the large game of Montana and Wyoming, now the best game districts of the country, is—aside of the general metamorphosis of wild mountain country into cattle ranges—entirely dependent upon one condition, the price of "pelts." As long as the price of antelope and Deer skins per pound remains less than fifteen cents, and Elk skins less than twelve cents, net to the hunter, there will be few killed, except for food. When the price rises above these figures, the destruction will go on in a greater or less ratio, in proportion thereto.

A recent writer, in *Forest and Stream*, very truly says of the late rise in the prices of deer and antelope skins to twenty-five and thirty-five cents per pound, that the destruction of those animals has been commensurate. For the season of 1880 the shipment of hides on the Missouri and Yellowstone having been approximately 167,000, and for 1881, 143,000, representing about seventy-five per cent. of animals actually killed. The hard winters of 1879-80, and 1880-81, with their deep snows, peculiarly favoured this work, as during the winter months elk, deer, and antelope band together in large herds, and are the more easily bagged. During the summer they disperse into small bands, the two former disappearing into the timber of the foot-hills and of the most rugged mountains. Last spring, elk skins, which before that had been of small value, rose to twenty-two and twenty-five cents. per pound ($2.50 to $5 per hide)—this price giving a fine profit. Last summer the deer were even followed into the high and most precipitous mountains, their summer home (something that had never been done before), ten to twelve days' travel of packs being necessary to get the hides to market.

And so with the buffalo. During all seasons when their robes were good this work has been steadily going on, and mostly by men who have been engaged in the business for years on the southern buffalo ranges.

As a matter of statistical information, pains have been taken to gather the following facts, believed to be approximately correct, in relation to the shipment of hides from the Yellowstone and Missouri rivers for the years named, and which represent from seventy to seventy-five per cent. of the animals killed by men engaged in that business:—

	1880.		
Yellowstone River—deer and antelope		60,000	
Missouri River—deer and antelope		107,000	
			167,000
Yellowstone—buffalo (by whites)		22,700	
" " (by Indians)		5,000	
No report from the Missouri.			27,700
Total			194,700
	1881.		
Yellowstone—deer		20,000	
Yellowstone—antelope		53,000	
Missouri—deer and antelope		70,000	
			143,000
Yellowstone—elk		5,200	
			5,200
Yellowstone—buffalo (whites)		78,000	
" " (Indians)		15,000	
Missouri—buffalo		23,000	
			116,000
Total			264,200

In a subsequent portion of the article the writer says:—

"It is not probable that the price of pelts (with the decreasing annual supply) will again fall below a paying price to the pelt-hunter; so that the sequences before chalked out in this article will just as inevitably obtain as that day follows night, and a few years will witness the gradual extermination of the grandest game that ever existed on the earth."

Let me here say a few words on a different subject, *i.e.* that cruel and certainly very unsportsmanlike habit of careless shooting where game is so abundant, as in the West. Only too often men will pot away at a band of antelopes or deer, supremely indifferent regarding the ultimate fate of those animals they have happened to hit, but who failed to fall at the crack of the rifle. Then you will hear: "I think I hit half-a-dozen, but they all went off, and I can't bother to make sure what has become of them." And the mighty hunter, whose cheek would blanch, were he to be told that he had done something very unsportsmanlike—indeed, something which in point of torture inflicted to brute creation is far worse than cutting off a cow's tail, consoles himself with the thought, "Well, perhaps it won't hurt them much."

It is this very circumstance which makes me a strong partisan of Express rifles of larger bore even for the smaller species of game, such as our red-deer and chamois. For if hit, the wound is in nearly every case far more effective than that of smallbore solid balls. You instantly see that the game is hit, and the quantity of blood lost by the animal, if it can continue its flight, is infinitely greater than from those inflicted by the other species of arm, not only exhausting the victim much sooner, but making the tracking, even without a dog, comparatively easy.

In my eyes the misery inflicted on animals by careless shooting, and which many sportsmen hold in very slight regard, is infinitely worse than a shortcoming for which a favourite word in their selfish vocabulary is always ready. What this word is those who on one occasion were so singularly handy with it will best know.

MAUVAISES TERRES.

PROFESSOR GEIKIE puts the chief features of the geological formations of the West in such plain words, that I may be pardoned if I quote a few of his remarks. He says:—

"Granted that the solid materials out of which a mountain or table-land has been built were originally accumulated as sediment on the floor of the sea, how has this hardened sediment been fashioned into the well-known lineaments of the land? The solution of this question aroused some years ago a keen discussion, and has given rise to a portentous mass of geological literature. The combatants, as in most warfares, scientific or other, ranged themselves into two camps. There were the Convulsionists, or believers in the paramount efficacy of subterranean movement, who, starting from the universally admitted proofs of upheaval, crumpling, and fracture, sought an explanation of the present inequalities of the land in unequal disturbance from below. On the other hand, there were the Erosionists, or upholders of the efficacy of superficial waste, who maintained that besides the elevations due to subterranean causes, mountains, valleys, and all the other features of a landscape have been gradually carved into their present shapes by the slow abrasion of the air, rain, rivers, frosts, and the other agents of subaërial erosion. The contest, which was keen enough some years ago, has for a while almost ceased among us, though an occasional shot from younger combatants, fired with the old enthusiasm, serves to keep alive the memory of the campaign.

"Having long ago attached myself to the camp of the Erosionists, though by no means inclined to do battle under the extreme 'quietist' banners of some of its champions . . . I have long been convinced, that for the proper discussion of the real efficacy of superficial erosion in the development of a terrestrial surface, the geologists of Europe have been at great disadvantage. The rocks in these regions have undoubtedly been subjected to so many changes—squeezed, crumpled, fractured, upheaved, and depressed—that the effects of unequal erosion upon their surface has been masked by those of subterranean disturbance. The problem has thus become much more complicated than, with simpler geological structure, it would have been. Its solution has demanded an amount of knowledge of geological structure which can hardly be acquired without long and laborious training, the want of which on the part of many who have taken part in the controversy, has led to the calling in question or denial of facts, about the reality and meaning of which there should never have been any doubt at all. That, in spite of these obstacles, observers in this country should have been able to brush aside the accidental or adventitious difficulties, and to get at the real gist of the matter, as I am certain they have done, seems to me a lasting proof of their scientific prowess.

"Now, it is unquestionably true that had the birthplace of geology lain on the west side of the Rocky Mountains, this controversy would never have arisen The efficacy of denudation, instead of evoking doubt, discussion, or denial, would have been one of the first obvious principles of the science, established on the most irrefragable basis of patent and most impressive facts. Over thousands of square miles the strata remain practically unchanged from their original horizontal position, so that the effects of surface erosion can at once be detected upon their flat parallel layers. The country has not been under the sea for a vast succession of geological periods. It has not been buried, like so much of Northern Europe, and North-Eastern America, under a thick cover of ice-borne clays and gravels. Its level platforms of sandstone, shale, clay, or limestone, lie at the surface, bare to the wind and rain, and their lines can be followed mile after mile, as if the whole region were one vast geological model, to which the world should come to learn the fundamental laws of denudation."

"The *Mauvaises Terres*," or "Bad-lands," is the expressive name of the strangest, and, in many respects, the most repulsive scenery in the world. They are tracts of irreclaimable barrenness, blasted and left for ever lifeless and hideous. To understand their peculiar features, it is needful to bear in mind that they lie on the sites of some of the old lakes already referred to, and that they have been carved out of flat sheets of sandstone, clay, marl, or limestone that accumulated on the floors of these lakes. Everywhere, therefore, horizontal lines of stratification meet the eye, giving alternate stripes of buff, yellow, white, or red, with here and there a strange verdigris-like green. These strata extend nearly horizontally for hundreds of square miles. But they have been most unequally eroded. Here and there isolated flat-topped eminences or "buttes," as they are styled in the West, rise from the plain in front of a line of buff or cliff to a height of several hundred feet. On examination, each of these hills is found to be built up of horizontal strata, and the same beds reappear in lines of terraced cliff along the margin of the Plain. A butte is only a remnant of the original deep mass of horizontal strata that once stretched far across the Plain. Its sides and the fronts of the terraced cliffs, utterly verdureless and bare, have been scarped into recesses and projecting buttresses. These have been further cut down into a labyrinth of peaks and columns, clefts and ravines, now strangely monumental, now uncouthly irregular, till the eye grows weary with the endless variety and novelty of the forms. Yet beneath all this chaos of outline there can be traced everywhere the level parallel bars of the strata. The same band of rock, originally one of the successive floors of the old lake, can be followed without bend or break from chasm to chasm, and pinnacle to pinnacle. Tumultuous as the surface may be, it has no relation to underground disturbances, for the rocks are as level and unbroken as when they were laid down. It owes its ruggedness entirely to erosion.

"But there is a further feature adding to the repulsiveness of the "Badlands." There are no springs or streams. Into the soil, parched by the fierce heats of a torrid summer, the moisture of the subsoil ascends by capillary attraction, carrying with it the saline solutions it has extracted from the rocks. At the surface it is at once evaporated, leaving behind a white crust or efflorescence, which covers the bare ground and encrusts the pebbles strewn thereon. Vegetation wholly fails, save here and there a bunch of salt-weed, or a bunch of the ubiquitous sage-brush, the parched, livid-green of which serves only to increase the desolation of the desert."

THE BIGHORN.

THAT Bighorn rams fight among themselves during rutting-time, I had in my last trip, occasion to observe. I watched several such engagements; when the rams would run at each other with amazing force, striking each other's horns with such violence that I heard the sound two or three hundred yards off with quite a stiff breeze blowing athwart the intervening space. Port once shot a very big ram, shortly after the rutting season, who had an immense cut, extending from the shoulder to the middle of his back; a wound undoubtedly inflicted by a rival. Likewise was it the good fortune of one of the men to kill, three years ago, an hermaphrodite Bighorn, with very singular horns. Passing, twelve months afterwards, near the place where he killed it, I was anxious to secure the head, but it was gone; cayotes or wolverines having probably carried it off. According to the description given to me, the horns resembled those of a two or three-year-old ibex, lacking, however, the "rings" peculiar to the latter's headgear.

To speak of sizes given by English sportsmen, it would seem that many of the conflicting accounts would be brought to agree by taking the simple fact into consideration that the horns shrink, not only in girth at the base, but also, strange as it sounds, in length. An instance mentioned, if I am not mistaken, by Lord Dunraven in his "Great Divide," of the singular difference in the measurement of the same pair of horns, some time having elapsed between the first and second application of the tape, led me not only to examine every available source of information, but also to make accurate measurements myself, both of which proved to me beyond doubt that the girth decreases considerably more than the length of the horn measured along the curve. Even the ibex horn, which is more solid, shrinks, it seems, though to a much lesser degree, as can be seen by the silver and gold-mounted goblets, snuffboxes, and powder-flasks wrought by the expert German silversmiths of the sixteenth and seventeenth centuries, of the treasured "steinbock," all of which will be found to have shrunk from their mountings; and this in the moist climate of Europe, with a solid mass of horn. How much greater must the shrinkage be, therefore, of a horn supplied with a soft core, in a climate so dry that waggon wheels made of seasoned hickory fall to pieces if not frequently wetted? Nothing is easier, therefore, than to explain many of the apparently conflicting statements made by English sportsmen, who have omitted to state when the horns they speak of were measured—whether at once on the death of the animal, or a year or two afterwards. From what I saw, I should not in the least doubt that a heavy pair, shot in summer, would in one year decrease an inch in girth, especially if left in a dry climate.

An American author of a recent monograph on this animal, states that rams emit at rutting time "a long-drawn booming bark, not a signal of distress, but an amatory acclaim, an invocation of the *dulcis dea amathusia* when the mercury trembles at forty-five below zero." I have never heard this sound, but I am inclined to think the author intended to use not the word mercury, which, as everybody knows, congeals at 39° Fahr., but another one, say for instance gullibility. I give this contribution to Natural History with due reserve.

In Mexico the Bighorn is hunted with dogs. With this form of chase the author I have cited seems to be better acquainted than with that of the Northern Rockies. The dogs, he says, used are a special breed of fleet animals, called galgos, or *cimarroneros*, in Nueva Leon, and said to be descendants of those powerful sleuth-hounds that are used to chase the wolf and the Iberian ibex in the Eastern Pyrenees. In quiet winter nights the cimarróns often descend to the middle region of the sierra, but hurry back to the highlands at the first alarm; and, taking advantage of this habit, the hunting-party divide their forces. At a given signal the first galgos are slipped, and though they may fail to overtake the fugitives, they will put them to hard shifts before they reach the uplands, where they have to run the gauntlet of the second detachment. If the dogs understand their business, they will co-operate and keep their game together till they can make a simultaneous attack; for, if the herd scatters, the first victim will generally prove a scapegoat for the rest. Going straight up-hill the cimarróns often improve their start by dashing up a cliff where the pursuer has to turn to the left or right; but on level ground the tables are turned, and, once abreast of his game, the hound makes short work of it, dashing ahead ot the nearest good-sized sheep—often a nursing ewe—and, suddenly turning, flies at the throat in true wolf style and *le rasga la vida*, as the Spaniards express it—"tears out her life"—at the first grip. The galgo does not remove his prey, but stays on the spot and summons the hunter by a peculiar howl, repeated at shorter and shorter intervals if he has reason to fear that snow-drifts or prowling wolves will make his post untenable. Professional cimarrón-hunters generally carry a meat-bag, as contact with the hairy coat of the deer-sheep often afflicts the human skin with *cosquillas* ("sheep-tickle"), a persistent itch that sometimes spreads from the hands to the chest, but, strange to say, cannot be traced to any visible cause. Like mange and prurigo, it is probably caused by microscopic parasites.

ANTLERS AND HEADS.

ANTLERS should never be sawn off at the burr, a portion of the skull should always be included. As it is, of course, quite impossible to pack Wapiti antlers on packhorses, they must be separated by sawing through the skull-bone that has been left on them, thus each horn will have a piece of bone attached to it, which also facilitates mounting if the head is to be stuffed, and what is *most* important the correct angle of skull and horns is preserved. It is often supposed that to have an entire head stuffed it is necessary to take with you the whole skull, jaw-bone, &c. This is by no means the case. The antlers sawn off as advised, and the head-skin taken off well down to the chest, great care being taken in the vicinity of the eyes, is all that is wanted. For preserving these head-skins in the West, where the air is singularly dry, nothing more is necessary than to turn them inside out, so that the "snout" is of sack-like shape (also the ears have to be turned), and so let them dry. Not a single Wapiti head-skin of mine was in the slightest damaged, notwithstanding that ten or eleven months intervened before they reached the taxidermist's hands. If they have to be boxed while yet damp, a liberal coating of salt and alum will, I am told, protect them till they reach Europe.

With Bighorn heads, also very cumbersome things to pack, the mode is even simpler. If the whole head (and portion of the neck) is to be stuffed, skin the neck clear, and then sever the spinal cord at the top nearest to the skull, doing the same with the lower jaw-bone. A circular incision at the base of skull will enable you to get out the brain.

Two saws should be taken—one an eighteen-inch broad-bladed, the other a fifteen-inch butcher's saw, the blade of which can be screwed in; a few spare blades being taken.

ZOOLOGICAL COLLECTIONS IN ENGLAND.

REGARDING this subject much could be written. Their singular poorness has been often remarked by others. None of our great public zoological museums are, it would seem to unprejudiced observers, at all on a par with our national weakness for sport. While it is perfectly true that in many English country mansions there are collections of game animals and beasts of prey unrivalled, in their speciality, by any one of the chief museums in the world—in fact, at least half-a-dozen such private repositories could be named, each a matchless and complete collection of a large continent's quarry, the result of the life-long efforts of a single devotee—yet a country cousin, or foreigner on a visit to our metropolis, and desirous of examining our national zoological collections, cannot help being struck by the startling disparity between these ill-arranged shows of game animals—consisting generally of very inferior specimens in a bad condition, very poorly stuffed, and crowded together "as if," as a French *savant* once remarked to me, "we tried to pack them into the smallest possible space"—and the far-famed renown of the ubiquitous English sportsman, who, in the pursuit of game, traverses Oceans and Continents, expends riches, and braves untold dangers with a composure and determination worthy of great ends.

There would, I fancy, be perhaps less prating from radical platforms against the classes from which the sportsman is usually recruited, were the public made a little better acquainted with those features that legitimize the pursuit of the Nimrod; and while this would tend to raise the standard of sport in the eyes of the outside world, it would also create fresh and attractive fields for the unabating activity of that product of the British stamina-endowing soil—the English sportsman.

THE TETON BASIN.

Four or five months after my return to civilization, my attention was drawn to an article by one of the four gentlemen, members of the Hayden Exploration Party, who had ascended the Grand Teton in 1872. The account and the illustrations are rather of a sensational character. The party ascended the great chain from the West and not from the East, as I did, so of course I cannot speak of the first half of their work. From their accounts it was comparatively easy, the difficult part commencing on leaving the backbone to tackle the peak itself. This portion we had in common, at least to judge from their graphic and minute description; and it is here that the writer must allow me to differ with him. Had he confined himself to American mountains in his comparison of mountaineering difficulties, I would not have a single word to say, for probably the Teton is one of the most difficult peaks in North America, at any rate in the Rocky Mountains; but as he drew the Alps into his discussion, of which, as he confesses, he had no personal acquaintance, I have to remind him that what he says of them is not entirely correct. Among the statements he makes are the following: "No steeper ascents than those made by us have ever distinguished the Alpine climbers; and when Whymper states that the ascension of one mile in two miles of latitude is *prodigiously steep*, we may be forgiven a little pride in the accomplishment of a mile of ascent in somewhat less than *one* mile of latitude." Considering that one of the climbers was a gentleman "fresh from his home in England, who knew little of the properties of snow and ice," the author had, perhaps, less difficulty in persuading his audience of the truth of the above statement than he would have in the case of persons conversant with mountains. The expedition seemed to partake of the exceptional in the eyes of the writer, for even a surgeon had "considerately accompanied us to the base of the ridge, provided with instruments and bandages in case of accidents." Considering that "on the top of an adjacent pinnacle, but little lower than the one we occupied," they found signs of human architecture of a rude form, the words of the writer, "others might come after us, but to be the first where hundreds had failed was no braggart boast," are perhaps a little inconsistent, and on a par with the opinion he expresses that the ascent is more difficult than that of the Matterhorn.

The scenery on the range itself is of savage grandeur, and the peculiar clearness of the air makes this all the more apparent, for everything is thrown out far more distinctly than in the mellower, and unquestionably more picturesque light of the Alps. Even from the backbone of the chain a vast sweep of country is visible, and from the much higher altitude I gained on the peak the view was very fine; towards the West it is of melancholy desolateness, for you overlook the barren table-lands of Idaho, and vast stretches of *mauvaises terres*. Towards the North and East the view is far grander, and entirely of Alpine character. Beginning with the Yellowstone country, you see before you the Great Divide for a length of at least 200 miles, and it was pleasant to note the different peaks in the distant range I had ascended.

There are some small glaciers on the Teton; the few remaining refuges for these formations in the Central or Northern Rocky Mountains. I may still refer mountaineers to an interesting account of Alpine work in the Rocky Mountains of Wyoming and Idaho, by Mr. James Eccles, in No. 65 of the *Alpine Journal*.

There is a good deal of mystery about the locality of the Teton Basin. According to some accounts, it is on the Western slopes of the range, and is not the same place as Jackson's Hole, this supposition being shared by several map-makers. In Professor Hayden's last map of that region the name Teton Basin does not occur at all. The testimony of two trappers, who have known the locality for the last thirty or forty years, proves the terms to be synonymous, and each to refer to the place located on the Eastern slopes.

THE BEAVER.

THE beaver's castoreum, *i.e.* the contents of his musk-bag, was once, as everybody knows, a very valuable drug. Now it is no longer used by the druggist and apothecary, but the decline is comparatively of very recent date. Von Tschudi, the editor of Winkell's famous *Sporting Chronic*, mentions that as late as 1852 the castoreum of a European beaver fetched as much as 509 Rhenish florins (50*l*.). Singular to say, no Western trappers I had occasion to interrogate regarding the market value of castoreum knew anything about it, though many of them had trapped for thirty or forty years. It would appear that from Alaska 248 lbs. of castoreum were exported to Europe in 1852.

Not only to the naturalist, but also to the historian, does the beaver afford study. For two centuries or more the pelt of this animal was an important article in our mercantile annals, our upper classes wearing it exclusively for about 200 years. In Charles II.'s reign Parliament prohibited the use of any other material but beaver skins for hat manufacture. It was also frequently exercised in passing statutes on behalf of beaver fur and the protection of its trade. So, for instance, do I find in the Calendar for that year, that Sir David Cunningham received, A.D. 1638, new leases for twenty-one years of a duty of twelvepence, payable to his Majesty upon every beaver hat and cap made by the Company of Beaver Makers of London, with a moiety of the benefit of seizures of all foreign beaver hats imported. For this a yearly rent of 500*l*. was paid. Prices of beaver fur have kept up with the ruling fashions of the day. Thus, 200 years ago, during the Dutch occupation of New Amsterdam, beaver skins were worth about 10*s*. a-piece (a very high price), and were used in lieu of currency. In 1820, and again in 1834, they were worth on the trapping ground from 2*l*. to 3*l*.; while twenty or twenty-five years ago a good skin fetched but 8*s*., at which rate the sales of the Hudson Bay Company in 1854-5-6 amounted, it would appear, in London alone to 627,655 skins.

THE CATTLE RANCHE BUSINESS.

ACCORDING to a statement I append, made upon the spot, and submitted to the critical examination of several of the most reliable ranchemen I came across, it appears that a man starting with a capital of 10,000*l*. will, if he does not touch either capital or interest for three years, at the end of that period be the richer by 8800*l*. This, with moderate luck and careful handling.

ESTIMATE FOR CATTLE-RAISING IN WYOMING OR MONTANA TERRITORIES. CAPITAL INVESTED, 10,000*l*., AS FOLLOWS:—

	£	s.	£	£	£
A herd of 2000 good Oregon or Utah cows, 75 per cent. of which, if carefully selected, with calves, cost in 1879, delivered at ranche	3	10	7000		
1000 yearlings	2	0	2000		
35 good American bulls, Shorthorn or Hereford	10	0	350		
Cost of building log ranche and corrall	—		200		
Necessaries for ranche: 50 ponies at 6*l*. saddlery and branding iron and waggon	—		450	10,000	
Your stock-book would show at end of FIRST year:—					
The 1500 calves bought with the cows, of which 750 heifers and 750 steer calves would now be worth as yearlings	2	0	3000		
The 1000 yearlings would now be two-year-olds, worth 3*l*., or 1*l*. more than at first	—		1000	4000	
Expenses: ranche expenses, provisions for four men per annum	—		300		
Wages of three cow-boys, $35 per month=7*l*. per month=84*l*. per annum	—		252		
Other incidental charges and taxes	—		148		
Losses: usually fully covered by 5 per cent. on capital in cattle	—		470	1170	
PROFITS at end of FIRST year					2830
Your stock-book at end of SECOND year would show:—					
The 750 heifer calves, now two-year-olds, would be worth 2*l*. 15*s*., or 15*s*. more	—		560		
The 750 steer calves, now two-year-olds, would now be worth 3*l*., or 1*l*. more	—		750		
The 1000 yearlings, now three years old, would be worth 3*l*. 10*s*., or 10*s*. more	—		500		
The 2000 cows had calves the first year; take 75 per cent., would give 1500 calves, now yearlings, worth	2	0	3000	4810	
Ranche expenses, increased by 200*l*.; additional man's hire, losses above the first 5 per cent., increased by 100*l*. (300*l*.), added to 1170*l*.	—		—	1470	
PROFITS at end of SECOND year					3340

Your stock-book at end of THIRD year would show:—

The 750 heifer calves, now three years old, would be worth (increased) 15s.	— ...	560
The 750 steer calves, now three years old, would be worth (increased) 1l.	— ...	750
The 1000 yearlings, of which 500 heifers would have 375 two-year calves...	2 0 ...	750
500 steers, no increase.		
The 2000 cows had calves second year, 75 per cent. = 1500, worth	2 0 ...	3000
The first 1500 calves, now two-year-olds (750 heifers), worth 2l. 15s. (2060l.); 750 steers, worth 3l. (2250l.)	— ...	4310
The first 750 heifer calves, now three-year-olds, had calves (now yearlings) 560 at	2 0 ...	1120 ...10,490
Ranche expenses, increased by 300l. (purchase of bulls, horses, and additional men's hire).		
Losses above the first 5 per cent., increased by 200l. (500l.), added to 1170l.	— ... — ...	1670
PROFITS at the end of THIRD year	... ...	—— 8820

One or two items in my statement require a word of explanation. It will be seen that—at starting—I counted three cowboys, which, if the master is competent and understands his business, is ample. If he is not, and is only recently out from England, it is absolutely necessary for him to have, at least for the first year or two, a foreman. You can get capital men of this class, reliable and of long experience, for about $75 to $100 per month (180l. to 240l. per annum), and in no case would I advise men to engage in the business without first acquiring some of the most fundamental principles and details. This can be very easily done by a visit of two or three months *to one of the outlying* ranches, where the rough sides of life are best seen. Personal experience is very essential out West. Gross exaggeration on every subject is very generally the rule. Hear and see for yourself, is about the best advice that can be given to the immigrant. In a country where human fortune fluctuates so strangely, and where men of all classes, grades, and character, are thrown together—it is doubly incumbent upon the stranger to keep his eyes and ears skinned—in fact, to believe but what he himself sees.

As I have before pointed out, the profits of the business are only then great when sufficient capital is invested to "fill the corners." Men in a small way cannot expect to make more than fifteen or twenty per cent. No person who takes to ranching, solely as a money-making speculation, should think of starting in it with less than 1500 or 2000 head. Good judges maintain that the real profits come in only when you have 5000 or 6000 head to start on. The larger the herd, the less will be the cost per head of running the concern.

Wyoming and Montana, being further north than Colorado, have more snow in winter, notwithstanding that the summers and autumns are very similar in their delightful and invigorating effects. Snow, however, as I have clearly said, in most Western regions is very unlike our European commodity.

Great extremes are also common. A cold spell will for days take the thermometer down to 30° Fahr., while the following week fine sunny weather will set in, which continues for a month at a time. Often have I ridden about coatless on a December or January day. The winds in these portions of the West are at times extraordinarily high. But, as I have stated, they are the salvation of the country; but for them, the snow would remain on the ground, and not one single head of cattle be able to survive even a moderate winter. But at the same time, next to water, high bluffs, rocks, or mountain ranges, with the countless little ravines and gorges peculiar to the Rocky Mountain formation, are quite indispensable when selecting your range, for there alone can cattle find shelter from the fury of the elements. On the approach of one of these winter storms you will see them flock from considerable distances, fifteen or twenty miles, to these sheltering nooks.

Cattle-raising on the free public lands of the Western Territories is attracting general attention just now in the United States. New York, Boston, and all the great cities on the Atlantic, are naturally much interested in the raising of an improved stock for the European markets. Several books have appeared quite recently on this subject, and the magazines are full of papers picturing the delightful life and sure way of "trebling your capital in three years." The great fault an Englishman has to find with all these accounts is their more or less exaggerated descriptions. When speaking of the profits, they are all more or less unreliable. Thus, for instance, does the author of "Cattle Ranches in Colorado" give a very considerably over-estimated account of the profits that await the emigrant. According to him, a herd of 4000 cows and eighty Hereford bulls, costing \$76,000, will, at the end of three years, be worth \$233,800 How this happy result is to be achieved is detailed at great length in a very plausible and taking manner, very apt "to fetch" even the coolest reader, who happens to be ignorant on the subject.

Another writer in a book on Colorado, just published, gets entirely lost amongst the "000" of profits. According to him, \$72,000 invested in 4000 cows would in seven years swell to \$730,952, the profits of the last year alone amounting to \$254,792.

Unlike many of our European crafts, however, where long training and the experience of years precede the actual start, the majority of persons engaged in stock-raising have had no previous acquaintance whatever with its working details; and hence the perplexity consequent on an over-abundance of "good" advice, exaggerated accounts of profits, and the ease with which success is to be compassed, proves, as I often have had occasion to remark, a serious stumbling-block for new comers.

Locusts, an ever-threatening danger to the future farmers in Wyoming and Montana—for both Territories belong to what the Government Entomological Commission define as the permanent or native breeding-ground, where the species is always found—are for the cattlemen of those regions a source of very little anxiety.

The question of improving the breeds of Western cattle is receiving every year more attention. When Mr. L. F. Allen, President of New York State Agricultural Society, says, "The Americans (perhaps of all people so intelligent and active in their agricultural pursuits), have been the least enterprising in improving their breeds of cattle," this can hardly, with justice, be extended to trans-Missourian regions, where the whole business of raising cattle is of the most recent origin. No doubt the next ten years will see a very vast improvement in this matter.

While "prospecting" for a range or learning the details of the business, I would recommend the concealment as much as possible of one's object. Sight-seeing or "gunning" covers retreat in that respect. At many of the ranches the owners are not present; but this is no disadvantage, as much more can be frequently gleaned from the servant than from the master, who, if he does understand the business, is often of a suspicious cast, and does anything but tell the truth. It was from the mouths of the cowboys — mostly a genial, open-handed set of fellows, the best of company, and the best of story-tellers—that I learnt much of the details of the business. This, however, can only be attained if the stranger (I am speaking here to Englishmen) is willing to treat them as they want to be treated, which to a man who has no false pride about him, and the desire to give no offence, is the easiest of tasks. In four cases out of five they represent not only the hands, but also the head of the concern. The owner or "boss," in not a few cases, can perhaps hardly tell the difference between an Oregon and a Texas cow; he is often hundreds of miles away, following his regular occupation as hotel-keeper, doctor, or banker, in towns and cities, visiting his ranche for a week once a year; and many of the ranges I passed had never been seen by the owner of the cattle that grazed over it. It was looked up, located, and the ranche building erected by the foreman and his cowboys.

It is needless to point out what grave responsibilities are assumed by an author writing on a country as a field for emigration. Even with the most uninterested motives he is apt, by giving colour to one feature and passing over another, to mislead. In the foregoing notes and text I have been at pains to state all the pros and contras of the rough ranche business as fairly as I possibly could. What I have written appeared originally in the *Field* (January 31st and March 6th, 1880), and elicited many replies of which I propose to add one letter, published in the *Field* February 7th, 1880, as it puts the whole case into a nutshell.

"SIR,—I have read with interest the paper in your last issue by Mr. Baillie-Grohman on the cattle ranches of Wyoming, and quite agree with him, that before any person determines upon entering into cattle-raising on the frontiers in America he should have personal and practical experience.

"Many of the publications upon the subject are misleading and unreliable, as I have found from inquiries which I was induced to make in consequence of my son's determining to go into the business. Having made preliminary arrangements, I wrote to a friend in the State asking his advice, and, as it may interest some of your readers who feel inclined to go, I append his reply. A.

"'As to your inquiry about purchasing land, my opinion is that well-selected prairie-land in any of our promising Western counties cannot fail to prove a fairly profitable purchase on the capital invested, even if the land be left untouched, simply paying the State taxes thereon, for, at the rate the public lands are being taken up by settlers and purchased by speculators, and given away by Government as subsidies to railroads and other objects, not many years will elapse before no cheap lands worth having can be had; hence held, they must before many years bring a handsome profit. You will see that no land can be owned by non-residents that are so safe as prairie-land. Timber-land is robbed, mining-land is worked, but a virgin prairie cannot be stolen, burned, or injured—hence is the safest, if not occupied. The best advice I can offer in the more important step contemplated by you in reference to your son's engaging in cattle-raising on the frontier is to come and see for yourself. You must not believe any of the glittering generalities which you read in the various published accounts. Most of them are put forward from interested motives. I feel that it is too serious a matter for me to say one word which would induce you to send your son here, the result of which might be the reverse of what you anticipate. I have never advised any one to leave England and come here. There are some grave reasons why I could not do so, chief of which is the almost impossible conversion of an Englishman into an American. I came here, as you know, from England when I was ten years old, and have been educated, trained, and fully Americanized. The great difficulty in the way of success to an Englishman in America is that he remains an Englishman. Farming and stock-raising cannot be done by proxy. The old adage of Franklin is so truthful when applied to this country, that it must not be overlooked, viz :—

> He who by the plough would thrive
> Must either hold himself or drive.

"' We have no gentlemen farmers here. Our most prosperous farmers are out at work with their men early and late; never say 'Go and do,' but 'Come, let us do this.'

"' Stock-raising on the frontiers, such as you contemplate for your son, involves pluck, physical endurance, hardships, exposures, a frontier life among men of the roughest, hardest character, whose very calling is one of danger, making them reckless of life, both their own and others'; when on duty, isolated, living on the Plains away from settlements, watching their stock from bandits and Indians. When they come into town, like sailors from a long voyage, their earnings go like water; only life is often taken in their debauchery, for on the frontier it is a threat and a shot—often the shot first, and some poor wretch passes into eternity. Nothing is done about it; a frontier country makes its own laws, and 'Judge Lynch' is the only tribunal to hold them in check.

"'I say this, and do not overstate it; because you should know exactly what herding cattle on the frontier means. The day following the receipt of your letter I met a friend, who had been in Kansas buying up some seven-eighth pure blood shorthorns for a relative in Chicago, and had also been down to Fort Worth, on the Santa Fé Railway, to complete a purchase of 5000 acres, where he is going to raise cattle and sheep. He is an American, and thoroughly up in all questions of cattle herding, having been in every State and Territory of the Union, and his opinion is reliable. He confirms all I have written, and says that a man to have an even chance with others must be possessed of experience and reckless bravery, and be a frontiersman, while he would need have the moral courage to resist a thousand temptations of a frontier cattle-town; and, as an instance, a little town he went to had only eight places of legitimate business, and forty-three places for gambling, drinking, and kindred vices; and I am afraid this description applies generally to the great cattle-raising section of the country.

"'There are many places nearer settlements where the business of stock-raising or mixed farming can be carried on by experienced persons with success, and there can be, I think, no doubt there is a great future for this country, and that any person with a moderate amount of capital, who can adapt himself to the American customs and ideas, is bound to succeed if he is industrious and frugal.

"'Again I say, come and see for yourself. The journey to New York is not worth a consideration, and when you arrive there write or telegraph; but if you come on to us without doing either, you will find us, as Western people say, with 'Our latch-string on the outside always.'"

I have given this letter in full, and though some of the points are, to my idea, a little overdrawn, there is yet a great deal of truth about it. The *reckless bravery* might be toned down to a *firm will;* and the *thousand temptations of a frontier cattle-town* have to be reduced to three, the most prominent being the vilest of whiskey, while the two others, gambling and worse, are of a similarly wretchedly poor description, and could hardly be called temptations for the class of men who are likely to be guided by these Notes.

LIST OF SOME AUTHORS ON THE WEST CONSULTED BY THE WRITER.

Audubon, 7 works.
Bachmann, 3 works.
Baird, F. S., 7 works.
Barker, Ch.
Bartlett, J. R.
Batty, H.
Beach, W. W.
Beadle, J.
Berkeley, Hon. C. G. F.
Black, Capt.
Blackmore.
Bonaparte, Prince C. L.
Bosgood.
Brackenridge.
Bradley, R. T.
Bradbury.
Brown, Robert.
Campion, J. S.
Cass.
Catlin, G., 5 works.
Caton, J. D.
Cox, Ross.
Custer, G. A.
De Lafrenaye.
D'Obigny.
De Vere.
Doane, Lieut.
Duden, G.
Dunraven, Earl of.
Elwyn.
Fleming, G.
Fosset.
Franklin, S. C.
Fremont, J. C., 4 works.
Garfielde.
Gilmore, P.
Goodman.
Haliburton, T. C.
Hall, W.
Harlan.
Hind.

Hittel, J. S.
Kenney.
King, Clarence, 3 works.
James, Ed.
Jones, W. A.
Long, Major.
McKenney.
Mallery, Garrick, 2 works.
Maxey, R. 2 works.
Morgan, L. H.
Morse, Dr.
Murray, Hon. C. A.
Newhouse, J.
Nicollet.
Parker.
Pickering.
Poeppig.
Powell, J. W., 9 works.
Redfield, H. V.
Richardson, A. D.
Richardson, H.
Richardson, J.
Rowan, J. J.
Ross.
Say.
Schoolcraft, H. R., 12 works.
Southesk, Earl of.
Stansbury, H.
Strahorn.
Tanner, S.
Townsend, J. K.
Up de Graff.
Vere, Dr. M. Schele De.
Volney.
Warden.
Wheeler.
Whetham, Boddam.
Whittaker, F.
Wied, Prince of.
Wilkes, C. J.
Wyeth, Capt.

INDEX.

ABSENCE of nobs and snobs, 30.
Advice to English settlers, 322.
Air of the West—its qualities, 3.
Antelope, tasteless venison, 4.
Appetite, glorious, 61.
Appetite, sound, 47.
Appetite, veteran, 48.
Application of the Beaver's hydrostatics, 240.
Arrangement in strings, 367.
Arrival my, at Settlement, 376.
Arrappahoes the, reported on the war-path, 272.
Arrappahoe the, and his squaw, 273.
Audubon, 407.
Authors on the West, 432.

BABY the, giving me an impression, 365.
Bad-land—its aspect, 155.
Bad Medicine the, 42.
Baking, 56.
Baldfaced-Hattie, 99.
Baldfaced-Hattie—how she was rope broke, 99.
Beans, the pot of, 190.
Beans is pison, 192.
Bear chase, a, 184.
Bearclaw Joe, his get-up, 13.
Beauty of outline in antlers, 136.
Beaver, the, 233.
Beaver influence of, upon landscape, 259.
Beaver pelt, prices of, 252.
Beaver an historical animal, 425.

Beaver work, 242.
Beaver town, my night at a, 256.
Beaver, the traits of, 239.
Beaver medicine, 250.
Beaver, trapping of, 250.
Beaver timber, 242.
Beaver, the teeth of, 241.
Beaver, the instinct of, 235.
Beaver dam and bank, 233.
Beaver, what trees are gnawed by, 247.
Beaver, the castoreum of, 424.
Beds, how to make them, 408.
Beds, making of, 63.
Beds, sharing, 64.
Bedfellow troubles, 64.
Bedmaking under difficulties, 188.
Bibleback, 90.
Bighorn, the, 160.
Bighorn, stalk of the largest, 167.
Bighorn, my largest head, 167.
Bighorn fighting, 420.
Bighorn, its coat, 166.
Bighorn hunting in Mexico, 421.
Bighorn, the scab of the, 178.
Bighorn rutting, 164.
Bighorn, horns of the, 161.
Big Wind River Mountains, 123.
Big Wind River, 50.
Bite of the skunk, 109, 110, 401.
Black Coal, 272, 278.
Blue-winged teal, 80.
Bone carpenter, Henry's dream of, 47.
Boreas finds a camping place, 53.
Boreas's character, 95.

F f

Boreas's bump of locality, 96.
Boreas, trading for him, 89.
Boreas's dislike of grizzlies, 97.
Borrow to, trouble, 187.
Boss's the, thundering jump, 107.
Boy stalker, the, 139.
Boy sentry, the, 377.
Brands of cattle, 359.
Bridge, the $700, 288.
Brillat-Savarin's story, 202.
Bucking, 100.
Bucked off, getting, 100.
Bags, 212, 214.
Building your ranche, 361.
Burying children, 41.

CAMP bucket, 411.
Camps, different sorts of, 73.
Camp duties, 62.
Camp, naming of, 69.
Camp, return to, 173.
Camp, telescoping of, 74.
Canyons of the Colorado River, 297.
Careless shooting, 417.
Cartridges, 410.
Castoreum, 424.
Cattle brands, 359.
Cattle business, origin of, 324.
Cattle business, profits of, 426.
Cattle business, letter on, 429.
Cattle business, unreliable accounts of, 428.
Cattle, choice of, 346.
Cattle, cutting-out, 343.
Cattle, getting your, 346.
Cattle, number of, in the U.S., 324, 325.
Cattle plague, 334.
Cattle-raising, profits of, 329.
Cattle-raising, losses, 338.
Cattle-raising attracting attention, 348.
Cattle-ranche, the first, in Colorado, 353.
Cattle, stampeding of, 358.
Cellar fort, the, 378.
Charm of trapper travelling, 52, 55.
Choice of cattle, 346.
Cities, their aspect, 5.

Civilization, my return to, 289, 290.
Cleanliness of Western men, 381.
Climbing order, light, 113.
Climate of Wyoming, 409.
Climate of the uplands, 198.
Cliff swallow, the, 312.
Clothing, 411.
Cold mutton comfort, 27.
Cold snap, 131.
Cold in 1880, 34.
Colorado River, the, 296.
Colorado, rapid growth of, 354.
Connexion of Nature's works, 134.
Cooking, 56, 60.
Coroner's, the, *good story*, 370.
Coureurs de bois, names given by, 72.
Cowboys at work, 341.
Cowboys, independence of, 363.
Cowboys, two classes of, 344
Crossing rivers, 42, 44.
Crossing the Wind River (Indians), 273.

DANGERS threatening cattle-raising, 334.
Dawn in the West, 131.
Deadly instruments, three, 216.
Dead man's boots, playing for, 388.
Deadman's Claim, 21.
Death of the trapper, 15.
Debut, my, 147.
Desperado, 29.
Destruction of game, 416.
Diphtheria, 41.
Discovery of Sheepeaters, 177.
Disvobulations, 75.
Doctrines of Western morality, 29.
Dressing-room, sitting down the 187.
Dressing, story of, 47.
Drop, getting the, 27.
Dry Camps, 38.
Dry stores, 54.
Dug-out, life in a, 261.
Dunraven's, Lord, white collar civilization, 295.
Dunraven, Lord, opinion of the Wind River Country, 400.
Dust, bones, and flesh, 293.
Dutch Cent, 386.

Index. 435

EAGLE of Lewis and Clarke, 78.
Eaten too much dinner, 88.
Edd, 18.
English faces, seeing again, 291.
English settlers, difficulties of, 363.
Ethics of the West, 20.
Evenings in trapper camps, 62.
Experimentalizing of the Western man, 22.
Expedition over to the Colorado, 302.
Exploration, previous, 51, 396.
Express bullets, 411.

FAVOURITE playground, my, 154.
Fill your boots, 195.
Finding of water, 36.
Fires on the Plains, 36.
Fire driving us out, 223.
First dinner, 50.
First impressions, 365.
Fish, how to carry them, 218.
Fish, where I saw most, 220.
Fish-in-Bed Camp, 71.
Fishing, my, 215.
Fishing in the Rockies, 211, 214.
Flaming Gorge, 304.
Forests, in dense, 201.
Forked lightning, untangling, 125.
Fort Washakie, 49, 276, 286.
Founding a home, 394.
Four-bull-Camp hunger, 121.
Four bulls, the, 115.
Four Wapiti, the, 115.
Fremont's Peak, 196.
French Louy's skunk, 110.
Frontier settlements, origin of, 374.
Fur Company voyageurs, 15.

GAME, preservation of, 415.
Game country, wonderful, 149.
Game, unsophisticated, 151.
Gang of moving Wapiti, 139, 141, 145.
Getting up names, 13.
Getting your cattle, 346.
Geikie, Professor, 417.
Geikie, Professor, description of bad-lands, 157.
General Sheridan, 31.

Geological speculations, 318.
Glorious appetite, 61.
Go! And I went, 280.
Going to bed, 63.
Going straight on Meat, 20.
Gold, walking on, 197.
Gold pan, the, 197.
Good stories, life of, 369.
Good stories, where one hears them 369.
Government exploration party, 209.
Grace, a strange, 385.
Grand Canyon, 315.
Grazing land, 336.
Great gun, the, and small boy, 141, 377.
Grizzly, close encounter with a, 220.

HABITATIONS in the Lower Canyons, 317.
Half-breed trappers, 257.
Headwaters of three great streams, 195.
Head of the great stag, 122.
Heap, heap, 268.
Henry's humour, 47, 59.
Henry, 18.
Henry, unadmiring, 211.
History of the Colorado explorations, 297.
Hold-all, the, 65.
Home, 393.
Hoosier, poisoning, 60.
Horsebreaking, profession of, 100.
Horseshoe Canyon, 308.
Horns of the Bighorn, 161.
Hovey, Rev. H., 404.
Humour of Henry, 19.
Humour of the West, 368.
Hydrographical point of interest, 196.

ILIFF, Mr., 349.
Indians and beaver, 253, 255.
Indians, curiosity of, 270.
Indian languages, 282.
Indian love of the beaver, 237.
Indian no lost, Indian here, wigwam lost, 203.
Indian panic, an, 377.

Indian philosophy, 271.
Indian reservations, 276.
Indians, the Sheepeater, 176.
Indians, stoical, 270.
Indian, the Soshoné, 266.
Indian trails, 183.
Indians trying my Express, 270.
Indians and travellers, 400.
Inspiring sight of big stag, 121.
Interview, a ludicrous, 19.
Iron store, 131.
It will keep, 367.

JACKSON'S Hole, romance of, 205.
Jackson's Hole, wintering in, 222.
Janeway, Dr., on the skunk, 404.
Jennie's Lake, 217.
Jerusalem Overtaker, the, 382.
Jones, Capt., the explorer, 399.

KATE, 103.
Kitchen pony, the, 202.

LADY of the Rocky Mountains, 367.
Lakes on the Wind River Chain, 77.
Lake scenery, 79.
Languages of the North American Indians, 282.
Landseer's sketches, 136.
Land tenure and laws in the United States, 331.
Laramie Peak country, 148.
Lawn tennis shoes, 412.
Leading subject, a, 385.
Le Mars Colony, the, 321.
Life in a dug-out, 261.
Light-pack camps, 73.
Lightness of the air, 114.
Loafer Dick's death, 391.
Losing oneself in forests, 203.
Losses in cattle-raising, 338.

MAKING bed, 63.
Market hunters' home, 143.
Market hunters, a family of, 141.
Main Divide snowstorm, 183.
Mauvaises terres, 42, 50, 155, 175, 194, 417.
Mavrick, 360.
Measuring horns, 174.

Meat, going straight on, 20.
Mishaps to the hold-all, 68.
Misunderstanding, my, with *Black Coal*, 279.
Misinterpretation of good intentions, 281.
Monarch of the Divide, death of, 132.
Moonlight ramble, a, 225.
Moonlight stalking, 157.
Mosquitoes, 48.
Mountain lion, wail of, 83.
My first stalk, 150.

NAMES, corruption of, 72.
Names, getting up of, 13.
Naming camp, 69.
Newberry, Prof., 318.
Newland, 144.
Newness of the West, 155.
Night-camping, 131.
Night-scene, a, in the Colorado canyons, 312.
Nobs and snobs, their absence, 30.
Notabilia venatoris, 135.
November, 1880, great cold in, 273.

OLD Christmas, 19.
Old John, 104.
Origin of the cattle business, 324.
Outfit for sportsmen, 410.
"Outfit," the Western use of that word, 1.

PACKING horses, 45.
Pelt prices, influence of, 416.
Pet skunk, 110.
Pioneer settlements, origin of, 374.
Pitcairn Islanders, 291.
Plains fires, 36.
Plains, the, as grazing land, 336.
Plains waggon, 39.
Poker, game of, 388.
Poisoning wolves, 268.
Poisoning hoosier, 60.
Port, his youth, 16.
Port, his humour, 18.
Post-office regulations, 289.
Pot, the, of beans, 190.
Potamology, peculiarities of, 196.

Index.

Powell's Major, Exploration of the Colorado, 297, 306.
Preservation of game, 415.
Preparing heads, 422.
Pre-empting land, 332.
Profits of cattle business, 329.
Putting out fires by counterburning, 37.
Purgatorial wavework, 194.

RABIES mephitica, 402.
Raising cattle on free land, 327.
Ramble, a, on the Divide, 76.
Rattlesnake Hills, 104.
Rattlesnakes, their rattle, 105.
Reback-action of water, 58.
Reservations of Indians, 276.
Retrospective glances, 293.
Return to civilization, 289, 290.
Return to camp, 84.
Revolver, 411.
Reynold Capt., 399.
Ridgepole of North America, 182.
Riding over to the dead stag, 133.
Riding on trail, 355.
Rifles, 410.
Rifle the, always with you, 226.
Rifle, anxiety for the, 106.
Rifles, different names of, 144.
Rocky Mountain lady, 61.
Ropebreaking of a horse, 99.
Round-up, the, 339.
Rücksack, 411.
Ruskin of the chase, 134.

SALERATUS, 56.
Saratoga, the, 66.
Scab on bighorn, 178.
Scarcity of game, 45.
Scenery in daylight, 228.
Schloss in Tyrol, 122.
Secrets of beaver medicine, 251.
Secundum, 267.
Sharing beds, 64.
Sheepeater Indians, 176.
Shipping beeves, 343.
Shooting of my first wapiti, 137.
Shot at the big stag, 129.
Sierra Soshoné, 50.

Silence in the canyons of the Colorado, 310.
Skunk, 401.
Skunks, their peculiarities, 108, 109, 110.
Snowstorms on the Plains, 337.
Snowstorm, a, is upon us, 185.
Soap, how *not* to make, 199.
Speaking wapiti, a, 138.
Sportsmen, outfit for, 410.
Squatter's, the right, 332.
Shirley Basin, 41.
Shooting stories, 25, 26.
Sierra Soshoné, 123.
Sleigh ride, a cold, 286.
Snowstorm, early, 119.
Soshoné Mountains, 397.
Soshoné Indians, 266.
Soshoné reservation, the, 277.
Stag, the great, 123.
Staglore, 134.
Stalking at moonlight, 151.
Stalker's bag, 411.
Stalking of four wapiti, 115.
Stampeding of cattle, 358.
Stare, an uncomfortable, 169.
Start, a bad, 7.
Starting for wapiti hunt, 112, 114.
Stock-raising business, the, 320.
Strange old customs, 135.
Streams, running dry, 35.
Strychnine, use of, 268.
Sunset, 80.

TAKING root, 200.
Telescoping camp, 74.
Tenderfoot, his difficulties, 12.
Teton, the great, 210.
Teton, the ascent of, 423.
Teton, the partial ascent of, 223, 424.
Teton basin, 205, 423.
Teton basin, locality of, 207.
Teton basin, romance of, 205.
Texan and Yorkshireman, 392.
Thanksgiving-day dinner, 379.
Thunderstorm, 257.
Time, lost reckoning of, 392.
Togwotee pass, 398.
Tool-box, 411.
Topshelfer's outfit, 1, 9.

Index

Tourists not to carry revolvers, 26.
Tracking the great stag, 126.
Trading, 91.
Trading for Boreas, 89.
Trading Jack's death, 384.
Trading Jack's grace, 385.
Trapper travelling, charm of, 53, 55.
Trapper, death of the, 15.
Trapper, the old, gone up, 16.
Trappers, engaging them, 11.
Traveller's questions, 25.
Tricks of wolf poisoners, 269.
Tricks of fur hunters, 252.

UNSURVEYED land, 330.
Untangling forked lightning, 125.
Upper Shirley basin, 71.
U. P. train, 293.
Usefulness of man relapsing into semi-savagery, 293.

VALET, no man is a hero to his, 294.
Vicious horses, 45.
View from peak on the Divide, 194.
View of the Teton basin, 208.
Visit my, to *Black Coal*, 279.
Voyageurs Fur Company, 15.

WADS, 410.
Waggon-sheet, 408.
Walton's art in the Rockies, 211, 214.
Wanton waste, 150.
Wapiti, a big band, 127.
Wapiti antlers, size of, 150.
Wapiti breaking cover, 129.
Wapiti, cleaning-time of horns, 412.
Wapiti, fighting, 127.
Wapiti, good climbers, 413.
Wapiti, moving bands of, 139, 141, 145.
Wapiti, poorness of skins, 415.
Wapiti, shedding time, 412.
Wapiti, stalking of four bulls, 115.
Wapiti, throwing horn, 231.
Wapiti, whistling, 82, 123.

Watching beaver at work, 243, 244.
Water-finding, 36.
Watson, Sir T., 401.
Washakie reservation, 277.
Weather fine, 198.
Weight of the bighorn, 162.
Wengeren Alp in the Rockies, 77.
West, authors on, 432.
West, turning it into a cattle-yard, 232.
Western humour and lingo, 368.
Western hunter's idea about game, 151.
Western judge, story of, 65.
Western man, 20, 21, 23.
Western man acts as his own executioner, 28.
Western man starting into crime, 29.
Western man's love of trading, 91.
Western man's achievements, 31.
West, newness of the, 155.
Western repartee, 19.
Western waggons, 39.
Western woman, a, *coup*, 383.
Western woman's the, *savoir faire*, 382.
Whistle of the Wapiti, 82.
Whistling of the Wapiti, 82, 123.
Whiskey tales, 6.
Windfall, corralled in a, 201.
Wind River Mountains, 50, 397.
Wind River Mountains scenery, 194.
Wind River, Indians crossing the, 273.
Wintering in Teton Basin, 222.
Winter of 1880, 34.
Wolves, poisoning of, 268.
Woman, respect shown to, 28.
Work of the evening, 62.
Wyoming, climate of, 409.
Wyoming, size of, 397.

YELLOWSTONE, the, 195.

ZOOLOGICAL collections in England, 422.

THE END.

www.ingramcontent.com/pod-product-compliance
Lightning Source LLC
Chambersburg PA
CBHW022136300426
44115CB00006B/217